Yale Historical Publications

Miscellany, 90

Prelude to Populism: Origins of the Silver Issue, 1867–1878

by

Allen Weinstein

New Haven and London, Yale University Press, 1970

Library of Congress catalog card number: 70–99846
Standard book number: 300–01229–2
Designed by Marvin Howard Simmons set in Garamond type, and printed in the United States of America by The Carl Purington Rollins Printing-Office of the Yale University Press, New Haven, Connecticut.
Distributed in Great Britain, Europe, Asia, and Africa by Yale University Press Ltd., London; in Canada by McGill-Queen's University Press, Montreal; and in Mexico by Centro Interamericano de Libros Académicos, Mexico City.

TO SARAH AND SAMUEL WEINSTEIN

Acknowledgments

A number of people provided me with aid and comfort from start to completion of this book. I mention some below, although none should be implicated in the book's various shortcomings.

Library staffs throughout the country lightened the burdens of research, but I owe a special debt for their help over a period of several years to the capable staff of the Library of Congress Manuscripts Division.

Discussions with friends and associates helped clarify my own views on the silver question, although any factual or doctrinal errors in the book are my own. Among those friends who, as past or present colleagues, helped me to press forward at critical moments, the following must be mentioned: Daniel Aaron, Louis Cohn-Haft, Stanley M. Elkins, Frank Otto Gatell, Paul W. Glad, Joel Silbey, and Jack Wilson. Other friends and historians who have offered valuable criticisms include Irwin F. Unger, Ari Hoogenboom, Harold M. Hyman, Robert Marcus, H. Wayne Morgan, Martin Ridge, and Robert Sharkey. Mrs. Hilda McArthur typed the various drafts of the manuscript with great skill and intelligence.

The book began as a Yale University dissertation. Yale provided generous fellowship assistance. At a later stage, a grant from the Earhart Foundation and grants from the Smith College Faculty Research Committee helped speed the book's completion. The manuscript took final shape during a summer's service in 1968 as a Fulbright Lecturer in Australia, where I learned a great deal about both the art of hospitality and the practice of American Studies from my various hosts: Paul Bourke, Brian Dalton, Norman Harper, Phil Lockwood, Jim Main, Trevor Wigney, and especially Frank Willcock.

I had the privilege of studying while at Yale with John Morton Blum, Henry W. Broude, Edmund S. Morgan, Norman Holmes Pearson, and David Potter. I remain grateful to them all. Professors Blum and Broude criticized an earlier draft of the manuscript and suggested a number of ways to improve it, not all of which their stubborn student has adopted. The staff of Yale University Press—particularly Mrs. Ruth Kaufman, Mrs. Ellen Vowles, and Mr. Robert Zangrando—helped prepare the book for publication with impressive skill.

I owe my greatest debt, however, to Professor C. Vann Woodward of Yale. As director of my dissertation, he supervised its progress with patience and tact. He offered help whenever needed, and his criticisms maintained a level of judiciousness that guided the project at every stage. The book's weaknesses remain my own responsibility, while anything of value in the work must be attributed largely to his wise counsel.

For my wife Diane, no repayment is possible.

A. W.

Northampton, Massachusetts
July 1969

Contents

Tables

Prologue: The Treacherous Baron Rothe

Said Mr. RothSchild, hell knows which Roth-schild 1861, '64 or there sometime, "Very few people 'will understand this. Those who do will be occupied 'getting profits. The general public will probably not 'see it's against their interest."

Ezra Pound, Canto XLVI

The plot was hatched at Baron Rothe's mansion one evening in 1869. The baron, "a portly, well-fed, brainy diplomat and financier," had invited to dinner the equally unscrupulous banker and bondholder, Sir William T. Cline, to enlist Cline's support in a daring scheme. "If the United States and the principal governments of Europe adopt [the gold standard]," Baron Rothe informed his guest, "it will double your fortune and mine." Furthermore, if the United States should demonetize silver quickly, "with the fall in [monetary] values we will destroy their balance of trade." But if the United States managed to keep both silver and gold as monetary standards, Baron Rothe warned, within thirty years she—not England—would dominate the world's economy. "Demonetize her silver. It is the key to the situation. All the rest will follow."

How could this be done, Sir William asked, without the Americans' knowledge and consent? "Do you believe that a man can be persuaded to cut his own throat?" Baron Rothe had prepared the answer. "One man on the finance committee in the Senate, and one on the same committee in the House, and one hundred thousand pounds, and the job is done. Once enacted into a law, we are safe." Sir William remained skeptical. Surely his host had underestimated the integrity of American congressmen? Wouldn't they expose the baron's agents and, thus, the entire plan? Rothe then explained his strategy. "A bill can be presented to reform the coinage laws—a bill innocent on its face . . . The bill, on its face, would not demonetize silver, but *as enrolled,* it would. Congressmen would vote for it under the impression of [revising] the coinage laws . . . I doubt whether [its true purpose] would become known for several years." After all, the American public had not used gold or silver widely since the Civil War, when the country abandoned the specie standard and had issued hundreds of millions worth of greenback paper money. "They are off their guard," Baron Rothe insisted, "and this is the opportune time to strike the blow." But when they do discover it, Sir William objected, "a cry will go up and repeal will be inevitable. The public will—" "The public be damned," shouted his host. "Once enacted into a law it can be maintained . . . To repeal the law, it will require both Houses and the President to be in favor of the repeal. You can risk our friends in Wall Street to take care of one of these three." Persuaded finally of the scheme's chance for success, Sir William pledged his financial support.

The American legislator chosen to steer the coinage measure safely through Congress was a midwestern senator, John Arnold, then visiting London: "one of the recognized leaders of his party, a leader of leaders . . . in a small way, a successful financier, and by his party associates . . . generally recognized as an authority on matters of finance." Fortunately, it took Baron Rothe little effort to persuade Arnold to assist in demonetizing silver. They sealed the bargain with a twenty-five thousand dollar bribe, a first installment on the hundred thousand promised the senator for his services.

Arnold returned to Washington and began working immediately to pass a bill nominally "revising" the outmoded coinage laws but actually demonetizing silver. Three years passed and the measure remained before Congress when a young English associate of Baron Rothe's, Victor Rogasner, arrived in Washington in November 1872 carrying an additional twenty-five thousand dollars for the senator. "I am here," Rogasner mused after delivering the money, "on the greatest mission an Englishman, military or civil, has ever been sent . . . I am here to destroy the United States [by eliminating its silver coinage] . . . I will drag them down and choke the life out of their industries and commerce . . . I will destroy the last vestige of national prosperity among them, and humble that accursed pride with which they refer to their revolutionary ancestors, to the very dust."

The Coinage Act demonetizing silver passed Congress finally in February 1873, fulfilling Baron Rothe's original prophecy: "No one had discovered what had been done . . . Not a whisper was to be heard—not a word in print was to be seen, about the demonetization of silver." Only the small group of conspirators—Baron Rothe, Sir William Cline, Victor Rogasner, and two others "working for the same end in France . . . and in Germany"—recognized at the time the impact that demonetization would have on the American economy. Even Senator Arnold and his corrupt counterpart in the House believed only that gold now became the sole monetary standard, a fact that Baron Rothe had assured them would merely benefit bondholders and men of capital like themselves. That demonetization might also "bankrupt the nation neither entered their minds nor was considered in their money grasping natures." Rogasner, his mission accomplished, departed Washington for other assignments, leaving a secretary there to "watch with a hawk's eye for the first sign of discovery." Three years passed with no hint of detection when, in August 1876, Rogasner received a cablegram from America that bore the single word, "DISCOVERED." Thus began the silver issue.

Introduction

Only one aspect of this fanciful account of silver's demonetization, taken from William Hope ("Coin") Harvey's novel *A Tale of Two Nations,* had any basis in fact.[1] When Congress demonetized silver in 1873, it did so without an audience. Few Americans cared about the matter, and none marked the occasion in public. By the time President Grant signed the mint bill into law on February 14, 1873, Congress had turned its attention to other business, allowing a measure that figured prominently in later Gilded Age political debate to pass unnoticed at the time. Politicians who dominated silver debate during subsequent decades, except for Senator John Sherman of Ohio, the "John Arnold" of Harvey's novel, displayed little interest in 1873 in the obscure coinage statute that almost none of them had bothered reading.

Twenty-three years of controversy lay ahead before the final confrontation of gold and silver advocates during the nineties, and neither party's standard bearer in 1896 had even begun his political career when Congress passed the mint bill. "McKinley, that respectable McKinley," as Vachel Lindsay characterized him, "The man without an angle or a tangle, / Who soothed down the city man and soothed down the farmer," still practiced law in Canton in 1873 while awaiting the birth of his second

1. William H. Harvey, *A Tale of Two Nations* (Chicago, 1894), passim.

child.[2] As for Bryan, "that Heaven-born Bryan, / That Homer Bryan, who sang from the West," then thirteen years old, he prepared to enter Illinois' Whipple Academy where, four decades later, a favorite teacher would recall "that it was not [I] who taught Bryan that man descended from a monkey." Despite the general indifference toward demonetization in 1873, within three years silver had been "discovered" and quickly became a major political issue, remaining one until the end of the century.

The facts concerning the monetary standard issue, once recognized, contained few surprises for most Americans. Contemporaries and subsequent historians viewed the "battle of the standards" as a clearly defined contest in which agrarian inflationists and silver miners waged a long, but ultimately fruitless, struggle against conservative eastern business interests to restore bimetallism, a demand defeated ultimately in the presidential election of 1896. McKinley's victory over Bryan's Democratic-Populist coalition, as generations of schoolboys have learned, shattered the American farmer's dream of securing "free and unlimited coinage" of the 412.5 grain silver dollar, a coin its enthusiasts christened "the dollar of the daddies." "Defeat of western silver, / Defeat of the wheat," Vachel Lindsay lamented of 1896, "Defeat of my boyhood, defeat of my dream."

For most observers, the origins of the silver movement presented no particular mystery. "The demand for the coinage of silver dollars began [in 1876] where the cry for unlimited paper money left off," ran one typical account of the episode. "The movement which resulted in the [Bland-Allison] act of 1878 was but another manifestation of the . . . hot and fierce debates between the inflationists and contractionists."[3] Most historians have accepted substantially this version of the silver issue's

2. "Bryan, Bryan, Bryan, Bryan," in Vachel Lindsay, *Collected Poems* (New York, 1930), pp. 103–04.

3. J. Laurence Laughlin, *The History of Bimetallism in the United States* (New York, 1893 ed.), p. 188.

genesis.[4] The campaign to restore legal bimetallism, according to most narratives, was led and endorsed from the outset primarily by two groups, southern and western agrarians seeking currency inflation and western miners demanding a guaranteed government market for their product.

The following chapters examine the formative years of the silver movement. They explore the myths that evolved regarding the coinage question in American politics. At the same time, they trace the development of coinage politics and policy making during the 1870s, when the issue first arose. Many stark contrasts emerge between the actual nature of the early silver movement and the portrait drawn by later scholars, most of whom were concerned primarily with the more dramatic events of the 1890s. Certain important episodes such as the "Crime of 1873," considered mythical by most historians, prove to contain a factual basis while, on the other hand, available evidence fails to support much of our traditional version of early silver politics.

Most misunderstandings have stemmed basically from the fact that previous scholars, having examined the silver issue during the nineties, assumed generally that the coalition of agrarian inflationists and mineowners they detected in that decade had taken root during the embryonic silver drive two decades earlier. This was not the case, however, as a study of the actual birth and evolution of the silver movement during the 1870s demonstrates. The present work focuses on the politics and sociology of the first silver drive, not on the economic merits or deficiencies of bimetallism, a problem of revived interest to some recent economists. The struggle for remonetization in the

4. See, for example, the following: Richard B. Morris, ed., *Encyclopedia of American History,* rev. ed. (New York, 1961), p. 254; John D. Hicks, George E. Mowry, and Robert E. Burke, *The American Nation,* 4th ed. (Boston, 1963), 2, 58–59; John A. Garraty, *The American Nation: A History of the United States* (New York, 1966), pp. 613–14; Richard Current, T. Harry Williams, and Frank Freidel, *American History: A Survey* (New York, 1966), p. 559.

seventies served as seedtime for the silver movement, a period during which the myths, ideologies, and policies that dominated money politics in the United States for two decades first took root. Although William Jennings Bryan called his 1896 campaign on behalf of silver "the first battle," this fight had actually been waged twenty years earlier. The limited victory won by American bimetallists with passage of the Bland-Allison Act raised their hopes for complete restoration of silver as a monetary standard. In so doing, the campaign of the seventies fueled a twenty-year struggle among many Americans to reach an elusive "silver Zion."

1

Silver Abandoned: The "Crime of 1873" as Myth and History

American historians have tabulated a surprisingly large number of suspected plots and conspiracies running throughout our national folklore Thus students of political history continue to debate the meaning of supposedly "corrupt bargains" that decided presidential elections in 1800, 1824, and 1876; while equally alert sentries have detected at key moments in the American past that silent but malign phenomenon, "the Money Power." The most dramatic "Money Power" myth concerns the demonetization of silver. According to bimetallists, the Coinage Act of 1873, which discontinued the silver dollar as a monetary standard, passed Congress through the corrupt influence of a cabal of powerful government bondholders who conspired with Treasury officials and influential congressmen. By establishing a single gold unit of account, the cabal presumably hoped to raise the market value of its public securities.[1] The silverites labeled this version of demonetization the "Crime of 1873."[2]

1. Ignatius Donnelly, *The American People's Money* (Chicago, 1895), pp. 150–64.

2. The earliest hint of a conspiracy surrounding the demonetization of silver in 1873 came from George Melville Weston in a letter to the Boston *Globe* on Mar. 2, 1876. Weston's charge was quickly endorsed by several leading newspapers, most importantly the New York *Graphic,* Joseph Medill's Chicago *Tribune,* and Murat Halstead's Cincinnati *Commercial.* Horace White, the Liberal Republican editor, was the "Crime's" earliest critic, writing a rebuttal of Weston's letter in the New York financial weekly, the *Public.*

While the Senate debated the House-passed Bland bill remonetizing the silver dollar in February 1878, a troubled Delaware manufacturer confessed to Senator Thomas F. Bayard that "at the beginning of the agitation . . . I was totally ignorant of all that related to the silver question . . . so much in fact that (I find now like almost everyone else, not excluding Congressmen) I did not know Silver had been demonetized."[3] Prior to 1876 few Americans understood that the 412.5 grain silver dollar had lost its place in the monetary system as full legal tender alongside gold. Throughout the Reconstruction era, supporters of the gold standard had jousted with advocates of greenback inflation for control of national monetary policy.[4] During the struggle over specie resumption, however, silver lacked its own group of political and economic partisans, largely because the American silver dollar commanded $1.03 or more in gold prior to 1873. Because of its high market value and consequent

---

For early commentary on the "Crime of 1873," see Weston's Boston *Globe* letter, reprinted in George M. Weston, *The Silver Question* (New York, 1878), pp. 105–09; also Horace White's article, *Public,* 9 (Mar. 23, 1876), 198–99. For a small portion of the many 1876 editorials on silver's "surreptitious" demonetization, see the New York *Graphic,* Mar. 14, May 9, 15, June 19, July 11. See also the Cincinnati *Commercial,* June 6, July 8, 13, 18, 23, 1876. Two excellent discussions of the literature and background of the "Crime of 1873" are found in Irwin Unger, *The Greenback Era: A Social and Political History of American Finance, 1865–1879* (Princeton, N.J., 1964), pp. 328–32, and in Richard Hofstadter's introduction to W. H. Harvey, *Coin's Financial School* (Cambridge, Mass., 1963), pp. 36–43. Paul Barnett places the first use of the term "Crime of 1873" at a later date, neglecting the substantial body of literature concerning the "Crime" which accumulated during the silver drive of the 1870's. Paul Barnett, "The Crime of 1873 Reexamined," *Agricultural History, 38* (1964), 178–81.

3. Wilbur H. Burnite to Thomas F. Bayard, Feb. 9, 1878, Thomas F. Bayard Papers.

4. Unger, *Greenback Era,* passim. See also Robert P. Sharkey, *Money, Class, and Party: An Economic Study of Civil War and Reconstruction* (Baltimore, 1959; paperback ed., 1967).

disuse in domestic commerce from 1865 to 1873, the silver dollar possessed little appeal to monetary inflationists until 1876, by which time the metal's market price had dropped well below that of gold.[5]

Silver's price on the world's exchanges slumped steadily after 1873 as a result of vastly expanded American production and a steadily narrowing international demand for the metal.[6] Germany had begun changing from a silver to a gold standard late in 1871, and its demonetized coinage began competing with the product of American silver mines for the world market. In 1874 competition for available outlets became even more intense when the members of the Latin Monetary Union—France, Belgium, Greece, Italy, and Switzerland—closed their mints to further silver coinage.[7] The United States became a gold-standard nation when, in 1873, the coinage act discontinued minting the 412.5 grain silver dollar and when, the following year, the United States Revised Statutes limited the legal tender of all existing silver coins to five dollars in a single payment.[8]

Between 1873 and 1876 no American protested demonetization or argued that a "crime" had occurred three years earlier through collusion among bondholders, treasury officials, and

5. *Historical Statistics of the United States, 1789–1945* (Washington, 1952), Series N 179–84, p. 277.

6. Ibid., Series G 118–24, p. 152.

Silver Production in the United States, 1869–76

	Quantity in fine ounces	Value in dollars		Quantity in fine ounces	Value in dollars
1869	9,281,200	12,297,600	1873	27,650,400	35,881,600
1870	12,375,000	16,434,000	1874	28,868,200	36,917,500
1871	17,789,100	25,588,300	1875	24,530,300	30,485,900
1872	22,236,300	29,396,400	1876	29,996,200	34,919,800

7. J. Laurence Laughlin, *The History of Bimetallism in the United States* (New York, 1885), pp. 146–60.

8. Ibid., Appendix III, pp. 231–32, reprints the provisions of the Coinage Act of 1873 and those of the U.S. Revised Statutes of 1874 which concern the demonetization of silver.

congressmen.[9] Most late nineteenth-century economic historians found no evidence of this conspiracy. Horace White, for example, noted that:

> The [coinage] law of 1873 was not passed surreptitiously, or secretly, or without due consideration. Some of the hottest silver men were members of Congress at that time and voted for it. . . . The silver dollar [in 1873] was an obsolete coin . . . worth two cents more than the gold dollar. *Nobody could then anticipate that it would ever be worth less than the gold dollar.*[10]

Recent historians have also denied the charge that public officials and government creditors schemed to insure payment of the bonded debt entirely in gold. Neil Carothers ridiculed the notion that dropping silver as a monetary standard was "the result of a sinister plot." Practically all subsequent economic historians have agreed with Carothers that "there is no evidence . . . the silver dollar had been dropped from the coinage by fraud and collusion."[11] Richard Hofstadter, generally accepting Carothers' conclusions, even suggested that instead of compiling further proofs of its absurdity, historians turn their attention to those cultural factors which encouraged widespread belief in the "Crime of 1873."[12]

9. Unger, *Greenback Era,* pp. 328–32.

10. Horace White, *Money and Banking Illustrated by American History* (Boston, 1895), pp. 218–19. Italics not in original. See also Laughlin, *History of Bimetallism,* pp. 92–108; David K. Watson, *History of American Coinage* (New York, 1899), pp. 113–38; Davis Rich Dewey, *Financial History of the United States,* 7th ed. (New York, 1920), pp. 403–05.

11. Neil Carothers, *Fractional Money: A History of the Small Coins and Fractional Paper Currency of the United States* (New York, 1930), p. 235. See also Unger, *Greenback Era,* p. 331; Paul Studenski and Herman E. Krooss, *Financial History of the United States* (New York, 1963), p. 187.

12. Hofstader's introduction to *Coin's Financial School,* pp. 39–40.

Was there a "Crime of 1873"? Historical controversy over demonetization has centered on the question of foreknowledge and intent. Was the silver dollar eliminated in the Coinage Act of 1873 without awareness of the market forces which would soon bring a substantial reduction in the metal's price? Or were these forces understood? By 1874 the market price of silver had dropped below the established government rate of purchase, and bullion sales to the mint for coinage had become profitable again for American silver producers. By then, however, the metal was no longer legal tender for an unlimited amount.[13] Since treasury officials who drafted the act of 1873, and legislators who sponsored it, later claimed to have been ignorant of this impending market downturn prior to 1873, economic historians have concluded that elimination of the 412.5 grain silver dollar in the coinage act did not represent a conscious scheme.[14] Silver's demonetization, according to the traditional account, came as an unplanned if fortunate by-product of a complex and largely technical revision of the mint laws in the Coinage Act of 1873.

Most economic historians have accepted this version of the demonetization of silver and have remained skeptical of the conspiracy charge leveled by silverites concerning the "Crime of 1873." Only one writer in recent years, Paul M. O'Leary, has found the accusation even partially credible.[15] O'Leary argued

13. Studenski and Krooss, *Financial History,* p. 187.

14. Laughlin, *History of Bimetallism,* pp. 197–220. See also Milton Friedman and Anna Jacobson Schwartz, *Monetary History of the United States, 1867–1960* (Princeton, N.J., 1963), pp. 114–15.

15. Paul M. O'Leary, "The Scene of the Crime of 1873 Revisited: A Note," *Journal of Political Economy, 68* (1960), 388–92. Walter T. K. Nugent, in a study completed after submission of the dissertation on which this book is based, verified my own findings on silver's demonetization. Walter T. K. Nugent, *The Money Question During Reconstruction* (New York, 1967), pp. 65–92. See also the same author's *Money and American Society, 1865–1880* (New York, 1968), pp. 65–171.

that the "legislation of 1873 was deliberately aimed at striking down the silver dollar just when it was apparent to those in a position to know that it was about to make a comeback."[16] To support this contention, he offered discrete pieces of evidence, primarily connected with the behavior of Henry Richard Linderman, a leading mint official who helped draft the provision which discontinued coinage of the silver dollar. Linderman, in an 1877 treatise, not only denied that the men responsible for the coinage act had anticipated the market slump in silver but also insisted that the decline in price "could have had no influence in determining the question."[17] O'Leary challenged this denial and pointed out that by 1872 Linderman had shown a clear understanding of the increase in silver coinage which its imminent market depreciation would bring and that the mint official clearly anticipated the metal's future appeal to monetary inflationists. To support his argument that treasury officials foresaw the slump in world silver prices, O'Leary cited as evidence two reports containing this insight written late in 1872, one by Linderman and the other by Secretary of the Treasury George S. Boutwell.[18]

Having reopened the case for a "Crime of 1873," O'Leary failed to offer a complete alternative analysis of the demonetization episode, thereby leaving many vital questions unanswered. Milton Friedman and Anna Schwartz have noted, for example, that O'Leary did not demonstrate that Linderman's foreknowl-

16. O'Leary, "Scene of the Crime of 1873 Revisited," pp. 390, 392.

17. Henry Richard Linderman, *Money and Legal Tender in the United States* (New York, 1877), cited in O'Leary, "Scene of the Crime of 1873 Revisited," p. 391.

18. See especially Linderman's comments on the silver market in Linderman and John Torrey (technical adviser), House *Special Report of Examination of Branch Mints on the Pacific Coast* (transmitted to Secretary of the Treasury George S. Boutwell on Nov. 19, 1872), reprinted in *Banker's Magazine, and Statistical Register,* 7, 3d ser. (1873), pp. 710–716. See also Francis Bowen, Minority Report, *Report of the United States Monetary Commission, 1877, 1,* 148; O'Leary, "Scene of the Crime" pp. 391–92.

edge had any direct influence upon legislative treatment of the coinage act.[19] If those who drafted the Coinage Act of 1873 anticipated the market decline of silver, when did this slump become of concern to them? More pointedly, did the possible awareness by Treasury officials of the market forces affecting silver influence congressional handling of the coinage act? An investigation of the available evidence suggests that O'Leary was substantially correct. Government officials in the Treasury and in Congress, aware by 1872 of silver's imminent decline, strove to eliminate it as a monetary standard before its coinage became attractive to monetary inflationists.

Secretary of the Treasury Boutwell, Linderman, who was Boutwell's special advisor on coinage, and John Sherman, chairman of the Senate Finance Committee, had all recognized the imminent depreciation of silver by late 1872. Together, they worked to complete congressional action on the pending coinage bill before their expert and specialized information became public knowledge. They revised the measure's silver-coinage provisions in December 1872 and helped to secure the final passage of the bill in February 1873 without explaining to Congress the essential reason for their actions—the expected market downturn in silver. Sherman and his associates acted to demonetize silver not for corrupt private gain but in order to secure a domestic gold standard before the anticipated flood of depreciated silver bullion began arriving at government mints for coinage into legal-tender silver dollars. In doing so, however, they possessed information of which most congressmen were not aware. Although they were not self-interested rascals, as advocates of the "Crime of 1873" later charged, neither were they economic innocents, as most historians have portrayed them, caught without warning by a sudden and fatal decline in the silver market.

Nowhere was their knowledge of the impending market

19. Friedman and Schwartz, *Monetary History,* p. 115.

slump discussed more pertinently than in Boutwell's published report for 1872:

> As the depreciation of silver is likely to continue it is impossible to issue [silver] coin redeemable in gold without ultimate loss to the Government; for when the difference becomes considerable holders will present the silver for redemption [in gold], and leave it in the hands of the Government to be disposed of subsequently at a loss.[20]

How Boutwell gained his understanding of trends in the bullion market, how the Treasury determined monetary policy, and how Congress handled the Coinage Act remains the untold story of demonetization. The history of the "Crime of 1873," as it actually unfolded, was both more complex and less dramatic than the simple morality tale of agrarian folklore.

It began in January 1870, when Boutwell requested his Deputy Comptroller of the Currency, John Jay Knox, to prepare a bill "revising the laws relative to the mints, assay offices, and coinage of the United States."[21] Assisted by Linderman, Knox condensed the bulk of coinage legislation then on the statute books into a fifty-five section bill which Boutwell submitted to Congress in April 1870. Knox's first draft of the measure retained the silver dollar but removed its parity as a monetary standard with gold by limiting the coin's legal tender in a single payment to "five dollars except [for] duties on imports." The first draft also reduced the weight of the silver dollar from 412.5 to 384 grains, roughly equivalent to the weight of two silver half-dollars.[22] Both provisions were designed to eliminate

20. *Annual Report of the Secretary of the Treasury for 1872* (Washington, 1872), p. xii.

21. See either House Exec. Doc. 307, 41st Cong., 2d sess. or Senate Misc. Doc. 132, 41st Cong., 2d sess. Both contain the draft of the bill submitted to Congress by the Treasury Department as well as all correspondence solicited by treasury officials while compiling the bill.

22. House Exec. Doc. 307, pp. 30–31, 44. Boutwell himself requested that Linderman come to Washington to assist Knox in drafting the mint

the double standard and make silver subsidiary to gold in the monetary system. Most coinage experts and mint officials who were consulted by Knox and Linderman before writing their final draft favored retaining the silver dollar as a subsidiary coin, reduced in weight and with limited legal tender power.[23] Linderman, however, urged Knox to discontinue the silver dollar entirely on the grounds that

> the gold dollar is really the legal unit and measure of value. Having a higher value as bullion than its nominal value, the silver dollar long ago ceased to be a coin of circulation; and, being of no practical use whatever, its issue should be discontinued.[24]

The two officials agreed after consultation to omit the coin entirely from the final draft of the measure sent to Congress and explained their reasons in an accompanying commentary on the bill, one section of which Knox entitled "Silver Dollar—Its Discontinuance As a Standard."[25]

Linderman's career as a mint official spanned six presidencies from 1853 to 1879. From 1870 to 1873 he acted as Boutwell's chief advisor on coinage matters, even making a semiofficial inspection tour of European mints for the treasury in 1870–71. He became the first director of the centralized Bureau of the Mint in 1873, a post established by the Coinage Act. Because of his matchless knowledge of mint procedures, price trends in

---

bill. Boutwell to Linderman, Mar. 5, 1870, Mint Correspondence of the Secretary of the Treasury, Record Group 56 (National Archives). Hereafter, records in the National Archives are indicated by the record group (RG) number.

23. For letters favorable to retaining the silver dollar in some form, see Andrew Mason to Charles J. Folger, Jan. 27, 1870; George F. Dunning to John Jay Knox [n.d.]; James Ross Snowden to Boutwell, Mar. 10, 1870; Officers of the San Francisco Mint to Boutwell, Feb. 4, 1870, RG 56, pp. 50–51, 40–45, 34–40, 52–53, respectively.

24. Linderman to Knox, Jan. 25, 1870, RG 56, p. 31.

25. Knox to Boutwell, June 25, 1870, Senate Misc. Doc. 132, p. 11.

the bullion market, and monetary standard theory, Linderman played a major role in formulating government economic policy during the decade and a half following the Civil War.[26]

Linderman's basic ideas on monetary standard theory varied only in minor detail during his long career as a mint official. As early as 1867, he advocated a gold standard for the United states and endorsed swift demonetization of the 412.5 grain silver dollar as a unit of account.[27] As a devoted Anglophile, he argued in report after report during the years preceding demonetization that British commercial prosperity was founded in large measure on economic advantages which the English derived from their gold-based currency. Linderman stressed that establishment of the gold standard would improve the commercial and financial position of the United States relative to Great Britain. Throughout his long career as a Treasury official, he labored to make the American coinage system more closely resemble the British model.[28] The market decline of silver which began in 1872 only confirmed his previously-held belief that the United States could not restore specie payments without first abolishing legal bimetallism.

26. For useful discussions of Linderman's career, see Allen Johnson and Dumas Malone, eds., *Dictionary of American Biography,* 22 vols. (New York, 1932), *11,* 273; *Pennsylvania Magazine of History and Biography,* vol. 51 (No. 1, 1927); his Personnel Folder, RG 69. Linderman's Treasury Department activities from 1869 to 1873 can be traced in his voluminous correspondence found in the records of the Philadelphia mint and the papers of the Secretary of the Treasury. His influence on treasury policy during the 1870s has been discussed most perceptively in Carothers, *Fractional Money,* passim, and in O'Leary, "Scene of the Crime of 1873 Revisited."

27. *Annual Report of the Director of the Mint* (Philadelphia, 1867), pp. 9–10.

28. *Annual Report of the Director of the Mint* (Philadelphia, 1868), pp. 8–11. See also *Report on Examination of the San Francisco Branch Mint,* Oct. 8, 1869, reprinted as Senate Exec. Doc. 51, 41st Cong., 2d sess.; Henry Richard Linderman, *The Free Coinage of Gold and Its Importance in Connection with the Resumption of Specie Payments and Commerce of the United States* (Philadelphia, 1872).

Linderman's interest in demonetizing silver was directly related to its increased domestic production. He shared the views of American mining and coinage experts in the 1860s, such as Senator E. D. Morgan of New York, who wrote in an 1868 congressional report on coinage: "Authorities unite in the conclusion that a fall in the value of the precious metals, in consequence of their rapidly increasing quantity, is inevitable."[29] Linderman, himself, had predicted in 1867 that once the Indian wars ended and railroads penetrated the major western mining regions, American bullion extraction would increase "to an extent hitherto unknown," a prognosis confirmed during the following years by the large expansion in production of the precious metals.[30] The increase in domestic silver mining during the following years fulfilled Linderman's most optimistic forecast.[31] Production of the metal increased by almost five million ounces yearly, reaching 27,650,400 ounces by 1873, and Linderman understood that the market price of silver varied with the supply and demand.[32]

Treasury records from 1870 to 1873 indicate that the Director of the Philadelphia Mint, James Pollock, and other high mint officials often reminded Boutwell of the increase in domestic silver output; but Linderman remained Boutwell's major source of information on mining conditions and price trends in the

29. Senator E. D. Morgan, Minority Report, reprinted in *International Coinage* (Washington, 1868), pp. 11–12. On the expected increase in mining production and consequent fall in price, see also J. Ross Browne to Secretary of the Treasury Hugh McCulloch, Nov. 24, 1866, reprinted in *A Report Upon the Mineral Resources of the States and Territories West of the Rocky Mountains,* House Exec. Doc. 29, 39th Cong., 2d sess., p. 9.

30. *Annual Report of the Director of the Mint* (Philadelphia, 1867), pp. 4–5.

31. Linderman to Boutwell, Apr. 26, 1870, RG 104.

32. Linderman to J. F. Schirmer, Apr. 5, 1873, Letterbooks, Director of the Mint, RG 69.

bullion market.[33] Following an official inspection tour of western mints in 1872, Linderman prepared the report which figured prominently in Boutwell's subsequent concern for demonetizing silver as quickly as possible. Linderman noted in this November 1872 report to Boutwell "several causes . . . at work, all tending to an excess of supply over demand for silver, and its consequent depreciation." He pointed especially to silver's "increasing production, its demonetization [beginning in December 1871] by the German Empire, and continued disuse in this country, except to a limited extent, as part of the circulating medium. . . . The facts above stated indicate the gradual but eventually certain adoption of the gold standard and consequent demonetization of silver by all commercial nations."[34] He later suggested to Boutwell the disturbing possibility that deposits of silver for coinage, which had increased substantially each year from 1868 to 1873, would expand still further once silver's premium over gold had disappeared.

The mint official urged the government to seek an expanded Oriental outlet for America's increased silver production by coining a new 420 grain silver dollar to be known as the "trade dollar," a coin which could compete on roughly equal terms with a Mexican dollar of similar weight then popular in Asian commerce. The trade dollar, Linderman felt, would "afford some relief to our mining industries from the serious decline and further apparent depreciation in the value of silver."[35] Although

33. James Pollock to Boutwell, Jan. 9, 1871; Boutwell to Pollock, Jan. 21, 1871; Thomas C. Acton to Pollock, Nov. 14, 1871; Boutwell to James A. Garfield, Jan. 20, 1872; Boutwell to Pollock, Feb. 9, 1872; William Richardson to Thomas Hillhouse, Aug. 5, 1872; Boutwell to Hillhouse, Oct. 21, 1872, RG 104.

34. *Banker's Magazine,* 7 (1873), 710.

35. Ibid., p. 711. Linderman's own figures show the substantial increase in silver-dollar coinage in the years before passage of the coinage act.

he believed that both increased domestic production and the recent German demonetization of silver were responsible for the metal's anticipated drop in market price, the mint official felt that the latter had triggered its original downturn on the world's exchanges.[36]

In his report, Linderman noted that a recent drop in silver's premium over gold to less than two percent had occurred in the London market.[37] Within a few days after filing the November 1872 report, however, the mint official dispatched an urgent personal letter to Boutwell on the same problem which reported still another loss and concluded that "at a further decline of about 1¼ cents per ounce the Silver dollar can be coined and issued advantageously to owners of bullion."[38] Boutwell, recognizing the dangers of inaction under these circumstances, inserted in his December 1872 annual report to Congress the recommendation that the Senate substitute Linderman's 420 grain *trade* dollar for a lighter-weight 384 grain subsidiary dollar contained in the mint bill passed by the House. "As the production of silver is rapidly increasing," Boutwell acknowledged in the report, "such a coinage [the trade dollar] will at once furnish a market for the raw material and facilitate commerce between the United States and China." He urged Congress to pass the Coinage Act quickly. Further delay, he pointed out, would

---

Number of silver dollars coined

1868—	52,800	1871—	657,929
1869—	231,350	1872—	1,112,961
1870—	588,308	1873—	977,150 (Jan.–March only)

Linderman, *Money and Legal Tender,* p. 49. For a more reliable breakdown of silver-dollar coinage during those years, see Carothers, *Fractional Money,* p. 317. Carothers' estimates for the same period are generally even higher than those made by Linderman.

36. *Report of the Monetary Commission, 1877,* 2, 194.

37. *Banker's Magazine,* 7 (1873), 713.

38. Linderman to Boutwell, Dec. 2, 1872, in "Knox" correspondence of H. S. Lansing file (National Bank Examiner), RG 69.

result in the mints being flooded with depreciated silver bullion. He warned that this was a grave threat to the public credit and to successful resumption of specie payments.[39]

At the same time that the Secretary of the Treasury pressed Congress for swift action on the coinage bill late in 1872, he rejected several requests from Director of the Philadelphia Mint Pollock for an increase in that agency's supply of silver bullion and informed Pollock only that the treasury did not wish to authorize additional purchases for the moment.[40] Boutwell's hesitation to stockpile silver was based on his expectations concerning the probable market decline in the price of bullion. He was right. The premium held by silver over gold had disappeared completely by mid-1873 and, once more, the metal's coinage became profitable to its producers. By then, however, the mint bill which ended legal bimetallism had safely passed Congress and Linderman, now director of the Bureau of the Mint, could boast to his subordinates: "The decline is what I have expected for some time past."[41] Both Boutwell and John Sherman could have made similar claims.[42]

The coinage bill, first introduced in April 1870, remained in Congress for three years before final passage in February 1873. The Senate approved a version of the bill in January 1871 that followed the Treasury's draft in discontinuing the standard 412.5

39. *Report of the Secretary of the Treasury* (Washington, D.C., 1872), pp. xi–xii.

40. Boutwell to Pollock, Dec. 9, 1872; Boutwell to Linderman, Feb. 24, 1873, Mint Correspondence of the Secretary of the Treasury, RG 69.

41. Linderman to J. B. Floyd, Aug. 7, 1873, RG 104. See also *Annual Report of the Director of the Mint* (Washington, 1873), pp. 18–19; *Annual Report on the State of the Finances* (Washington, 1873), p. xxxii.

42. For Boutwell's later expression of this knowledge of silver's imminent market decline in 1872, see George S. Boutwell, *Mr. Boutwell's Speech on the Mint Bill of 1873* (Boston, 1896), pp. 6–7, delivered before the Twentieth Century Club on Oct. 14, 1896. See also, George S. Boutwell to the Boston *Herald,* July 9, 1896.

grain silver dollar, thus eliminating legal bimetallism.[43] Debate on the measure in 1871, however, centered around an amendment by John Sherman which substituted a minting charge on both gold and silver for the "free coinage" provision of the Treasury draft. Most of the bill's remaining sections attracted little comment. Western mining-state senators angrily attacked Sherman's amendment as an unjust tax on gold producers, citing the Treasury's argument that retaining a government profit on coinage—"seigniorage"—would encourage the export of domestic bullion to countries like England which allowed "free coinage." After rejecting Sherman's proposed minting charge, the Senate enacted the entire coinage bill. Because of the controversy stirred by the seigniorage amendment, however, Senator William M. Stewart of Nevada and other mining-state senators supported passage of the measure in January 1871—while Sherman, its Senate floor manager, voted against it.[44]

Debate in the House over the mint bill did not begin until the following January and, again, there was little discussion of the change in monetary standards proposed by the measure.[45] The Pennsylvania protectionist William Darrah "Pig-Iron" Kelley, who became closely identified with the congressional silver bloc in later years, served for a time as floor manager for the coinage bill and informed his colleagues at one point during debate that fluctuations in the bullion market made it "impossible" to retain the double standard.[46]

Kelley surrendered House direction of the bill in April 1872 to Congressman Samuel Hooper of Massachusetts, a Boston

43. Sherman introduced the measure on Apr. 28, 1870, as Senate Bill no. 859. *Cong. Globe,* 41st Cong., 2d sess., p. 3051 (Apr. 28, 1870). On Jan. 10, 1871, the Senate passed the mint bill, 36 to 14. For the debate see ibid., 3d sess., pp. 368–78, 394–99 (Jan. 9, 10, 1871).

44. Ibid., p. 337 (Jan. 9, 1871); ibid., p. 399 (Jan. 10, 1871).

45. For the liveliest portion of the House debate, see *Cong. Globe,* 42d Cong., 2d sess., pp. 322–28, 336–40 (Jan. 10, 1872).

46. Ibid., p. 2311 (Apr. 9, 1872).

merchant-millionaire who amended the Senate measure to include a new coin—a 384 grain subsidiary silver dollar which would be legal tender for only five dollars along with other minor silver coins.[47] In Hooper's revised draft, therefore, despite his inclusion of the lighter-weight silver dollar, the gold dollar remained the sole unit of account and gold the single monetary standard. Boutwell and Treasury officials, of course, opposed the 384 grain coin. Hooper insisted on retaining it, however, and the coinage bill which passed the House in May 1872 included this subsidiary dollar.[48]

There is some evidence that Hooper included the 384 grain silver dollar at the suggestion of an important English coinage expert, Ernest Seyd, who sent the Massachusetts congressman a detailed commentary on the revised mint bill prior to its introduction in the House. Among other suggestions, Seyd strongly recommended that Hooper add a silver dollar to the coinage bill, whatever weight or legal tender was assigned to it, in order to keep the coin in circulation. Seyd's apparent influence on Hooper, if true, would add an ironic touch to the story of demonetization, since many silverites later condemned the English bimetallist as a central figure in the conspiracy which they believed had eliminated legal bimetallism. In this traditional silverite version of the "Crime of 1873," Seyd served literally as the "bag man" who traveled across the Atlantic in 1872 to place

47. For House debate over Samuel Hooper's revised mint bill, H. R. 1427, see *Cong. Globe,* 42d Cong., 2d sess., pp. 2304–17 (Apr. 9, 1872).

48. Boutwell to Hooper, Feb. 3, Apr. 9, 1872, RG 69. See also *Cong. Globe,* 42d Cong., 2d sess., pp. 3882–83 (May 27, 1872). When Hooper brought the measure up for a second round of House debate on May 27, 1872, he prevented a resumption of the earlier inconclusive squabbling by introducing a substitute bill for which he requested immediate House approval. Since the two bills were practically identical, there is good reason to believe that Hooper drew up the substitute primarily to avoid another wearing round of floor debate. The measure was passed overwhelmingly, 110 to 13, and sent to the Senate.

British gold in American hands in order to guarantee congressional approval of the coinage bill![49]

Six months elapsed after House passage of the measure before the Senate Finance Committee brought Hooper's version of the mint bill up for floor debate in December 1872. By then the 384 grain subsidiary domestic dollar had been eliminated and in its place Sherman's Senate Finance Committee had substituted the 420 grain trade dollar. Sherman was also aware of the anticipated drop in silver's market price through information provided him and perhaps other members of his committee by Boutwell and Linderman. Sherman informed the Senate in December 1872, however, when the amended measure reached the floor, that he had replaced the 384 grain subsidiary coin with the trade dollar primarily at the request of the California state legislature.[50] This assertion was challenged immediately by Eugene Casserly, the California senator whom Sherman named as the legislature's spokesman. Casserly seemed unaware of the request, and Sherman had to explain the amendment's provisions to his California colleague during Senate debate.[51] Sherman had not bowed to the single petition that he received from the California Assembly while his committee was proposing the trade coin but had accepted the urgent recommendation of the Treasury which drew up the actual amendment.

The process by which this Treasury policy decision became translated into legislative action took less than two weeks to com-

49. Seyd to Hooper, Feb. 2, 1872, reprinted in *Documentary History of the Coinage Act of February 12, 1873* (Washington, 1893), pp. 95–106. Hooper acknowledged Seyd's helpfulness during House debate in 1872 and noted that the English banker had "furnished many valuable suggestions which have been incorporated in this bill." *Cong. Globe,* 42d Cong., 2d sess., pp. 2304–05 (Apr. 9, 1872). For an excellent discussion and refutation of the Seyd myth, see Hofstadter's introduction to *Coin's Financial School,* pp. 62–63.

50. *Cong Globe,* 42d Cong., 3d sess., p. 672 (Jan. 17, 1873).

51. Ibid., pp. 672–73 (Jan. 17, 1873); John M. Willem, Jr., *The United States Trade Dollar* (New York, 1959), p. 84.

plete. Several days after Boutwell submitted his report to Congress in December 1872, Sherman invited both the secretary and Linderman to testify before the Senate Finance Committee on the pending coinage legislation. Although no records have survived of the closed meeting, four days later Boutwell submitted to Sherman, at the Senator's request, alternate drafts of the amendment providing for a a 420 grain trade dollar.[52] Boutwell's draft "B" was almost identical to the version submitted by Sherman to the Senate later that month and undoubtedly served as its model.[53] Only a single clause distinguished the Treasury draft from the amendment finally introduced by Sherman. Boutwell wished to withhold making the coin a domestic legal tender in any amount, while Sherman, probably to make the substitution more acceptable to Hooper, retained the five-dollar legal tender limit given to all subsidiary silver coins in the House bill. Sherman and the Treasury officials expected the trade dollar to absorb the bulk of domestic silver production in excess of the supply used for subsidiary coinage. In Linderman's words, "It will be seen that a safe outlet [for silver] would thus be secured [through the trade dollar], and the perplexing proposition as to the decline in price of the metal, and its increasing production, be at once solved in a most satisfactory manner."[54]

Samuel Ruggles, the only informed witness to the demonetization episode who knew all three principals, confirmed the fact that Sherman had introduced the trade-dollar amendment

52. Linderman came to the Dec. 10 meeting of the finance committee at Boutwell's request. Boutwell to Linderman, Dec. 6, 1872, Mint Correspondence of the Secretary of the Treasury, RG 69. See also Boutwell to Sherman, Dec. 14, 1872, enclosing Knox to Boutwell (Dec. 14). Letters to Congressional Committees, RG 69.

53. On the trade dollar's origins, see Willem, *United States Trade Dollar,* pp. 55–82; Porter Garnett, "The History of the Trade Dollar," *American Economic Review,* 7 (1917), 91–97.

54. Boutwell to Sherman, Dec. 14, 1872, and Linderman to Boutwell, Nov. 19, 1872, RG 69.

at the suggestion of Treasury officials who were concerned with the prospective market fall in silver. A New York City financier and currency expert who helped to launch the campaign to eliminate legal bimetallism in the United States while serving as American delegate to the Paris Monetary Conference of 1867, Ruggles had watched the progress of the coinage bill through Congress with great interest.[55] Shortly after the measure's passage, he told a meeting of the New York Chamber of Commerce that the trade dollar had replaced the House bill's 384 grain subsidiary coin "on the recommendation contained in the valuable report to the Secretary of the Treasury in November last [1872] by DR. LINDERMAN."[56]

Although the Treasury Department's policy decisions clearly prompted Sherman's subsequent inclusion of the trade dollar in the mint bill, the senator probably was aware of the impending market depreciation of silver even before his December meeting with Boutwell and Linderman. In the summer of 1872 Sherman had traveled throughout the Far West. He visited the area's financial center, San Francisco, where Linderman had obtained from local bankers and financiers much of his own information on conditions in the bullion market.[57] Sherman also visited the major silver-producing mines at Virginia City,

55. For a detailed discussion of Samuel B. Ruggles' role in the demonetization episode, see D. G. Brinton Thompson, *Ruggles of New York: A Life of Samuel B. Ruggles* (New York, 1946), pp. 139–51.

56. Report of the Committee on Coinage, Samuel B. Ruggles, Chairman, Apr. 30, 1873, in "Proceedings," *Annual Report of the New York Chamber of Commerce, 1873–1874* (New York, 1874), pp. 3–4. Ruggles stressed the connection between Linderman's report and Sherman's trade-dollar amendment in even more glowing terms at the Chamber of Commerce's 1873 annual dinner. *Annual Dinner of the Chamber of Commerce of New York* (New York, 1873), pp. 15–19.

57. John Sherman, *Recollections of Forty Years in the House, Senate and Cabinet* (Chicago, 1896), pp. 408–14. See also Sherman to Cornelius Cole, Aug. 3, 1872, Cole MSS; Effie Mack, "The Life and Letters of William Morris Stewart, 1827–1909" (doctoral diss., University of California, 1930), p. 170.

Nevada. This extended tour, occurring at a time when knowledgeable western stockbrokers and mining experts had begun calling attention to the expected flood of bullion from the Comstock, may have given Sherman firsthand insight into the market slump that Linderman and Boutwell described at the December 1872 meeting of the finance committee. The Ohio Republican, however, waited until late in life to relate the sequence of events which led to his last-minute alteration of the coinage bill. In a debate over silver policy in 1893 Sherman told the Senate:

> [Grant's] Secretary of the Treasury, his chosen officer, in a document . . . in December, 1872, just before the passage of this [coinage] act, urged Congress to pass the act, and gave as a reason that, unless it was passed, we would be disturbed by the falling of silver in the markets of the world. Gen. Grant might have said that he did not read the report of the Secretary of the Treasury, but how can members of Congress make such a plea as that? . . . Sir, I would rather stand this day before you defending a law which has been denounced and vilified, as this has been . . . than to plead the baby act, and say I did not know what was pending here before us for two or three years as an act of legislation.[58]

58. *Cong. Record,* 53d Cong., 1st sess., p. 1059 (Aug. 30, 1893). President Ulysses S. Grant, on the occasion to which Sherman referred, wrote a "Mr. Cowdrey" eight months after having signed the Coinage Act of 1873, wondering why "silver is not already coming into the market" following its recent depreciation in value. Grant's remarks were often used by silverites for the next two decades as proof that demonetization had proceeded so secretly that even the President, who signed the measure approving it, lacked awareness that it had taken place! Edward McPherson, *A Hand-Book of Politics for 1874* (Washington, 1874), pp. 134–35. Sherman had denied "foreknowledge" of this price decline in earlier speeches and writings. John Sherman, Senate speech, reprinted as *The Coinage Act of 1873* (Washington, 1888), p. 7, delivered on Mar. 13, 1888. For a similar assertion, see Sherman, *Recollections,* p. 395.

Sherman did "plead the baby act," however, when the mint bill came up for Senate debate in January 1873. Preferring to obscure the real purpose behind the trade-dollar amendment, he left the distinct impression among his Senate colleagues that the revised coinage bill, which most of them had not bothered to read, now contained *both* the 384 grain and 420 grain silver dollars, both Hooper's subsidiary dollar and Linderman's trade coin.[59] Sherman also disclaimed personal responsibility for revisions made in the House-passed measure, including the trade-dollar amendment, observing only that the changes had been prepared by the Treasury Department. "I do not like myself to break in upon this plan," he told the Senate modestly, "or to change it in the slightest degree, but prefer to leave it to the proper officers of the Mint."[60] Above all, at no time during Senate debates did Sherman mention the purpose behind the trade-dollar amendment as stated in Linderman's and Boutwell's reports, their belief that increased domestic production and the declining world-market value of silver made necessary both its swift elimination as a monetary standard and the creation of a foreign market for American bullion.

Had the market decline been noted by inflationists during discussion of the coinage bill, the demonetization of silver would have been infinitely more difficult to secure. It would certainly have provoked an extensive debate over monetary-standard policy. Most senators voted for the amended measure ignorant of the facts needed for an intelligent judgment on the change in monetary standards. The Senate passed the revised mint bill in January 1873. Following a joint-conference committee meeting which retained the trade-dollar amendment, the measure received final congressional approval on February 6. Six days later President Grant signed the Coinage Act, placing the United States on the gold standard.[61]

59. *Cong. Globe,* 42d Cong., 3d sess., p. 672 (Jan. 17, 1873).

60. Ibid.

61. Ibid., pp. 674, 868, 871, 1150, 1189, 1214, 1282 (Jan. 17, 27, Feb. 6, 7, 12, 1873). The Senate conferees were Sherman, John Scott,

Three years elapsed before Congress recognized the silent revolution in American monetary policy to which it had unwittingly assented in 1873. When Sherman later wrote that "no one then contemplated the enormous yield of silver from the mines, and the resulting fall in the market value of silver," he probably spoke accurately about most of his former congressional associates.[62] Few had troubled to familiarize themselves with readily available information regarding the reasons behind demonetization, material such as the 1872 Treasury Department report. But Sherman's remark did not apply to himself. In view of his admitted knowledge of Boutwell's 1872 report and considering his meeting in December 1872 with Linderman and Boutwell, a talk which produced the trade-dollar amendment, Sherman's later plea of ignorance is not credible. It represented the same type of self-serving lie resorted to by William Stewart and "Pig-Iron" Kelley once remonetization became a political issue, when all three men found themselves politically embarrassed by their earlier positions on the Coinage Act.[63]

Was there, then, a "Crime of 1873"? On the one hand, mining-state senators failed to keep properly informed of major trends in the world bullion market important to their constituents. On the other hand, Linderman and Boutwell helped place

---

and Thomas F. Bayard. Representing the House were Hooper and Williams Stoughton. No conference-committee records have survived. Ruggles, in an 1873 report to the New York Chamber of Commerce, noted that the Senate amendments, including the trade-dollar provision, had been accepted by the conferees only "after much discussion." Samuel B. Ruggles, Report to the Chamber of Commerce, Mar. 6, 1873, in "Proceedings," *Annual Report for 1873,* p. 2.

62. Sherman, *Recollections,* p. 397.

63. For William D. Kelley's defense, see *Cong. Record,* 44th Cong., 2d sess., pp. 167–71 (Dec. 13, 1876). For Stewart's apology see "True History of the Demonetization of Silver" delivered Sept. 5, 1893, reprinted as *Speech of Hon. William M. Stewart of Nevada* (Washington, 1893). Thompson has observed wryly, "The attempt of legislators in the late seventies to deny knowledge of what had been going on was, in view of the record, a confession of bad memory, untruthfulness, or gross inattention to business." Thompson, *Ruggles of New York,* p. 158.

the United States on the gold standard knowing that the market slump would soon make silver coinage profitable to holders of bullion if the 412.5 grain silver dollar remained as a monetary standard.[64] Had the majority of congressmen in 1872 recognized the inflationary potential of a depreciated silver currency, the mint bill probably would not have been approved without first restoring the discontinued legal tender silver dollar. The market premium on silver relative to gold disappeared completely before the end of 1873; within three years, a continuing decline made silver coins even less valuable than greenbacks. The silver question, however, no longer remained the exclusive concern of monetary experts by 1876. It had become supremely political and remained the most perplexing economic policy issue in national politics for the next two decades. Those who championed remonetization now dubbed the demonetized 412.5 grain silver dollar the "dollar of the daddies," while the Coinage Act which eliminated it became known as the "Crime of 1873."

Linderman, Boutwell, and Sherman broke no laws, nor did they plot a fate for the old silver dollar that the mint bill did not already have in store for it. Nevertheless, while demonetization was included in the measure's original draft in 1870 largely because of the monetary standard theories of its authors, Linderman and Knox, by late 1872 the basic factor behind the elimination of legal bimetallism in the Coinage Act had become the impending price decline in silver. Linderman observed, shortly before his death in 1879, that silver's demonetization helped

64. One major recent study of American monetary history and policy has questioned the underlying assumption of government officials who worked to demonetize silver in 1873. "The decline in the gold price of silver," Friedman and Schwartz observed, "itself reflected the demonetization of silver and the widening adoption of the gold standard. The adoption of silver by the U.S. would have reduced the monetary demand for gold and increased the monetary demand for silver and in both respects would have contributed toward a higher gold price of silver. And this would have been intensified by the effects of American action on other countries." Friedman and Schwartz, *Monetary History,* p. 134.

explain the Treasury's notable success in selling millions of dollars worth of low-interest government bonds to European investors between 1873 and 1879, bond sales that helped to underwrite the successful resumption of specie payments.[65] Boutwell and Sherman shared this estimate. If silver had remained a monetary standard, Sherman wrote in 1877, "the United States would now be compelled to suspend the free coinage of silver dollars, as the Latin nations did [in 1874], or to have silver as the sole coin standard of value."[66] Fearful that the United States would resume specie payments while a depreciated legal tender silver currency continued to circulate on a par with gold, Sherman and the Treasury officials had worked to eliminate the double standard "upon grounds of public policy," hoping to dispatch the bulk of the nation's expanded silver production abroad through the trade dollar.[67]

Richard Hofstadter, commenting on Paul M. O'Leary's article, recently acknowledged that "the considerations raised by O'Leary do indicate gold-standard malice aforethought, at least by one significant actor on the scene [Henry Linderman]."[68] Boutwell and Sherman, it must be added, shared Linderman's "gold-standard malice aforethought." Yet is it possible to measure precisely the extent to which the United States stumbled into demonetization, as most historians assert, and the extent to which it was pushed? Interpretation of the episode has been influenced generally by the historian's moral sympathies or economic prejudices, and most American monetary historians have favored either the gold standard or *international* bimetallism. Furthermore, the facts concerning the "crime" show that more of

65. Linderman, *Money and Legal Tender*, pp. 44–45.

66. *Annual Report of the Secretary of the Treasury, 1877*, p. xxiii. See also Sherman, *Recollections*, pp. 397–98.

67. *Annual Report of the Secretary of the Treasury, 1872*, p. xii.

68. Richard Hofstadter, "Free Silver and the Mind of 'Coin' Harvey," *The Paranoid Style in American Politics and Other Essays* (New York, 1965), p. 280.

a conspiracy existed than goldbugs cared to admit—yet less of one than silverites preferred to believe.

The evidence of some collusion among public officials prior to passage of the Coinage Act suggests that money power myths such as the "Crime of 1873" reflect more than the paranoid fantasies of partisan contemporaries. Myth making, after all, "results from man's efforts to make his experience intelligible to himself."[69] The historian's scrutiny of money myths, therefore, may uncover what Marianne Moore called "imaginary gardens with real toads in them." Both silverites and goldbugs presumed the existence of conspiracies in order to clarify otherwise-confusing sets of events. As the silver issue evolved in the 1870s, both groups developed not only policies on the monetary standard question but also ideologies that imputed to their opponents motives such as secret plots against the public interest. The "Crime of 1873," only the first of several conspiratorial schemes that marked debate on the monetary standard question, raised vital and complex economic questions that protagonists on both sides preferred to answer only in the simplest terms.

69. Paul W. Glad, *McKinley, Bryan, and the People* (Philadelphia, 1964), p. 34.

2

Silver Rediscovered: The Resumption Act of 1875

Often American histories find it difficult to determine the exact moment at which a specialized economic policy question becomes a national political issue and the reasons for its emergence. The political factors responsible for the opening of debate on tariff or currency questions have often seemed unpremeditated and even accidental. The silver question arose during the 1870s in precisely this offhand manner, as a president and a congress strikingly ignorant of monetary standard problems laid the groundwork for future controversy on the subject. This absence of economic awareness was sometimes almost whimsical, as when President Grant, who signed the 1873 mint bill which demonetized silver, wrote one correspondent the following year expressing concern that legal tender silver coins were not circulating in sufficient numbers to relieve a temporary shortage of fractional money![1] Most Americans remained indifferent, however, to the problem of silver coinage until 1876, when Congress first discussed the question, a debate triggered by a little-noticed provision in the previous year's Resumption Act.[2]

With little fanfare the silver question entered national politics

1. Grant's letter is reprinted in Edward McPherson, *A Hand-Book of Politics for 1874* (Washington, 1874), pp. 134–35.

2. For this first 1876 debate over silver coinage policy, see *Cong. Record,* 44th Cong., 1st sess., vol. 4, pt. 2, pp. 1762–74, 1985–96, 2042–48, 2049–50, 2082–88, 2129–30, 2254, 2341–53, 2360, 2389, 2418, 2513.

in 1875 through the provision which authorized replacement of fractional greenbacks by subsidiary silver coins. This section, considered both minor and uncontroversial at the time, had barely been discussed during the heated congressional struggle over the Republican-sponsored measure. For over a year following passage of the Resumption Act, the Treasury purchased substantial quantities of bullion and stockpiled millions of dollars worth of the newly-minted subsidiary coins without attracting public or political attention. In February 1876, however, congressional bickering over release of these silver coins opened the door to a long struggle over the future of silver as a monetary standard. Demands that the silver dollar be restored as a unit of account were first heard during the legislative discussions early in 1876 over the expediency of issuing subsidiary coins in place of fractional paper notes, which supporters of the policy viewed as a first step toward specie resumption.[3]

According to the charge hurled most often in early debate by congressional opponents of the new subsidiary coinage, western mineowners, notably the powerful Bonanza Kings, secured the provision's insertion in the Resumption Act in order to provide a guaranteed government market for their bullion.[4] This accusation of mineowner complicity, leveled without a single piece of evidence, was widely accepted, nevertheless, among a number of eastern gold standard congressmen, newspapers, and journals of opinion.[5] Although mineowners like the Bonanza Kings

3. Ibid., pp. 2341–53. See also the notes made by Senator Justin S. Morrill of Vermont on early senatorial response to the problem of remonetizing silver, found on the back of a copy of Morrill's bill, Senate no. 157, 44th Cong., 1st sess., ca. Jan. 5, 1876, in Morrill MSS, Library of Congress, hereafter referred to as LC.

4. See, for example, the accusations against the Bonanza Kings by Representatives Abram S. Hewitt of New York, a Democrat, and William D. "Pig-Iron" Kelley of Pennsylvania, a Republican, made during House debate over issuing the subsidiary coinage in March, 1876. *Cong. Record,* 44th Cong., 1st sess., vol. 4, pt. 2, pp. 1764–67, 1770.

5. Ibid., New York *Tribune,* Feb. 18, 1876; *The Nation,* Apr. 20, 27, 1876; *Iron Age, 18,* July 20, Aug. 3, 1876; Baltimore *Sun,* Aug. 3, 1876. Many bankers and businessmen also held this view of the mine-

profited handsomely as a result of this proposal, it originated elsewhere and received most of its support from other, more unexpected, groups in the business community. Whatever its genesis, the attempt to implement the silver coinage section of the Resumption Act triggered a fierce congressional battle over remonetizing the metal completely, a battle which flared intermittently as a national issue between 1876 and 1896.

The section of the Resumption Act replacing fractional greenbacks with subsidiary silver appeared relatively unimportant to legislators at the time, however, and attracted little attention during debate on the measure.[6] No senator challenged the remark by Ohio Republican John Sherman, the bill's floor manager in the upper chamber, that silver redemption of existing fractional currency was likely to "meet the general concurrence of every member of the Senate."[7] Even some Democrats who opposed the Republican-sponsored bill still favored replacement of minor paper notes with silver, and one hard-money Democrat, Allen Thurman of Ohio, confessed during debate that he knew of no senator who did not approve that particular section of the measure.[8] Only two senators, Hamilton and Schurz, raised questions about the provision; both attempted to extract a promise from John Sherman that the fractional greenbacks, once redeemed, would not be reissued, thereby inflating the currency

---

owners. See especially August Belmont to Thomas F. Bayard, Nov. 18, 1877; W. G. Deshler to John Sherman, Jan. 13, 1877; G. L. Foote to H. C. Fahnestock, Nov. 8, 1877; all in John Sherman MSS, LC; John Curtis to James A. Garfield, Feb. 7, 1878, James A. Garfield MSS, LC; Morris H. Cook to Thomas F. Bayard, Dec. 29, 1877, Thomas F. Bayard MSS, LC.

6. Unger, *The Greenback Era,* p. 254; Alonzo B. Hepburn, *A History of Currency in the United States* (New York, 1924), pp. 222–23; Davis R. Dewey, *Financial History of the United States* (New York, 1934), pp. 372–74.

7. *Cong. Record,* 43d Cong., 2d sess., vol. 3, pt. 1, p. 194. For the full Senate debate on the Resumption Act, ibid., pp. 186–88, 194–208.

8. Ibid., p. 197; James Garfield to [name illegible], July 15, 1875, *Garfield Letterbooks,* Garfield MSS, LC.

still further. Sherman pledged to answer this question during floor debate, yet he was aware that the Resumption Act's major attraction to a divided Republican party lay in its ambiguous silence on the important question of whether it would effectively expand or reduce the volume of circulating currency. The party's inflationist and contractionist wings both found the measure acceptable partly because it left this fundamental question unanswered, and Sherman therefore decided against responding to the inquiries of Senators Hamilton and Schurz.[9] However, apart from these embarrassing queries concerning possible reissue of the fractional greenbacks, the subsidiary coinage provision was not discussed during either Senate or House debate on the Resumption Act.[10]

A major factor in accounting for widespread congressional acceptance of the silver coinage section was the belief, shared by supporters and opponents of the Resumption Act, that the provision represented sound monetary policy. Democratic Senator Thurman, one of the measure's most effective critics, viewed the subsidiary coinage provision as the only portion of the bill which could conceivably help in achieving specie resumption. Both Thurman and his fellow-Ohioan John Sherman noted that the section had been recommended both by the Director of the Mint and by the Secretary of the Treasury.[11] Unlike the other, more controversial, sections of the act, the subsidiary coinage section was included at the explicit request of Secretary Benja-

9. *Cong. Record,* 43d Cong., 2d sess., vol. 3, pt. 1, pp. 194, 197. See also Carothers, *Fractional Money,* p. 248, and Unger, *Greenback Era,* pp. 256–57.

10. Republican leaders rushed the bill through the House with less than ten minutes of debate, refusing to allow even the introduction of amendments. Most of the brief House debate concerned the right of congressmen to print their unintroduced amendments in the *Congressional Record! Cong. Record,* 43d Cong., 2d sess., vol. 3, pt. 1, pp. 233–34, 317–19.

11. Garfield to [name illegible], July 15, 1875, *Garfield Letterbooks,* Garfield MSS, LC; *Cong. Record,* 43d Cong., 2d sess., vol. 3, pt. 1, p. 197.

min H. Bristow, who wrote in his December 1874 report to Congress: "With a view to the resumption of specie payments, it is important to manufacture a large quantity of silver coins to take the place of the fractional notes . . . and to gradually withdraw the fractional notes." This action, the secretary believed, in conjunction with removing mint charges on gold coinage, would retard the flow of domestic gold and silver bullion abroad into more profitable foreign markets.[12] The Director of the Mint, Henry Richard Linderman, made a similar recommendation in his November 1874 report to Bristow.[13]

With respect to the other features of a resumption measure, however, Bristow was reluctant to saddle Congress with an official administration plan for returning to specie payments. His 1874 *Report* generally avoided specific recommendations on this question and left in the hands of Republican congressional leaders the difficult task of framing a compromise resumption bill acceptable to both the party's hard money and soft money factions. "My desire is to get the support, in the first instance, of all friends of resumption," Bristow wrote a business associate in November 1874 concerning his forthcoming report to Congress, "and avoid, if possible, provoking any antagonism among that class of people by presenting details of methods about which there would almost certainly be differences of opinion."[14]

Securing the support of "all friends of resumption" behind a compromise measure may have been Bristow's desire, but it also mirrored the strategy actually employed by John Sherman to secure passage of a resumption bill during the session of Congress which began in December 1874. Fraternal squabbles between opposing wings of the Republican party on the resumption question had proven costly in the November congressional

12. *Report of the Secretary of the Treasury for 1874* (Washington, D.C., 1874), p. xxii.

13. *Report of the Director of the Mint for 1874* (Washington, D.C., 1874), pp. 15–16.

14. Benjamin Bristow to E. H. Stoughton, Nov. 18, 1874, Bristow MSS, LC.

elections, and control of the House of Representatives passed into Democratic hands for the first time since the Civil War.[15] Fearful that continued battling on financial issues would impair Republican chances in the 1876 presidential election, Sherman and other party stalwarts returned to Washington in December 1874 and searched for some formula to unite opposing monetary factions behind a single Republican-sponsored resumption measure. This would remove the issue from abrasive congressional debate before the 1876 campaign.[16] Following several days of informal conferences among a small group of influential Republican legislators—most notably, Sherman, Senator Timothy Howe of Wisconsin, Senator George F. Edmunds of Vermont, and Representative Henry L. Dawes of Massachusetts—a senatorial caucus representing every shade of financial opinion within the Republican party assumed the task of framing a compromise bill reflecting party policy on the problem of returning to specie payments.[17]

The wide divergence of views among the eleven members of the caucus dramatized the importance of arriving at some mutually acceptable plan for resumption, however vague and unworkable its details, before the issue split the Republican party wide open. "The necessity of an agreement," Sherman later wrote, "was so absolute that a failure to agree was a disruption of the Republican party."[18] Many leading Republicans, conscious of

15. Unger, *Greenback Era,* pp. 249–50.

16. The most complete and incisive analysis of the Resumption Act's background is in Unger, *Greenback Era,* pp. 249–63. See also Sherman, *Recollections,* pp. 426–39.

17. The group included soft-money Midwesterners like Oliver P. Morton of Indiana, Thomas W. Ferry of Michigan, and John A. Logan of Illinois, along with stern monetary contractionists like George S. Boutwell of Massachusetts, George F. Edmunds of Vermont, Roscoe Conkling of New York, and Frederick T. Frelinghuysen of New Jersey. Pragmatic middle-ground opinion on resumption and the proper volume of currency was represented by Sherman, Timothy Howe, William Boyd Allison of Iowa, and Aaron Sargent of California. Sherman, *Recollections,* p. 428; Unger, *Greenback Era,* p. 252.

18. Sherman, *Recollections,* p. 428.

the long-standing antagonism between the midwestern inflationist and eastern contractionist wings of the party on the resumption issue, questioned the caucus' ability to achieve a compromise solution. "I should be glad if the Republican Party could take some conservative step looking toward specie payments," Congressman James A. Garfield wrote one correspondent shortly after the caucus began its deliberations, "but I doubt if anything can be secured this winter."[19] Faced, however, with the prospect of a disastrous party split which might pull Republicans of all financial persuasions down to defeat in 1876, a majority of the senatorial caucus accepted the compromise draft of a resumption act prepared by the group's chairman, John Sherman, with the assistance of George F. Edmunds.[20]

Sherman's measure sought the broadest possible consensus among Republicans on matters involving resumption and made important concessions both to hard money and soft money advocates. The first two sections of the bill did not appear of special political interest, however, to most members of the caucus committee. They provided for the replacement of fractional greenbacks with subsidiary silver and for the repeal of the existing seigniorage or minting charge on gold bullion, both of which had been requested by Treasury and mint officials for several years.[21] A provision of Sherman's draft which legalized "free banking" had special appeal to the party's inflationist wing. In other sections, however, the bill remained deliberately ambiguous on the question of monetary inflation. It called for the Treasury to redeem $80 in greenbacks for every $100 in new

19. Garfield to J. W. Schuckers, Dec. 19, 1874, Schuckers MSS, LC.

20. Unger, *Greenback Era,* p. 253; Sherman, *Recollections,* p. 428. See also Don Carlos Barrett, *The Greenbacks and Resumption of Specie Payments, 1862–1879* (Cambridge, Mass., 1931), pp. 182–83.

21. On the subsidiary coinage recommendation, see the following *Annual Report(s) of the Director of the Mint* [included in the yearly volume of reports of Treasury officials bound with the *Report of the Secretary*], 1869, pp. 349–50; 1870, pp. 421–22; 1871, p. 432; 1874, p. 200. See also *Report of the Secretary* (1874). On the abolition of seigniorage, ibid.

bank notes issued until the circulating stock of government paper money had been reduced to a minimum of $300 million. Once this greenback minimum had been achieved, the act placed no restrictions on the total amount of bank-note issue. The final clause of the measure authorized the Treasury Department to employ both surplus revenues and funds secured through bond sales to stockpile a gold reserve for use in purchasing any greenbacks presented for redemption after January 1, 1879.[22] This stipulation, that actual resumption would not begin for four years, offended a small group of bitter-end Republican contractionists, like Carl Schurz, who refused to accept the caucus' compromise measure and condemned as unworkable the measures for returning to specie payments that the bill authorized.[23]

Most Republicans in Congress, especially those from the Midwest, felt generally satisfied with the compromise Resumption Act. Not only did it sanction free banking, long a popular rallying point in the agrarian districts, but it also gave the region's Republican officeholders a comprehensive plan for specie resumption which they could endorse without being forced to take a position on the politically sensitive question of currency contraction, on which the measure remained silent.[24] At a time when current hard money dogma held that specie resumption could be achieved only by contracting the greenback supply, the bill's managers had discreetly avoided facing the problem of whether paper money redeemed under provisions of the act would be reissued or destroyed. To most observers, hard-money Republicans appeared to have gained less than their inflationist brethren by accepting the caucus committee's resumption scheme: "At all events, the soft-money Republicans received immediate free banking, for which they had long agi-

22. *Coinage Laws of the United States, 1792 to 1894,* 4th ed., Senate Report no. 235, 53d Cong., 2d sess. (Washington, D.C., 1894), pp. 61–62.

23. Unger, *Greenback Era,* pp. 256–63.

24. Ibid., pp. 256–59. See also Sherman, *Recollections,* p. 428.

tated, in exchange for a problematical resumption in 1879, four years away."[25] In view of the many bitter wrangles among Republicans on the resumption question since the end of the Civil War, however, the bill's managers maintained remarkable discipline over their unruly troops, and the Resumption Act swept through both houses of Congress on a strict party vote: 32 to 14 in the Senate and 136 to 98 in the House. President Grant signed the measure into law on January 14, 1875.[26]

None of the party's discordant currency factions claimed the bill as an undisputed victory for its own views, but most Republicans expressed relief that the resumption question—or so they hoped—had been removed from Congress for the moment and dropped into the lap of the Treasury Department, which had responsibility for administering the deliberately vague provisions of the compromise measure. Republican supporters of resumption felt that Treasury officials could proceed with preparations for a return to specie payments without injecting the question into congressional debate again until the party fought the presidential campaign of 1876 on a more familiar and comfortable battleground, namely the Southern Question. As Sherman wrote to a political associate following Senate passage of the Resumption Act in December 1874, "the Finance bill is a compromise . . . and although not what I considered the *best* yet is a *good* measure and the only one that could unite Republican senators. I hope it will pass the House without amendments and thus leave us to consider the much more difficult problem presented by the state of affairs in the South."[27] Although effective in staving off a disastrous split in party ranks before the

25. Unger, *Greenback Era,* p. 255. London *Times,* Dec. 26, 1874, in Bristow MSS, LC. See also New York *Tribune,* Dec. 21, 22, 23, 24, 28, 31, 1874.

26. *Cong. Record,* 43d Cong., 2d sess., vol. 3, pt. 1, pp. 208, 319, 459.

27. John Sherman to Isaac Stingem, Dec. 28, 1874, Sherman MSS, LC. See also James A. Garfield, Diary, entry for Dec. 23, 1874, Garfield MSS, LC.

election of 1876, few of the Resumption Act's Republican supporters felt confident that the measure represented a final solution, or even a sensible one, to the vexing task of restoring specie payments. "We must do the Senate of the United States the justice," the London *Times* avowed while criticizing the act, "of remembering that they do not look upon . . . their bill as the means of accomplishing the result they desire."[28]

The section providing for the redemption of fractional greenbacks with subsidiary silver was probably written by John A. Logan, an Illinois inflationist and a member of the Senate caucus committee which drafted the resumption measure. Apparently, the caucus decided against using an earlier Treasury Department draft of the same provision. The entire question of the Resumption Act's authorship, in fact, remains uncertain. John Sherman, in his *Recollections,* claimed to have written the key section of the bill, which outlined procedures leading to resumption of specie payments, assisted only by George Edmunds of Vermont. Sherman remembered that this "important and closing clause of the bill was referred to Mr. Edmunds and myself."[29] For his part, Senator Edmunds later disparaged Sherman's role in the proceedings, claiming after the Ohioan's death that he, Edmunds, had drafted the measure's central provisions without Sherman's assistance. According to Edmunds, Sherman had functioned merely as an intermediary, transmitting the measure from the caucus to the full Senate in his role as spokesman for the ad hoc committee. Edmund's account of the committee's deliberations is admittedly self-serving, but it remains the only surviving discussion of the group's procedures during its work on the bill. Interestingly, the Vermont Republican did not claim to have authored the entire Resumption Act, only its important final section. Edmunds noted that the caucus committee had

28. London *Times,* Dec. 26, 1874, in Bristow MSS, LC. See also Unger, *Greenback Era,* pp. 260–63.

29. Sherman, *Recollections,* p. 429.

assigned John A. Logan to assist him in preparing the remainder of the measure and that Logan drew up the subsidiary coinage provision.[30]

"Black Jack" Logan, Civil War general and Republican stalwart from Illinois for two decades following the war, never publicly acknowledged that he wrote the subsidiary coinage clause, but certain aspects of his life in the 1870s suggest that he may have been more concerned with this particular provision than were other members of the Republican caucus. During the post-Civil War period, Logan speculated constantly in Colorado silver mines, investing much of his time and his small supply of capital in pursuit of quick bonanzas that he never achieved. In the summer of 1874, Logan traveled to Colorado, combining a vacation with local legal business. While there, he explored possible mining development in the state. "I could see enough silver with the eye," he wrote his wife after examining one mine, "to make any one as rich as they ought to be . . . I could get a mine here that would make a constant profit, but you cannot trust anyone to act for you." Logan apparently overcame his anxieties, since he purchased half-interest in a Georgetown, Colorado silver mine and mill that same winter.[31] If Edmunds is correct in attributing authorship of the subsidiary coinage section to Logan, the Illinois Republican prepared the provision while himself deeply involved in private silver mining investment. Whatever his personal motives, however, Logan's draft followed closely the previous recommendations concerning subsidiary coinage made by both the Director of the Mint and the Secretary of the Treasury. "Black Jack" Logan's career in mining consisted of a series of unsuccessful speculations as a mineowner during the 1870s and 1880s. His widow observed despondently after his

30. Barrett, *Greenbacks and Resumption of Specie Payments,* pp. 182–85.

31. John A. Logan to Mary Logan, Aug. 15, 1874, May 25, 1875, Logan MSS, LC.

death that she held "enough beautifully engraved certificates of stock in mines, for which he paid cash, to paper a good-sized room, which were, of course worthless."[32]

Whether Logan, or some other member of the Republican caucus, actually wrote the subsidiary coinage provision of the Resumption Act, of course, cannot be shown conclusively. It is likely, however, that the section was drafted by its congressional sponsors without first consulting Secretary of the Treasury Bristow or Director of the Mint Linderman, despite the fact that it substantially followed earlier Treasury recommendations. Evidence of congressional authorship comes from a letter of Linderman's to John Sherman, written on the day the Resumption Act passed the Senate, in which the mint director suggested several possible changes in the subsidiary coinage provision that might clarify its meaning. Linderman felt troubled especially by its vague wording, which seemed to exclude redemption of the fifteen cent fractional paper note. He proposed that Sherman amend the section to include specific reference to this odd denomination of greenback and acknowledged its caucus committee authorship by observing: "The words 'standard value' on the sixth line I infer means silver coins of the *fineness* and *weight* as prescribed in the Coinage Act of 1873. If I am correct in assuming this as the meaning of the words referred to, it is all right."[33] Sherman, aware of Linderman's technical ability in the drafting of coinage legislation, evidently called upon the mint director

32. Mary S. Logan, *Reminiscences of a Soldier's Wife, An Autobiography* (New York, 1913), p. 329. For informative discussions of Logan's career as a mining investor see pp. 327–29, and George Francis Dawson, *Life and Services of Gen. John A. Logan* (Chicago and New York, 1887), pp. 217–18. A personal account of Logan's frustrations as a Colorado mineowner can be drawn from Logan's letters to his wife in the spring and summer of 1875. See especially John A. Logan to Mary Logan, May 31, June 1, June 7, June 8, July 6, July 31, Aug. 7, 1875, Logan MSS, LC.

33. Henry Linderman to John Sherman, Dec. 22, 1874, Letterbooks, Director of the Mint, National Archives, RG 104.

to clarify any obscure details of the subsidiary silver clause prior to Senate passage of the Resumption Act.

The apparent absence of consultation between Treasury officials and the Republican caucus on this provision reflected the strained political atmosphere among congressional Republicans when the caucus committee met in December 1874 to formulate party financial policy in the wake of a shattering electoral defeat. Any attempt by the Treasury to impose an administration-sponsored resumption bill upon Congress would have proven disastrous, given the bitterness which many party stalwarts felt toward the Grant regime following the president's veto of the inflation bill prior to the 1874 election, an action which had cost the party dearly in the midwest.[34] Even before Congress convened in December 1874, Secretary Bristow indicated to friends that he intended to provide only general guidelines for a resumption bill and leave the details to be worked out by Republican congressional leaders, in order to insure wide support for any measure which emerged from the party caucus.[35] The senatorial caucus evidently drafted the entire resumption measure, including its subsidiary coinage provision. Nevertheless, without support from some Republican faction, the subsidiary silver clause would probably have been dropped from the version of the bill presented to Congress. It becomes important, therefore, to understand which groups were most interested in the section which proposed redemption of up to fifty million dollars worth of fractional greenbacks in subsidiary silver. What were the "silver interests" in 1875 that actively promoted the subsidiary coinage feature of the Resumption Act?

Some historians have viewed the section as a quid pro quo to insure support for the entire measure by Pacific coast silver-state Republicans. According to Neil Carothers, the leading authority

34. Unger, *Greenback Era,* pp. 249–51.

35. Bristow to E. H. Stoughton, Nov. 18, 1874, Bristow MSS, LC. See also Linderman to Bristow, Jan. 25, 1875, Bristow MSS, LC.

on American subsidiary coinage, "the silver interests of the West, well represented in Congress, were quite ready to support any measure that revived silver coinage." In the compromise worked out by Sherman's caucus committee, Carothers goes on to say, the sections which provided for subsidiary silver to replace fractional greenbacks and which abolished minting charges on gold coinage "were, although excellent in themselves, to a large extent merely concessions to the inflationist and mining interests."[36] Most economic historians have either omitted discussing the background of the subsidiary coinage provision or have called it simply "minor and non-controversial," born out of concern for western mining companies and mining-state congressmen.[37] Actually, the provision enjoyed a great deal of support from some unexpected quarters in the lobbying which preceded passage of the Resumption Act.

The subsidiary coinage section, not surprisingly, received strong backing in the silver-producing regions of the West. The two leading mining-state newspapers, both Republican journals, endorsed the provision. However, both dailies made it clear that they based their approval not on the potential value of newly minted subsidiary coinage to western mining but rather on the stimulus which expanded silver coinage would provide for a swift resumption of specie payments. "The idea of supplying silver in the place of the fractional currency, though of secondary importance," the Virginia City *Territorial Enterprise* observed, "is a good thing for Nevada, though we are never troubled with fractional [paper] currency here. Such a demand for our chief product will cause it to advance a little in price [but] there is some satisfaction in feeling that one lives within sight of what will restore the nation to a healthy financial basis, even if [one] has no stock in either the California or Consolidated Virginia [mines]."[38] Similarly, Denver's *Rocky Mountain Daily News*

36. Carothers, *Fractional Money* (New York, 1930), p. 248.
37. Unger, *Greenback Era,* p. 254.
38. Virginia City (Nevada) *Territorial Enterprise,* Dec. 9, 1874.

praised passage of the Resumption Act partially because of the silver coinage provision but noted that "the greatest good that will be effected by the bill is the assurance that it gives to the community that there will be no further inflation of the [paper] currency."[39] Both newspapers recognized that the measure was "more of a political than financial act" but considered it "nevertheless a step in the right direction, and perhaps as good a bill as could be expected on account of the discordant views which exist both in and out of congress."[40] There is no sign, however, in these or other western papers, that the redemption of fractional greenbacks with subsidiary coinage had been of special concern to the mining community prior to passage of the Resumption Act, nor do the mining state journals appear to have advocated such a policy before the Republican senatorial caucus produced its bill. States depending for their prosperity upon silver mining obviously responded favorably to the provision, but there is no evidence that "western mining interests" either initiated or lobbied for the subsidiary section.

On the other hand, certain eastern and midwestern business groups did actively sponsor this portion of the Resumption Act. Weeks before the Republican caucus committee prepared its compromise measure, Vermont's Republican Senator Justin S. Morrill, a firm contractionist like his colleague George Edmunds, forwarded to Secretary Bristow the draft of a resumption plan developed by a mutual acquaintance, George Harrington. Harrington was Assistant Secretary of the Treasury during the Civil War under Salmon P. Chase and in 1874 became president of a New York City telegraph company. Among other features, Harrington's proposal called for introducing fifty million dollars worth of subsidiary silver coin into the monetary system at the rate of one million per month and simultaneously withdrawing

39. *Rocky Mountain Daily News* (Denver, Colo.), Jan. 16, 1875. See also Dec. 21, 1874 edition.

40. Ibid., Jan. 16, 1875. See also *Territorial Enterprise*, Dec. 24, 1874; Jan. 8, Jan. 19, Jan. 20, 1875.

forty million dollars worth of fractional greenbacks at the same rate. Fearing a contraction of available coinage prior to resumption, Harrington also urged that the government increase the legal tender limit of silver coins from five dollars to fifteen: "Thus you protect the Importer from any undue advance in coin [i.e., in the market value of silver coins] during the preparatory period."[41]

Business support for replacement of fractional greenbacks with an expanded silver coinage also emerged from a meeting of the National Board of Trade held in Washington on December 9, 1874. Representatives of boards of trade from Baltimore, Boston, Buffalo, Chicago, Milwaukee, Philadelphia, Portland, St. Louis—with only the New York Board of Trade absent among the major eastern and midwestern mercantile groups—prepared a resumption plan to present to the Treasury Department and to the forthcoming session of Congress. The main feature of their proposal suggested that the government borrow "four hundred millions in gold as a means of resuming specie payments." Like Harrington, the National Board of Trade called for redemption of all fractional greenbacks with newly minted subsidiary silver coins as a necessary first step toward specie resumption. The group stressed the contractionary effect of its silver coinage proposal by demanding "the cancellation and destruction of all the fractional currency . . . that shall be redeemed."[42] Secretary Bristow received a copy of the National Board of Trade's plan on December 15, before the Republican caucus met, along with a recommendation from the board's Executive Council that Congress legislate on the subject of resumption without delay so that "it may have the support of the Commercial and other press."[43] Since the board drafted its

41. Justin S. Morrill to Benjamin H. Bristow, Dec. 7, 1874, enclosing George Harrington to Bristow, Dec. 4, 1874, Bristow MSS, LC.

42. *Banker's Magazine,* Feb. 1875, pp. 587–91.

43. B. F. Nourse to Benjamin Bristow, Dec. 15, 1874, Bristow MSS, LC.

scheme while meeting in the nation's capital, and since the organization's leading officials remained in Washington to lobby for swift congressional action on resumption, some members of the Republican caucus probably were familiar with its proposals.

Even after introduction of the Resumption Act, certain eastern businessmen took special interest in its silver coinage section. The provision's most ardent defender, in fact, was a New York City national banker, H. C. Fahnestock, who had been associated with Jay Gould in the sale of government bonds during the Civil War. In December 1874, when the Resumption Act was before Congress, Fahnestock was vice-president of New York's powerful First National Bank. Fahnestock, replying to a New York *Tribune* editorial that month criticizing the caucus-sponsored measure, wrote the newspaper's publisher Whitelaw Reid complaining about the journal's opinions. The influential national banker objected especially to the *Tribune's* opposition to the subsidiary coinage clause. Fahnestock believed that the paper's editorial writer was "not 'level' on the silver question," and he advised Reid to send this journalist to the First National Bank for instructions on the subject. "It *is* possible," Fahnestock insisted, "for the Govt. now, without disadvantage, to substitute silver of the present [subsidiary weight and] standard for fractional [paper] currency, if it is undertaken in the right way." The *Tribune* editorial had argued that any increase in the metal's world market price would make silver so much more valuable as bullion that the new coins, once issued, would quickly disappear from circulation and be melted down. The *Tribune* insisted that, for this reason, the new subsidiary coinage would not fulfill the expectations of those who wrote the Resumption Act.[44]

Fahnestock, on the other hand, approved of the entire resumption measure as a helpful step in moving toward a return to

44. New York *Tribune,* Dec. 21, Dec. 22, Dec. 23, Dec. 24, Dec. 28, Dec. 31, 1874. H. C. Fahnestock to Whitelaw Reid, Dec. 21, 1874, Reid MSS, LC.

specie payments, and he questioned the *Tribune's* understanding of prevailing financial conditions. Like the National Board of Trade, the New York banker believed in the value of a cautious but deliberate program of substituting subsidiary coinage for fractional greenbacks, and in a second letter to Reid he argued:

> My point in the former note was to call your attention to what has since been made clear enough in the press discussion; viz., that, with gold at say 110, the Treasury could, without loss, coin silver to retire the fractional currency, and any purchases below 110 for gold would show a profit. To pay it out in driblets before accumulating a supply sufficient to ensure the success of the operation would of course be unwise as would be the redemption of fractional currency where gold rules higher than at present.
>
> Remember that if the govt had on hand enough bullion to replace the 40 odd millions fractionals, it wd take at least two years to coin it. Hadnt we better *begin* then sometime?[45]

In the months following passage of the January 1875 Resumption Act, New York banking and financial houses supplied the bulk of silver bullion purchased by the government for minting the new silver coins, although their support for the subsidiary coinage provision was based on considerations other than economic gain, as Fahnestock's letter to Reid makes clear. However, Fahnestock was not alone during the following months in attempting to secure a government market for bullion owned by his bank. Several other large eastern banking and investment concerns vied with "western silver interests" for substantial shares of the government's new silver purchase program. Thus, the First National Bank of New York sold half a million ounces of silver to the Treasury in March 1875 and, the same month, August Belmont and Company, American agents for the Rothschilds, disposed of one and a half million ounces of bullion to

45. Fahnestock to Reid, Dec. 26, 1874, Reid MSS, LC.

the government. Then, within a week after its huge purchase from August Belmont and Company, the Treasury added to its growing stockpile of silver by acquiring almost three hundred and fifty thousand ounces from the investment house of Drexel, Morgan and Company. Throughout the following months, the mint acquired additional, smaller, amounts of bullion in a steady procession of purchases from such eastern holders of silver as the Fourth National Bank of New York; the Bank of the State of New York; J. and W. Seligman and Company; Kidder, Peabody and Company; and the two major New York bullion dealers, J. B. Colgate and Parker Handy.[46] Although in time these eastern bullion sellers did not sell as much silver to the Treasury as the major western mining companies, they nevertheless represented a significant percentage of total government purchases in the year following passage of the Resumption Act.

The actual volume of eastern sales, however, is less significant than the clear concern for expanding silver coinage evident prior to passage of the Resumption Act among hard-money, pro-resumption mercantile interests in the East and Middle West as well as among influential firms within the eastern banking community, firms like August Belmont and Company and the First National Bank of New York which later, in 1877, organized

46. Benjamin F. Bristow to F. O. French (First National Bank), Mar. 3, 1875, Mint Letterbooks, Secretary of the Treasury, National Archives, RG 104. Bristow to August Belmont, Mar. 15, 1875 and Mar. 16, 1875, RG 104. In both sales, the Treasury Department raised their purchase offer over fifteen cents an ounce more than their original quotations at the request of the two sellers. See Bristow to French, Mar. 3, 1875; Bristow to Belmont and Company, Mar. 16, 1875; and Charles F. Conant to Belmont and Company, Feb. 5, 1875; RG 104. For details of the large Drexel, Morgan and Company sale, see Charles F. Conant to Drexel, Morgan and Company, Mar. 23, 1875, and Bristow to J. Pierpont Morgan, Mar. 30, 1875; RG 104. For a complete accounting of Treasury silver purchases from New York bankers and financiers following passage of the Resumption Act, see *Record of Silver Purchases, 1875–1880, U.S. Assay Office* (New York City), National Archives, RG 104.

banking opposition to silver's *complete* remonetization. Several years earlier, in 1874 and 1875, these same banking and investment houses apparently felt that redemption of the fractional greenbacks in silver coin posed no real danger to the resumption of specie payments in gold.

In this manner, the silver question entered national politics through the subsidiary coinage provision of the 1875 Resumption Act, sponsored originally by Treasury officials as a means of advancing toward specie resumption through redeeming the fractional greenbacks. The provision was apparently written by an inflationist midwesterner, John A. Logan, himself deeply implicated in mining investments. Active support for the section, however, came mainly from commercial groups and eastern financiers who saw both economic advantage and sound financial policy in an expanded government silver purchase program. Few of those who sponsored and favored the subsidiary coinage section of the Resumption Act anticipated the national political importance that the silver question would take on even before the election of 1876.

3

The First Bimetallist: John Percival Jones of Nevada

An article of political faith among western politicians in Congress has been their devotion to silver coinage. "My boy," Arizona Senator Henry F. Ashurst informed the new Secretary of the Treasury in 1933, "I was brought up from my mother's knee on silver and I can't discuss that any more with you than you can discuss your religion with me."[1] The campaign to remonetize silver began during the 1870s, and it might have surprised men like Ashurst, weaned on its traditions, to learn that at the beginning few western politicians rallied behind the silver standard.

Only one mining state legislator in Congress, Senator John Percival Jones of Nevada, vigorously supported remonetization during the first silver drive. Jones served as the sole western apostle of bimetallism in the congressional struggle which opened in April 1876, helping to propogate doctrines later identified with the entire mining West. Although a mineowner himself, Jones championed the issue more for political advantage and ideological reasons than on economic grounds, and he played a crucial role in calling public attention to silver in the early years of the struggle. Nevadans called him "the daddy of our dollars," a pun on their nickname for the 412.5 grain silver dollar which had been demonetized in 1873, "the dollar of our daddies." Jones played a pivotal role in the emergence of silver as a national issue in 1876, an issue whose origins can be under-

1. John Morton Blum, ed., *From The Morgenthau Diaries, Years of Crisis, 1928–1938* (Boston, 1959), p. 186.

stood fully only against the political background of Nevada politics and within the economic context of an existing depression.

The Congressional drive to remonetize silver began in 1876 largely as an expansionist response of hard money specie resumptionists to the worsening depression. The problem of returning to specie payments without further reduction in the monetary supply troubled many of these resumptionists, since they viewed any additional currency contraction as an impediment to swift recovery from the protracted economic downturn which began in 1873. Silver politics in the United States arose in this depression setting. Reflecting the social and economic tensions that have marked such periods in American history, the remonetization struggle of the 1870s represented something other than an episode in agrarian discontent alone. The drive to restore the 412.5 grain silver dollar as a legal unit of account, essentially a demand for return to the monetary status quo before 1873, attracted to its ranks a variety of groups within American society for moral and political as well as economic motives. Traditional historical analysis of the silver issue, which has drawn a simple line of cleavage between "hard" and "soft" money forces—"not Republican against Democrat, but East versus West, banker versus farmer, creditor versus debtor"—has failed to portray accurately the social forces present in the campaign to remonetize silver from 1876 to 1878.[2] The silverites are viewed usually as little more than latter-day greenbackers: "If they could not have paper instead of coin, they were determined to have silver coin at a parity with gold."[3] Yet to identify the

2. Davis S. Muzzey, *James G. Blaine: A Political Idol of Other Days* (New York, 1934), p. 136; Don Carlos Barrett, *Greenbacks and Resumption of Specie Payments* (Cambridge, Mass., 1931), p. 212–13; William J. Schultze and M. R. Caine, *Financial Development of the United States* (New York, 1937), p. 376; Paul Studenski and Herman E. Krooss, *Financial History* (New York, 1963), pp. 186–88; John D. Hicks, *The Populist Revolt* (Minneapolis, 1931; Bison edition, 1959), p. 315 and passim.

3. Muzzey, *James G. Blaine.*

supporters of remonetization simply as disguised greenback inflationists fails to recognize the economic complexity of the silver movement.

Supporters of remonetization included both inflationists and contractionists, greenbackers and anti-greenbackers. Numbered among the silverites were substantial groups of farmers, businessmen, and bankers as well as politicians, publishers, and publicists. The drive to restore silver as a monetary standard derived this broad appeal not from economics alone but from its compelling moral symbolism. Underlying the silver drive's emotional attractiveness to many Americans of different class backgrounds in the 1870s lay a more general hostility among many Americans of varied economic backgrounds toward the new industrial society, which was changing or had already changed many older economic patterns, numbered among which was the demonetization of silver itself. The slogans used by the silverites during this decade referred to restoration of the double standard as "an act of justice"—*restore* legal bimetallism, *remonetize* the dollar of the daddies, *redress* the "Crime of 1873"—and silverites preferred to call themselves "old fashioned hard-money men."[4] As financial conservatives, many among the leaders and supporters of the silver drive were more interested in the favorable impact which they believed that remonetization would have on specie resumption than in profiting personally from an expansion of silver coinage. An ideological faith in bimetallism had roots that extended back to the early days of the American republic. Economic historians have considered this traditional veneration of metallic money a major reason for the failure of the Greenback party, and this affection for silver coinage served as a symbolic link for Americans of different classes, sections, and political affiliations who joined forces to support remonetization during the political tempest over silver in the late 1870s. "The restoration of the 'silver dollar of the Fathers,'"

4. James T. Worthington to Thomas Ewing, Feb. 25, 1878, Salmon P. Chase MSS, Pennsylvania Historical Society (Philadelphia); *Cincinnati Commercial,* July 17, 1876.

one of John Sherman's correspondents wrote shortly after the election of Rutherford B. Hayes, "is a very popular idea with the masses; *Republican* and Democratic." Sherman's correspondent went on to observe that the essential root of the agitation lay in the fact that "right or wrong, [silver's] demonetization is regarded as a grand error if not a crime."[5]

The battle to remonetize silver opened during the lowest point of the six-year national business decline which began after the Panic of 1873, the most serious of three major late nineteenth-century downturns in the American business cycle.[6] Later statistical measurement has corroborated the severity of economic collapse during the 1870s, with the "general price index" alone declining from 100 in 1873 at the depression's start to 77 by 1879, when the economy began its upswing.[7] By 1876 almost every aspect of production and commerce had felt the impact of this decline. The total number of New York City bank clearings, "one of the more precise mathematical tests for measuring the ebb and flow of the economy," declined from $35,461,000 in 1873 to $21,597,000 by 1876, while new railroad construction fell to its lowest point since the Civil War, from 7,379 miles of track laid in 1873 to 1,711 in 1876. The production of pig iron, a key barometer of economic trends in an industrializing society, decreased similarly from 2,868,279 net tons in 1873 to 2,093,236 net tons by 1876, and few Americans expected a quick recovery from the general economic stagnation.

5. H. S. Bundy to John Sherman, Dec. 23, 1876, Sherman MSS, LC.

6. A. R. Eckler, "A Measure of the Severity of Depressions, 1873–1932," *Review of Economic Statistics, 15* (1933), 77, 81; Edward C. Kirkland, *Industry Comes of Age: Business, Labor, and Public Policy, 1860–1897* (New York, 1961), pp. 6–7.

7. Bureau of the Census, *Historical Statistics of the United States, 1789–1945,* p. 231. Smaller dips in the general price index took place during subsequent nineteenth-century depressions, with an eleven point decline from 1882–86 and a seven point drop from 1890–96. See also Kirkland, *Industry Comes of Age,* p. 8.

Although production of many refined metals slumped considerably, the output of silver bullion from the western mines during these same years reached continually higher levels, increasing from 17,789,100 ounces in 1871 to 27,650,400 ounces in 1873 and expanding to 29,996,200 ounces by 1876. Because of silver's demonetization by both Germany and the United States during the early 1870s, at a time when American production of the metal soared yearly, the market price of silver depreciated steadily after 1873. The bullion value of the demonetized 412.5 grain silver dollar declined from a fraction more than the gold dollar in 1873 to less than ninety cents in gold by 1876, a drop in the commercial ratio of silver to gold from 15.93 to 1 in 1873 to 17.75 to 1 by the latter year.[8]

Many contemporaries traced the severity of the depression in American business to such factors as overproduction, the decrease in new railroad investment, the slump in the price level and general loss of confidence in the economy.[9] Often, however, these same analysts believed that a return to economic prosperity depended primarily upon adoption of proper financial policies by the national government. Believers in the prevailing quantity theory of money—whether greenbackers, gold standard men, or silverites—viewed the business collapse as intertwined somehow with earlier changes in the stock of available capital. "The true and only cause of the stagnation in industry and commerce now everywhere felt," declared the congressional Monetary Commission in 1877, "is the fact everywhere existing of falling prices, caused by a shrinkage in the volume of money."[10] The relationship between this declining money stock, more

8. Kirkland, *Industry Comes of Age*, p. 6; *Historical Statistics*, pp. 149, 151–52, 270, 277.

9. For a review of contemporary opinion on the causes of the depression which began in 1873, see United States Senate, Report No. 703, *Report of the Monetary Commission*, 44th Cong., 2d sess., vol. 1, pp. 117–24.

10. *Report of the Monetary Commission*, p. 121; see also Kirkland, *Industry Comes of Age*, p. 26.

accurately a monetary stock which contemporaries *thought* to be declining, and the country's low level of economic activity received special attention on the Pacific coast in early 1876, where suggestions were first heard concerning the possibility of utilizing silver coinage to supplement the existing circulating stock of currency. By February 1876, at a time when the West began to feel the impact of the national business slump, the San Francisco business community and the city's leading newspapers were debating strenuously the possible effect of remonetizing silver upon western economic conditions.[11]

Even in Nevada, despite the state's continuing high level of employment until mid-1876, there was widespread anxiety over the future of the country's largest silver producing region. In Virginia City, center of the Comstock Lode, by 1876 only the two Bonanza-owned mines, the California and Consolidated Virginia were issuing dividends to their stockholders among the hundreds of mines in the area. "The city was subject to marked fluctuations [even] in prosperity," one writer observed, "and there were frequent labor troubles."[12] The historian of the Comstock Lode has also noted the area's widespread unemployment and poverty at the peak of the region's phenomenal mining boom in 1876: "The complaint of hard times on the Comstock during the height of the big bonanza sounds strange, yet the newspapers constantly dwell upon the lack of employment for many that had flocked in."[13]

A torrent of editorial comment on "the silver problem" poured from the press of the Virginia City *Territorial Enter-*

11. Letter from the Editor of the San Francisco *Alta* to the Washington, D.C. *National Republican,* Feb. 23, 1876. See also *Alta,* Feb. 9, 1876, cited in *National Republican,* Feb. 19, 1876. Also Jan. 11 and Mar. 2, 1876.

12. Francis Phelps Weisenburger, *Idol of the West, The Fabulous Career of Rollin Mallory Daggett* (Syracuse, 1965), p. 79.

13. Grant H. Smith, "History of the Comstock Lode, 1850–1920," *University of Nevada Bulletin,* Vol. 37, No. 3, Geology and Mining Series No. 37 (Reno, 1943), p. 212. Also ibid., pp. 212–17.

prise, Nevada's most influential mining daily in the early months of 1876. The paper expressed the fear shared by the region's miners that a continued decline in silver prices, if left unchecked, would ruin the industry and intensify economic distress in the state. This price depreciation, the *Enterprise* volunteered in February 1876, could only be stemmed through congressional action, and the paper first suggested that "congress . . . pass a law for the issuance of silver notes" in exchange for bullion, the notes to be legal tender in the same way as existing gold notes.[14] That same month, the daily endorsed the notion of redeeming all greenbacks in silver, not simply fractional paper notes, as a preliminary stage toward eventual restoration of the gold standard. This plan was similar to the "silver resumption" scheme which Nevada's Senator John Percival Jones introduced into Congress in April 1876. By 1876 many Nevadans had come to believe that a revived system of silver coinage or of government notes backed by silver bullion would expand the available money stock, thus stimulating domestic commerce and industry while at the same time checking the precipitous slump in silver's market price. Pro-resumption and anti-greenback in its editorial policies, closely aligned to the state's Republican party, the *Enterprise* reflected the opinions of many thoughtful Nevadans at the outset of the drive to remonetize silver. Frankly concerned with securing a government market for the state's bullion to prevent the business depression from affecting Nevada's mining communities, the *Enterprise* campaigned vigorously for national action on silver during the early months of 1876.[15]

Most San Francisco bankers, business leaders, and the city's Chamber of Commerce, on the other hand, opposed remonetization from the beginning, fearing injury to the Bay City's foreign

14. *Territorial Enterprise,* Feb. 6, 1876. Also for the following 1876 dates: Jan. 29, Feb. 10 and Feb. 11.

15. Ibid. for the following 1876 dates: Feb. 12, Mar. 9, 11, 12, 21, 25, 26, 30.

trade as well as to their own domestic bond holdings and real estate investments.[16] California's congressional delegation, largely aligned with the San Francisco business community, therefore supported only the smallest extension of existing legal tender limits on subsidiary silver coins. As for Nevada, prior to John Percival Jones' first speech proposing remonetization in April 1876, the state lacked its own strong spokesman in national politics. Not only were the state's interests in Washington neglected generally by California's congressional delegation as well as by its own representatives, but one Nevada senator, William Sharon, who opposed remonetization, did not bother even taking his Senate seat in 1875 until nine months after his election![17] Little wonder that the *Enterprise* and other Nevada journals swiftly endorsed Senator Jones' April 1876 demand for restoration of the 412.5 grain silver dollar as a monetary standard. Although the millionaire Republican had been a somewhat distant figure previously to most Nevadans, spending almost all of his time either in Washington or, when west, in California, he now became a political hero to Nevadans deeply troubled by the state's future economic prospects.[18] The silver question first emerged clearly as a national issue in April 1876 with Jones' elaborate Senate speech on the problem, and it remained a controversial political question for the next two years, when discussion abated temporarily with passage of the Bland-Allison Act in February 1878.

Although formal congressional debate over remonetization began in April 1876, the silver question had entered legislative

16. On the opposition of San Francisco's business community toward remonetization, see *Territorial Enterprise* for the following 1876 dates: Feb. 6, Feb. 12, Apr. 18. See also Washington *National Republican*, Feb. 19, 1876.

17. On the lukewarm attitude of most Western congressmen toward silver legislation during the 1870s, see Philadelphia *Inquirer*, Nov. 26, 1877.

18. *Territorial Enterprise* for the following 1876 dates: Apr. 1, 7, 11, 18, 26, 27, 29, 30; May 2, 4, 5.

discussion of other financial measures several months earlier. The first proposals for restoration of legal bimetallism emerged actually during informal cloakroom conversations in January 1876. One such colloquy in the halls of Congress preceded formal consideration of a Senate bill sponsored by Justin S. Morrill of Vermont on the specie resumption issue. Morrill's measure, introduced on January 5, authorized the Secretary of the Treasury to sell 4.5 percent long-term bonds in exchange for greenbacks which the Treasury would then withdraw from circulation, thus further contracting the currency.

On the day the Senate debated his proposal, January 6, Morrill scribbled some hasty notes recording his fellow senators' private comments on the question of how to secure swift resumption of specie payments. Curiously, most of the legislators talked of the role that silver coinage would have to play in the resumption process, and their remarks foreshadowed later public statements on remonetization:

> Gen. Logan [the notes begin] thinks silver should be made a legal tender. Believes Banks would retire their circulation.
>
> Mr. Jones [of Nevada] favors the general principles of the bill. He would make a trade dollar legal tender. Silver, he says, will not fluctuate, while gold will.
>
> Senator Kernan thinks silver legal tender would be easier for the debtors, etc., etc.
>
> Senator Boutwell sees nothing that can be done to aid resumption but that paper and gold will be mainly at par but he does not agree with Logan, or Jones about silver. Our chief business is with countries who use gold. Silver would leave us as we are now with paper.
>
> Senator Sherman the first thing he would do would be to redeem fractional greenbacks in silver . . . Would increase the legal tender *limit* to $20.00.[19]

19. See Morrill's own notes on Senate response to his bill, Senate No. 157, 44th Cong., 1st sess., ca. Jan. 5, 1876, in Morrill MSS, LC.

The Vermont Republican's notes reveal great interest among congressmen early in 1876 in the possibility of utilizing silver coinage more extensively in preparing for specie resumption. Thus, months before legislative debate began over remonetizing the metal, the silver issue entered political discussion as an aspect of the broader financial problem of returning to specie payments. At least three congressmen returned from the Far West in December 1875 for the opening of the Forty-Fourth Congress prepared to introduce measures raising the current five-dollar legal tender limit on subsidiary silver coins, hoping by this means to alleviate the commercial depression on the West coast while at the same time aiding in the resumption process.

Who first proposed remonetizing the old 412.5 grain silver dollar remains unclear even among economic historians: "How and when the agitation to restore silver to free coinage actually began seems in doubt."[20] The earliest 1876 proposals to raise the legal tender power of silver coins did not suggest restoring the old silver dollar, only that the legal tender powers of existing silver coins, including the 420 grain trade dollar, be increased slightly. Two California Republicans, Senator Aaron Sargent and Congressman William A. Piper, introduced identical bills in January 1876 which increased the current five-dollar legal tender limit on silver coins to twenty dollars for the trade dollar and ten dollars for the half-dollar piece. By raising the legal tender limit on existing silver coins without returning completely to the double standard, Piper and Sargent hoped to stimulate an expanded use of silver in the American monetary system, thereby halting the metal's downward slide in market price.[21]

20. A. Barton Hepburn, *History of Currency in the United States* (New York, 1924), p. 275; Irwin Unger, *The Greenback Era*, pp. 328–30; J. Laurence Laughlin, *History of Bimetallism*, pp. 179–81.

21. Sargent introduced his measure on Jan. 17, 1876 and Piper acted on the following day. *Cong. Record*, 44th Cong., 1st sess., vol. 4, pt. 1, pp. 428, 476; San Francisco *Chronicle*, Jan. 30, 1876. On the motives behind the Piper-Sargent bill, see the editorial on "The Silver Problem," San Francisco *Bulletin*, Feb. 15, 1876.

Because it promised to aid specie resumption without at the same time endangering the gold standard, the Piper-Sargent proposal received Mint Director Henry Linderman's endorsement. Linderman wrote Piper that his "bill if passed will make our [coinage] systems—Gold the standard and unlimited tender; and silver subsidiary, and limited as to tender and issue—perfect."[22]

The Piper-Sargent bill conflicted, however, with the mint director's efforts to remove the five-dollar legal tender power possessed by the 420 grain trade dollar. That coin, placed in the Coinage Act of 1873 shortly before its adoption in order to divert an expected increase in silver production into foreign trade by allowing mineowners to coin an unlimited number of 420 grain "trade" dollars, had been allowed the same five dollar legal tender power as domestic subsidiary silver coins. The decline in silver's market value during the three years following passage of the Coinage Act had reduced the bullion value of the 420 grain trade dollar to about 94 cents in gold by 1876, making it profitable for western silver producers to circulate the coin domestically as well as in foreign trade, since the holder of the trade dollar could "use it at par" because of its five dollar legal tender value. The mint director hoped to choke off this inflationary loophole in the coinage laws by depriving the trade dollar of this legal tender power, forcing holders of the coin to use it solely in export trade. However, until Congress acted on Linderman's request later in the 1876 session, western businessmen and bankers often found themselves forced to accept depreciated trade dollars in payment for debts contracted originally in gold. "In consequence of this margin of profit [for holders of trade dollars]," Linderman wrote Secretary Bristow in February 1876, "the tendency on the Pacific Coast, where the business is conducted on a gold basis, is, to force the Trade Dollar into circulation, and being at a discount as against gold,

22. Linderman to W. H. Piper, Feb. 17, 1876, Letterbooks, Director of the Mint, National Archives, RG 104.

inconvenience in retail transactions is experienced."[23] To correct this situation, Bristow sent to Congress in February 1876 a bill prepared by the mint director which eliminated the trade dollar's legal tender power and substituted as a legal tender coin a 384 grain subsidiary silver dollar "of the same standard [and legal tender powers] as the present subsidiary silver coin."[24]

Linderman attempted to combine the Piper-Sargent bill, which increased slightly the legal tender of subsidiary coins, with his own measure removing the mischievous domestic circulation of the trade dollar. In a revealing letter to Congressman Piper, the mint director assured the California Republican that through adoption of this combined measure, the government would provide an adequate market under the existing gold standard for any surplus domestic stocks of silver bullion. According to Linderman, mint purchases of subsidiary coinage would assure that both American silver producers and Treasury policy makers remained content: "After the substitution of silver coin for fractional notes, say $40,000,000, which will be readily absorbed for change purposes, these coins would be issuable only in exchange at par for gold coin, and which will always prevent redundancy and keep their purchasing power in retail transactions equal to Gold."[25] Had the Sargent-Piper-Linderman measure been the only silver coinage plan before Congress at this time, political controversy over the issue would have been minimal. Congress had already accepted in the Resumption Act of 1875 the principle of substituting subsidiary silver for fractional greenbacks. Even increasing the legal tender powers of existing silver coins to twenty dollars or providing for a new subsidiary silver dollar would have had only minor economic effects as long as gold remained the sole monetary

23. Linderman to Secretary of the Treasury Bristow, Feb. 7, 1876, RG 104.

24. Bristow to John Sherman, Feb. 7, 1876, RG 104.

25. Linderman to Piper, Feb. 17, 1876, RG 104.

standard of value. The New York *Graphic,* reporting Linderman's proposal for a 384 grain subsidiary dollar, gave as "the reason assigned for this . . . a desire to increase the market for silver."[26] By offering Treasury support for the Piper-Sargent plan, Linderman apparently hoped to assure western bullion interests of his intention to help reverse the market decline in silver without making any fundamental changes in the American coinage system.

Another western legislator, however, had returned from the Pacific coast in January 1876 concerned with the depreciating world market price of silver and equally determined to force congressional action on the problem. John Percival Jones, Nevada's senior Republican senator and an ardent specie resumptionist, considered the Piper-Sargent scheme an inadequate approach to the problem of fully utilizing silver coinage as part of the circulating currency. Jones proposed instead that a temporary silver monetary standard be established as a transitional step toward eventual specie resumption in gold. "Of the two propositions," noted the San Francisco *Chronicle,* "the most popular will be that of Senator Jones, who came in third hand, 'seeing' Sargent's and Piper's blinds, and 'raising' them to an unlimited amount."[27] Although the actual relationship between the two silver coinage schemes remains obscure, Piper and Sargent placed their bills on the congressional calendar soon after the session opened while Jones publicized his ideas in the press, waiting until April 1876 before he finally presented them to the Senate.

The Nevada Republican called at this time for the immediate resumption of specie payments in silver as "an intermediate stage between paper and gold coin." This new standard of value would have a dual unit of measure, a fully remonetized 412.5

26. New York *Graphic,* Feb. 26, 1876.

27. San Francisco *Chronicle,* Jan. 30, 1876. See also Henry D. Barrows, "The Silver Question—A New Departure," San Francisco *Express,* Feb. 10, 1876.

grain silver dollar as well as a silver certificate to be issued in exchange for bullion deposited at the mints, the latter a direct transcription of the earlier "silver note" scheme developed by the *Territorial Enterprise.* Jones proposed that the five dollar legal tender limit be removed from all silver coins and that they be made unlimited legal tender, with the new silver certificates—notes representing bullion deposited at current market value—used to handle large transactions.[28] Jones did not envision his "silver standard" as inflationary, since he proposed replacing and retiring the bulk of the greenbacks as the new silver currency was issued. "It seems to contemplate the substitution of silver for the paper now in circulation," the San Francisco *Bulletin* wrote of Jones' plan.[29] The Nevada senator expected to see silver rise in market price once remonetized and, thereafter, to hold a relatively steady price level until the country had returned to specie payments in gold.

The ingenuity of Jones' scheme attracted attention among supporters of specie resumption who opposed further contraction of the monetary supply, and some newspapers on both coasts commented approvingly on "the practical hard money views of Senator Jones."[30] Despite scattered discussion of Jones' proposal, however, most journals of opinion remained silent on the question of silver coinage until Congress first debated the question. Even Jones' Pacific coast colleagues either held aloof from his silver resumption scheme or actively opposed it. Nevada's other Republican senator, William A. Sharon, expressed his opposition almost immediately both to Jones' plan and to the

28. Washington *National Republican,* Jan. 17, 1876. See also the discussion of Jones's earliest plan in the San Francisco *Bulletin,* reprinted in the New York *Graphic,* Jan. 27, 1876.

29. San Francisco *Bulletin,* Feb. 15, 1876; Washington *National Republican,* Jan. 27, 1876.

30. See, for example, the San Francisco *Chronicle,* Jan. 30, 1876; Washington *National Republican,* Jan. 27, 1876; Virginia City (Nev.) *Territorial Enterprise,* Mar. 11, 1876; and the New York *Graphic,* Jan. 27, 1876.

Piper-Sargent bill. "That [i.e. the two proposals] seems to me to be a mistake," Sharon informed an interviewer in February 1876,

> for while other nations are demonetizing it, we, in the event of the adoption of [these] plans, should be raising its value. You cannot enhance the value of silver by legislation. It is regulated by great international laws of trade. If we give silver a fictitious value, the silver coins of the world will flow in upon us and flood us.[31]

Sharon, despite his extensive holdings in Nevada mining stock, played no role in the subsequent drive to remonetize silver. The "King of the Comstock," as he was known, spent most of his time in San Francisco tending to vast banking and real estate investments while quietly opposing remonetization.[32] He and Jones had been bitter economic and political antagonists in Nevada since the early 1870s, when Jones built his first mining fortune while nominally serving as one of Sharon's mine superintendents. Hostility between the two men flared up again when Jones outbid Sharon in the Nevada 1872 senatorial contest for the votes of Nevada's extremely marketable legislature.[33] A strong supporter of the gold standard, Sharon sided with the contractionist wing of Republican resumptionists and opposed any government effort to raise the market value of silver through remonetizing the metal. "Sell bonds enough to retire the greenbacks," he told one newspaperman in 1876, "and let commercial interests and the relative value of gold and silver take care of themselves."[34] Throughout his single Senate term Sharon "spent little time at his duties in Washington and demonstrated no real concern for the welfare of Nevada." In 1881, when his term

31. San Francisco *Chronicle,* Feb. 14, 1876.
32. Philadelphia *Inquirer,* Nov. 16, 1877.
33. Gilman M. Ostrander, *Nevada: The Great Rotten Borough, 1859–1964* (New York, 1966), pp. 69–70.
34. San Francisco *Chronicle,* Feb. 14, 1876.

ended, the Democratic "Bonanza King" James G. Fair defeated Sharon's bid for reelection.[35]

William A. Piper, the California congressman who sponsored the original January 1876 House bill raising the legal tender power of silver coins, quickly abdicated leadership on the question to the measure's Senate managers. Piper remained silent on the remonetization issue once it arose, advocating instead a new system of free banking and greenback contraction as the best means of achieving specie resumption.[36] Aaron Sargent of California, who sponsored Piper's bill in the Senate, also sat on the fence during early legislative debates over restoring the double standard. During the silver drive which followed, however, Sargent became a bitter opponent of remonetization and voted against the Bland-Allison act in the Senate.[37] When James T. Farley, who supported the double standard, won Sargent's California Senate seat in the fall of 1877, silverites hailed his election, regretting only that Farley would not take up his post until after final congressional action on the question.[38] In opposing silver, both Sargent and Sharon reflected the almost unanimous opposition to remonetization among the banking and commercial interests of San Francisco to which both legislators held close economic and political ties.[39]

California's senior senator, Newton Booth, also opposed restoration of the double standard, advocating instead a more traditional greenbacker's plan for achieving specie resumption by floating an "interconvertible bond," "making greenbacks redeemable in government bonds bearing a low rate of interest

35. James W. Hulse, *The Nevada Adventure, a History* (Reno, Nev., 1965), p. 118.

36. *Cong. Record,* 44th Cong., 1st sess., vol. 4, pt. 3, May 3, 1876, pp. 2960–63.

37. Ibid., Mar. 30, 1876, pp. 2061–62; *Territorial Enterprise,* Feb. 14, 1878.

38. New York *Graphic,* Dec. 22, 1877.

39. San Francisco *Chronicle,* Oct. 20, 1877.

in gold."[40] Booth, the Greenback party's vice-presidential candidate in 1876, endorsed replacement of fractional greenbacks with subsidiary silver but opposed full remonetization of the metal.[41] The Californian, elected to the Senate as an Anti-Monopolist Democrat, urged that the government work to raise the market price of greenbacks to par with gold and then maintain the single gold standard rather than change to a bimetallic valuation:

> The funded debt of the Government should be paid in gold . . . gold by the common consent of the commercial world is the ultimate standard by which all values are measured . . . we ought to use the national credit directly in the form of national notes [greenbacks] and not lend it to the banks for that purpose, and [we ought] to make national notes good as gold.[42]

Of all the California and Nevada congressional representatives, then, legislators from the two far western mining states most seriously affected by the continuing decline in silver's market value, only John Percival Jones actively supported the campaign to restore the metal as a monetary standard. Although remonetization aroused considerable enthusiasm among western voters throughout the silver drive that followed, only Jones, who initiated the campaign in Congress, championed bimetallism among the entire Pacific coast delegation. The absence of widespread support for remonetization among western congressmen in the 1870s challenges the assumption held by most historians that western mining interests and their representatives in Congress helped originate and actively sponsor the legislation.

Of the two major mineowners in Congress at the time, Sharon opposed remonetization while Jones served as its earliest spon-

40. *Territorial Enterprise,* Jan. 13, 1876.

41. *Cong. Record,* 44th Cong., 1st sess., vol. 4, pt. 4, 3678–83, June 8, 1876. See also Unger, *Greenback Era,* p. 308.

42. *Cong. Record,* 44th Cong., 1st sess., vol. 4, pt. 4, 3681.

sor. After first proposing a temporary silver standard, by April 1876 Jones had begun advocating a permanent double standard and immediate restoration of the 412.5 grain silver dollar, abandoning the silver certificate portion of his original scheme. During the agitation which followed the Nevada Republican became the most influential congressional supporter of the double standard. In the two years between his first speech on the subject and passage of the Bland-Allison Act, Jones served as chairman of the monetary commission which Congress appointed in August 1876 to study the silver question. He wrote its majority report endorsing remonetization and was the most militant Senate advocate for the Bland silver bill, once that measure had cleared the House in November 1877.

Contemporary opponents of remonetization and most historians have charged that Jones raised the issue primarily for economic motives, to protect his own silver mine investments from further losses due to the metal's continued depreciation in market price. The commentators have noted that, as an important Comstock Lode mineowner, Jones stood to profit handsomely from the expected increase in silver's market quotations following remonetization: "The mine operators had much to gain from restoring silver, particularly if they could pocket the difference between the market price of silver and its par value."[43] One influential wing of the silver movement, according to J. Laurence Laughlin, consisted "chiefly of Senators [and their followers in the House] whose constituents were interested in silver mines."[44] Despite evidence that among all the Pacific coast mining state legislators, only Jones actively supported the silver drive, even the most perceptive study of currency politics during the Reconstruction era has asserted: "Needless to say, the miners and their friends in Congress supported remonetiza-

43. Unger, *Greenback Era,* p. 335.

44. Laughlin, *History of Bimetallism,* p. 193.

tion."[45] According to historians, the congressional representatives of western mining interests favored restoration of silver as a monetary standard in order to shelter their product from world market forces, just as manufacturing groups protected their industries against foreign competition through the high tariff wall.[46]

Since Senator Jones of Nevada served as the lone congressional voice of the mining West during the earliest struggle for remonetization, a closer examination of his motives in promoting the silver drive might help to clarify the political origins of the movement. Was Jones governed primarily by concern for his personal mining investments in sponsoring the silver issue, or were there also compelling political and ideological factors behind his campaign to remonetize the metal? Jones' influential role in the silver agitation of the 1870s has been accepted both by contemporaries and subsequent historians. "He found the country without opinions, and without any special knowledge of the facts bearing upon the question of the metallic standards," one leading silverite wrote in 1878, "and he was able, not to change its opinions, but to form and fix them."[47] The question, however, remains. Why did the "father of the silver drive" foster a congressional campaign to restore the double standard?

Jones possessed substantial investments in Comstock Lode

45. Unger, *Greenback Era,* p. 335. See also Studenski and Krooss, *Financial History,* p. 187. Philip E. Buckner, however, questioned whether mine owners had involved themselves in silver politics during the 1870s, although he presented no evidence on the subject. Philip E. Buckner, "Silver Mining Interests in Silver Politics, 1876–1896," Master's Thesis, Columbia University, 1954, esp. Chap. I.

46. Laughlin, *History of Bimetallism,* pp. 193–95. In illustrating this point with citations from congressional debate, however, Laughlin quoted several legislators from Midwestern and Southern states but none from a major mining area except for John Percival Jones!

47. George Weston, *The Silver Question* (New York, 1878), p. 61.

mining property. He owned a controlling interest in the Crown Point mine at Gold Hill, Nevada, from which he drew millions in the early 1870s.[48] The Crown Point, however, paid its last dividend in 1875 and, along with all but the two extraordinarily profitable Bonanza firm mines on the Comstock Lode, it began assessing stockholders in order to meet production expenses.[49] On still another part of the Comstock, Jones owned the equally unprofitable Save Mine, which had almost run dry by 1875, and he also controlled ore-crushing mills owned by Virginia City's Nevada Mill Company.[50] Despite his holdings, throughout the silver drive, Jones denied having sponsored remonetization primarily to increase the value of these extensive Nevada silver investments, which he enjoyed calling "insignificant."[51]

By 1876, Jones' Comstock Lode properties formed only a portion of his overall wealth. Along with other Comstock millionaires, Jones had begun investing heavily in other enterprises during the mid-1870s. William A. Sharon, for example, although a senator from Nevada, actually spent little time in that state supervising his extensive mining property. Sharon lived usually in San Francisco, helping to direct the widespread economic interests of the Bank of California which he controlled. Similarly, by 1876, the four "Bonanza Kings" had started channeling most of the profits from their Nevada mines into less speculative holdings elsewhere. James C. Flood and his three partners invested heavily in government resumption bonds and San Francisco real estate, storing additional millions in gold coin in the vaults of their private San Francisco bank. In similar fashion, John Percival Jones began by the middle of the decade to divert his personal fortune into investments other than silver mines. When

48. William Wright (Dan DeQuille, pseud.), *The Big Bonanza* (1876; repr. New York, 1947), p. 407; Harry M. Gorham, *My Memories of the Comstock* (Los Angeles, 1939), p. 113.

49. Smith, "History of the Comstock Lode," pp. 169, 199.

50. Wright, *The Big Bonanza*, p. 407.

51. Interview with John Percival Jones, Detroit *Evening News*, May 18, 1876.

he entered the Senate in 1873, Jones left his Nevada properties in the hands of a brother, Samuel L. Jones, superintendent of the Crown Point Mine, who became the senator's chief Nevada lieutenant, charged with administering the mines and mending political fences in the state.[52] The senator himself spent an increasing amount of his time on the Pacific coast in California rather than on the Comstock Lode.

To categorize John Percival Jones solely as a "silver mine owner" is hardly accurate, considering the range of his economic investments and projects. For example, Jones always asserted, probably with accuracy, that his "investment in nonproductive silver mines [was] less extensive than in mines which produce gold exclusively."[53] Most of his gold mining property was located in the Panamint Mountains of California near Death Valley, where he reputedly lost almost two million dollars during the late 1870s while in partnership with another important Nevada political figure, William Morris Stewart.[54] From 1875 on Jones also held a $25,000 seat on the San Francisco Stock and Exchange Board where he speculated in a variety of projects.[55] One unfortunate gold mining venture alone cost him $750,000—"too much water and not enough gold" as his nephew put it—a Panama Railroad stock purchase drained off another quarter of a million and a matching amount was lost in an unsuccessful attempt to develop a new rotary ore-crushing mill.[56]

52. Gorham, *Memories of the Comstock,* p. 113. Gorham, the Senator's nephew, wrote one of the most vivid memoirs of life on the Comstock Lode during the 1870s.

53. Philadelphia *Inquirer,* Feb. 15, 1878, interview with Jones. See also his remarks to the Detroit *Evening News,* May 18, 1876.

54. Gorham, *Memories of the Comstock,* pp. 108–09; Wright, *The Big Bonanza,* pp. 407–08; Wells Drury, *An Editor on the Comstock Lode* (New York, 1936), p. 291; J. P. Jones to Georgina Jones, Sept. 28, 1877, Jones Family MSS, Huntington Library.

55. Joseph L. King, *History of the San Francisco Stock and Exchange Board by the Chairman* (San Francisco, 1910), p. 325.

56. Gorham, *Memories of the Comstock,* pp. 110–11.

Actually, his most absorbing economic project during the years from 1875 to 1878 was a new artificial ice-making process on which he lost over three-quarters of a million dollars while devoting to it countless hours of personal attention stolen from his labors in Congress.[57] In less than two years, while Jones worked on the remonetization struggle in Congress, he poured close to a million dollars into experimental ice-making plants at New Orleans, Galveston, and Dallas, confessing often in letters written to his wife in 1877 a desire for quick success in the project: "I am longing to have the ice business fairly started so that I can bid farewell and forever to the harrassing business of mining and stock dealing."[58]

Jones' economic interest in his ice-machine process during the late 1870s was matched by a similar passion for his real estate and town planning venture at Santa Monica, California. Of all his properties during the decade, the Nevada senator probably devoted more time and energy to the development of Santa Monica than to any other, including his mining investments. Jones founded the town in 1875, laid out its first streets and began selling parcels of land on the thirty thousand acres of the Santa Monica and San Vincente ranches which fronted the Pacific Ocean fourteen miles from Los Angeles.[59] For the remainder of his life, the senator spent most of his free time away from Congress building and promoting the growth of Santa Monica.[60] Although most of his economic investments after 1875 involved enterprises removed from the Comstock Lode

57. Gorham provides a lively and detailed account of his uncle's financial speculations. Ibid., pp. 108–13.

58. J. P. Jones to Georgina Jones on the following 1876 dates: July 29, Aug. 26 and Aug. 28, Jones Family MSS, Huntington Library. See also J. P. Jones to Georgina Jones on the following 1877 dates: Feb. 2, Feb. 13, Aug. 26, Sept. 28, ibid.

59. Gorham, *Memories of the Comstock,* pp. 112–13, Drury, *Editor on the Comstock Lode.*

60. Gorham, *Memories of the Comstock;* George Lyttleton Upshur, *As I Recall Them, Memories of Crowded Years* (New York, 1936), p. 123.

and unconnected with silver mining, Jones continued to speculate in Nevada silver stocks as well. His mining investments from 1875 to the end of the decade, however, whether in gold or silver, proved grandiose failures. The bull market for Nevada mining stocks in San Francisco had begun declining precipitously in 1877, ruining many large Comstock investors. "Now everything is dull—blue—discouraging—the outlook in mining matters is the worst I have ever seen," one of Jones' associates wrote from San Francisco in November 1877. "There is great suffering here . . . We [all on this coast] are watching with keen interest your noble fight for the silver dollar. It is our only hope of relief."[61] Thus, although the remonetization of silver appealed to Jones partly because it promised relief for himself and other investors in silver mines from a severe plunge in the value of their stock holdings, it is equally significant that the bulk of his own economic investments lay elsewhere by this time.

Jones confidently expected that the market price of silver would rise once the metal again became a monetary standard, climbing until it reached the government's mint price and thus restoring financial stability under bimetallism without further inflation of the currency:

> If we have to accept a limitation of the coinage [Jones wrote Murat Halstead of the Cincinnati *Commercial* in January 1878 while the Senate considered the Bland bill], I propose to have the Senate amendment amended so as to make three millions per month the minimum coinage and whenever the market price and mint price shall coincide, *which they soon would do,* the mint to be open to free coinage. This will satisfy those who clamor that the government shall receive the difference between the two and will be the best for us if the coinage is to be restricted.[62]

61. J. P. Jackson to J. P. Jones, Nov. 4, 1877, Jones MSS, Huntington Library.

62. J. P. Jones to Murat Halstead, Jan. 18, 1878, Halstead MSS, Cincinnati Historical Society (italics added).

Jones was certain that restoration of the double standard would raise the market price of silver substantially, quelling the anxieties of western bullion producers without triggering depreciation in the market value of existing gold coinage.

Political considerations, however, were as important as any economic factor in stimulating Jones' energetic involvement in the congressional campaign to remonetize silver. After entering the Senate in 1873, the Nevadan quickly became a leading member of the stalwart, pro-Grant wing of the Republican party.[63] During the congressional struggle over the inflation bill of 1874, which provided for a modest expansion of greenback circulation, Jones played a conspicuous role in Congress among hard money opponents of the measure.[64] The Nevadan enjoyed national influence as a member of the President's inner circle of political cronies, serving as Grant's leading adviser on western affairs, a position held formerly by William Morris Stewart of Nevada until his Senate term expired in 1874. Yet despite his national prominence, the previous political history of Nevada afforded Jones little hope for a long career in the Senate.

When Nevada achieved statehood in 1864, William Morris Stewart and James W. Nye received its first Senate seats, and both men subsequently won full six-year terms only to be defeated in bids for reelection—Nye in 1872 by Jones and Stewart by William A. Sharon in 1874. By 1876 it appeared certain that Jones would face stiff competition for reelection in 1878 from several other Comstock millionaires interested in purchasing a Senate seat from which to join Washington's more elegant

63. Charles Carroll Goodwin, *As I Remember Them* (Salt Lake City, 1913), p. 285.

64. For an exhaustive discussion of the congressional battle over the 1874 "Inflation Bill," see Unger, *Greenback Era,* pp. 233–48. Jones' speech on the measure was reprinted as *Banking and Currency* (Washington: U.S. Govt. Printing Office, 1874). The Nevadan kept a scrapbook filled with clippings from the nation's press praising him for standing behind the gold standard, hard-money forces on the "Inflation Bill." Jones Scrapbooks, UCLA Library.

social world. Often mentioned as possible successors to Jones were Democrats James G. Fair, the Bonanza King who eventually squelched William A. Sharon's bid for reelection in 1880, and Adolph Sutro, developer of the Comstock Lode's Sutro Tunnel.[65] Jones' close association with Grant meant little in Nevada political life, as Stewart's enforced retirement in 1874 had shown. "From what [had] gone before," the state's earliest historian observed, "it will be perceived how really little national politics had to do with politics in Nevada [in the 1870s] during the rule of the Comstock firms."[66] Jones' own 1872 election campaign had given him an indispensable education in the political realities of a state that was still completely dominated by the great mining and railroad kings of San Francisco, who ventured across the mountain passes into Nevada mainly to check their balance sheets and purchase ballots.

Jones and William A. Sharon, who battled for the state's senatorial prize in 1872, both spent prodigious sums estimated at more than a million dollars to influence and buy votes for sympathetic state legislators, who in turn elected the U.S. senator.[67] No Nevada politician at this time enjoyed state-wide popularity except the type paid for by the generosity of his previous campaign. Political party machinery hardly existed in the state during the 1870s, and candidates for state-wide or national office waged essentially independent campaigns. Few Nevada congressmen or senators ever spent enough time in the state to develop a personal following, and even Jones' supporters acknowledged that he rarely visited the state after his election to

65. Drury, *Editor on the Comstock Lode,* p. 270–74; Ostrander, *Nevada: The Great Rotten Borough,* pp. 66–74; Hubert Howe Bancroft, *History of Nevada, Colorado and Wyoming* (San Francisco, 1890), pp. 188–92.

66. Bancroft, *History of Nevada, Colorado and Wyoming,* p. 198.

67. Ibid., pp. 190–92; Drury, *Editor on the Comstock Lode,* pp. 270–71; Ostrander, *Nevada: The Great Rotten Borough,* pp. 69–70. A detailed file of political correspondence on the 1872 senatorial race can be found in the Jones papers at the UCLA Library.

the Senate in 1872.[68] Although it is improbable that Jones raised the silver question in Congress solely to meet his coming political challenge in Nevada and help his chances for reelection, the senator's struggle to remonetize the silver dollar secured his political future in the state by transforming a previously indifferent or venal group of voters into a passionate and issue-conscious electorate. Through his campaign to restore the double standard, whether by design or accident, Jones struck an immediate response among Nevada voters, who had been content until then to allow their state to remain a rotten borough for San Francisco tycoons with national pretensions. After 1876, largely through the efforts of Jones in Congress, Nevada began to develop its own political style and identity. No longer could a Comstock millionaire or any other politician assume political prominence in the state without first demonstrating that he was "sound" on the silver question.

Jones' campaign to remonetize silver offered the promise of eventual relief from the business depression which reached Nevada's populous mining districts in 1876 and 1877. Stock values, mining production, and local commerce in the towns on the Comstock Lode all suffered from the hard times. Hundreds of unemployed miners roamed the streets of Virginia City, Gold Hill, and other Nevada towns searching unsuccessfully for any available work. Even "in the flush year of 1876 . . . when winter came two or three thousand people [in Virginia City alone] remained without work and without means . . . One hundred and thirty mines were levying assessments, and only the [Bonanza-owned] Con. Virginia and the California [were] paying dividends." Local newspapers painted bleak portraits of the effect which this mining depression had on Comstock life. "Strong, able-bodied men call daily at the dwellings of citizens, asking for food or the chance of a night's lodgings. The funds

68. Drury, *Editor on the Comstock Lode;* New York *Graphic,* Feb. 28, 1878.

of the Relief Committee are exhausted."[69] Under these conditions most Nevadans felt that remonetization would inevitably stimulate mining production, and both Democrats and Republicans alike in the state supported Jones' efforts in Congress. The silver drive seemed to crystallize and channel economic discontent among the state's merchants and businessmen as well as among the miners themselves. Recognizing his constituency's enthusiastic response to the silver issue, from 1876 on Jones devoted his energies in Congress almost entirely to sponsoring remonetization, both as chairman of the Monetary Commission created to study the question and as the chief Senate enthusiast for silver. In his efforts the Nevada Republican spent large personal sums to study and propagate the silverite cause.[70] These activities paid both immediate and lasting political dividends for Jones in his home state. "From the many letters and telegrams I am daily receiving from all parts of the Pacific Coast," he informed ex-Senator Cornelius Cole of California shortly before final passage of the Bland-Allison Act, "I am persuaded that my course on this question of remonetizing silver meets the approval of nine-tenths of our people."[71]

Following passage of the Bland-Allison Act, Jones' popularity among Nevadans soared still further, and he toured the state as a returning hero in July 1878, hailed by citizens of both parties for his partially victorious labors on behalf of silver. Several thousand people jammed the streets of Virginia City in front of the senator's hotel to pay him an unpurchased political tribute

69. Virginia City *Chronicle*, cited in *The Iron Age*, May 10, 1877, p. 7; Smith, "History of the Comstock Lode," pp. 212–13; George Thomas Mayre, Jr., *From '49 to '83 in California and Nevada* (San Francisco, 1923).

70. New York *Graphic*, Feb. 26, 1878; Speech of (Nevada) Congressman Rollin F. Daggett, Jul. 20, 1878, copy in Daggett MSS, Bancroft Library (Berkeley); Gorham, *Memories of the Comstock*, p. 111; Drury, *Editor on the Comstock Lode*, p. 273.

71. John P. Jones to Cornelius Cole, Feb. 16, 1878, Cole MSS, UCLA Library.

without precedent in the state's history, and large crowds greeted his arrival in Gold Hill, Reno, and other towns.[72] Although partisan ties remained strong in Nevada politics during subsequent decades, Jones ceased to be affected by them. He won his 1878 race for the Senate after receiving support from many Democratic mining district residents and newspapers along with the almost unanimous, unpaid for, endorsement of his own Republican party, an inconceivable achievement prior to the appearance of the silver issue.[73] Through raising the question in Congress, Jones not only insured his own Senate future but, in the process, altered fundamentally the political life of the mining West by providing the dominant theme for its future involvement in national affairs.[74]

Still a third factor other than political and economic ones entered into Jones' decision to advocate remonetization in 1876. Like many congressmen, Jones believed himself an expert on currency questions, skillful at doctoring the country's battered monetary system to financial health using simple and relatively painless remedies. He periodically changed his prescriptions, recommending large doses of gold in 1874, shifting to greater amounts of silver by 1876 and, for a brief period in 1877, to an even more drastic tonic of greenbacks.[75] Throughout the 1870s

72. Among the many accounts of Jones' reception in Nevada, see the following: New York *Graphic,* Feb. 26, 1878; *Nevada State Journal* (Reno), July 20, 21 and 23, 1878; *Gold Hill News,* July 18, 22, and 29, 1878; San Francisco *Bulletin,* July 29, 1878; Virginia City *Chronicle,* July 29, 1878; and *Territorial Enterprise,* July 29, 1878.

73. San Francisco *Bulletin,* July 29, 1878; Gold Hill *News,* July 26, 1878.

74. Drury, *Editor on the Comstock Lode,* p. 273; Bancroft, *History of Nevada, Colorado and Wyoming,* pp. 198–99; Ostrander, *Nevada: The Great Rotten Borough,* pp. 104–05.

75. On Jones' brief commitment to greenbackism, see Jeannette P. Nichols, "John Sherman and the Silver Drive of 1877–78: The Origins of the Gigantic Subsidy," *Ohio State Archaeological and Historical Quarterly, 46,* No. 2 (1937), pp. 160–61; and Jones's Interview with "Gath" (George Alfred Townsend), Cincinnati *Daily Enquirer,* Dec. 31, 1878.

Jones believed himself a leading authority on American monetary policy and, after having endorsed restoration of the double standard, his credibility as an economic expert rested increasingly on the validity of these new bimetallist doctrines, a fact he undoubtedly recognized during the many tedious months of work as chairman of the congressional monetary commission.[76]

Ironically, while preparing the monetary commission's majority report in 1877 endorsing remonetization, Jones for a time lost his own belief in the double standard! A temporary convert to greenbackism, the Senator continued his labors on behalf of silver for political and economic reasons, although he no longer found bimetallism an adequate solution for the nation's financial ills.[77] Jones struggled to compose the report's final draft for over a year, finally completing it in the fall of 1877. By this time he had come to realize that his Nevada constituents, silvermen and not lumbermen, would refuse to accept his conversion from the double standard to a greenback standard. Political necessities prevailed over Jones' fleeting attraction for the "rag baby." The demands of Nevadan political life reinforced an earlier commitment to bimetallism, and Jones remained silver's most ardent Senate champion for the duration of his long career.

76. John Percival Jones to David A. Wells, July 24, 1876, Wells MSS, LC.

77. J. P. Jones to Georgina Jones, Sept. 2, 1877, Jones MSS, Huntington Library.

4

Old Standards for New: Congress and Silver, 1876

First Thoughts

When the silver issue first reached Congress in 1876, it involved not the lofty question of monetary standards but one of petty change. The problem of remonetization first intruded into legislative debate in March 1876 over one measure concerning the subsidiary coinage and another that stripped the 420-grain trade dollar of its legal tender quality.[1] In still a third connection, Democrat Lewis Bogy of Missouri took the Senate floor in March to recommend increasing the legal tender powers of existing silver change to one thousand dollars in a single payment while nominally retaining the gold standard.[2] Bogy felt that limited remonetization of silver would aid eventual resumption of specie payments, and his argument anticipated the rhetorical identification of silver as the "people's money," which would characterize subsequent bimetallist appeals: "The large transactions between bankers and those between this and foreign nations would continue to be in gold, but the silver would remain here as the coin of the people and the laboring man as well as of the small dealer, and indeed of all those persons who do not deal with millions at a clip."[3] Bogy's major contribution to the

1. *Cong. Record,* 44th Cong., 1st sess., vol. 4, pt. 2, Mar. 6, 1876, pp. 1479–82.

2. Senate Bill No. 57, ibid., p. 1479.

3. Ibid., p. 1482.

silver drive derived less from this early advocacy of limited remonetization than from his role as a tutor in monetary questions to the young Missouri House Democrat, Richard Parks Bland, who sponsored a bagful of congressional silver bills over the next two decades. Bland, appointed in December 1875 as chairman of the House Committee on Mines and Mining, sponsored the measure that dominated congressional debate over remonetization during the 1870s.[4]

Silver emerged as a distinct issue in Congress, however, not because of Bogy's demand for a significant expansion of its legal tender powers but through the legislative debates in March and April 1876 over issuing the subsidiary silver change authorized by the 1875 Resumption Act. In both houses of Congress representatives who began by discussing the effect of replacing fractional greenbacks with subsidiary silver ended by confronting cautiously the possibility of completely restoring bimetallism. Thus advocates of remonetization emerged in Congress by April 1876, primarily among hard money supporters of specie resumption who favored currency expansion but opposed issuing additional greenbacks.

The controversy over issuing more subsidiary silver change began with the Resumption Act in January 1875. After its passage, the Treasury Department purchased in 1875 almost 8,250,000 ounces of silver bullion for minting into subsidiary coins. By the time Congress reconvened in December 1875, ten million dollars worth of these coins, presumably earmarked for the retirement of fractional greenbacks, had accumulated in the Treasury's vaults. Secretary Bristow refused to issue the coins, however, and noted in his 1875 report that he believed it "im-

4. "The first information I had of the demonetization of silver," Bland later stated, "came from Senator Bogy." For a discussion of Bland's role in the silver drive of the 1870s, see Harold Alanson Haswell, "The Public Life of Congressman Richard Parks Bland," unpublished Ph.D. dissertation, University of Missouri, 1951.

practicable" to circulate them because of the current sharp depreciation in market rate of both greenbacks and silver relative to gold, a fact which caused Bristow to question whether greenbacks and silver could stabilize in price at an equivalent level. Without such stability, the new subsidiary coins and the old paper notes would not be interchangeable as fractional money, and the silver change, then worth more than fractional paper money, "would now be hoarded for shipment abroad, or converted into plate and jewelry, or reduced to bullion."[5]

Many congressmen did not share Bristow's anxiety that the subsidiary coins, once issued, would disappear from circulation because greater in value than the minor paper notes. It struck these legislators as supreme irony that at a time when coinage was in scarce supply among American merchants, the Treasury's vaults overflowed with the new silver coins while the government still spent more than $100,000 a month to replace worn fractional greenbacks with new ones. A number began demanding that the Treasury issue these new silver pieces immediately, and when Bristow requested an additional congressional appropriation of $163,000 to replace tattered paper money in March 1876, the House Committee on Appropriations appended instructions to its authorization calling on the secretary to begin exchanging subsidiary silver immediately for the minor greenbacks.[6] How ludicrous that the Treasury should coin millions in silver tokens, the House committee reasoned, only to hoard them while the nation's commercial community starved for an adequate amount of specie to transact normal business.

While preparing this appropriation bill, the committee also debated the wisdom of extending the legal tender powers of subsidiary silver coins, then limited by the Coinage Act of 1873 to five dollars for a single payment. In the end, it made no recom-

5. *Report of the Secretary of the Treasury for 1875,* p. xxvii. See also, Carothers, *Fractional Money,* pp. 250–53.

6. Carothers, *Fractional Money,* p. 253; *Cong. Record,* 44th Cong., 1st sess., vol. 4, pt. 2, p. 1414.

mendation but decided simply to allow amendments during House debate on the subject. When the measure reached the House floor that same month, however, discussion of the broader monetary standard issue occasionally threatened to overshadow the question of redeeming the fractional greenbacks. Although House members recognized that the market value of silver had fallen below the greenbacks relative to gold, both supporters and opponents of issuing the subsidiary coinage assumed that this decline would be only temporary. "The moment this bill passes," one critic of the bill observed, "[silver] will go above par and it will be withdrawn from circulation as currency."[7] Although the March 1876 measure simply restated the subsidiary coinage provision of the 1875 Resumption Act, a section considered uncontroversial at the time, it created a furor in Congress and aroused passionate stump oratory from the opposing currency factions in both parties. Republican-greenbackers like William D. Kelley and hard money Democrats such as Abraham S. Hewitt joined in denouncing the proposed release of subsidiary coinage as a dangerous subsidy for "bonanza mine owners." Most Republicans, on the other hand, including House Minority Leader James A. Garfield, and a number of hard money Democrats like Samuel J. Randall of Pennsylvania defended the proposed exchange of minor silver coins for fractional greenbacks as a necessary first step toward resuming specie payments.[8]

House debate on the "silver resumption" bill, as the subsidiary coinage act became known, proceeded in passionate but leisurely fashion for several weeks, laying bare fundamental disagreements in both parties but especially among the Democrats over specie resumption. "We are in a bad way on the money question," Democratic Congressman William Morrison confided to David

7. *Cong. Record,* 44th Cong., 1st sess., vol. 4, pt. 2, p. 1414.

8. Debate on the measure, H.R. 2450, occupied several long meetings of the House and one in the Senate before its final approval. Ibid., pp. 1762–74, 1985–96, 2042–48, 2049–50, 2082–88, 2129–30, 2254, 2341–53, 2360, 2389, 2418, 2513.

A. Wells following the first House debate over silver resumption, "and the only satisfaction we have (if it be a satisfaction at all) is that our Republican friends are fast tending toward the same bad end."[9] Morrison's last comment undoubtedly referred to "Pig-Iron" Kelley's opposition to "silver resumption," but apart from Kelley, a long-standing party maverick, Republican ranks held firm during House debate over the silver resumption bill. Leading Republicans like Hale of Maine, Page of California, and Garfield of Ohio—the latter being the party's major House spokesman on financial issues—all disputed vigorously Kelley's charge that the subsidiary coinage measure had been advanced primarily to benefit silver mine owners. Far from enriching the Bonanza Kings, asserted Congressman Page of the mineowners' home state, the exchange of subsidiary silver for fractional notes would actually prove costly to holders of coin on the Pacific coast: "the Government now proposes to sell its silver to the people of this country for paper, while California has paid in gold coin for her $4,000,000 of silver, so that she will suffer by this measure a loss of between $400,000 and $500,000."

House Democrats quarreled furiously, unlike their Republican colleagues, over the merits of silver resumption. Congressmen Reagen of Texas and Burchard of Illinois, both inflationists, recommended returning completely to bimetallism in order to utilize America's silver production fully in the resumption process. Other Democratic inflationists like Landers of Indiana proposed that the subsidiary coins simply be released, without at the same time retiring an equivalent amount in fractional greenbacks. Still other paper money advocates like Dunnell of Minnesota opposed issuing the subsidiary coinage under any conditions. Joining Democratic inflationists in their hostility to increased silver coinage were hard money Democrats like Abram Hewitt and Fernando Wood of New York, who favored immediate return to specie payments but insisted that the proposed

9. William Morrison to David A. Wells, Mar. 16, 1876, Wells MSS, LC.

replacement of fractional notes with minor silver coins was merely a "Bonanza" scheme to increase mineowner profits through government silver sales. Opponents of the measure remained too divided among themselves to align against it, however, and the subsidiary coinage bill passed a Democratic-controlled House on March 31 by a 123 to 100 majority, with most Republicans supporting the administration-backed measure while a majority of Democrats opposed it.

Almost as an afterthought the bill opened the monetary standard question itself. Before final passage, the House incorporated into the silver resumption scheme an amendment introduced by Congressman Reagen of Texas raising the 420 grain trade dollar legal tender limit to fifty dollars in a single payment and increasing that of all subsidiary silver coins to twenty-five dollars. The Senate Finance Committee, to which the House bill was referred, threw out this section and substituted an amendment calling for coinage of a 412.8 grain silver dollar, to be legal tender for twenty dollars except for payment of customs duties or interest on the public debt.[10] Another Senate Finance Committee amendment abolished the existing legal tender powers of the trade dollar. These Senate changes in the House's silver resumption bill, written by John Sherman, reflected Sherman's effort to satisfy rising congressional demands for increased silver coinage without restoring bimetallism on a de facto basis, which might have occurred had the trade dollar's legal tender been raised to fifty dollars as the House bill had provided.[11] By the time the full Senate began discussing the House silver resumption act on April 10, the subsidiary coinage question had been overshadowed

10. For the debate, see *Cong. Record,* 44th Cong., 1st sess., vol. 4, pt. 2, especially pp. 1764–73, 1990–93, 2043–48, 2084–88, 2130, 2341–42.

11. Carothers, *Fractional Money,* p. 255. Carothers called the Reagen Amendment "an attempt to revive bimetallism surreptitiously by raising the legal tender limit of the [existing] trade dollar to a sum that would cause its unlimited coinage for circulation in the United States."

completely, as a growing number of legislators demanded complete restoration of the double standard.

The question of redeeming fractional greenbacks in subsidiary silver, the original purpose of the House bill, never entered Senate debate over the measure, and legislators in the upper chamber concentrated almost exclusively on Sherman's Finance Committee amendment creating a 412.8 grain silver dollar. As the Ohio Republican acknowledged, his amendment "presents the most difficult question in political science . . . the question of the single or double standard." Senate discussion of Sherman's amendment foreshadowed the lengthier congressional debate over remonetization that occurred later in the session. Four distinct viewpoints emerged during discussion of Sherman's proposed limited remonetization of the silver dollar, and the arguments employed in April 1876 reflected the four major strands of congressional opinion on the silver question that re-emerged during subsequent legislative tussles over bimetallism for the remainder of the decade.

Sherman himself denied that limited recoinage of a domestic silver dollar would endanger resumption or threaten the existing gold standard. He asked support for his partially remonetized 412.8 grain silver dollar on the grounds that it would bring the market price of silver up to par with gold while adding to the existing stock of circulating hard money, thus helping to bring about specie resumption "without contraction." Sherman insisted, probably with good reason, that his decision to press for a new silver dollar was made reluctantly, "forcibly, against our will," because of the House silver resumption bill's provision raising the legal tender limit of silver coin.

Rather than delay congressional passage of the entire subsidiary coinage measure or "risk a controversy with the House" by striking out completely their silver clause, Sherman preferred to alter it. He considered the silver dollar amendment a "fair compromise" with the House provision that increased the legal tender limit of existing silver coin. The Ohio Republican opposed complete remonetization of silver but favored instead a substantial expansion of the metal's use as money, both through subsidiary coinage and through the partly restored domestic silver dollar. Sherman also urged an international monetary agreement regulating the legal mint ratio of gold and silver in all Western nations as an ultimate solution for the silver question, but he expressed doubts over the feasibility of securing such an agreement in the near future and saw his present compromise plan for partial remonetization as a stopgap measure.

Sherman spoke for those congressional moderates who, although supporters of the gold standard, were anxious for political reasons to allow a carefully controlled expansion of silver coinage. The three other senators who joined in this debate over the House "silver resumption" bill resisted such compromise. One of the two Republicans who spoke was an opponent of resumption who favored greenback inflation while the second, a gold standard advocate, believed resumption possible only by contracting the currency. The third speaker, a Democrat, proposed immediate and full restoration of the double standard. All three questioned the merits of Sherman's compromise amendment and called for its rejection in favor of more extended debate on the entire silver question. "This bill," complained gold-standard Republican Justin Morrill of Vermont, "comes here with a proposition at the head to supply a deficiency in the Treasury for the printing of legal-tender notes; yet attached to it is a proposition that is to revolutionize our whole established custom from the foundation of the Government in relation to legal tender in coin." Silverite Lewis Bogy of Missouri also called the subject "too important . . . too vast and too complicated" for settlement after such brief debate on a single amendment to a minor House measure.

Bogy and Morrill held positions on the monetary standard question that were clear-cut, if diametrically opposed, but Indiana Republican Oliver P. Morton's remarks reflected the persistent ambiguity that was to plague greenback inflationists in coming to grips with the silver issue. Morton, although avowing his sympathy for eventual remonetization, reacted to Sherman's measure in a manner curiously similar to the gold standard advocate, Morrill of Vermont. Thus, Morton and Morrill both agreed that Sherman's proposed 412.8 grain dollar seriously undervalued silver in relation to gold at their current market quotations, insuring that gold coin would disappear once the less valuable silver dollars began to circulate with expanded legal tender powers:

> If we are to make new silver coins, why not make them of the value of gold coin? Put enough silver into them and make them the equivalent of gold coin, so that they can circulate together and be interchangeable the one for the other. Then you can make it a legal tender for a large amount.

Morton noted that subsidiary silver coins had recently dropped several cents below fractional greenbacks relative to gold, and he wondered whether Sherman's new silver dollar would rise to par with gold rapidly enough to prevent speculation in gold coin. Morrill had entered a similar objection and chided Sherman for "a blundering attempt to introduce nothing but silver as the legal tender of the country and to utterly abolish the use of gold."

Other than their shared hostility toward any rapid expansion of silver coinage, however, the Indiana and Vermont Republicans agreed on few points of financial doctrine. Morton called for a return to specie payments only after substantially increasing the greenback supply, and he denounced the House bill's replacement of fractional paper notes with subsidiary silver. Morrill, on the other hand, supported redemption of the minor greenbacks in subsidiary silver as a prelude to eventual resumption in gold. The third participant in this brief debate, Lewis Bogy, called instead for the complete remonetization of silver and alluded to the 1873 "blunder" responsible for demonetizing silver in the first place. All three men, however, rejected Sherman's patchwork solution and requested separate congressional consideration of the entire monetary standard question.

Attacked on all sides, Sherman moved to strike down both his own silver dollar amendment and the House provision that raised the legal tender limit of existing silver coins. The Senate accepted these changes and proceeded to approve the remainder of the House bill, which consisted of the Treasury appropriation for subsidiary coinage and specific instructions for the department to begin redeeming fractional notes with these subsidiary silver coins. The House quickly passed the Senate's version of the silver resumption bill, despite objections from members who favored extending the legal tender power of silver coins, and the President signed the measure on April 17.[12]

"This is the entering of the silver wedge," wrote one New York newspaper following the bill's passage, and indeed, Congress had begun to debate the entire question of remonetization while disposing of the subsidiary coinage question.[13] Until April 1876, however, this debate over increasing silver coinage had been concerned primarily with the merits of replacing fractional notes with subsidiary coins, a policy commended even by many monetary contractionists. One such legislator, James A. Garfield, who led the House fight for the silver resumption bill, confided in his diary after final passage of the revised measure that the hard money men had won a splendid victory, and National Board of Trade official B. F. Nourse, an ardent gold-standard resumptionist, wrote Secretary Bristow calling it "both proper and expedient" for the secretary to begin implementing the statute immediately.[14] Whitelaw Reid's influential New York *Tribune,* which had opposed the sub-

12. For this Senate debate over the subsidiary coinage bill, see *Cong. Record.,* 44th Cong., 1st sess., vol. 4, pt. 2, pp. 2254, 2341–53, 2389, 2418, 2513.

13. New York *Graphic,* Apr. 11, 1876.

14. Garfield Diary, Mar. 31, 1876, Garfield MSS, LC; B. F. Nourse to Benjamin H. Bristow, Apr. 3, 1876, Bristow MSS, LC.

sidiary coinage provision when it was first included in the 1875 Resumption Act, now reversed itself and called for swift retirement of fractional greenbacks by the new silver coins.[15]

Even most opponents of silver resumption believed that the bill's enactment would soon lead to an increase in the metal's market price, a rise that some feared would remove the new subsidiary coins from circulation because of their premium over fractional notes. "If the silver should disappear into the melting pot," the liberal Republican editor Horace White warned Secretary Bristow, "and the people were left without very small change . . . the consequence . . . would be an incalculable but dangerous element in the approaching election."[16] Still other supporters of specie resumption, however, cautioned against releasing the subsidiary coins until silver stopped depreciating, lest the decline prove to be permanent. The Washington *National Republican,* for example, complained about "hard money men [who] are anxious to compel the people to take silver for fractional currency, because silver is cheap and plenty," and warned that silver might become still cheaper and more plentiful before its market depreciation halted.[17]

Almost all of these early congressional and public reactions to the silver resumption bill revealed a deep note of uncertainty concerning the economic and political complexities of the monetary standard question. "It is hardly too much to say that public opinion is in the process of transition on this subject," wrote the New York *Graphic* late in March 1876, "and it is scarcely safe to venture a prediction as to its final conclusion."[18] The shifting tides of popular sentiment found expression in the

15. New York *Tribune* Mar. 21, 1876. See also Baltimore *Sun,* July 12, 1876.

16. Horace White to Benjamin Bristow, Mar. 1, 1876. See also Isaac Sherman to Bristow, Mar. 3, 1876; both Bristow MSS, LÇ.

17. Washington *National Republican,* Mar. 2, 1876; *Bankers' Magazine,* April, 1876, pp. 830–31.

18. New York *Graphic,* Mar. 31, 1876. See also *Graphic,* Apr. 1, 1876.

uncertain actions of economic publicists like Horace White, who was originally an opponent of silver resumption but reversed himself by April 1876 and demanded for a brief time not only redemption of the fractional greenbacks in subsidiary coins but a complete return to legal bimetallism.[19] Congressional leaders forced to debate the issue, often without clear understanding of earlier government silver coinage policy, were even more uncomfortable with the silver question than private citizens. When the Senate began considering on March 30 a bill introduced earlier in the session by California Republican Aaron Sargent to increase the legal tender of existing subsidiary coins, the degree of legislative confusion on the monetary standard question quickly became apparent.

Sherman's Finance Committee had previously reported an amended version of Sargent's measure. Instead of the original proposal which increased the legal tender of existing domestic silver coins, Sherman's amended bill provided only for removing the 420 grain "trade" dollar's legal tender. Few Senators understood Sherman's precise intention, and some viewed it as the opening wedge of a campaign to abandon completely the use of legal tender silver money. One such protest came from Senator Cockrell of Missouri who proclaimed: "I believe in silver as a currency, and I should like to see it a legal tender for sums larger than $5. I am opposed to its being demonetized and driven out of the country."[20] Several other silverites, including Lewis Bogy, expressed similar reservations over Sherman's amendment, which in fact had been designed only to prevent *domestic* circulation of the *trade* dollar, a coin intended by its sponsors in 1872 only to circulate in export trade. Bogy urged that Congress, instead of remitting the trade dollar's domestic circulation, raise its legal tender limit along with that

19. Horace White to John Sherman, Apr. 28, 1876, Sherman MSS, LC.

20. *Cong. Record,* 44th Cong., 1st sess., vol. 4, pt. 2, pp. 1999, 2060–61.

of all subsidiary silver coins from $5 to $1,000. For the first time in Senate debate, on March 30, John Percival Jones raised Bogy's ante to the limit by demanding that Congress return completely to a bimetallic monetary system.

As Senate debate rambled on over stripping the trade dollar of its legal tender, it became apparent that even those senators interested in the measure shared the bewilderment of most congressmen over silver coinage policy. Few of them felt comfortable discussing the new issue. Even Lewis Bogy, an early advocate of remonetization, became confused during debate over the exact meaning of the term "subsidiary silver coinage," and during the discussion, Roscoe Conkling of New York asked his fellow senators, three years after passage of the Coinage Act that demonetized silver, "is it true that there is now by law no American [domestic silver] dollar?" Following Conkling's inquiry several senators—notably Sherman, Bogy, and Jones—muddled the debate still further by offering three different explanations for silver's demonetization.

Sherman was questioned sharply by other senators concerning his reasons for advocating removal of the trade dollar's legal tender, and he received support from a surprising source when Republican John Percival Jones of Nevada defended the proposal. "By having the trade dollar a legal tender for $5, the full amount that the subsidiary coins are now a legal tender for," Jones observed, "the effect is to degrade the two half dollars that had cost the citizen [on the Pacific coast] $1 in gold . . . to the bullion value of the trade dollar [ninety-two to ninety-four cents]."[21] Therefore, Jones urged passage of Sherman's measure removing the trade dollar's domestic legal tender so that regular small silver change would continue to circulate at parity with gold on the Pacific coast. The Nevada Republican wanted Congress to consider the subject of remonetizing silver as a distinct issue unconnected with the trade dollar and sub-

21. Bogy's remarks are woven through the entire debate. Ibid., pp. 2060–64. For Jones' comments, ibid., pp. 2062–64.

sidiary coinage questions, and he remarked during debate over Sherman's trade dollar amendment that "on another occasion, it will be time enough to introduce bills, and advocate them, restoring the silver dollar and declaring the double standard."[22] The Senate refused to pass Sherman's trade dollar measure during its March 30 debate, however, and the following month the Finance Committee attached the trade dollar legal tender repeal provision to Sherman's earlier bill calling for a partly remonetized domestic silver dollar.[23]

Jones had preferred to wait until Congress disposed of the trade dollar question before demanding restoration of the double standard, but the Senate Finance Committee's decision to link the former issue to Sherman's earlier silver dollar proposal forced his hand. After recognizing that the other silver coinage issue would not be disposed of quickly, Jones finally unveiled his plan in April 1876 for the complete reestablishment of American bimetallism.

Before Jones took the Senate floor, Lewis Bogy spoke on the same issue, anticipating the Nevadan's demands by proposing that Sherman's 412.8 grain silver dollar, instead of being limited in legal tender to twenty dollars, be made an unlimited legal tender. Bogy called for complete restoration of the double standard "in payment of all contracts whatsoever, both public and private," and he reviewed in an extensively prepared speech the background of American bimetallism from the founding of the Republic to the Coinage Act of 1873. Bogy acknowledged that his ideas followed substantially the analysis of "Mr. George M. Weston, a friend of mine in Boston," especially Weston's denial that Congress had possessed legal authority to change the monetary standard in 1873 without a constitutional amendment. The Missouri Democrat also questioned the integrity of those government officials who, three years earlier, had steered

22. Ibid., p. 2063. See also the interview with John Percival Jones, Detroit *Evening News,* May 18, 1876.

23. *Cong. Record.,* 44th Cong., 1st sess., vol. 4, pt. 2, pp. 2587, 2735.

through Congress the act that demonetized silver. He raised the spectre of a conspiracy for the first time in Congress by claiming that the "law of 1873 was surreptitiously interjected into a bill pending at that time before the Senate in relation to the mint."[24]

John Percival Jones offered his own remonetization proposals in an April 24 speech that followed Bogy's talk. Both Jones and Bogy acknowledged their debt to George Melville Weston, a Boston importer and former abolitionist Republican newspaper editor from Maine. Weston, in a letter which appeared on March 2, 1876, in the Boston *Globe,* first raised publicly the notion of the "Crime of 1873," when he charged that elimination of silver as a monetary standard in the mint bill of 1873 "was as selfish in its origin as it was surreptitious in the manner of its introduction." Demonetizing silver, Weston wrote in the *Globe,* "was undoubtedly intended to augment the burden of [American] public and private debts," and demonstrated the "flagrant and audacious . . . control exercised by foreign and domestic bankers over national legislation in these recent and evil days." Weston asserted that bimetallism had been replaced by the gold standard in 1873 solely to insure that government bonds would be repaid in gold alone, an action which he termed "unconstitutional as respects private debts, and scandalously corrupt as respects the national debt, the burden of which [increased] by a heavy percentage."[25] The Boston publicist played a major role in marshaling public support for silver during the opening phase of the campaign for remonetization. Even before he became secretary of the Monetary Commission appointed by Congress in August 1876 to explore the entire question, Weston's stream of newspaper letters and magazine articles on the silver

24. For Bogy's speech, ibid., pp. 2062–66, 2642–45, Apr. 20, 1876. See also Weston's articles attacking the demonetization of silver in the following newspapers: Boston *Globe,* Mar. 2, 1876; Boston *Herald,* Mar. 19, 1876; and Boston *Commercial Bulletin,* Apr. 8, 1876. All had been published prior to Bogy's speech.

25. Boston *Globe,* Mar. 2, 1876.

issue influenced strongly the ideas of many bimetallist congressmen, notably Lewis Bogy and John Percival Jones, the two earliest legislative supporters of remonetization.[26]

Weston, who had edited a Washington antislavery newspaper during the 1850s, lost no time in circulating his ideas on the silver question among old government friends and political associates. "I enclose letter on constitutional aspects of silver," he wrote Montgomery Blair in March 1876, two days after the letter's publication in the Boston *Globe*. "I have great confidence that my legal points are well taken, and I trust you may have time to look at them carefully." Of the three congressmen most closely identified with bimetallism in 1876—John Percival Jones, Lewis Bogy, and Richard Parks Bland—only Jones had advocated complete restoration of silver before the Boston importer began publishing his views on the question.[27]

Jones' lengthy April 24–25 Senate speech on silver, which opened formal congressional debate on the monetary standard question, touched on a variety of subjects: the nature and function of money, the historical relationships of gold and silver as monetary standards, changes in the world's supply of precious metals, "the relative value of gold and silver from the earliest times to the present . . . and how constant that relation has been," and, finally, the Nevada Republican's explanation of the current decline in silver below par with gold, a phenomenon that Jones traced to "the various edicts or enactments which in various

26. Weston wrote twenty-two articles or long public letters on aspects of the silver question that he republished in the Appendix to his later book. Weston, *The Silver Question*.

27. George Melville Weston to Montgomery Blair, Mar. 4, 1876, Blair Family MSS, LC. Lewis Bogy, who tutored his fellow Missourian Richard Bland on the facts concerning silver, acknowledged taking Weston's advice freely, *Cong. Record,* 44th Cong., 1st sess., vol. 4, pt. 2, p. 2644. Furthermore, John Percival Jones relied heavily on four of Weston's previously published articles for ideas and arguments in his exhaustive Apr. 24–25 Senate speech, which opened congressional debate over remonetization.

countries" had demonetized the metal.[28] Restoring the double standard, Jones believed, would help immeasurably in returning to specie payments while, at the same time, ending the long business depression. Asserting that silver had been removed as a monetary standard "in the interest of . . . creditors at home or abroad," Jones referred to the Coinage Act of 1873 as "a grave wrong . . . committed no doubt unwittingly, yet no less certainly, in the interests of a few plutocrats in England and in Germany . . . a mere caprice of legislation."

The Nevada Republican insisted repeatedly in the speech that without remonetization, returning the United States to a coin standard of monetary values would prove impossible. He believed that the country's current monetary stock of gold was hardly adequate to guarantee the success of resumption without adding the supply of silver that would accrue if bimetallism were restored. Therefore, although Jones endorsed the 1875 resumption statute as "a very proper act of itself," he considered resumption in gold alone of benefit only to foreign and domestic creditors, a process "gratuitously and needlessly enhancing the value of the mortgages which, in the name of Government bonds, they hold upon the industries of this country."

The Nevada Republican asserted that once the bimetallic standard had been restored, a satisfactory equilibrium in market price between gold and silver would be established swiftly, thereby allowing both metals to continue circulating without either one depreciating significantly. Wrapping his argument in the accepted cloak of Manchesterian liberal doctrine, he insisted that international market forces would naturally and automatically restore the lost price balance between gold and silver if only government legislation did not tamper with the bullion market: "*Laissez-faire* in money is as important to the well being

28. *Cong. Record.,* 44th Cong., 1st sess., vol. 4, pt. 6, Appendix pp. 67–99, reprinted as *Resumption and the Double Standard* (Washington, n.p., 1876). Subsequent citations are taken from the printed volume.

of the world as *laissez-faire* in corn."[29] Jones also accepted a prevailing version of the quantity theory of money when he insisted that the Coinage Act of 1873 had "artificially diminished" the money stock by demonetizing silver, thereby impeding free operation of the international bullion market.[30] Remonetize silver, and not only would the "natural" level of domestic legal tender coinage be restored but the volume of business transactions would increase correspondingly.[31] Jones concluded his paean to silver coinage by predicting confidently that as a direct result of remonetization,

> prices [will] rise; exchange or commerce is stimulated; new enterprises are set afoot; the products of agriculture, manufactures, and mining are increased; the commercial and industrial classes find abundant employment and earn remunerative profits and wages; bankruptcies and suicides rarely happen; marriages are promoted; the newly born survive in greater numbers; population increases in quicker ratio; letters, the fine arts, and the sciences make most rapid strides; education, intelligence and morality, and the observance of religion are promoted; and the general happiness of mankind becomes greatly enhanced.[32]

Even before the brief Senate debate that followed Jones' two-

29. Ibid., pp. 1, 8, 47, 67–79, 81, 92–93.

30. "In general terms, then, the value of money varies inversely with its quantity," W. A. L. Coulborn, *A Discussion of Money* (London, 1950), p. 85. Coulborn's chapter on the quantity theory of money provides a clear brief review of the subject. Ibid., pp. 84–91. For two excellent treatments of monetary flows in the United States, see Friedman and Schwartz, *Monetary History*, esp. pp. 15–134 on late nineteenth-century finance; also Phillip Cagan, *Determinants and Effects of Changes in the Stock of Money, 1875–1960* (New York, 1965), esp. pp. 1–117.

31. According to the traditional theory of money, MV=PT, or the volume of money multiplied by the velocity of its circulation equals the price-level multiplied by the volume of transactions. Coulborn, *A Discussion of Money*, pp. 88–89.

32. Jones, *Resumption and the Double Standard*, pp. 92–93.

day oration had ended, clear divisions had emerged over the question of restoring silver as a monetary standard. Supporters of complete remonetization led by Jones, Bogy, and John Logan of Illinois had seized the initiative by demanding a complete return to bimetallism, a policy unacceptable to limited restorationists such as John Sherman. More fervent gold standard advocates like Morrill of Vermont, on the other hand, viewed with undisguised alarm any attempt to increase silver's legal tender powers, whether made by Sherman or Jones.[33] Within a month after the Nevadan's opening speech, the lower chamber would also begin to form ranks on the question, and the House campaign to remonetize silver—led primarily by inflationist, anti-resumption Democrats—succeeded with remarkable speed against only scattered opposition.

First Triumphs

Historians of the silver movement during the seventies have focused attention in the past primarily on the bitter congressional debates over remonetization which took place in the winter of 1877–78, neglecting the earlier legislative controversy over restoring legal bimetallism during the spring and summer of 1876.[34] Yet even before the election of 1876 a surprising amount of congressional agreement had emerged over the silver question, especially in the House of Representatives. Several extremely important votes had taken place on the issue in Congress months before the presidential campaign began.

33. *Cong. Record,* 44th Cong., 1st sess., vol. 4, pt. 2, p. 2734.

34. The fullest account is in Laughlin, *History of Bimetallism,* pp. 181–83, devoted mainly to quoting from the early silver bills. See also Unger, *Greenback Era,* pp. 343–44; Hepburn, *History of Currency in the U.S.,* p. 275; Dewey, *Financial History of the U.S.,* p. 406. All of these authors merely note the date that Bland first introduced *his* remonetization measure and then discuss only the 1877–78 debates. In her article on the silver drive, Jeannette Nichols does not mention the 1876 debates. Nichols, "John Sherman and the Silver Drive," *Ohio State Arc. and Hist. Quarterly,* passim.

In the House, with its large Democratic majority, anti-resumption Democrats supported remonetization as an inflationist wedge that might undermine Republican efforts to implement the 1875 Resumption Act. This Democratic concern for restoring the double standard stemmed not from the prior mandate of agrarian constituents for an increased circulation of silver—eastern Democrats largely joined their southern and western colleagues in these efforts—but from unrelenting partisan hostility in a presidential election year toward the Republican's Resumption Act, which most Democrats believed an inept and dangerously contractionist approach to the problem of returning to specie payments. Senate supporters of remonetization, on the other hand, took their direction primarily from a small group of anti-inflationist and pro-resumption legislators, mainly Republicans, led by John Percival Jones, William Boyd Allison, John A. Logan, and Lewis Bogy.

Congressional silverites quickly recognized the potential public impact of the charge leveled by Jones that silver had been demonetized through fraud and collusion, and from the start of the controversy they stressed the popular theme of restoring the old 412.5 grain "dollar of the daddies." Although the Nevada Republican spoke confidently in 1876 about ultimate victory on the silver question, he warned his constituents in a public letter to the *Territorial Enterprise* that "success is by no means certain at this session."[35] As a rule, early supporters of remonetization in the upper chamber found it easy to caucus and to plan strategy because of their smaller numbers, while House silverites scrambled for leadership positions, undoubtedly keeping in mind the popularity which such roles appeared to assure. Missouri Democrat Richard Parks Bland and Pennsylvania Republican William D. Kelley were the two most prominent contenders throughout the spring and summer of 1876 for control of the remonetization drive in the lower chamber. Both introduced measures restoring legal bimetallism

35. Virginia City *Territorial Enterprise*, May 3, 1876.

and worked feverishly to place them before the House until Bland, as chairman of the powerful Committee on Mines and Mining, finally emerged as the proposal's sponsor and leading advocate.[36]

It became apparent almost from the beginning of the campaign that Senate supporters of full restoration did not control a clear majority of the upper house in 1876 and that only by arriving at some compromise plan with moderates like John Sherman could they hope to pass a remonetization measure. In the House silverites held a comfortable majority almost from the moment the issue arose. Even before Congress had adjourned in August 1876, the lower chamber's Democratic majority had already voted twice to restore legal bimetallism only to have the Republican Senate refuse to accept such a swift change in monetary standards. Senate Republicans were concerned that undue attention to the silver issue might complicate Hayes' election campaign by forcing a party stand on the question. They succeeded in sidetracking final disposition of the matter until after the election by securing congressional approval of an interim Monetary Commission to study the problem. Presumably, when Congress reconvened after the presidential election, it remained only to frame a suitable compromise bill acceptable to a Senate majority that favored restoring some measure of bimetallism.

John Percival Jones' April 24 speech, which opened the drive to restore silver as a monetary standard, quickly attracted attention among his fellow legislators and on the Pacific coast. The day following Jones' address, California's Republican party endorsed remonetization at its state convention but called at the

36. Bland and Kelley fought a verbal duel on the House floor over whether bills concerning remonetization came under the control of Kelley's Committee on Banking and Currency or Bland's Committee on Mines and Mining. *Cong. Record,* 44th Cong., 1st sess., vol. 4, pt. 4, June 3, 1876, pp. 3555–56.

same time for specie resumption and payment of government bonds in gold coin alone.[37] Jones' speech undoubtedly influenced the convention's silver plank, but its demand for gold payment of federal securities indicated the California party's reluctance to break completely with its earlier gold-standard position. At the same time, while preparing for the impending debate on silver, several congressmen made persistent inquiries at the Mint Bureau for the latest quotations of the metal's market value. Mint Director Linderman's correspondents included both Congressman Richard Parks Bland of Missouri, who introduced one of the first free coinage measures on May 3, and John Sherman, to whom Linderman expressed anxiety over silver's continual depreciation on the London exchanges: "The currency value of one [silver] dollar in subsidiary coins [worth one gold dollar] is eighty-four cents and four mills. Gold value of greenback dollar eighty-eight and a half cents."[38]

Weeks of private discussions in Washington followed Jones' speech before Congress began public debate over remonetization. Representative Benjamin F. Butler of Massachusetts informed Jones during this interval that after talking with President Grant early in May, he felt that the chief executive held no definite views on the subject despite appeals by his old political allies, Butler and Jones, for support.[39] The controversy over restoring bimetallism resumed on June 8 when the Senate again took up Aaron Sargent's January 1876 measure, which had provided originally for a slight increase in the legal tender of subsidiary silver coins. By June, the bill bore little resemblance to this earlier version, having been amended in the intervening months by all three major factions in the silver controversy—

37. San Francisco *Bulletin,* Apr. 27, 1876; Virginia City *Territorial Enterprise,* Apr. 27, 1876.

38. Linderman to Bland, Apr. 28, 1876, and Linderman to Sherman, May 2, 1876; Letterbooks, Director of the Mint, RG 104, NA.

39. Benjamin F. Butler to John P. Jones, May 4, 1876, Butler MSS, typescript, LC.

supporters of full remonetization, advocates of limited restoration, and gold monometallists.

To review the situation, John Sherman had proposed in April that the silver dollar be recoined with its legal tender restricted to twenty dollars. Lewis Bogy and John Percival Jones then demanded full remonetization of the metal. When debate resumed on June 8, Justin Morrill of Vermont, a bitter opponent of silver coinage, confused Sargent's original bill still further by proposing two amendments, one that continued the existing five dollar legal tender limit and another that provided for a 467.8 grain silver dollar, an overweight coin equivalent in its silver bullion content to the current market value of the gold dollar. Republican-inflationist Oliver P. Morton of Indiana and Newton Booth of California, an Anti-Monopolist Independent, also opposed remonetization when debate reopened, while Sherman defended the soundness of his original proposal for limited restoration as "specie resumption in the old time-honored standard of silver dollars of full weight and fineness [which] will prepare the way for full resumption in gold." Sherman pleaded with Jones and Bogy not to "embarrass" his amended bill by demanding complete remonetization "at this time, when we cannot pay our debt in either gold or silver." With Bogy ill at the time and Jones absent from Washington, Sherman's plea went unanswered, and the June 8 Senate debate ended with no action taken on the Sargent measure.[40]

In order to avoid confusion, both Sherman and Jones wished to dispose of two earlier and collateral silver coinage matters still pending before Congress, the subsidiary coinage and trade dollar questions, before raising the more basic problem of restoring silver as a monetary standard. The House, also troubled by this welter of related coinage bills, passed two measures on June 10 designed to dispose of these secondary issues, one to relieve an existing shortage of subsidiary coins in commercial

40. *Cong. Record,* 44th Cong., 1st sess., vol. 4, pt. 4, pp. 2684, 3673–78, 3685–86.

channels and the other removing the legal tender power of the trade dollar. With many hard-money Democrats in the lower chamber abstaining, a rare Republican House majority pushed through a joint resolution substituting ten million dollars in subsidiary silver coin for an equal number of dollar note greenbacks, supplementing earlier legislation which had allowed the exchange of subsidiary coins only for fractional paper notes. The House resolution provided for eventual destruction of the redeemed greenbacks rather than their reissue, thereby preventing the new silver change from further inflating the currency.[41]

Another House measure, more ambiguously worded, won approval the same day. It authorized issuing twenty million dollars worth of additional subsidiary coins without specifying any equivalent redemption of greenbacks. The bill's sponsor, Democrat Samuel J. Randall of Pennsylvania, expressed surprise when other congressmen suggested that his measure would allow eventual retirement of an equal number of greenbacks and claimed that his "object is to put the silver coinage into circulation, not to destroy the greenbacks."[42] S. S. "Sunset" Cox of the Banking and Currency Committee, the bill's floor manager, reported Mint Director Linderman's endorsement of the proposal and added that the new outlay of subsidiary coins was both "imperative and popular," made indispensable by the urgent need for more coinage in "the daily and hourly interests of trade and business."[43] Cox blocked efforts by his fellow Democrats, Richard Bland and Franklin Landers, to amend the bill so that it would remonetize the silver dollar, and the Randall measure

41. House discussion of these oft-amended measures, Joint Resolution No. 109 and HR 3398, filled many pages in the *Cong. Record.* On the joint resolution, see especially ibid., pp. 2861, 2898, 3746–47, 3897, 3945–46, 3975–76, 4211–15, 4318, 4432, 4550–63, 5028. For HR, 3398, see ibid., pp. 3027, 3747–52, 4132, 4155, 4177–81, 4195–4209, 4225–28.

42. Ibid., p. 3751.

43. Ibid., p. 3748. See also Henry R. Linderman to S. S. Cox, June 8, 1876, Letterbooks, Director of the Mint, RG 104, NA.

passed by voice vote, going to the Senate where it eventually died in the Finance Committee.[44]

Although the Senate never considered the Randall bill, it acted quickly on the House's joint resolution authorizing an additional ten million dollars in subsidiary coins, further amending the measure on June 21 at Mint Director Linderman's recommendation to include a provision that repealed the trade dollar's legal tender powers and limited the export coin's minting at the discretion of the Secretary of the Treasury. Linderman insisted that without this amendment the mint would find it impossible to produce quickly enough "the necessary amount of subsidiary coin," should the joint resolution pass both houses of Congress.[45] Following a brief debate, the Senate concurred in the amended resolution and dispatched it to the lower chamber, which resumed discussion of the measure that same day.

New York Democrat "Sunset" Cox moved for immediate House concurrence in the Senate changes, but his Indiana party colleague Franklin Landers rose to challenge the amendments, especially the removal of legal tender powers from the trade dollar. Landers objected to demonetizing the export dollar before Congress had first remonetized the old 412.5 grain domestic coin. He suggested that Senate action had been influenced by the same "bondholders" who had presumably been responsible for eliminating the silver dollar from the Coinage Act of 1873. Landers opposed specie resumption in gold alone and, like many inflationist Democrats, viewed remonetization as a second line of attack on Republican resumption policy, important enough to be held in reserve if attempts to repeal the 1875 Resumption Act failed: "I also hold that the currency of the country should

44. *Cong. Record,* 44th Cong., 1st sess., vol. 4, pt. 4, p. 3748. For the Senate history of the bill, see pp. 3751–52, 3814, 4132, 4155, 4177–81, 4195–4209, 4225–28.

45. Linderman to Sherman (telegram), June 21, 1876, RG 104; *Cong. Record,* 44th Cong., 1st sess., vol. 4, pt. 4, pp. 3945–46.

be based upon its credit, upon all its gold, silver, real estate, labor, and everything possessing value." The Indianan, ideologically close to the Greenbackers, acknowledged that his support for silver was largely a tactical move to insure that "if the 'hard money men,' as they are styled, are to succeed . . . [they have] a broader basis than gold alone can give."[46] From the beginning of the controversy, House Democrats like Landers used the silver question as a partisan stalking-horse in an effort to impede progress toward resumption under the terms of the Republicans' 1875 statute. For this reason Landers and his Democratic colleagues prevented immediate House ratification on June 21 of the Senate's amended joint resolution providing for subsidiary coinage expansion, and the measure returned to the Committee on Banking and Currency. Since they endorsed remonetization largely for these tactical political reasons and not on economic grounds, inflationist Democrats in the lower chamber had little interest in whether or not silver coinage actually increased in circulation.

The two houses of Congress acted in tandem on the two subsidiary coinage measures during the following month, with the House considering the joint resolution while the Senate debated Randall's bill, H.R. 3398, shuttling both pieces of legislation between the two chambers. When the Randall bill, which provided for an additional twenty million dollars in minor silver coinage, came up for Senate discussion late in June, the Finance Committee introduced amendments incorporating Sherman's plan for remonetizing the silver dollar as a legal tender for twenty dollars, the new coins to be issued only in exchange for greenbacks which would then be destroyed. Silverites Lewis Bogy, John Percival Jones, and John A. Logan then renewed their earlier demands for full restoration of the 412.8 grain dollar, while Vermont's two Republican senators,

46. *Cong. Record,* 44th Cong., 1st sess., vol. 4, pt. 4, pp. 3946, 3975–76.

George F. Edmunds and Justin S. Morrill, again attacked all forms of remonetization.

Caught as usual in the middle of this intraparty debate among sound-money Republican resumptionists, Sherman pleaded for passage of his compromise measure and expressed weariness with the manner in which, like some ill-timed Jack-in-the-box, the monetary standard question kept intruding into discussion of subsidiary coinage measures. "I thought I should not say anything more about this silver bill," he remarked at one point, "for I am as tired of it as I ever was of any bill in my life." He called limited remonetization of the silver dollar merely a convenient way of increasing the subsidiary coinage, for which public demand was "continuous." Sherman clearly recognized the symbolic meaning for many of his Republican colleagues of restoring some version of the "dollar of the daddies," even though its legal tender power might be restricted.[47] Yet the Ohio Republican professed outrage at the charges of "fraud" being hurled with increasing vehemence by Republican senators at party opponents on the silver question. Jones and Logan harped on the "surreptitious" demonetization of the metal in 1873, while Justin Morrill, in turn, denounced Jones' demand for a return to legal bimetallism as privileged legislation in the "single interest" of large bullion holders.[48] Such backbiting among Republicans had to end before the presidential election campaign began, Sherman believed, or a party gravely divided on financial issues would award the contest by default to the Democrats.

In the House the struggle to restore bimetallism resumed on June 28, when the lower chamber again approved its earlier joint resolution on subsidiary coinage, this time incorporating a simple amendment that fully remonetized the silver dollar. The

47. Ibid., pp. 4177, 4206–07. For the June 27–29 Senate debate over HR 3398, see vol. 4, pt. 5, pp. 4177–81.

48. For a typically abrasive exchange of charges and countercharges, see ibid., pp. 4205–09. Jones' second major speech on remonetization delivered on June 28, contained a demand for "free coinage," pp. 4195–4205.

provision, which was introduced by Franklin Landers and made the silver dollar "legal tender in payment of all debts, public and private," received a 111 to 55 majority, with 123 members not voting.[49]

Debate in the House over the entire joint resolution confused many representatives, a factor that may have encouraged abstentions, since three distinct questions were now incorporated in the same measure: repeal of the trade dollar's legal tender power, provision for issuing ten million dollars in additional subsidiary coinage, and complete restoration of the double standard. Anti-silver congressmen like Henry Payne of Ohio and John A. Kasson of Iowa tried unsuccessfully during debate to delay consideration of the monetary standard issue by calling attention to the more pressing public demand for an immediate expansion of subsidiary coinage. "Letters come to us from all over the Northwest imploring us to hasten this matter of supplying the people with 'change,'" Kasson reminded his colleagues. "We have stopped issuing fractional currency, and there is not 'change' enough." A series of votes on the subsidiary coinage and trade dollar legal tender repeal questions, however, revealed a majority of House Democrats unsympathetic to either proposal. After passing the Landers Amendment restoring a bimetallic standard with little prior discussion, the lower chamber approved another amendment by Samuel Randall to issue an additional twenty million in subsidiary coin, the substance of Randall's earlier bill which had remained neatly bottled up in the Senate.[50] The original joint resolution then passed the House again but with the Landers and Randall amendments included among its provisions (see Tables 1 and 2).

49. Ibid., pp. 4214–15. For House debate prior to passage of the Landers amendment, see pp. 4211–15. The Virginia City *Territorial Enterprise* believed it more than coincidental that the House passed the Landers amendment on the same day Jones presented his Senate address. *Territorial Enterprise,* June 30, 1876.

50. *Cong. Record.,* 44th Cong., 1st sess., vol. 4, pt. 5, pp. 4212, 4214–15.

Table 1

Vote on the Reagen Amendment (Partially Remonetizing Silver), House of Representatives, March 30, 1876

	Ayes			Nays		
	Rep.	Dem.	Ind.	Rep.	Dem.	Ind.
New England States						
Massachusetts	1			3	3	1
Maine				4		
New Hampshire	1	1				
Vermont				3		
Connecticut		1				
Rhode Island				2		
TOTALS	2	2		12	3	1
Middle Atlantic States						
New York	2	3		11	4	
Pennsylvania		14		8	1	
Maryland		2				
Delaware					1	
New Jersey		3		2	2	
TOTALS	2	22		21	8	
Midwestern States						
Ohio	2	9		4	1	
Illinois	2	10	1	4	1	
Indiana	5	6				
Wisconsin	1		1	3		
Minnesota				2		
Michigan	4	1		2		1
Iowa	1			6		
Kansas	1	1		1		
Nebraska				1		
TOTALS	16	27	2	23	2	1
Border States						
Kentucky	1	6			2	
Tennessee		7		1		
West Virginia						
Missouri		7			3	
TOTALS	1	20		1	5	

Table 1—Continued

	Ayes			Nays		
	Rep.	Dem.	Ind.	Rep.	Dem.	Ind.
Southern States						
Virginia		3		1	4	
North Carolina	1	7				
South Carolina				2		
Georgia		2			3	
Alabama		6				
Mississippi	1	3		1		
Florida						
Louisiana		3		2		
Texas		3				
Arkansas		1			1	
TOTALS	2	28		6	8	
Far Western States						
California				1	2	
Nevada						
Colorado						
Oregon						
TOTALS				1	2	
GRAND TOTALS	23	99	2	64	28	2

TOTAL AYES: 124

TOTAL NAYS: 94

Comparison of House voting on the March 30 Reagen amendment which provided for limited remonetization and balloting on the Landers Amendment for full restoration of silver suggests the impact of intervening congressional and public debate. The Democrats endorsed both proposals overwhelmingly, by a 99 to 28 margin in March and by an 84 to 17 vote in June. Although early support for remonetization seemed stronger proportionately within the party among southern and border state representatives, substantial numbers of Atlantic seaboard and Middle Western Democrats also favored the two proposals.

Table 2

Vote on the Landers Amendment (Completely Remonetizing Silver), House of Representatives, June 28, 1876

	Ayes			Nays		
	Rep.	Dem.	Ind.	Rep.	Dem.	Ind.
New England States						
Massachusetts				3	3	1
Maine				1		
New Hampshire						
Vermont				3		
Connecticut		1		1		
Rhode Island				1		
TOTALS		1		9	3	1
Middle Atlantic States						
New York	1	1		10	2	
Pennsylvania		6		3	2	
Maryland		1				
Delaware						
New Jersey	2	4				
TOTALS	3	12		13	4	
Midwestern States						
Ohio	1	5		1	1	
Illinois	5	4	1		1	
Indiana	4	4				
Wisconsin	1	1		1		
Minnesota	1			1		
Michigan	5			2	2	1
Iowa	3		1	3		
Kansas	1	1		1		
Nebraska	1					
TOTALS	22	15	2	9	4	1
Border States						
Kentucky		6				
Tennessee		8		1		
West Virginia		2		1		
Missouri		9			1	
TOTALS		25		2	1	

Table 2—Continued

	Ayes			Nays		
	Rep.	Dem.	Ind.	Rep.	Dem.	Ind.
Southern States						
Virginia		5				
North Carolina		6				
South Carolina				2		
Georgia		5			2	
Alabama		5				
Mississippi				1		
Florida		1				
Louisiana		2				
Texas		2			2	
Arkansas		2				
TOTALS		28		3	4	
Far Western States						
California		2			1	
Nevada						
Colorado						
Oregon		1				
TOTALS		3			1	
GRAND TOTALS	25	84	2	36	17	2
TOTAL AYES: 111						
TOTAL NAYS: 55						

Certain striking shifts in voting patterns occurred, however, even in these early tallies, especially among House Republicans. Although Republicans had disapproved of the Reagen Amendment by a hefty 23 to 64 margin in March, the balloting for Landers' more extreme proposal in June showed a much reduced Republican opposition margin of 25 to 36. Republican abstentions on the Landers Amendment increased significantly in almost every section, most notably in the midwest, where powerful party dailies and local business leaders had emerged as champions of silver. Thus, although midwestern Republicans had opposed limited restoration by a 16 to 23 margin in March, they favored complete remonetization in June by an even larger 22 to 9 tally. The basically partisan nature of voting patterns on the two amendments can be seen by comparing intrasectional balloting. Only in New England did a majority of the congressmen in both parties take the same side on both votes, although the area's small Democratic contingent came close to fulfilling the overall pattern of party voting elsewhere. Republicans and Democrats divided on the two remonetization proposals in almost all sections, with Reagen and Bland receiving substantial support from their Democratic colleagues while Republicans rallied against the amendments. Midwestern Republicans and California Democrats, who endorsed restoration of the double standard in increasing numbers, constituted the major exceptions to the general thread of partisan response to early silver legislation in the House.

The Republican-controlled Senate did not share the House's anxiety for swift disposition of the monetary standard question and was caught unprepared by the lower chamber's passage of the Landers Amendment. Senate Republicans, whatever their views on silver coinage, agreed that no useful purpose could be served by further congressional debate of this new and preplexing currency issue until after the presidential election. Rather than report the House's joint resolution back to the floor for still another round of amendments, therefore, the Finance Committee recommended on July 1 that the Senate simply refuse to concur in the House amendments and that the upper chamber request a joint conference committee. After the Senate approved this proposal, it appointed conferees representing the three major schools of opinion on the silver question: Lewis Bogy, who favored complete remonetization; John Sherman, a supporter of limited remonetization; and George S. Boutwell, who urged maintenance of the gold standard. The House managers on the conference committee were both hard money Democrats: Samuel J. Randall, a silverite, and Henry Payne, a gold monometallist.

The committee's July 13 report on the House's joint resolution represented a carefully designed compromise between advocates of expanded silver coinage and opponents of remonetization. In place of the Landers Amendment which restored the silver dollar as a full legal tender, the conference committee substituted an amendment authorizing an additional issue of subsidiary coinage that, when added to existing fractional notes and silver coins, "shall in the aggregate not exceed at any time $50,000,000." As a quid pro quo, exacted in return for this great enlargement of subsidiary silver coinage, those who supported complete restoration of the double standard agreed in the report to remove the trade dollar's legal tender power. They further agreed, tacitly, to postpone discussion of remonetization until after the election of 1876, when it could be debated as a separate question. Senate opponents of silver consoled themselves with this delay and with the conference committee's stipulation that any minting profits from the increased subsidiary silver coinage would be paid into the Treasury and not returned to bullion sellers.[51]

The House passed the conference committee's amended joint resolution only after vigorous debate. Although a procession of speakers from both parties rose to demand remonetization, House silverites disagreed among themselves over whether to accept the amended resolution and then raise the monetary standard question again at a later date. Henry Payne, who presented the conference report to the House, pointed out that all three Senate managers on the committee, including the silverite Lewis Bogy, had voted to drop the Landers Amendment restoring the silver dollar on the grounds that no subsidiary coinage bill with that or any similar provision could pass the Senate before the election of 1876. Payne also questioned the House's wisdom in voting for remonetization without first debating the problem at some length, especially since silver had begun depreciating substantially on the London market in recent months.

Some silverites, notably Franklin Landers and "Pig-Iron"

51. Ibid., pp. 4225–28, 4318, 4550.

Kelley, challenged Payne's estimate of the Senate's temper and even claimed erroneously that without inclusion of the Landers Amendment, the upper chamber would reject the conference committee report. Because the conference committee had eliminated the provision for remonetization, Landers and other anti-resumptionist soft-money advocates, mainly Democrats, voted against the amended joint resolution. Pro-resumption silverites in both parties, including Democrats Cox and Randall as well as Republicans Horatio Burchard and Joseph Cannon, combined with gold monometallists to push the compromise joint resolution through the House on July 13 by a 129 to 76 margin.

Many House silverites supported the joint resolution, even without a remonetization clause, not merely because they felt that expansion of subsidiary coinage would aid in the resumption process but also because of their growing concern over the absence of an adequate amount of fractional currency, silver or paper, to meet the needs of domestic and foreign commerce in the existing depression. "When we have secured the $50,000,000 subsidiary silver coin," silverite Horatio Burchard of Illinois remarked, "we will see what can and ought to be done about the silver dollar." Even the leading House opponent of an expanded silver coinage, Abram Hewitt of New York, voted in favor of the conference committee's compromise. The New York City industrialist explained with some embarrassment that American merchants preferred any sort of change, even silver, to correct the current shortage, and that the business community —even his own Manhattan constituents—would consider the House "a parcel of blunderers" unless they passed the joint resolution "as a measure . . . of absolute necessity."[52]

52. Ibid., pp. 4550–63. Speaking in favor of restoring legal bimetallism were Democratic congressmen Landers, Holman, Randall and S. S. Cox, along with Republicans Burchard, Cannon, Fort, Kelley, Phillips and Willard. Only Democrats Payne and Townsend along with Republicans Kasson and Garfield opposed remonetization in this early debate over monetary standard policy. See also Garfield Diary, July 13, 1876, Garfield MSS, LC.

The Senate concurred in the conference committee's report with little debate. The chamber's two leading silverites, Lewis Bogy and John Percival Jones, voiced their disagreement on the question. Bogy, a member of the conference committee, defended its recommendations, asserting the generally held belief that immediate provision for commercial purposes of an increased subsidiary coinage was "a matter of absolute necessity . . . as a matter of relief." With the first session of the Forty-Fourth Congress "very far advanced" and the Senate bitterly divided on remonetization, Bogy also implied that even some silverites now believed the metal's market price too low to justify immediate restoration of the double standard, and he urged that consideration of the issue be delayed until after the presidential election. The Missouri Democrat restated the basic argument of pro-resumption silverites, however, when he insisted that eventual return to specie payments was possible only when Congress provided a sufficient number of remonetized silver dollars in place of the existing greenback circulation.

Jones, on the other hand, denounced the conference report and criticized any increased use of subsidiary coinage prior to remonetization. The Nevada Republican called the subsidiary coins "promises to pay gold printed on silver" and suggested that "they had better be printed on paper; it is cheaper." Instead of fifty million dollars in additional subsidiary coinage, Jones urged immediate restoration of the legal tender silver dollar as a more adequate cure for the nation's currency famine. Despite his objections, however, the Senate swiftly approved the joint resolution and avoided further discussion of the silver question until its adjournment in August.[53]

Passage of the joint resolution disposed of the subsidiary coinage and trade dollar questions, but House silverites continued to press the remonetization issue in the waning days of the 1876 session. Both Richard Bland and "Pig-Iron" Kelley brought forward their previously introduced measures for the restoration of

53. For the entire Senate discussion, ibid., pp. 4565–68.

legal bimetallism. Silverites in the lower chamber were more reluctant than their Senate counterparts to delay consideration of the issue until after the election, especially since they already controlled a large majority favorable to immediate remonetization. Even before passage of the Landers Amendment in June, Richard Bland began asserting his claim to leadership in the House silver drive. He introduced a measure on May 3 which provided for legal tender "silver notes" to be issued in exchange for bullion deposited at the mint at the 16 to 1 ratio of 412.8 grains of silver bullion for each dollar note.[54] Bland's bill, a substitute for an earlier silver certificate measure introduced by Massachusetts Congressman Nathaniel P. Banks, underwent further changes before it came up for House debate on July 19.[55]

While Bland's substitute awaited floor action, Republican William D. Kelley, the Missouri Democrat's arch-rival for House direction of the silver issue, introduced another remonetization bill that provided simply for recoinage of the 412.8 grain silver dollar and restoration "of its legal-tender character." Bland's measure reached the House floor first, on July 19, by which time, it called not only for issuing of silver certificates but also for coinage of the legal tender silver dollar. Earlier in the session Kelley made one last-ditch effort to sidetrack Bland's measure when, on June 24, the Pennsylvania protectionist moved to suspend the rules and vote immediately on his proposal. Silverites in the lower chamber failed by only six votes at that time to muster the two-thirds majority required to suspend House rules, dividing 119 to 68 in favor of Kelley's motion, with 97 members not voting[56] (see Table 3).

Voting patterns followed substantially the previous month's balloting on the Lander's Amendment, especially in continuing

54. Ibid., vol. 4, pt. 3, p. 2917; vol. 4, pt. 5, p. 4733.

55. For the legislative history of changes in the Bland bill, see ibid., vol. 4, pts. 2–5, pp. 1811, 2917, 3555–56, 4733. The final bill bore the title HR 3363.

56. Ibid., vol. 4, pt. 5, pp. 4705, 4733, 4855.

several trends already observable in the June tally. An increasing number of Democrats from eastern states joined their Republican counterparts in opposing remonetization, while midwestern Republicans began flocking to the bimetallist standard. Furthermore, for the first time, both Democrats and Republicans from the mining states of the far west began voting as a cohesive block in the House on the silver question, as California's two Republican representatives supported their state party's previously announced pro-silver position. But after Kelley's aborted bid for leadership, the remonetization issue in the House remained largely in Democratic hands, properly so since the party had endorsed the Kelley motion 82 to 37 while Republicans split 34 to 37 against the proposal.

The major danger faced by House bimetallists concerned efforts by Democratic opponents of specie resumption in the lower chamber to combine the two financial questions. On the resumption issue, House silverites divided almost completely along party lines. Even before debate began on the Bland bill in August, Franklin Holman of Indiana attempted unsuccessfully to attach an amendment repealing the 1875 Resumption Act to the silver bill. When floor discussion began on the Bland bill, Holman renewed this effort, modifying his amendment now to repeal only the key section of the Resumption Act which specified the day—January 1, 1879—on which specie payments would resume. Bland supported the amendment but refused to allow it to be attached to his remonetization measure, expressing fears that his bill would be "embarrassed by it" and that Republican votes needed for its passage would be lost. The Missouri Democrat considered his silver certificate scheme sufficient balm for those inflationists concerned with expanding the circulation of paper money as well as silver coinage.[57]

After debate began on his measure, however, Bland soon dis-

57. Ibid., p. 4876, July 25, 1876; ibid., vol. 4, pt. 6, p. 5047; Haswell, "The Public Life of Congressman Richard Parks Bland," pp. 59–63.

Table 3

Vote on the Kelley Motion to Suspend the Rules, House of Representatives, July 24, 1876

	Ayes			Nays		
	Rep.	Dem.	Ind.	Rep.	Dem.	Ind.
New England States						
Massachusetts				4	3	1
Maine				4		
New Hampshire					2	
Vermont				1		
Connecticut		1		1		
Rhode Island				2		
TOTALS		1		12	5	1
Middle Atlantic States						
New York				9	6	
Pennsylvania	1	10		3	2	
Maryland						
Delaware					1	
New Jersey	1			1	3	
TOTALS	2	10		13	12	
Midwestern States						
Ohio	2	5		3	1	
Illinois	5	6	1		1	
Indiana	5	5				
Wisconsin	2	2	1	3		
Minnesota	1					
Michigan	4				2	1
Iowa	4		1			
Kansas	2	1				
Nebraska						
TOTALS	25	19	3	6	4	1
Border States						
Kentucky	1	7				
Tennessee	1	7				
West Virginia		1				
Missouri		8			1	
TOTALS	2	23			1	

Table 3—Continued

	Ayes			Nays		
	Rep.	Dem.	Ind.	Rep.	Dem.	Ind.
Southern States						
Virginia		4		1	1	
North Carolina		5				
South Carolina				2		
Georgia		5				
Alabama	1	4				
Mississippi		1		2	1	
Florida	1	1				
Louisiana		1		1	1	
Texas		2			2	
Arkansas		2				
TOTALS	2	25		6	5	
Far Western States						
California	2	3				
Nevada	1					
Colorada						
Oregon		1				
TOTALS	3	4				
GRAND TOTALS	34	82	3	37	27	2

TOTALS AYES: 119

TOTAL NAYS: 66*

*The Congressional *Record* claims 68 Nays on the Kelley motion but lists only 66 names.

covered that pro-resumption silverites in the House, including some eastern Democrats, not only agreed with the Senate's decision to postpone consideration of the question until after November but also supported creation of a joint congressional commission to study the entire question, a group that would issue its report only after the presidential election. "Sunset" Cox's Banking and Currency Committee debated this proposal for a joint commission early in August while Bland struggled unsuccessfully to generate House enthusiasm for still another vote on remonetization.[58] The lower chamber's silverite majority had disbanded for the moment, however, and Bland's measure lost the House floor once the Banking and Currency Committee had completed action on its concurrent resolution providing for a Monetary Commission. In a carefully designed strategem, "Sunset" Cox presented the Monetary Commission scheme on August 5 along with another measure that repealed the resumption-day clause of the 1875 Resumption Act, insisting that the two proposals be considered jointly.[59] House debate, as Cox anticipated, centered on the latter proposal, with anti-resumption Democrats mustering a majority to pass the bill.[60]

The New York sound-money Democrat knew that the resumption-day repeal measure stood no chance of approval by the Republican Senate, but by attaching it to the Monetary Commission scheme, he succeeded in diverting the passionate oratory of House inflationists from the newer silver issue to their earlier and more cherished legislative objective, resumption repeal, thereby gaining approval of the Monetary Commission. Although a few Democrats like Bland and Holman continued to demand an immediate vote on remonetization, most House silverites willingly followed Cox's lead in delaying consideration of the touchy question until voter sentiment could be tested in the fall elections. On August 5 the House passed Cox's concurrent resolution establishing a joint Monetary Commission by an

58. For floor debate on Bland's bill from Aug. 1–8, see *Cong. Record,* 44th Cong.,1st sess., vol. 4, pt. 6, pp. 5047, 5080, 5186–88, 5216–27, 5323–24.

59. Ibid., p. 5218. Other congressmen including two later members of the Monetary Commission, had introduced measures setting up a similar commission in the two weeks before the Aug. 15 adjournment of Congress: Representative Randall Gibson's Joint Resolution No. 159, Senator George S. Boutwell's Senate Bill No. 1032, and John Sherman's Senate Bill No. 1037. Ibid., pp. 5033, 5193, 5304.

60. For the key votes on repeal of the resumption-day clause, which passed by a 106 to 86 majority with 98 members not voting, see ibid., pp. 4230–32.

overwhelming 132 to 31 margin. Bland attempted to raise his silver bill again several days later, but the lower chamber failed to see the need to keep the issue alive at its present session and quickly dropped debate amid a general clamor for swift adjournment. Most House members faced more pressing issues than silver in the election drive which had already begun, and congressmen were anxious to return home to begin their re-election campaigns.

The Senate concurred in the House resolution without debate on August 15 shortly before its own adjournment. The Monetary Commission established by the resolution included Senators Jones, Bogy, and Boutwell along with Bland and two House colleagues, Democrat Randall Gibson of Louisiana and Republican George Willard of Michigan.[61] Commission members also included two nonpolitical "experts," Republican William S. Groesbeck, an Ohio businessman, and Yale University economist Francis Bowen. A majority of the commission favored remonetization from the outset, with only Boutwell and Bowen opposing immediate restoration of the double standard, and the group reflected its bimetallist bias by selecting John Percival Jones as Chairman and George Melville Weston as Secretary.[62]

Although Congress failed to resolve the silver question before the election of 1876, legislative divisions on the issue had already become clear, pointing toward the controversy's probable outcome. After several victorious skirmishes in the House led by Democratic inflationists during the spring and summer of 1876, the major congressional contest over remonetizing silver shifted to the Senate after the fall elections. In the upper chamber, moderate Republican bimetallists, solidly entrenched in the Finance Committee, began their cautious, and ultimately successful, campaign to restore silver as a monetary standard without seriously inflating the currency.

61. Ibid., pp. 5240, 5323–24, 5667.
62. *Report of the Monetary Commission, 1*, 1.

5

Urban Publicists: Origins of the Silver Movement

The debate over silver policy which began in Congress during the spring of 1876 spread quickly throughout the country, engaging the attention of numerous currency experts and enthusiasts. Businessmen, economic publicists, newspaper editors, reformers, and an occasional local politician detected the issue's future importance months before the general public became aware of its existence. The silver issue's major battlegrounds in 1876 were in the private correspondence of public officials and in the statements of a small number of influential newspapers, periodicals, and organizations.

George Weston's March 2 letter, which opened public discussion of the issue, provoked several immediate rebuttals, including a widely circulated critical letter of editor Horace White's to the New York financial journal, *The Public.*[1] Within weeks after they had first been published, Weston's observations on silver had been reprinted, praised and criticized by newspapers in Boston, New York, Chicago, and San Francisco, thus beginning the Boston importer's new career as an influential publicist for remonetization.[2] More than a dozen articles by Weston ap-

1. *The Public,* 9 (1876), 198–99; Weston, *The Silver Question,* pp. ix–x.

2. Chicago *Times,* Mar. 14. 1876; San Francisco *Commercial Herald,* Mar. 16, 1876; New York *Public,* Mar. 23, 1876; New York *Evening Post,* Apr. 1 and 7, 1876.

peared during 1876 in such prominent periodicals and dailies as the Boston *Journal of Commerce,* the New York *Commercial Advertiser,* the Philadelphia *American Exchange and Review,* Forney's *Washington Chronicle,* the Chicago *Tribune,* and the nationally circulated *Bankers' Magazine.*[3] Weston, more than any other single individual, helped stimulate public interest in the silver question through his writings.

Clear divisions within the business community on silver policy emerged only after the election of 1876, although from the beginning of the controversy, "silver was winning converts among commercial men and industrialists."[4] The restoration of bimetallism appealed to those businessmen and business spokesmen who opposed further contraction of the currency while the depression lasted, and many pro-resumption, hard money newspapers believed that the loss of legal tender silver coin after 1873 had been a chief cause of the prolonged business slump.[5] William B. Dana, editor of the widely read New York *Commercial and Financial Chronicle,* for example, raised the remonetization issue in his columns during the spring of 1876 "merely for the purpose of exciting discussion" among the business community. "If we can reach specie payments quicker and with less suffering thro' silver," Dana wrote David A. Wells, "may it not be wise to use it?"[6] Baron Edmund de Rothschild, later head of

3. A complete list of Weston's writings on silver in the seventies can be found in the table of contents to his 1878 book. Most of his articles are reprinted in the Appendix to that volume, passim.

4. Unger, *Greenback Era,* p. 333.

5. New York *Graphic,* June 7, 1876. The *Graphic,* the Cincinnati *Commercial* and the Chicago *Tribune,* for example, editorialized almost daily on the need for remonetization from June 1876 to passage of the Bland-Allison Act, passim.

6. William B. Dana to David A. Wells, May 9, 1876, Wells MSS, LC. New York *Commercial and Financial Chronicle* for the following 1876 dates: Mar. 18, Apr. 22, Apr. 29, May 27, Sept. 3. Dana later answered his own question in the negative, and by 1877, the *Commercial and Financial Chronicle* had become an outspoken critic of remonetization.

the syndicate which marketed American resumption bonds in Europe and himself a substantial holder of these securities, advised Treasury Secretary Bristow in March 1876 that the expansion of silver coinage in the United States "would be a great relief for the commercial world." Rothschild advocated both increasing the amount of subsidiary coinage and remonetizing the silver dollar in order to check the metal's market decline.[7] Bristow responded to Rothschild's letter two months later, by which time Congress had taken up the silver issue. He assured the French banker that "the tendency of our legislation [is] in the direction which you so strongly favor."[8]

The American banking community remained generally silent on the problem in 1876, although from the beginning of the silver drive, I. S. Homan's *Bankers' Magazine* opened its columns to George Weston and to other bimetallists.[9] Homan's journal remained sympathetic toward restoration of the double monetary standard throughout the 1870s, and in May 1876, the magazine published an editorial article endorsing restoration of legal bimetallism on grounds of economic nationalism. "In our National monetary arrangements," the anonymous *Bankers' Magazine* author maintained, "it is our duty to consult only what is advantageous for us, and being so largely a debtor nation, and producing so freely of silver, it seems clearly our interest to maintain for ourselves, and strive to induce other nations to follow us in maintaining, the silver valuation."[10] The influential bankers' publication practically supported remonetization officially in June 1876, when it asserted that Americans "have no

7. Baron Edmund de Rothschild to Benjamin Bristow, Mar. 6, 1876, Bristow MSS, LC.

8. Bristow to Baron Edmund de Rothschild, May 2, 1876, ibid.

9. Weston published articles in the following issues of the *Bankers' Magazine:* July 1876, Aug. 1876, Sept. 1876, Oct. 1876, Aug. 1877, Nov. 1877 and Feb. 1878. See also an unsigned article by "Argonaut," May 1876, esp. p. 868.

10. *Bankers' Magazine,* May 1876. "Argonaut" may have been Weston, himself, or I. S. Homan, editor of the journal.

contract with the world which requires us to use only gold for money."[11] The views of *Bankers' Magazine* on the silver question, however, did not reflect the dominant sentiment of New York's national bankers, most of whom opposed the double standard. However, the banking community of New York and other eastern cities did not begin organizing opposition to the silver drive until the fall of 1877.[12]

Quarrels among mercantile groups over remonetization also remained muted until after the election of 1876, although several large commercial bodies proclaimed their opinions at an earlier date. The silver issue created divisions among American merchants similar to earlier fissures over resumption policy; "the traditional rift between [the business groups of] East and West once again appeared."[13] More accurately, the quarrel over silver eventually divided merchants in the seaboard centers of foreign trade—including the Pacific coast metropolis of San Francisco—from those in inland commercial cities. Even before the presidential campaign had begun, the New York and San Francisco Chambers of Commerce, the Boston Board of Trade, and the executive committee of the National Board of Trade—the latter group closely aligned that year to the New York Chamber of Commerce—had all petitioned Congress "against making silver coin an unlimited legal tender."[14] The Boston Board of Trade and the New York Chamber of Commerce proposed instead that an international monetary conference be summoned immediately to consider the monetary standard question. The National Board of Trade opposed even this concession to silverite sentiment and demanded instead that the five-dollar legal tender

11. *Bankers' Magazine,* June 1876, pp. 961–62.

12. Unger, *Greenback Era,* pp. 260–61.

13. Ibid., p. 333.

14. "Memorial of the Boston Board of Trade," Jan. 5, 1877. See also "Resolutions of the Chamber of Commerce of the State of New York," May 4, 1876; "Memorial of the National Board of Trade," June 29, 1876; and "Resolution of the Chamber of Commerce of San Francisco," Senate Finance Committee Records, 44th Cong. NA.

limitation on subsidiary coins be retained without additional legislative action. Representatives of Boston, New York, and Philadelphia commercial groups dominated discussion of silver policy at the National Board of Trade's June 1876 meeting in New York City. Several of those present placed blame for the remonetization campaign solely on the mineowning Bonanza Kings, whom they believed had incited the issue in order to secure a larger government market for surplus bullion.[15]

Many western merchant groups, on the other hand, not only endorsed specie resumption along with their eastern counterparts but, at the same time, supported the silver drive, considering restoration of the double standard a legitimate means of expanding the circulating stock of hard money. The Cincinnati and St. Paul-Minneapolis Chambers of Commerce, for example, petitioned Congress for remonetization early in the campaign, and most midwestern business groups remained favorable to silver throughout the controversy.[16] A. L. Conger, an Ohio manufacturer and Republican party wheelhorse, warned James A. Garfield in March 1877 that Garfield's opposition to bimetallism had cost him the "almost unanimous" support of Ohio's business community in the legislator's bid for a Senate seat. "I have mixed a great deal with the business community in Ohio, and throughout the [Mid]west for the past six months," Conger noted, "and I think I am not mistaken when I say to you that the people want the silver dollar as it used to exist."[17]

American manufacturers, unlike the commercial groups, did

15. *Proceedings of the National Board of Trade* (Chicago, 1876), p. 78. See also Senate Finance Committee Records, 44th Cong., NA, pp. 78–84.

16. "Memorial of the Chamber of Commerce of St. Paul and Minneapolis," Dec. 18, 1876, Senate Finance Committee Records, 44th Cong., Cincinnati Chamber of Commerce, *Twenty-Ninth Annual Report,* p. 29. Unger, *Greenback Era;* Martin Ridge, *Ignatius Donnelly, The Portrait of a Politician* (Chicago, 1962), pp. 176–77.

17. A. L. Conger to James A. Garfield, Mar. 3, 1877, Garfield MSS, LC.

not respond in any clear pattern to the silver question when it first arose. Iron and steel industry publications, although often sympathetic to greenback expansion, viewed remonetization with suspicion. *Iron Age* considered the entire campaign a corrupt "job" in the "interests of the Bonanza mineowners," while James Swank's American Iron and Steel Association *Bulletin* condemned even the "silver resumption" of minor paper notes, defended the fractional greenbacks and demanded retention of the existing five dollar legal tender limit on silver coins.[18] The vast majority of manufacturers, merchants, and other businessmen refrained from declaring themselves on the silver question until after the electoral crisis of 1876–77. Only when faced in 1877 with imminent congressional action on Richard Bland's silver bill did the business community react strongly to remonetization. In the process, it drew clear, often surprising, battle lines on the issue across the broad spectrum of American entrepreneurship.

The "academic-reform" community, unlike the moneyed interests, expressed its ideas on the bimetallist controversy even before the 1876 presidential election.[19] Soon after the issue arose in 1876, in fact, a passionate war of words over silver policy began among economic publicists, liberal Republicans, genteel reformers, and other elements in the American intelligentsia. The academic reformers could not agree either on the merits or the dangers of remonetization.

Among the American members of England's exclusive reform association, the Cobden Club, for example, at least fourteen favored continuation of the gold standard while eight supported

18. *Iron Age,* vol. 18, July 20 and Aug. 3, 1876; American Iron and Steel Association, *Bulletin* (Philadelphia), Mar. 22, 1876, p. 92; Mar. 29, 1876, p. 98. See also the pro-silver editorials during 1876 that appeared in *Railway World,* a leading transportation trade journal, cited in Nugent, *Money and American Society, 1865–1880,* pp. 206–07.

19. Unger, *Greenback Era,* p. 337.

either immediate restoration of the silver dollar as a unit of account or some form of international bimetallism. This small sampling included many of the country's most respected reform politicians, economists, and businessmen. Among the gold monometallists were the historian Henry Adams, Massachusetts insurance executive and economist Edward Atkinson, Congressman James A. Garfield, ex-Secretary of the Treasury Hugh McCulloch, free trade theorist David A. Wells, liberal Republican editor Samuel Bowles, and New York City's reform Democratic newspaperman Manton Marble. International bimetallists included the economists Francis Amasa Walker and William Graham Sumner, as well as the banker and corporation president George A. Walker. Numbered among the advocates of immediate, unilateral American remonetization of silver were President Grant's first Secretary of the Interior, Jacob D. Cox of Ohio, Democratic Congressman Samuel S. "Sunset" Cox of New York, liberal Republican William H. Grosvenor of Missouri, Kentucky editor Henry S. Watterson and Thomas Olcott, the respected Albany Jacksonian banking leader.[20] Other gold standard reformers, not members of the Cobden Club, included the economists Francis Bowen and Henry Varnum Poor, while among the more prominent early bimetallists were Rutherford B. Hayes' Ohio friend S. Dana Horton and Boston businessman Benjamin F. Nourse.[21]

This sharp division within the academic-reform community on the silver question in 1876 contrasted starkly with its previous record of basic agreement on major national policies under political debate. Most reformers of the era favored a program of tariff reduction, return to specie payments, use of "coin" money as opposed to greenbacks, civil service reform, and removal of

20. The source of these identifications was a list of Cobden Club members taken from the club's official journal and reprinted by the anti-free trade *Bulletin* of the American Iron and Steel Association. *Bulletin,* Dec. 6, 1876.

21. Unger, *Greenback Era.*

the remaining federal troops from the South.[22] Almost without exception they acted together during the Reconstruction period's earlier monetary struggles against inflationists, anti-resumptionists, and greenbackers. Coming to grips with the silver question, however, proved difficult for many of them. For one thing the monetary standard question had arisen suddenly and lacked a dominant orthodox position among expert economists—themselves divided between monometallists and bimetallists—forcing the American academic reformers to respond as individuals to the issue, with little benefit of approved "scientific" dogma.

The absence of agreement among financial experts, American and European, on the monetary standard question became apparent at the September 1876 annual meeting of the American Social Science Association, which sponsored an open forum on the silver issue. Whitelaw Reid's New York *Tribune,* itself strongly opposed to bimetallism, acknowledged after the meeting that "its chief result is to bring out more clearly than ever before the fact that the highest financial authorities are themselves disagreed on the subject of the single or double standard."[23] The difficulties faced by academic reformers in confronting the silver question can be seen in the response of three representative members of the intelligentsia—George A. Walker, Horace White, and Jacob D. Cox—all of whom had campaigned together in the past for specie resumption and considered themselves sound money men yet who arrived at completely different conclusions on the merits of remonetization.

George A. Walker had been assistant Secretary of the Treasury under Salmon P. Chase during the Civil War years, became

22. A sophisticated analysis of the temperament and ideals of the American reformers can be found in Irwin Unger's study of Reconstruction finance. Passim, especially pp. 127–44. See also Ari Hoogenboom, *Outlawing the Spoils: A History of the Civil Service Reform Movement, 1865–1883* (Urbana, Ill., 1961), esp. 20–22, and John C. Sproat, *"The Best Men": Liberal Reformers in the Gilded Age* (New York, 1968).

23. New York *Tribune,* Sept. 16, 1876.

president of a Massachusetts national bank following the war and, in 1876, was an executive of two New York City firms, president of the Provident Savings Life Insurance Company and vice-president of the Gold and Stock Telegraph Company.[24] Walker had been a gold monometallist and hard money enthusiast throughout the Reconstruction years, to the extent of supporting Treasury Secretary Hugh McCulloch's unpopular 1866 policy of contracting the volume of greenbacks in circulation as a prelude to eventual resumption.[25] The New York businessman remained a gold standard advocate until January 1876, submitting a proposal to Secretary of the Treasury Bristow that month which called for an international monetary standard based on the American gold dollar.[26]

In the months following submission of this plan, however, Walker began reading extensively in European literature on the coinage question to prepare several articles on monetary standard policy for the New York *Tribune*.[27] He planned to review for the paper the major arguments on both sides of the monetary standard question made by leading European financial experts such as Michael Chevalier, Henri Cernuschi, and Ernest Seyd. "My own opinion has always leaned to the single standard," Walker wrote *Tribune* publisher Whitelaw Reid in May 1876, "though all of its opponents I have named are personal friends for whose opinions I have a high respect."[28] Although poor health prevented Walker from completing his *Tribune* articles immediately, he confessed to Reid in July 1876 that he also

24. Carl Schurz to Benjamin H. Bristow, Jan. 23, 1876, RG 104, Letters Received "T," NA.

25. George Walker to Hugh McCullock, Dec. 4, 1866, McCulloch MSS, LC. On McCulloch's career as Secretary of the Treasury, see Unger, *Greenback Era*, pp. 41, 42 ff, 124, 160, 161, 163, 403. See also Sharkey, *Money, Class and Party*, passim.

26. Carl Schurz to Benjamin H. Bristow, enclosing George Walker to Bristow, Jan. 23, 1876, RG 104. Letters Received, "T," NA.

27. George Walker to Whitelaw Reid, May 18, 1876, Reid MSS, LC.

28. Walker to Reid, May 28, 1876, ibid.

wished to study the issue further before expressing his own views due to "the increased importance which the silver question has assumed since . . . April."[29]

At the American Social Science Association meeting in September, Walker presided over the silver debate and delivered a paper that presented all sides of the controversy without expressing any personal preference.[30] At the time, he cautioned Whitelaw Reid to keep the *Tribune* "guarded" in its comments on the double standard, observing: "I thought I was opposed to it three months ago but the more I have studied the more I have doubted. The array of authority in its favor in Europe is immense, and I think rapidly gaining ground."[31] By the following year Walker advocated international bimetallism. Although he remained sympathetic toward unilateral American remonetization, favoring a 400 grain silver dollar which would have adjusted the American silver-gold ratio to that of Europe's bimetallic Latin Union nations, Walker opposed the Bland bill because it called for a 412.5 grain dollar. This would overvalue silver, he felt, thereby driving gold from the United States and eventually forcing the Latin Union itself to demonetize silver completely.[32] Walker lobbied vigorously among government officials both in Congress and in the executive branch for this remonetized 400 grain dollar whose 15.5 to 1 ratio to gold, the Latin Union ratio, would ease the path to international bimetallism. He corresponded extensively with leading Washington officials involved in the fight to modify or defeat the Bland bill from 1876 to 1878, and his advocacy of international bimetallism placed him among those reformers who were "moderates" on the silver issue, neither opposed to restoration of the silver

29. Walker to Reid, July 23, 1876, ibid.

30. Walker to Reid, Sept. 7, 1876, ibid. See also letter by S. Dana Horton to the Cincinnati *Commercial,* Sept. 15, 1876.

31. Walker to Reid, Sept. 8, 1876, Reid MSS, LC.

32. George Walker to James A. Garfield, Nov. 10, 1877, Garfield MSS, LC.

dollar entirely like Horace White nor silverites like Jacob Dolson Cox who favored the Bland bill.[33]

Horace White's views on the silver issue themselves underwent several transformations in 1876. Within six months, he had swung from a belief that silver's *high* market value made subsidiary coins too expensive to remain in circulation to a qualified endorsement of the double standard and finally, reversing the pendulum, to complete rejection of remonetization. He concluded ultimately that silver's *low* market value would drive gold coinage from the country if it began circulating widely. White's gyrations were caused more by shifting political instincts on the monetary standard question than by sustained economic analysis, but they reflected the degree to which the silver issue confused many orthodox American sound money advocates.[34] Although White remained nominally an international bimetallist during the silver drive which followed, he differed from men like George Walker in firmly opposing any form of unilateral remonetization until silver had risen in market value. White favored retaining the gold standard for the foreseeable future, and Walker's proposed 400 grain "international" dollar seemed just as objectionable to the liberal Republican editor as the Bland bill's 412.5 grain "domestic" coin.[35]

Reformers like Jacob Dolson Cox, on the other hand, supported immediate restoration of the silver dollar as a monetary standard both for political and economic reasons. Cox, once a Civil War general, Secretary of the Interior under Grant and

33. On Walker's later role in the congressional struggle to remonetize silver, see Chap. 10.

34. Horace White to Benjamin Bristow, Mar. 1, 1876, RG 104; Horace White to John Sherman, Apr. 28, 1876, Sherman MSS, LC; Springfield *Republican,* quoted in Cincinnati *Commercial,* Sept. 12, 1876.

35. See, for example, Dana Horton's account of the debate at the American Social Science Association's Sept. 1876 meeting, where White delivered a speech opposing remonetization in any form prior to an international monetary agreement. Cincinnati *Commercial,* Sept. 15, 1876.

congressman-elect from Ohio after November 1876, endorsed international bimetallism in theory but felt unilateral action fully justified if an attempt to arrive quickly at a monetary standard treaty with the European states met with failure.[36] In an exchange of letters with his friend and gold standard advocate, David A. Wells, Cox defended his support for bimetallism as a logical extension of the earlier anti-greenback, hard money doctrines which both men held in common.[37] For although Cox's attitude to the silver issue was influenced by the popularity that remonetization enjoyed among his Ohio constituents, he also believed bimetallism an economically sounder policy for the United States than Wells' gold monometallism.[38]

When the American Social Science Association assembled in September 1876, most of those academic reformers who attended the Saratoga, New York, meeting had already recognized the future significance of the monetary standard question in American political life. George A. Walker, who served as chairman of the panel discussion on remonetization, suggested to his fellow delegates that "after the [presidential] election, the silver question is the vital question of the day."[39] Few of those participating in the panel discussion of silver policy opposed re-

36. Jacob Dolson Cox to R. B. Hayes, Feb. 10, 1877, copy in Hayes MSS, LC: J. D. Cox to James A. Garfield, July 23, 1877, Garfield MSS, LC.

37. For their first exchange of letters on this subject, see David A. Wells to Jacob D. Cox, June 10, 1877, Cox MSS, Oberlin College Library (Ohio), and Cox to Wells, June 17, 1877, Wells MS, LC.

38. Ibid. See also James Monroe to James A. Garfield, July 18, 1877, Garfield MSS, LC; and Cox to Wells, Feb. 28, 1878, Wells MSS, LC. Cox supported the Bland bill enthusiastically and, by mid-1877, advocated immediate American restoration of the double standard. He voted for remonetization whenever the House balloted on the subject.

39. S. Dana Horton, letter to Cincinnati *Commercial,* Sept. 15, 1876. In this communication, Horton perpetrated the worst pun made during the entire silver drive, apparently without intention, when he described George Walker as having spoken in a manner "which should have put the advocates of gold monometallism, if such they were, upon their mettle."

storing the double standard through an international monetary agreement. S. Dana Horton, B. F. Nourse, William Graham Sumner, Horace White, and others spoke in favor of such a treaty, and only one member of the association, the Boston merchant Elizur Wright, advocated maintaining the gold standard. The Philadelphia merchant Thomas Balch, also alone, called for immediate remonetization of silver. Most of the reformers, economic publicists, and academics at the meeting appeared to concur with S. Dana Horton in hoping that Congress would avoid "hasty action, but [they also] hoped that American diplomacy would prove equal to the task of securing [an international bimetallic agreement] from European power."[40]

The Social Science Association itself took no public stand as an organization on remonetizing silver throughout the political agitation which followed, although a majority of members who spoke on the subject at its 1876 and 1877 meetings clearly favored some form of international bimetallic agreement. Addresses by George Walker, B. F. Nourse, S. Dana Horton, and others urged this course, and when the association's executive committee voted to prepare an information manual on the monetary standard question after its fall 1876 meeting, "the gentlemen who undertook this found that the ground had been fully covered by [the international bimetallist] Dana Horton, one of the members" in a pamphlet entitled *Silver and Gold*.[41] F. B. Sanborn, the Social Science Association's executive secretary, acknowledged in 1877 that during the previous winter, when "Mr. Cernuschi, the French economist, had visited the United

40. Even Elizur Wright could hardly be classed as a monetary contractionist. "His idea was that we should have a new coinage (to meet the wants of trade) at ninety cents on the dollar; or, in other words, to cling to gold, but clip or debase the coinage ten per cent." Cincinnati *Commercial*, Sept. 15, 1876.

41. Report of the Secretary, F. B. Sanborn, Sept. 5, 1877, reprinted in *Journal of Social Science*, containing the *Transactions of the American* [*Social Science*] *Association*, No. 9, (Boston, 1878), p. 8. See also S. Dana Horton, *Silver and Gold* (New York, 1878).

States [to testify before the congressional monetary commission, he] had made many converts to his theory of international bimetalism."[42] Whatever their individual views, the academic reform community was solidly committed to swift resumption of specie payments and considered the new question of silver's remonetization primarily in terms of its possible impact upon government resumption policy.[43] Many became international bimetallists while some remained gold standard advocates, and there was little agreement among the best informed American economic writers over the merits of bimetallism.

Newspaper support for restoring silver when the issue first arose in 1876 came predominantly from hard money, pro-resumptionist journals. At the time, most greenback and inflationist dailies either held aloof from the campaign or actually opposed it. The two newspapers which first advocated remonetization, The New York *Graphic* and Murat Halstead's Cincinnati *Commercial,* shifted from gold standard to bimetallist views in 1876 only after the issue had been raised in Congress. Editors like Joseph Medill of the Chicago *Tribune* along with a flock of less prominent newspapermen studied the *Commercial's* daily catechisms on silver carefully, and Halstead quickly became the most influential silverite journalist in the country.

Newspaper response to the bimetallist crusade, however, did not divide along clear sectional lines, despite the usual classification made by historians of a pro-silver press in the West and South opposed by a gold standard group of northeastern dailies. Nor were silverite journals closely aligned with agrarian interests or organizations during the 1870s. Not only were the two earliest bimetallist papers, the *Commercial* and the *Graphic,* both hard-money, anti-greenback journals throughout the Reconstruction period, but both had close ties to their respective mercantile communities in Cincinnati and New York City.

42. Report of the Secretary, p. 9.
43. Cincinnati *Commercial,* Sept. 15, 1876.

Both the *Graphic* and the *Commercial* began supporting the double standard in the wake of John Percival Jones' April 1876 Senate speech. During the preceding months, neither paper had been consistent in its views on silver. The *Graphic,* probably the first newspaper east of the Rockies to advocate remonetization, began to shift from gold monometallism in February 1876 when it endorsed "silver resumption" of fractional greenbacks.[44] The New York tabloid continued for several months, however, to refer to gold as "our fundamental standard of value."[45] Its editorials after March 1876 commented increasingly on the need to expand silver coinage, and it noted that Jones' April 24–25 talk was "universally admitted to have been the great speech of the session."[46] By that time, the paper had come full circle and supported remonetization.

The *Graphic* took pains to deny that it favored bimetallism for inflationist motives. Thus, the paper agreed in June 1876 that the monetary standard problem ultimately "calls for international solution." When the gold standard New York financial weekly, *The Public,* accused "men like Senators Sherman and Jones, and journals like the Cincinnati *Commercial,* the Chicago *Tribune* and the New York *Graphic*" of unintentionally sponsoring currency inflation by endorsing remonetization, the *Graphic* lashed back at the charge. "For our part, we have urged that for every silver dollar issued a paper dollar should be retired and destroyed. This would be the first step toward resumption." The *Graphic* came to share with Halstead and other resumption-

44. New York *Graphic* for the following 1876 dates: Feb. 21, Feb. 24 and Feb. 26.

45. Ibid., Feb. 21, 1876. The silver question thrust itself into political debate among the newspaper fraternity almost from its inception as a national issue. Thus, on March 6, 1876, the *Graphic* discussed an article from the Chicago *Inter-Ocean* which had paraphrased George Weston's letter to the Boston *Globe*—although Weston's letter had appeared only four days earlier, on March 2!

46. Ibid., Apr. 26, 1876. See the *Graphic* also for the following April 1876 dates: Apr. 1, 7, 11 and 25.

ists who advocated bimetallism a belief that the "first great step" toward specie payments and general business recovery must be the full remonetization of silver.[47]

Murat Halstead's Cincinnati *Commercial* viewed with equal distaste the policies of greenbackers and other opponents of resumption. During the previous decade's political battles over specie payment policy, the *Commercial* and Joseph Medill's Chicago *Tribune,* probably the two most widely circulated Republican dailies in the Middle West, led the region's hard money journals in opposing all forms of paper money expansion or any "repudiation" of government debts through cheapening the value of existing currency.[48]

Halstead never abandoned his hostility toward legal tender greenbacks. During the spring of 1876, however, with the country facing its third year of severe business depression, he joined other hard money bimetallists in considering remonetization as a means of stimulating economic recovery. Senator Jones' April speech crystallized many of Halstead's ideas on the subject, as it had done for the *Graphic,* by providing elaborate economic and moral arguments to buttress the Cincinnati editor's mounting enthusiasm for silver. Only days before Jones' address, in editorial after editorial, the *Commercial* still declared itself a gold standard paper, and until the Nevada senator had presented his arguments for "restoration," Halstead continued to oppose reintroducing legal bimetallism.[49]

47. Ibid., June 21 and Aug. 12, 1876.

48. Unger, *Greenback Era,* p. 342. Medill's chief editorial writer at this time was Henry Demarest Lloyd, who became a nationally prominent reformer during the 1880s following publication of his widely-distributed tract attacking the Standard Oil trust, *Wealth Against Commonwealth.*

49. As Halstead later wrote of Jones's six-hour oration, "he aroused the attention of all thoughtful citizens to the importance and pertinence of 'the restoration of the double standard'." Cincinnati *Commercial,* July 7, 1876. On the paper's earlier gold standard views, see *Commercial* on the following 1876 dates: Apr. 3, Apr. 4, Apr. 7, Apr. 12, Apr. 19, Apr. 21, Apr. 22 and Apr. 26.

The precise moment of the *Commercial's* conversion on the silver question remains obscure, but by early May Halstead considered himself a bimetallist. Only two weeks after declaring government bonds payable in gold alone, the Cincinnati daily reversed itself in May 1876 and asserted that all securities sold prior to silver's demonetization in 1873 were redeemable legally in either metal.[50] After first rejecting Senator Jones' assertion that the silver dollar had been omitted from the Coinage Act of 1873 surreptitiously and through collusion, the *Commercial* began to accept this version of the episode, the so-called "Crime of 1873." Reprinting Senator Jones' speech on May 11, 1876, the paper endorsed its conclusions and called remonetization "the great financial question."[51] From May 1876 until passage of the Bland-Allison Act in February 1878, hardly a week passed without several editorials and news articles in the paper on the silver question. Both supporters and opponents of the double standard acknowledged the journal's position as the country's leading and most articulate silverite daily.[52]

The *Commercial,* like the New York *Graphic,* demanded that legal tender silver dollars be issued only in exchange for greenbacks, and at no time during the silver drive did Halstead advocate an inflationary use of silver by issuing legal tender silver coins *without* redeeming a corresponding number of greenbacks. The Cincinnati editor's views on remonetization were accorded great respect, especially in the Midwest, and often endorsed over the next few years by other resumptionist, anti-greenback Republican bimetallists in the region.[53] Halstead, like fellow resumptionist-silverites George Weston, John Percival Jones, and

50. Ibid., May 8, 1876. See also Apr. 28 and May 3, 1876.

51. For the paper's change in position, see Apr. 28 and May 11, 1876.

52. See, for example, the following editorials in May and June, 1876: May 15, 17, 20, 24, 25, 27, 30 and 31; June 1, 6, 9 and 13.

53. Ibid., July 13 and 18, 1876. On the *Commercial's* pro-resumption and non-inflationary bimetallist position, see also the following July 1876 editorials: July 12, 13, 14, 15 and 23.

Jacob D. Cox, argued that specie resumption in gold alone would deprive the country of half its legitimate hard coin, legal tender silver which it needed desperately to stimulate business recovery from the protracted depression. Often the Cincinnati editor sounded strikingly reminiscent of Jacksonian publicists like William Gouge in his obsessive hatred for paper money and in his insistence on returning to a business system transacted entirely on a coin basis, "in order to restore the country to financial health."[54]

One recent writer on the silver movement in the 1870s observed of Halstead and fellow silverite editor Joseph Medill of the Chicago *Tribune* that "to the extent that they propagated their honest convictions they helped create the enthusiasm for silver which they shared." The writer argued moreover that both men were "as much products as authors of the public mood" on the silver question:

> As good Republicans, they feared the political repercussions of resisting the silver movement. With the whole trans-Allegheny region and the South caught up in the frenzy [by 1877], they saw remonetization as an immediate political problem, not an abstract exercise in ethics or theory.[55]

The *Commercial* swung solidly behind remonetization in May 1876, however, when discussion of the question had not yet penetrated deeply into local or national politics. Halstead became almost immediately the new silver movement's leading journalistic advocate and worked to stimulate public awareness of the issue. "We propose to press it upon the people," Halstead observed in May 1876.[56] Rather than being "caught up in the

54. Ibid., July 23, 1876 and Oct. 1, 1877. On Gouge's views, see Arthur M. Schlesinger, Jr., *The Age of Jackson* (Boston, 1946), pp. 117–22.

55. Unger, *Greenback Era,* p. 343

56. Cincinnati *Commercial,* May 15, 1876.

frenzy" over silver that swept through the West and South, Halstead was instrumental in creating the country's frenzied enthusiasm for restoration of "the old silver dollar."

"Congress can soon restore the silver standard, if it will," he warned the national legislature in July 1876, "and if this Congress refuses, a Congress can be provided that will not refuse, and that will provide amply for the coinage of silver dollars."[57] Following the postponment of a free-coinage measure in the House that month, Halstead cautioned that "members of the House who vote against this honest proposition have no political future of any consequence."[58] Throughout the campaign of 1876, while most Republican newspapers kept silent on the remonetization issue, the *Commercial* editorialized almost daily on the problem. From May 1876 to mid-1877, in other words, for more than a year before silver became a burning political question in the Midwest, Halstead worked to create the "public mood" of support for bimetallism that later characterized his region. The Cincinnati editor's relentless advocacy of silver preceded any meaningful public response to the issue by many months and, to a great extent, helped provoke that response.

Resumptionist hard money journals like the *Commercial,* the *Graphic,* and the Chicago *Tribune* that supported remonetization in 1876 soon came under attack from both greenback and gold standard dailies. No clear sectional lines in this newspaper quarrel emerged, however, during the early months of the silver drive, which indicated that the political "fire" historians claim the silver issue "lit in the West and South" did not begin burning until after the election of 1876.[59] Conservative eastern sound money journals like the Boston *Transcript,* for example, commented during the presidential campaign on the "growing

57. Ibid., July 14, 1876.

58. Ibid., July 25, 1876. Hardly a day went by from the opening of the silver drive to passage of the Bland-Allison Act without several editorials by Halstead on the need for immediate remonetization.

59. Unger, *Greenback Era,* p. 339.

sense throughout the land of the justice and propriety of the double standard," while the Albany *Evening Post* recommended a return to bimetallism "in order to protect our miners and preserve the value of our immense silver mines."[60] At the same time, some midwestern pro-resumption newspapers strongly opposed remonetization. The St. Paul *Pioneer Press* criticized "the pervading fallacy of all the [Cincinnati] COMMERCIAL's argument for Silver," Halstead's belief that gold would remain in circulation once silver was remonetized.[61] In the Western Reserve area, the Cleveland *Herald* insisted that the typical greenbacker had begun trading "his rag baby for a silver dime . . . if he can't get greenbacks he will take silver, now it is cheap."[62] Even the Chicago *Tribune*, one of the staunchest early supporters of bimetallism, suggested that the silver dollar's grain content be increased in order to counter objections by gold monometallists to the coin's depreciated market value, although Joseph Medill soon changed his paper's position on this point under the insistent editorial prodding of Halstead's *Commercial*.[63]

Although remonetization secured widespread support in 1876 among hard money dailies through the Midwest and East, many greenback journals held aloof from the new cause, complaining about the silverites' scorn for paper currency and about the opposition of leading bimetallists such as Halstead and Jones to monetary inflation.[64] Supporters of the rag baby like the

60. Boston *Transcript*, Aug. 7, 1876. Albany (N.Y.) *Evening Post*, Apr. 29, 1876. See also *Transcript*, July 22, 1876.

61. St. Paul *Pioneer Press, Dec.* 20, 1876; cited in Cincinnati *Commercial*, Dec. 24, 1876.

62. Cleveland *Herald*, n.d., cited in Cincinnati *Commercial*, July 23, 1876.

63. Chicago *Tribune*, n.d., cited in Cincinnati *Commercial*, July 12, 1876.

64. See, for example, the following newspapers for the early hostility of greenback journals toward remonetization: Rushville (Ind.) *Republican*, July 27, 1876; Chicago *Inter-Ocean*, Apr. 29, 1876 and *Spirit of Democracy* (Ohio), June 6, 1876, both cited in Cincinnati *Commercial*, June 9, 1876.

Terre Haute *Express* and the Ironton, Ohio *Democrat,* thus, criticized the silverites repeatedly for opposing additional issues of government paper notes and, for their part, bimetallists like Halstead maintained that the two financial schemes were irreconcilable. "The silver dollar movement," the Cincinnati editor wrote in July 1876, "is a real honest money movement . . . opposed to the greenback delusion. We, of course, cannot add the silver dollar to the mass of greenback trash . . . we would issue silver dollars, destroy greenbacks."[65]

Eastern gold monometallist journals became as aroused as some western greenback papers over the increasing demands for restoration of a double monetary standard. The Boston *Globe,* which had printed George Weston's original letter, expressed its bewilderment that, "strange as it may appear, several members [of Congress] regarded as uncompromising hard-money men are in favor of it."[66] The Baltimore *Sun,* which had favored the earlier "silver resumption" of fractional notes, opposed full remonetization with the familiar gold standard argument that making silver coin legal tender in a falling market would debase the coinage and drain the country of its limited supply of gold. The New York *Sun* similarly denounced the proposed 412.5 grain silver dollar as a "fraud pretending to be a dollar" while worth considerably less in current market value of its bullion content.[67] More than one eastern gold standard paper considered the entire silver drive simply a scheme to fatten "the pockets of the Bonanza Senators" and their rich mineowner associates.[68]

65. Cincinnati *Commercial,* July 22, 1876. For the criticisms of silver made by the greenback papers, see July 21 and 22, 1876 editions.

66. Boston *Globe,* July 26, 1876.

67. Baltimore *Sun,* July 12 and 27, 1876; New York *Sun,* cited in Cincinnati *Commercial,* July 11, 1876.

68. Brooklyn *Argus,* July 25, 1876; New York *Tribune,* Mar. 17, 1876; *The Nation,* Apr. 27, 1876.

From the beginning of the silver drive, the most articulate and influential journalist opposed to remonetization was E. L. Godkin, editor of *The Nation,* the weekly journal of opinion published in New York City that served as a political bible for the nation's academic reform community. Godkin denounced "the proposed silver swindle" from the moment Congress began considering the question. He considered the drive to remonetize silver merely a subterfuge of paper money "repudiationists," a tactical device adopted by greenbackers once silver had declined sufficiently in market value so that it possessed "that delicious flavor of broken faith which many of the inflationists so much prize in any large pecuniary transaction."

Godkin's anti-silver editorial sermons, regularly preached in the columns of *The Nation,* were reprinted, paraphrased, and quoted throughout the country's gold standard press. The typical bimetallist, according to Godkin, was nothing more or less than a greenbacker with a thin white metallic coating, an inflationist mountebank and fraud strutting uncomfortably in new bullionist garments. "As soon as a specie of coin presented itself with which they could cheat as effectually as with paper," the *Nation* thundered in August 1876, "[the greenbackers] dropped the paper and became hard-money men. We do not say that every silver resumptionist is a knave or inflationist, but we are quite sure that there is no knave or inflationist in the country who is not a silver resumptionist."[69]

Godkin believed that the country's leading silver mine owners, the Bonanza Kings, had initiated the bimetallist agitation in order to insure a fat government market for their surplus bullion. The New York reformer felt confident in 1876, however, that the greenback movement was dying and that the country would also reject "silver inflationism . . . before undue harm had been done to its finances or its morals." Indeed, because of the metal's

69. *The Nation,* Aug. 10, 1876.

intrinsic market value, Godkin believed that "no inflationist can be as dangerous as a silver man as he was as a paper man."[70] Despite these qualifications, the editor of *The Nation* denounced the silver drive regularly in its columns. He held a position of leadership among gold standard journalists in the 1870s analogous to Halstead's role among the bimetallists. Godkin eventually forgave individual bimetallist apostates like Jacob Cox, Halstead, and other former associates in earlier Reconstruction battles for sound money, considering these reformers to be only temporarily deranged on the silver question. But he never tired of firing off editorial salvos at the majority of "knaves" and "fools," inflationists all, who, in his opinion, sponsored and supported the campaign for remonetization.

Monometallists like Godkin were often astounded by the background of many influential silverites, including several important elder statesmen of the Republican party like Grant's Vice-President Schuyler Colfax, Thurlow Weed, onetime leader of the Whig party in New York state, and former New York Governor John A. Dix. Colfax endorsed remonetization partly because of its popularity among the Republican rank and file but also because demonetization in 1873 was "a wrong that should be righted."[71] Weed actively campaigned for restoration of the double monetary standard in a series of articles published by the *Tribune* and other New York journals.[72] Weed also

70. Ibid., See also for Apr. 27 and July 27, 1876. Godkin, like Halstead on the silverite side, editorialized in almost every issue on the silver question.

71. Ovando James Hollister, *Life of Schuyler Colfax* (New York, 1886), p. 472. See also Schuyler Colfax to Murat Halstead, Sept. 2, 1877, Halstead MSS, Cincinnati Historical Society.

72. See, for example, Weed's letter to the New York *Tribune,* n.d., reprinted in the Cincinnati *Commercial,* Aug. 10, 1876. Three Weed letters advocating remonetization were published in the New York *Tribune*—dated July 25, 1876, Aug. 5, 1876, and Nov. 23, 1877—and reprinted as "Demonetization of Silver" in an 1889 bimetallist pamphlet, *The Silver Dollar of the United States* (New York, 1889), pp. 18–32.

believed in the "Crime of 1873" but denounced demonetization primarily on economic grounds, believing that it had seriously contracted the stock of hard coin at a time when American business required currency expansion to restore prosperity. Like other hard money silverites, he believed that with the return of bimetallism, a sufficiently large supply of silver would begin circulating alongside gold to stimulate business recovery and insure the success of specie resumption.[73] Weed, Colfax, and Dix all lobbied for remonetization in the press and in private correspondence to old political associates. Most importantly, as founders of the party, their activities lent the sanction of traditional Republican doctrine to the bimetallist campaign.[74]

The presence of so many leading supporters of sound money and specie resumption among the front ranks of the silverite forces within months after the controversy had broken out in Congress—men like Weed, Colfax, Dix, Jacob Cox, Halstead, and Joseph Medill—suggests that traditional accounts of early silver agitation have overstressed the movement's agrarian and inflationist origins. For one thing, not only did businessmen and business periodicals disagree on the problem of remonetizing silver, but the academic reform community and the nation's hard money press also split badly on the question. Newspaper editors, economists, bankers, and merchants from all sections of the country championed the "old silver dollar" many months before southern and western agrarians discovered the issue.

The drive to remonetize silver, which began in Congress during the spring of 1876, did not become "a popular craze threatening to sweep all before it" among the agrarian electorate until mid-1877. Initial support for restoring legal bimetallism

73. Cincinnati *Commercial,* Aug., 10, 1876.

74. Hollister, *Life of Schuyler Colfax.* See also George Melville Weston to Thurlow Weed, Dec. 13, 1876. Weed MSS, New York Historical Society (New York City); also John A. Dix to Rutherford B. Hayes, Aug. 11, 1877, Hayes MSS, Fremont, cited in Unger, *Greenback Era,* p. 337ff.

did not come from the country's farmers nor did the silver drive ignite an immediate political fire in rural America.[75] A variety of individuals endorsed remonetization in 1876, most of them articulate and economically knowledgeable men from urban environments who spread the bimetallist message through their newspaper editorials, chamber of commerce resolutions, political gatherings, and privately printed broadsides. Through this massive, largely unorganized educational process—undertaken separately by journalists, businessmen, reformers, and politicians throughout the country—the ordinary voter became conscious of the silver question and, by mid-1877, a mass movement supporting remonetization had developed cutting across traditional party and class alignments.

The image of a "Crime of 1873," for example, came first from the Boston journalist and importer, George Weston. It passed quickly in 1876 into Senate and House debate, then into newspaper editorials and discussions among academic reformers, before eventually being absorbed into agrarian folklore. Similarly, the economic arguments for remonetization were first developed by these same sound money advocates in the urban middle class—newspapermen, businessmen, bankers, publicists, and politicians. Months before greenback-minded agrarian legislators like Ignatius Donnelly and Thomas Ewing began stumping the hinterlands during the 1877 congressional campaign drumming up support for the Bland bill, hard money advocates of specie resumption like George Weston, John Percival Jones, Murat Halstead, and Thurlow Weed had outlined the silver movement's monetary doctrines.

The first party convention to declare its support for remonetization was not an inflationist conclave in the South or Midwest but California's conservative, sound money, pro-resumption Republican party, which endorsed bimetallism only two days after John Percival Jones' maiden speech on the question in

75. Ibid., p. 336.

April 1876.[76] The drive to remonetize silver did not originate among agrarian inflationists or galvanized greenbackers. It emerged as a moderate proposal for monetary expansion supported largely by "coin money" advocates of specie resumption deeply concerned over the existing business depression.

California had been one of the few states in the Union to maintain specie payments on state debts and local financial transactions throughout the Civil War and Reconstruction years, and it served as a model of conservative financial practices for eastern and midwestern supporters of resumption. The California Republican party had previously demanded at each convention a swift return to specie payments for the entire country and had consistently opposed all inflationary schemes for greenback expansion proposed in Congress. Its 1876 endorsement of bimetallism, therefore, indicated that many dedicated hard money men in California, most of whom held no personal stake in the mining industry, now believed along with supporters of remonetization elsewhere in the country that specie resumption and economic recovery were both impossible without first restoring legal bimetallism.

76. San Francisco *Bulletin,* Apr. 27, 1876.

6

The Bonanza King Myth: Western Mineowners and Remonetization

Two conflicting "devil theory" versions of history, both of which originated in the 1870s, influenced later political debate on the silver question. One concerned the demonetization of silver, which, according to bimetallists, had been secured by a conspiracy of bondholders who had bribed leading public officials to gain adoption of the gold standard, the "Crime of 1873." Gold standard advocates countered with their own conspiracy theory, which concerned the origins of the campaign to restore legal bimetallism. Many goldbugs believed that a small group of western silver mineowners, led by the powerful Bonanza Kings of San Francisco, had helped to incite and finance the drive to remonetize silver in order to secure a guaranteed government market for their bullion.[1] Until recently most historians have been skeptical of the "Crime of 1873," yet almost every student of American silver politics has accepted the notion that mineowners, especialy the Bonanza Kings, helped sponsor the remonetization demands of the late 1870s.[2] Historians have pro-

1. Among the earliest references to this belief in mine owner responsibility for raising the silver issue, see the following: New York *Tribune,* Feb. 18, 1876; *Cong. Record,* 44th Cong., vol. 4, pt. 2, 1764–71, Mar. 16, 1876; *The Nation,* Apr. 20 and 27, 1876; New York *Graphic,* Mar. 17, 1876.

2. Historians who have accepted the notion of basic mine owner involvement in the silver drive include the following: Jeannette P. Nichols, "John Sherman and the Silver Drive of 1877–1878: The

duced almost no evidence to support this belief, however, relying instead on a *post hoc, ergo propter hoc* argument, namely that the coalition of mineowners and agrarian inflationists which they detect in the silver drive of the 1890s had been formed two decades earlier.

The legend of mineowner complicity in silver agitation during the seventies, the Bonanza King myth, has been absorbed into almost every American textbook, economic history, and monograph which deals with the question.[3] This chapter examines the facts behind the legend, the extent to which the Bonanza Kings, the only important firm of silver bullion producers during the 1870s, actually attempted to influence government coinage policies. Did the large western silver producers really trigger and support these early demands for remonetizing silver, or have historians assumed too much on the basis of too little evidence concerning the political behavior of the western mining community?

The most powerful group of American silver mineowners in 1876, when political agitation began over the metal's future as a monetary standard, were the Bonanza Kings, who owned the only two major producing mines on Nevada's Comstock Lode.[4]

Origins of the Gigantic Subsidy," *Ohio State Archeological and Historical Quarterly,* 46 (1937), 149, 154, 160–61; Unger, *Greenback Era,* p. 335; Harvey, *Coin's Financial School,* p. 86; Carothers, *Fractional Money,* p. 253.

3. See, for example, Studenski and Krooss, *Financial History,* pp. 187–88; Friedman and Schwartz, *A Monetary History,* p. 115; and Current, Williams, and Freidel, *American History,* p. 559.

4. The fullest treatment of the colorful careers of the four Bonanza Kings can be found in Oscar Lewis, *Silver Kings, the Lives and Times of Mackay, Fair, Flood and O'Brien, Lords of the Nevada Comstock Lode* (New York, 1947). See also Rodman W. Paul, *Mining Frontiers of the Far West, 1848–1880* (New York, 1963), pp. 56–86; Grant H. Smith, "History of the Comstock Lode"; William S. Greever, *The Bonanza West, The Story of the Western Mining Rushes, 1848–1900* (Norman, Okla., 1963); Eliot Lord, *Comstock Mining and Miners*

Many goldbugs charged these four mineowners with initiating the congressional campaign to restore silver's full legal tender. As joint owners of the great Consolidated Virginia and California mines, the Bonanza Kings—James G. Fair, James C. Flood, John W. Mackay, and William S. O'Brien—had become the wealthiest men on the Pacific coast during the mid-seventies and among the richest men in the entire world.[5] With revenues from their Comstock mines and other jointly owned companies, they built palatial San Francisco mansions and sponsored the costly European presentation of socialite wives and children. In 1875, they opened the largest private bank in the West, the Nevada Bank of San Francisco, primarily as a depository for their vast bullion reserves. Contemporaries referred to the four Bonanza Kings as the "Lords of the Comstock," and from 1875 to 1878 they controlled the largest share of Nevada's mining production.[6]

(Washington: Government Printing Office, 1883); Ostrander, *Nevada: The Great Rotten Borough;* and Robert B. Merrivale, "Nevada, 1859–1881: The Impact of an Advanced Technological Society Upon a Frontier Area," unpublished Ph.D. dissertation, University of Chicago, 1957.

5. Lewis, *Silver Kings,* passim: Paul, *Mining Frontiers,* pp. 77–80; Greever, *The Bonanza West,* pp. 123–24. The classic narratives of the exploration and discovery of the Consolidated Virginia and California mines are found in Wright, *The Big Bonanza,* and in Charles Howard Shinn, *The Story of the Mine* (New York, 1896). See also C. B. Glasscock, *The Big Bonanza* (New York, 1934), pp. 242–54; and Joseph L. King, *History of the San Francisco Stock and Exchange Board,* pp. 73–83. The term "bonanza," in its most general sense, referred to any exceptionally rich ore deposit or pocket in veins that contained gold and silver. On the Comstock Lode, the term was applied only to a handful of mines. Of these, the Consolidated Virginia and California were commonly acknowledged to contain the richest "bonanzas" on the Lode.

6. Lewis, *Silver Kings,* passim. See also Paul, *Mining Frontiers,* pp. 79–80, for a concise, excellent summary of the Bonanza firm's swift rise to economic power in Nevada and California.

Historians have argued that the Bonanza Kings "connive[d], directly and indirectly, in inflation through the manipulation of silver," that "needless to say, the miners and their friends in Congress supported remonetization."[7] The most recent study of the first silver drive noted that the four Bonanza Kings "had much to gain from restoring silver, particularly if they could pocket the difference between the market price of silver and its par value. Free and unlimited coinage [or] even a limited Treasury purchase program [following remonetization] promised some relief from the low prices that the deluge of precious metals from Nevada had produced."[8] Fortunately, these assertions concerning the political role of the Bonanza firm in the silver drive can be easily tested.

The company was not merely one of several influential American silver mining companies in the late 1870s. For all practical purposes, from 1875 to the end of the decade, the Bonanza Kings alone represented the large producers of western silver. They owned the only two mines on the Comstock Lode which continued to pay dividends from 1876 to 1878, the dura-

7. Nichols, "John Sherman and the Silver Drive," p. 149; Unger, *Greenback Era,* p. 335. See also Studenski and Krooss, *Financial History;* Edward C. Kirkland, *Industry Comes of Age,* p. 37; Friedman and Schwartz, *A Monetary History,* and Harvey, *Coin's Financial School.*

8. Unger, *Greenback Era.* Unger qualifies this opinion somewhat by suggesting that "ambiguities in the mine operators' attitudes [existed] that make all generalization dangerous." He quotes without further comment a telegram from James W. Simonton of the Associated Press to Rutherford B. Hayes' Treasury Secretary John Sherman, in which Simonton portrayed the Bonanza kings as "against unqualified remonetization" and favorable only to a "moderate coinage" of silver. Unger remains uncertain, however, both about the accuracy and the general validity of this single piece of evidence, calling it "only one case, perhaps [which] underscores the dangers of accepting uncritically the familiar stereotypes." Thus he observes: "Needless to say, the miners and their friends in Congress supported remonetization" (pp. 335–36). See also James W. Simonton to John Sherman, Dec. 29, 1877, Sherman MSS, LC, cited in Unger.

tion of the silver drive, and they controlled and manipulated the lively speculative trade in mining shares on the San Francisco Stock and Exchange Board. Producing *two-thirds* of the silver bullion on the Comstock Lode in these years, the four Bonanza Kings were the unchallenged leaders of the nation's mineowners at the time that silver's remonetization first became a political issue.[9] As the director of the mint observed in 1877, the Bonanza-owned Nevada Bank of San Francisco remained "the only holder of any considerable quantity of [silver] bullion in this country," and thus they were practically synonymous with the "Western silver mining interest."[10]

The Bonanza Kings' attitudes toward remonetization remained a matter of dispute among contemporaries. In the months preceding passage of the Bland-Allison Act, many of their San Francisco banking associates came out against returning to legal bimetallism. One reporter from the San Francisco *Chronicle*, for example, discovered in a poll taken in the city's financial district that almost all the important bankers, including some who held substantial investments in western silver mines, favored retaining the gold standard. None of the Bonanza Kings would speak to the *Chronicle* reporter, however, because of the newspaper's many bitter attacks on their mining and speculative practices.[11] Still, the *Chronicle*, which supported

9. The dominant leadership of Bonanza firm mines in total ore production compared with other Comstock mines from 1876 to 1878, the period of the silver drive, is detailed in the *Annual Report of the Director of the Mint for 1878* (Washington, 1878), pp. 52–53. See also Paul, *Mining Frontiers*, pp. 78–80, and Greever, *The Bonanza West*, pp. 127–30.

10. Henry Richard Linderman to F. F. Low (Manager, Anglo-Californian Bank of San Francisco), Mar. 29, 1877, Letterbooks, Director of the Mint, NA, RG 104.

11. San Francisco *Chronicle*, Oct. 20, 1877. The *Chronicle* never succeeded in smoking out the views of the Bonanza firm on the silver issue, and when one of its reporters again toured the city's financial district after passage of the Bland-Allison Act seeking the opinion of local bankers concerning the legislation, he found only that "Louis McLane, of the Nevada Bank, had, as usual, little to say" (Mar. 3, 1878).

specie resumption in gold alone and opposed remonetization failed to single out the Bonanza firm as supporters of the silver drive. The paper called the hostility of the city's financial community toward the Bland bill "representative" of public opinion among Pacific coast businessmen, who had conducted their large economic transactions in gold throughout the Civil War and Reconstruction years, when the rest of the country had abandoned specie payments. "The wonder," observed the *Chronicle,* "is that a Senator [like John Percival Jones of Nevada] from this side of the continent could be found to advocate the other plan [i.e. remonetization]."[12]

Many eastern gold standard advocates insisted that the Bonanza Kings sponsored the silver agitation, however, and subsequent historians have given credence to this assertion.[13] The few contemporaries privy to inside information about the mineowners' views believed that the silver kings disagreed privately on the question.[14] Throughout congressional debate

12. Ibid., Oct. 29, 1877. Jones, himself, denied that he had ever communicated with the Bonanza Kings on the silver question "either collectively or individually, personally or through correspondence or otherwise on this subject." *Cong. Record,* 45th Cong., 2d sess., vol. 7, pt. 2, Feb. 14, 1878, p. 1025.

13. The vision of a conspiracy operating to influence government coinage policy haunted all sides in the monetary wars of the Gilded Age. "Do cats like cream?" the New York *Weekly Journal of Commerce* asked its readers in an allusion to the Bonanza Kings' reputed desire for a guaranteed government market for their bullion. For belief in Bonanza King involvement in the silver drive as expressed by gold standard journalists, bankers and businessmen, see the following: New York *Weekly Journal of Commerce,* Jan. 17, 1878 and Feb. 21, 1878; *Iron Age,* vol. 18, July 20, 1876 and Aug. 3, 1876; *The Nation,* July 13, 1876 and Aug. 17, 1876; August Belmont to Thomas F. Bayard, Nov. 18, 1877; W. G. Deshler to John Sherman, Jan. 13, 1877; G. L. Foote to H. C. Fahnestock, Nov. 8, 1877; all in Sherman MSS, LC; John Curtis to James A. Garfield, Feb. 7, 1878, Garfield MSS, LC; Morris H. Cook to Thomas F. Bayard, Dec. 29, 1877, Bayard MSS, LC.

14. For John Percival Jones' view, see *Cong. Record,* 45th Cong., 2d sess., vol. 7, pt. 2, Feb. 14, 1878. See also San Francisco *Bulletin*

on the Bland bill, the four lords of the Comstock made no public statements on remonetization nor have any fully reliable private accounts of their response to the silver drive yet appeared.

The reluctance of the Nevada Bank proprietors to support the Bland bill may have stemmed both from satisfaction with the silver purchase policies already being followed by the Hayes administration and from their unwillingness to endanger the close, profitable relationship which the Nevada Bank had cultivated with the Bureau of the Mint and Treasury Department. Contrary to prevailing belief, the Bonanza firm had few problems disposing of the vast silver production of its California and Consolidated Virginia mines in the years from 1875 to 1878.[15]

The Bonanza Kings sold millions of ounces in silver to the Treasury Department in exchange for premium five percent government bonds payable in gold between 1876 and January 1879, when the United States resumed specie payments. Both as individuals and through their jointly owned Nevada Bank, the four mineowners became substantial holders of these securities. Furthermore, between 1875 and 1878, the government served as a major customer for the product of the Consolidated Virginia and California mines. The Bonanza firm sold more silver to the United States mints in the four years following passage of the Resumption Act in 1875 than any other single producer of bullion, either domestic or foreign. Far from needing or seeking a new government market for their silver during the struggle over remonetization, the Bonanza Kings already possessed a reliable customer in the Treasury Department, to which it sold whenever more profitable sales in Indian and

[n.d.], cited by New York *Graphic,* Feb. 5, 1878; New York *Graphic,* Feb. 16, 1878; G. K. Fitch to J. W. Simonton, Dec. 17, 1877, in Simonton to John Sherman, Dec. 29, 1877, Sherman MSS, LC.

15. For a diametrically opposed view, which holds that the Bonanza Kings did have difficulty disposing of their bullion and therefore pressed the government constantly for additional purchases, see Nichols, "John Sherman and the Silver Drive," pp. 153–54.

Chinese trade did not absorb their available stock of silver bullion. To comprehend the probable reaction of the silver kings to remonetization, therefore, one must understand the close ties which already existed between the Bonanza firm, the country's largest producer of silver, and the Treasury Department from 1875 to 1878.

The Specie Resumption Act of January 14, 1875, contained a provision which called for the redemption of fractional greenbacks—ten, twenty-five, and fifty cent paper tokens—with subsidiary silver coins to be minted and issued "as rapidly as possible" at the discretion of the Secretary of the Treasury.[16] During the sixteen months following the passage of the Resumption Act, Treasury Secretary Benjamin Bristow and Director of the Mint Henry Richard Linderman purchased substantial amounts of silver bullion from both domestic and foreign holders, procuring it "as much below the equivalent of the London [market] rate as possible, and in no case [paying] above that rate."[17] The Bonanza firm's two largest Comstock Lode mining companies, the Consolidated Virginia and California, along with their newly acquired Pacific Refinery and Bullion Exchange in San Francisco, were among the largest sellers of bullion to the government during this period.[18]

Mint Director Linderman first purchased bullion from the Bonanza firm in 1875 in an effort to undermine the attempts by older bullion dealers in Europe, the eastern cities, and San Francisco to force up the market price. As "the only holder of any considerable quantity of bullion in this country," the Bonanza firm responded favorably toward these early govern-

16. On the economic and political background of the Resumption Act of 1875, see Unger, *Greenback Era,* pp. 249–85. See also Sherman, *Recollections,* pp. 507–18.

17. Henry Richard Linderman to John Sherman, Mar. 31, 1877, Letterbooks, Director of the Mint, NA, RG 104.

18. For government purchases from companies owned by the Bonanza Kings, see the list of silver purchases in Appendix I, covering the period from January 1875 to April 1876.

ment offers.[19] For a time the Treasury Department even utilized the firm's refining facilities in San Francisco to help process government bullion purchases, since the United States mints in San Francisco and Carson City lacked the capacity to handle completely its greatly expanded silver purchases. For a time in 1875 and 1876, thus, the Bonanza Kings not only sold huge quantities of their bullion to the government but the firm also held a virtual monopoly of bullion refining operations on the Pacific coast. The government not only purchased its silver but also paid the firm to process it![20]

At first the mint paid for silver purchases from the Bonanza Kings in gold coin. Hoping to conserve the Treasury's gold reserves to prepare for eventual specie resumption, Secretary of the Treasury Bristow changed this mode of payment in April 1876. In the process Bristow altered the economic direction of the Bonanza firm itself. Previously the Treasury had been selling government bonds in the world's major securities markets under terms of the Resumption Act, using a portion of the gold proceeds to purchase silver for subsidiary coinage purposes.[21]

19. Linderman to Thomas C. Action, Feb. 13, 1875, DM Lbks, NA, RG 104. For the Director of the Mint's earliest dealings with the Bonanza firm, see the following: Linderman to O. H. LaGrange (Superintendent, San Francisco Mint), May 17, 25, 29, 1875; June 1, 7, 1875; Linderman to Consolidated Virginia Mining Company, May 29, June 7, 1875; Linderman to Thomas C. Action, May 29, 1875; DM Lbks, NA, RG 104.

20. Linderman to Messrs. Flood and O'Brien, Oct. 4, 1875, DM Lbks, NA, RG 104. For a record of these negotiations, see also Linderman to Flood and O'Brien, Oct. 4, 21, 1875; Linderman to J. C. Flood, Nov. 2, 1875; Linderman to O. H. LaGrange, May 25, Oct. 10, Nov. 3, Dec. 18, 1875.

21. For a review of this Treasury policy, see John Sherman's interview as Secretary of the Treasury with the House Committee on Banking and Currency, Apr. 1, 1878, republished in *Resumption of Specie Payments,* 45th Cong., 2d sess., Misc. Doc. No. 62 (Washington, 1878), p. 24. See also *Banker's Magazine,* Aug. 1875, p. 2, "Notes on the Money Market."

In April 1876, however, Bristow decided instead to buy silver from the Bonanza firm with United States five percent bonds, payable upon maturity in gold, rather than paying in gold coin itself. That month Bristow and Linderman proposed to the Bonanza Kings that "all of the silver required for the subsidiary coinage would be purchased from [the Nevada Bank] at the equivalent of the London rate on the day of purchase," to be paid for in these five percent bonds.[22]

Despite the continuing decline in the metal's London market rate, the Bonanza Kings appeared less anxious than Treasury officials to commit in advance substantial portions of their silver bullion for regular sale at a prearranged price. Periodic demand by San Francisco merchants for large amounts of silver in the Asiatic trade coupled with the awareness that the government would have to turn for supplies to the Nevada Bank in any case—"the only holder of any considerable quantity of bullion in this country"—led the firm to demand more favorable terms from Bristow in April 1876, and negotiations for a Bonanza monopoly of government silver purchases soon broke down.[23] The major economic factor involved in the firm's decision was a simple one. As Louis McLane, president of the Nevada Bank, observed in August 1877: "In consequence of the demand for India and China, the price of silver has, during the last eighteen months, been at times higher in San Francisco than in New York or London." As it turned out, the mint still purchased silver

22. Linderman to John Sherman, Mar. 31, 1877, DM Lbks, RG 104 "On a sale of silver made to the government in exchange for 5-per-cent bonds, the price of the former was fixed at the equivalent of the London quotation, and of the latter by taking the average of the New York and London markets on day of sale." Louis McLane (President, Nevada Bank), sworn affidavit, in "Testimony of Leading bankers and others before the United States Treasury Commission in relation to purchase of silver bullion for the fractional coinage," Director of the Mint, *Annual Report, 1877* (Washington, 1877), pp. 56–57.

23. Linderman to F. F. Low, Mar. 29, 1877; Linderman to Sherman, Mar. 31, 1877, DM Lbks, RG 104.

bullion for coinage almost exclusively from the Nevada Bank between April and August 1876, often making payment in five percent gold bonds. The Bonanza firm's virtual monopoly of government silver purchases changed only in August 1876 when the Nevada Bank, anticipating a significant increase in the Chinese and Indian trade during the fall, stiffened its terms for government sales.[24]

When the congressional agitation for remonetization began in 1876, therefore, the Bonanza Kings were not overly concerned with securing a government market for their bullion. In previous months they had concluded substantial sales to the mint with obvious reluctance, since they preferred to hold their silver for more profitable later disposal to San Francisco exporters in oriental trade.[25] Throughout the remonetization drive, in fact, the Nevada Bank remained on extremely cordial terms with Director of the Mint Linderman. This relationship was so close that, during the period from April to August 1876, Secretary of the Treasury Bristow, upon Linderman's recommendation, gave the Bonanza firm a de facto monopoly of bullion sales to the government despite the absence of a formal contract.[26] During the months following this unofficial agreement on silver purchases between the Treasury Department and the Bonanza Kings in April 1876, while the question of remonetization first attracted the attention of Congress, the

24. Louis McLane, sworn affidavit, in Director of the Mint, *Annual Report, 1877;* Linderman to Louis McLane, Aug. 26, 1876, DM Lbks, RG 104.

25. Louis McLane, sworn affidavit, Director of the Mint, *Annual Report, 1877*. See also Linderman to Sherman, Mar. 31, 1877, DM Lbks.

26. Linderman to James Crawford (Superintendent, Carson City Mint), Apr. 18, 1876, DM Lbks. See also Linderman to the following Mint officials: O. H. LaGrange (Superintendent, San Francisco Mint), James Pollock (Superintendent, Philadelphia Mint), James Crawford (Superintendent, Carson City Mint), all Apr. 20, 1876; Linderman to N. K. Masten (Cashier, Nevada Bank), Apr. 20 and May 17, 1876.

Nevada Bank sold over seven million dollars worth of silver to the government.[27] Linderman continually pressed the Bonanza firm for even larger amounts of bullion than they had been supplying, telegraphing urgently at one point that government "consumption of silver at *all* the Coinage Mints, would be at the rate of 2,000,000 ounces of fine silver per month," and asking: "Can we depend on that amount?"[28]

During the entire silver drive, the government knocked regularly at the Nevada Bank's doors with silver purchase proposals, and seldom did the Bonanza Kings attempt to initiate sales to the Treasury. Linderman not only informed the Bonanza Kings regularly of mint bullion requirements but even corresponded with them on pending legislation as well and solicited their advice on Treasury coinage policy. The mint director was determined to tie the bullion resources of the great Bonanza mines to Treasury coinage needs, and he kept the mineowners in close touch with prospective congressional actions.[29]

If the Bonanza Kings favored any particular piece of silver legislation in 1876, they never mentioned this fact to Linderman, despite persistent requests for advice. Certainly they had no need for restoration of silver as a monetary standard in order to provide an adequate market for their available supplies of bullion. Both Louis McLane of the Nevada Bank and Director of the Mint Linderman later testified to the lively condition of the silver market from mid-1876 through early 1877. "In the fall of 1876," McLane observed before a special Treasury Department commission in 1877, "an active demand for silver sprang up here for export to China, lasting nearly three months, and at the same time an active demand existed in London for

27. For a record of government silver purchases from the Bonanza firm, through the Nevada Bank and other Bonanza-owned companies, see Appendix II for all purchases from April to August 1876.

28. Linderman to James G. Fair, July 27, 1876; Linderman to Louis McLane, July 29, 1876; both DM Lbks.

29. Linderman to Louis McLane, May 16 and Aug. 11, 1876, ibid.

export to India, the consequences of which was to keep this and the London markets comparatively bare of silver."[30] Linderman confirmed McLane's account in a March 1877 letter to John Sherman, the new Secretary of the Treasury, acknowledging that, at a time when support for remonetization grew in Congress that, throughout the country, the Bonanza Kings could choose among competing outlets for their entire bullion supply at high market prices. "The demand for India, China, Japan, and for coinage by the United States, from July 1876 to February 1877," Linderman wrote Sherman, "was sufficient to consume all the silver produced as well as part of the German supplies, and left the markets of Europe and this Country comparatively bare of silver, and no considerable amount could have been procured by us from December 1, 1876, to the close of February 1877, without advancing the price to a point at which we would not have been justified in purchasing under the law."[31]

When the Nevada Bank sold to the Treasury after August 1876, it generally received payment in gold coin rather than in government securities. However, the bank invested its profits from bullion sales increasingly in five percent gold bonds. Secretary Bristow had encouraged the exchange of bullion for bonds after concluding his de facto agreement with the Bonanza firm on silver purchases in April 1876.[32] Under this arrangement,

30. Louis McLane, sworn affidavit, Director of the Mint, *Annual Report, 1877*.

31. Linderman to John Sherman, Mar. 31, 1877, DM Lbks. Director of the Mint, *Annual Report, 1876* (Washington, 1876), p. 295, "The Silver Market at San Francisco."

32. Linderman to McLane, Apr. 5, 1876, DM Lbks. For a sampling of subsequent Mint transactions with the Nevada Bank based on the sale of silver for 5 percent government bonds, see the following: Linderman to Louis McLane, Apr. 5, 17, 18, 19, May 27, June 19, Aug. 23, 26, Sept. 5, 1876; Linderman to Superintendent, Carson Mint, Apr. 17, 19, 1876; Linderman to O. H. LaGrange, Apr. 19, 1876; Linderman to N. K. Masten, July 1, Aug. 20, 1876; Linderman to James Pollock, Apr. 19, 1876; Linderman to Benjamin H. Bristow (Secretary of the Treasury), May 25, June 8, 1876; Linderman to Lot M. Morrill (Secre-

the Nevada Bank acquired over six million dollars worth of government bonds by December 1876.[33]

The silver market declined noticeably in the spring of 1877, and for the first time since 1875, the Nevada Bank and other holders of bullion experienced difficulties in arranging sales to the mint. "Within the past thirty days," Linderman informed the superintendent of the San Francisco Mint in April 1877, "the condition of the market above referred to has completely changed and in the absence of an export demand for China or elsewhere, the producers of your section are compelled to sell to the U.S. or export to London." Under these conditions, the new Secretary of the Treasury John Sherman attempted to reduce the price paid to the Bonanza Kings and other bullion holders for their silver, a price which had approximated the current London market rate.[34] Apparently, the mint director did not follow Sherman's instructions carefully enough, for immediately following his purchase of one and a quarter million ounces of silver from the Nevada Bank in March 1877, the world market price declined over seven cents per ounce within a month.

---

tary of the Treasury), Aug. 18, 1876; Fred Eckfeldt (Acting Director, Bureau of the Mint) to Louis McLane, Aug. 8, 1876; Charles Conant (Acting Secretary of the Treasury) to John C. New (Treasurer of the United States), May 26, 1876; all DM Lbks.

33. For a record of government bonds acquired by the Bonanza Kings in 1876, see Appendix III. Also see Linderman to Benjamin Bristow, May 25, June 8, 1876; Linderman to Louis McLane, May 27, Aug. 26, Sept. 5, 1876; Linderman to N. K. Masten, July 1, Aug. 20, 1876; Linderman to Nevada Bank, June 19, Aug. 23, 1876; Charles F. Conant to John C. New, May 26, 1876, DM Lbks. On activity in the silver market late in 1876, see Linderman to Acting Director of the Mint Preston, Dec. 4 and 11, 1876, in letters received "T," NA, RG 104.

34. Linderman to La Grange, Apr. 5 and 19, 1877. Linderman to Sherman, Apr. 5, 1877, discusses the proposed reduction in the Treasury's rate paid for silver purchases. Linderman outlined the newly reduced rates and the policy underlying them in two memoranda to Mint officials on Apr. 2 and Apr. 18, 1877, in letters received "T." Also see Linderman to J. S. Cronise, Feb. 9, 1877. All in DM Lbks.

Linderman found himself severely criticized by Pacific coast business interests and by newspapers hostile to the Bonanza Kings.[35]

So blatantly did Linderman appear to favor the Nevada Bank in his silver purchase policies that the San Francisco *Chronicle* charged the mint director with holding stock in the Bonanza mines. Linderman, himself, denied any impropriety and defended his recent large purchase from the Nevada Bank on the grounds that the government mints had only enough silver on hand for one month's coinage and needed a swift substantial addition to its diminished bullion reserves.[36] With the silver market experiencing a serious slump, Treasury purchases of bullion declined, and the Nevada Bank lost temporarily its substantial share of the government silver market. Even now, it remained unwilling to accept Sherman's offers to purchase Bonanza bullion at a price below the full equivalent of the London market rate.[37] This situation changed in July 1877, when Linderman began negotiating with McLane and the Bonanza Kings in San Francisco for resumption of government silver purchases from the Nevada Bank. The mint director's efforts brought into the open some highly significant information concerning the economic interests of the secretive Bonanza firm.

At a meeting with the Silver Kings, described in a letter to

35. On Nevada Bank sales to the United States Mint in March 1877 see *Recordbook,* Silver Purchases, United States Mint, NA, RG 104.

36. San Francisco *Chronicle,* May 11, 1877; Linderman to F. F. Low, Mar. 29, 1877, DM Lbks.

37. See, for example, Linderman to Louis McLane, Mar. 31, May 16, 1877; Linderman to Nevada Bank, May 15, 1877; ibid. The San Francisco *Chronicle* kept up a steady barrage of criticism directed at Linderman's Treasury Department investigating commission, suggesting repeatedly that the Mint Director might begin his work by investigating, among other abuses, the favoritism he himself allegedly shown toward the Nevada Bank in silver purchases. *Chronicle* for 1877; May 16, July 1 and 2, Sept. 22, and Dec. 21.

Secretary Sherman, the mineowners discussed with Linderman their increasing purchases of government securities, investments they made with the profits of Treasury bullion sales. The conversation between the mint director and the two leading officials of the Nevada Bank, President Louis McLane and Bonanza King James C. Flood, offered a rare and revealing glimpse into the economic behavior of the firm. For one thing, it showed that the director of the mint, not the Bonanza Kings, initiated the proposal to renew the exchange of Treasury bonds for silver bullion, a practice begun under Secretary Bristow. It also suggested that the Comstock mineowners had not only been quietly increasing their portfolio of government securities but that they had even attempted, through New York agents, to participate in the syndicate of private bankers organized in 1877 to sell the Treasury Department's new four percent resumption bonds:

> I had some conversation today with the Bankers controlling Mines and Supplies of Silver [Linderman wrote Sherman], among them, the Bonanza Managers, Flood and McLane. In the course of the conversation, I stated to them in a general way that you had expressed a desire to have them take Bonds for Silver, also Gold—stating at the same time that I was not clothed with any authority to treat upon the subject. They informed me that Mr. Fry of the Bank of New York had seen you upon the subject and that no arrangement was arrived at. I infer that this conference was before the arrangement with Syndicate for the sale of 4%. They say that since then they have purchased 4½% Bonds to the Amount of $10,000,000 and are shipping gold coin against that purchase. They expressed their desire to meet your views but not through a third party [the Syndicate]. I deem it proper to state the tenor of this conversation. I introduced the subject with a view to see where they stood. If I had known that the matter had been before you through Mr. Fry I should not have referred to it. The matter is not

> of any importance but I could not understand their purchase of 4½ percents [when they had previously been receiving 5 percents in exchange for silver bullion].[38]

Flood exaggerated slightly, since the records indicate that the Nevada Bank actually purchased only *five* million dollars worth of 4.5 percent bonds in June and July 1877![39]

Sherman acknowledged to Linderman in his response that the Nevada Bank had attempted to purchase a large block of the new four percent resumption bonds, which had been awarded to the new syndicate for sale in June 1877.[40] Through their agents, the Bank of New York National Banking Association, the Bonanza Kings apparently attempted to join the resumption bond syndicate itself, although the facts on this point remain uncertain.[41] Sherman advised Linderman to continue discussing

38. Linderman to Sherman, July 2, 1877, Sherman MSS, LC.

39. Flood purchased the following amounts in 4.5 percent government bonds during June and July 1877 as personal investments:

June 28:	$1,000,000
June 29:	3,000,000
July 5:	250,000
July 21:	750,000
Total	$5,000,000

Recordbook, 4.5 percent 15-year funded loan of 1891 (due date), Individual accounts, Bureau of the Public Debt, NA, RG 53.

40. Sherman to Linderman, July 26, 1877, Sherman MSS, LC.

41. In 1877, the Treasury Department renegotiated an earlier contract for the sale of 4.5 percent bonds with a syndicate composed of leading American and European private banking houses—August Belmont & Company acting on behalf of the Rothschilds: J. & W. Seligman & Company; Drexel, Morgan & Company, acting for J. S. Morgan of London; and Morton, Bliss & Company. A group of New York national bankers attempted either to enlarge the old syndicate or, instead, to fund the entire new 4 percent bond loan themselves. This new syndicate included the First National Bank of New York, the Merchants' Bank of New York, the United States Trust Company and the Bank of New York National Banking Association, the latter firm representing its own interests and those of the Nevada Bank of San Francisco.

informally with the Bonanza Kings "any arrangement for the purchase of a considerable amount of gold and silver bullion to be paid for in four percent bonds," although he cautioned the mint director against concluding "any exclusive agreement . . . until I know and approve it."[42] With prospects favorable for congressional passage of a compromise bill remonetizing silver, both Sherman and Linderman wished to insure the Bonanza firm's support for Treasury efforts to accumulate a $100,000,000 gold reserve through the sale of government bonds, a gold fund which would be used to underwrite the resumption of specie payments scheduled for January 1879. Both officials preferred that the Nevada Bank invest its bullion reserves heavily in government bonds rather than hold them to finance later speculations in a rising silver market.[43]

In each letter during the summer of 1877, Linderman urged that substantial amounts of bullion be secured from the Nevada Bank and other San Francisco holders before he left San Francisco for Washington. After delaying action for several weeks, Sherman finally accepted Linderman's recommendation late in

---

After quiet and apparently unsuccessful overtures to the Treasury Department, Secretary Sherman turned down the national bankers' bid for the new bond contract and signed an agreement instead with the older syndicate led by Belmont. As an obvious concession to the New York national bankers, however, Belmont's new group included the First National Bank in its arrangement for funding the 4 percents. The Nevada Bank's agent, the Bank of New York, however, found itself completely shut out of the new syndicate, a fact that troubled Sherman. For the details of this complex bond sale negotiation, see the following: "Specie Resumption and Refunding of National Debt," House Executive Document No. 9, 46th Cong., 2d sess., reprinted (Washington, 1879), pp. 36–37, 61–62; Warner M. Bateman to John Sherman, July 23, 1877, Sherman MSS, LC; Unger, *Greenback Era,* p. 351; and especially Fritz Redlich, *The Molding of American Banking, Men and Ideas* (Ann Arbor, Mich., 1951), vol. 2, part II, pp. 367–68.

42. Sherman to Linderman, July 26, 1877, Sherman MSS, LC.

43. Linderman to Sherman, July 5, Sept. 14, 1877; Sherman to Linderman, July 26, 1877, Sherman MSS, LC.

August and approved an immediate purchase of 350,000 ounces of silver from the Nevada Bank as the first installment of an eventual three million ounce transaction.[44] On August 29, 1877, the same day the Nevada Bank received payment for its silver, the Bonanza Kings purchased an additional one million dollars in five percent government bonds, half in the name of the Nevada Bank and half as a personal investment for James C. Flood.[45]

Apparently Flood had more interest in investing his private capital in government securities than any of his associates, since only forty-eight hours after this half million dollar bond purchase, he began discussing with Linderman the possibility of acquiring an even more substantial amount in resumption bonds. Flood supervised the stock brokerage and banking interests of the Bonanza firm from San Francisco, leaving the Nevada management of the Consolidated Virginia and California mines in the hands of Fair and Mackay. As vice-president of the Nevada Bank and general business spokesman for Bonanza firm interests, Flood, according to the current president of the board, had become "the great leader" of the San Francisco Stock and Exchange Board by 1876.[46]

Flood instructed Louis McLane in August 1877 to approach

44. Linderman to Sherman, Aug. 3 and Aug. 7, 1877, ibid.; Linderman to K. E. Preston (Acting Director of the Mint), Aug. 21 and 22 (two dispatches each day), 1877, Letters received "L," DM Lbks. See also Preston memorandum, Aug. 22, 1877, ibid.

45. On August 29, 1877, ten $50,000 bonds were purchased for "Louis McLane, President, Nevada Bank, San Francisco" and ten other $50,000 bonds in the name of "J. C. Flood, San Francisco." *Ledgerbook,* Bonds Purchased, United States 5 percent funded loan of 1881, Bureau of the Public Debt, NA, RG 53.

46. Linderman to Sherman, Aug. 31, 1877, "Specie Resumption and Refunding of Public Debt," p. 138; King, *History of the San Francisco Stock and Exchange Board,* pp. 96, 105, 112, 213. Of the Nevada Bank's four principals, only Flood and O'Brien purchased seats on the San Francisco Stock and Exchange Board (at $25,000 each) according to King (p. 325).

Linderman with an offer to sell two million dollars worth of silver bars to the government, payment to be made in five percent government bonds. The mint director recommended that Secretary Sherman accept Flood's offer on the grounds that silver would "no doubt advance in price whenever a demand may again arise for export to the Indies or China; and a further advance would no doubt follow even the partial remonetization of the silver dollar."[47] Sherman's reply rejected purchasing additional Bonanza bullion with five percent bonds but approved slightly less favorable terms. "Will not sell five percent bonds for any purpose," Sherman telegraphed Linderman on September 8. "At present prefer to sell for silver, either four percent or gold."[48]

Within five days the Treasury purchased 1,650,000 more ounces of silver from the Nevada Bank under this arrangement, which Linderman hailed since it brought the Bonanza Kings into even closer association with the resumption aims of the Treasury Department. "I regard the purchase of silver from the Nevada Bank as a favorable one for the government," the mint director wrote Sherman. "Before recommending the purchase I satisfied myself that it was a question of whether these people [the Bonanza Kings] should put ten to 15 millions of dollars in Silver or in the U.S. Bonds. Now that the department met them on fair terms, they will put their idle money in U.S. bonds and will not use it to hold silver until such time as the price might rise to a point to suit them."[49] Unwittingly, Linderman had pre-

47. Linderman to Sherman, Aug. 31, 1877, DM Lbks. Flood had purchased privately four percent $50,000 bonds on each of the following occasions: Apr. 6, 7, 11 (twice), and 13, 1877; *Ledgerbook,* United States 5 percent funded loan of 1881, Bur. of Pub. Debt, NA, RG 53.

48. Sherman to Linderman, Sept. 8, 1877, "Specie Resumption and Refunding of National Debt," p. 141.

49. For the record of negotiations between the Treasury Department and the Nevada Bank surrounding these two major purchases, one for 150,000 ounces of silver and the other for almost 1,500,000 ounces, see the following: K. E. Preston to Linderman, Sept. 10, 1877; Preston to

dicted almost the exact amount of Bonanza firm investment in resumption bonds by the end of 1877. The four mineowners, either jointly through the Nevada Bank or privately in Flood's case, purchased nearly ten million dollars worth of five percent bonds in 1877 alone, increasing their accumulated holdings in government securities by the passage of the Bland-Allison Act to over twenty-two million dollars.[50] At the height of public agitation for remonetization in December 1877, the Bonanza Kings purchased $4,500,000 worth of the five percents, thereby demonstrating a faith in the success of specie resumption greater than many eastern and European investors, who feared that the silver bill would interfere with the Treasury's ability to resume specie payments in gold.[51]

Linderman evidently viewed his arrangement with the Nevada Bank during the summer of 1877 as a quid pro quo by which the Treasury purchased a substantial amount of silver from the Bonanza firm in return for a tacit agreement by the Nevada Bank to invest the proceeds heavily in government securities during the following months. Both sides kept to their part of the bargain, although the mining kings—or at least Flood—probably would have continued to purchase substantial amounts of resumption bonds even without the Treasury's decision to acquire large lots of silver from the firm in the fall.[52] By December 1877 the Nevada Bank held over $18,500,000

John Sherman, Sept. 12 and 13, 1877; DM Lbks and Letters received "L"; Sherman to Linderman, Sept. 13, 1877, Mint letters of the Secretary of the Treasury. See also Linderman to Sherman, Sept. 14, 1877.

50. For a detailed record of Bonanza King bond holdings through February 1878, see Appendix IV.

51. Ibid. See also Sherman to Linderman, Sept. 14 and 17, 1877, Sherman MSS, LC; San Francisco *Chronicle,* Sept. 16, 1877; Linderman to Sherman, Sept. 14, 1877, Mint letters of the Secretary of the Treasury. Most San Francisco bankers and bullion dealers *publicly* opposed the Bland bill as a threat to specie resumption. San Francisco *Chronicle,* Oct. 20, 1877; New York *Tribune,* Feb. 18, 1876.

52. San Francisco *Chronicle,* May 23, 1878, "Mining Stock News."

worth of 5 and 4.5 percent bonds, while Flood owned an additional $3,750,000 worth of resumption bonds as a personal investment.[53] Thus, if the Bonanza Kings sponsored the drive to remonetize silver, as many gold standard advocates charged, they did so at the risk of having $22,000,000 worth of government bonds repaid, principal and interest, in depreciated legal tender silver coinage after having acquired the bonds at their face value in gold or its full equivalent in silver bullion.

The charge raised by various gold standard newspapers that the Bonanza firm contributed a half-million dollar fund to secure passage of the Bland bill in the Senate is insupportable. Indeed, if the Nevada Bank ever contributed to the drive for remonetization, the money probably came fresh from the Treasury's own vaults, since the director of the mint continued making large-scale purchases of silver from the Bonanza Kings in the months preceding passage of the Bland-Allison Act. Linderman had warned Sherman in August 1877, when recommending an earlier transaction with the firm, that "if Congress should authorize the coinage of a silver dollar on a considerable scale I should expect the price of silver to advance probably three cents per ounce, possibly more."[54] This prediction proved accurate. With-

53. United States bonds held by the Bonanza Kings in various forms by December 1877 included the following amounts:

Bonds registered in the name of (total):	Total amount	Interest paid
John W. Mackay (for Nevada Bank)	$ 4,000,000	5%
Louis McLane (for Nevada Bank)	9,328,650	5%
James C. Flood (private?)	3,750,000	5%
James C. Flood (for Nevada Bank?)	5,000,000	4.5%
Total Bonds Held	$22,078,650	

Ledgerbooks, 4.5 and 5 percent funded loans, Bureau of the Public Debt, NA, RG 53.

54. Linderman to Louis McLane, Jan. 28, 1878; Linderman to Nevada Bank, Jan. 28, 1878, DM Lbks; *Recordbook,* Silver Purchases, Linderman to McLane, Dec. 8, 1877, Linderman to Sherman, Aug. 3, 1877, Sherman MSS, LC.

in a few days after congressional passage of the Bland-Allison Act in February 1878, the mint director purchased one million ounces of silver from the Nevada Bank at $1.205 an ounce or 2.5 cents more than the Bank's January price for the bullion.[55]

The Nevada Bank's February 1878 sale concluded an important chapter in Treasury silver purchase policy which began with the first substantial bullion sales by the Bonanza firm to the government following passage of the Resumption Act of January 1875. For thirty-eight months, from the passage of the Specie Resumption Act to final approval of the Bland-Allison Act, the United States Mint served as the largest and most faithful customer for silver produced in the Bonanza Kings' Nevada mines. The four "Lords of the Comstock" could hardly have pressed for remonetization in order to provide an adequate government market for their bullion, since they had enjoyed such an unchallenged market since 1875 with the enthusiastic cooperation of the director of the mint. The Bonanza Kings dominated the government's silver purchase program from 1875 to 1878, and the Nevada Bank, along with other firms controlled by the four Silver Kings, sold over half of the 31,600,000 ounces of silver acquired by the mint in the thirty-eight months between the passage of the Specie Resumption Act and final approval of the Bland-Allison Act.[56] Throughout the remonetization drive

55. Linderman to Nevada Bank, Feb. 22, 1878; Memorandum of the Director of the Mint to the Secretary of the Treasury regarding proposed silver purchases, Feb. 25, 1878; Linderman to McLane, Feb. 25, 1878; Linderman to Superintendent, Carson Mint, Feb. 26, 1878, DM Lbks.

56. "The total amount of silver bullion purchased by the government for coinage into fractional coins from January 1875 to February 28, 1878, at which time this coinage was intermitted, was 31,603,905.87 fine ounces, for which $37,517,148.04 was paid in gold coin, an average of 118,881 cents per ounce fine." Director of the Mint, *Annual Report, 1878* (Washington, 1878), p. 7. During this same period, the government purchased at least twenty-one million dollars worth of silver from the Nevada Bank and other Bonanza firm companies. *Recordbook,*

they enjoyed a close and profitable relationship with the Treasury Department, seldom finding it difficult to dispose of their bullion at satisfactory prices, either to the government or in foreign commerce.

On almost every economic policy question which concerned the Bonanza firm, James Flood directed the activities and decisions of the four partners, and there is striking evidence that the San Francisco stockbroker did not believe that the Bonanza firm's future lay in continued operation of its Nevada mines.[57] Flood made every effort beginning in 1876 to diversify the firm's investments, using a substantial portion of its profits to purchase San Francisco real estate and government bonds while at the same time even speculating against Bonanza stock on the San Francisco Exchange Board.[58] The Nevada Bank of San Francisco, opened by the Bonanza Kings in October 1875, became the major vehicle of Flood's efforts to diversify the firm's investments. The Bank opened for business with a paid-in capital of five million dollars in gold belonging to the four partners, which they increased to ten million dollars in 1876. To raise the

---

Silver Purchases, U. S. Mint, NA, RG 104. For a detailed record of government silver purchases from the Bonanza Kings during this period, see Appendix V.

57. Upshur, *As I Recall Them,* p. 84. Upshur, later an important New York banker and associate of J. P. Morgan, worked for the Nevada Bank from 1876 to 1880, serving as general manager of the Bonanza firm. See also King, *History of the San Francisco Stock and Exchange Board,* pp. 96, 105, 213; Lewis, *Silver Kings,* pp. 149–50, 157–58, 256–57.

58. On the Bonanza firm's efforts to diversify its investments and to transform the Nevada Bank from a clearing house for Bonanza bullion into a financial institution performing wider speculative and brokerage functions, see the following: Smith "History of the Comstock Lode," pp. 203ff; *Banker's Magazine,* Supplement, Dec. 1876, p. 9, and June, 1877, p. 991; Benjamin C. Wright, *Banking in California, 1849–1910* (San Francisco, 1910), pp. 52–53; Upshur, *As I Recall Them,* p. 103; San Francisco *Chronicle,* May 23, 1877; Myron Angel, ed., *History of Nevada* (Oakland, Cal., 1881), p. 595.

original five million in gold Flood sold Consolidated Virginia and California Mining Company shares secretly on the open market in San Francisco, disposing of a substantial amount of this Bonanza stock in the process.[59]

His unloading of Bonanza firm securities, however silent, did not pass unnoticed among the shrewder and more suspicious San Francisco brokers. Sharp speculators saw Flood's hand behind the large public sales of Consolidated Virginia and California stock made in 1876 and 1877, although they had no means of proving it. Grant Smith, the historian of the Comstock Lode, however, traced carefully the Bonanza firm's deliberate attempt to dump substantial amounts of their mining stock beginning in 1876:

> [By the Spring of 1876] the termination of the bonanza at the 1650-foot level, coupled with the continued criticisms [from San Francisco opponents of the Bonanza firm like the *Chronicle*], apparently caused the members of the Firm to lose all interest in bonanza stocks, except to unload more of their holdings, and the stocks drifted downward as the ore became depleted and the dividends grew smaller and smaller. They retained control of the mines, however, with the aid of their friends, and continued the search for another bonanza on level after level down to the 2,900.[60]

With their two producing mines becoming exhausted rapidly by 1876 and stock prices beginning a sharp decline on the San Francisco Exchange, Flood led his partners in searching for newer and more stable fortunes than those secured through silver mining and mining stock speculation. The Bonanza firm began to invest heavily in government bonds and real estate and to expand the banking functions of the Nevada Bank—hiring the

59. Upshur, *As I Recall Them*, pp. 111–12. See also "Biographical sketch of James Clair Flood," typescript, Hubert Howe Bancroft Collection, Bancroft Library.

60. Smith, "History of the Comstock Lode," pp. 199, 209.

respected president of Wells Fargo Express Company, Louis McLane, to serve as president of the bank. Of the four Silver Kings only James Fair remained hopeful of finding new and equally rich ore strikes in the late 1870s. Even in Fair's case, "well before the decade ended he, too, had reconciled himself to the inevitable and begun casting about for new fields of endeavor."[61] Did the Bonanza Kings, then, sponsor and finance a campaign to remonetize silver while at the same time reducing their mining investments as rapidly as possible?

The Nevada Bank's unsuccessful attempt in 1877 to join the resumption bond syndicate and to expand its government securities' portfolio symbolized the Bonanza firm's new concentration on banking, bond purchases, brokerage, and real estate operations. The Comstock heyday of the four mining kings had ended, as Flood and O'Brien recognized first, then Mackay, and finally Fair. Before the close of the decade, Flood's business career centered around the banking operations of the Nevada Bank. Mackay acquired "important real estate holdings in San Francisco and elsewhere in the West, became a director of the Southern Pacific [and developed] interests, as time went on [which] became less concerned with the region from which he had drawn his fortune."[62] The third surviving partner, James Fair, was elected to the United States Senate in 1879. Fair also invested heavily in both government and private securities. William Shoney O'Brien died in 1878.

By 1880 it had become rare for the surviving Bonanza Kings to speculate as a firm. On most occasions, the three old partners invested separately and moved into different fields. The original source of wealth, the California and Consolidated Virginia Mining Companies, paid final dividends in 1879 and 1880, by which time the trio of mining kings had already become important bankers, real estate promoters, government bondholders, and pri-

61. Lewis, Silver Kings, pp. 165–66.
62. Smith, "History of the Comstock Lode," p. 262.

vate speculators.[63] When John Percival Jones first raised the silver issue in Congress in 1876, they had already begun detaching themselves from the economic and political concerns of less affluent Comstock mineowners. Although the largest holders of silver in the entire country, the Bonanza Kings neither needed nor supported the Bland Bill, since they already possessed a secure government market for their available bullion through the subsidiary coinage provision of the 1875 Resumption Act. The Lords of the Comstock turned their money and attention instead to new investment projects, leaving "the silver question" to be settled by that small group of politicians and publicists who had raised it in the first place.

63. Ibid. The death of William Shoney O'Brien in 1878 left Flood in sole command of the Bonanza firm's San Francisco business affairs.

7

The First Battle: The 1876 Campaign and the Electoral Crisis

The people who held the time bonds we had given,
Determined to strengthen and tighten their hold;
A Congress, by bondholders hastily driven,
Declared that our coin should be nothing but gold.
Columbia then proved a very apt scholar,
Obeying at once the bondholder's command,
And blindly abandoned the old silver dollar,
The cherished old dollar that chinked in the hand—
The old silver dollar, the honest old dollar,
Our forefathers' dollar, that chinked in the hand.

Carl Brent, "The Old Silver Dollar,"
Cincinnati *Commercial, August 10, 1876*

During the 1876 presidential contest the major parties said nothing on the thorny issue of remonetization in their campaign platforms, and both the Republican and Democratic candidates failed to mention the problem in their letters of acceptance. Neither Rutherford B. Hayes nor Samuel J. Tilden wished to aggravate further the festering divisions of opinion on financial matters within his own party.

The Republican National Convention, meeting at Cincinnati on June 14, nominated Hayes of Ohio as their standard bearer, an outspoken foe of monetary inflation who had won the Ohio governorship the previous year in a campaign that centered on his endorsement of the party's 1875 Resumption Act.[1] The 1876 Republican platform, nevertheless, was deliberately vague on national finance, promising only "continuous and steady progress to specie payment" but avoiding a direct statement approving the previous year's resumption measure.[2] "This plank practically rules the hard-money issue out of the canvass," the New York *Graphic* predicted, "for the Democrats cannot agree to any plank that requires less in that direction."[3]

Hayes found himself caught in a crossfire of political pressures to strengthen in his letter of acceptance the convention's inoffensive currency resolution, but he preferred not to reopen old party wounds over resumption policy nor to provoke a fresh battle among Republicans over silver policy. "I am advised to harden by some, and to soften by others, the money plan, and so on," he wrote John Sherman. "Perhaps I would do well to approve it as it stands . . . My inclination is to say very little."[4] Thus, in his letter of acceptance, he did not endorse the 1875 act directly. Instead, he expressed personal support for a quick return to specie payments in somewhat more precise terms than the platform had done, using a draft prepared by reformer Carl Schurz as the basis of his remarks.[5]

The Democrats also decided not to discuss the monetary

1. Irwin Unger, "Business and Currency in the Ohio Gubernatorial Campaign of 1875," *Mid-America, An Historical Review,* vol. 41 (1959).

2. Edward McPherson, *A Handbook of Politics for 1876* (Washington, 1876), pp. 210–11.

3. New York *Graphic,* June 16, 1876.

4. R. B. Hayes to John Sherman, June 23, 1876, in Charles Richard Williams. ed., *Diary and Letters of Rutherford Birchard Hayes, Nineteenth President of the United States* (Columbus, Ohio, 1924), *3,* 328. See also Carl Schurz to R. B. Hayes on the following 1876 dates: June 21, June 25 and July 5, Schurz MSS, LC; also E. D. Morgan to Hayes, June 21 and 27, 1876; William D. Kelley to Hayes, Aug. 2, 1876; John Sherman to Hayes, June 26, 1876, Hayes MSS, Fremont.

5. Compare Schurz' draft, in Schurz to Hayes, July 5, 1876, Schurz MSS, with Hayes' remarks on currency in his letter of acceptance, July 8, 1876, in McPherson, *A Handbook of Politics,* pp. 212–13.

standard question at their St. Louis national convention in June 1876. After a bitter floor battle over financial policy, an overwhelming majority of delegates rejected a minority report that called for repeal of the entire 1875 Resumption Act, a report prepared by the party's leading midwestern inflationists, Thomas Ewing of Ohio and Daniel W. Voorhees of Indiana. Instead, the Democrats adopted a more general statement denouncing the Republican party for "financial imbecility and immorality" in failing to advance toward resumption during the previous eleven years. The resolution went on, however, to demand only repeal of the resumption-day clause in the 1875 measure. This compromise pronouncement both surprised and delighted eastern Democrats, who had not anticipated their triumph first in emasculating the inflationists' monetary plank and then in securing the presidential nomination for a strong hard-money resumptionist, Governor Samuel J. Tilden of New York. To placate the party's midwestern wing, the convention nominated as Tilden's running mate, Senator Thomas Hendricks of Indiana, an ardent soft-money inflationist.[6]

The two running mates disagreed on almost every aspect of financial policy. Tilden's letter of acceptance contained a ringing endorsement of sound money aims and a detailed program for securing a swift return to specie payments, while Hendricks' letter bitterly criticized the Resumption Act and cautioned against contracting the existing supply of greenbacks in order to resume specie payments.[7] This conflict in financial views between the two Democratic nominees amused political enemies and troubled supporters, because it exposed publicly the basic tensions that existed between the eastern and midwestern wings of the party.[8] Also, Hendricks' endorsement of "gold and silver" as "the real standard of values" suggested official Democratic en-

6. Unger, *Greenback Era,* pp. 309–10; McPherson, *Handbook of Politics,* pp. 214–17.

7. McPherson, *Handbook of Politics,* pp. 217–24.

8. Chicago *Evening Journal,* n.d., cited in Cincinnati *Commercial,* Aug. 7, 1876.

dorsement of remonetization while Tilden explicitly approved retaining the gold standard.[9]

Reformers in both parties, who had fought for over a decade to secure a return to specie payments, felt particularly pleased with the outcome of the two major party conventions. "It looks now as though we are already victorious," Isaac Sherman wrote David A. Wells, "[and] that we have captured the candidates of both parties and that we are destined to have a good honest hard money president unless Peter Cooper shall be elected."[10] Only the small Greenback party, which had nominated Cooper, the aging New York ironmaster, disturbed the sleep of hard money men during the campaign of 1876.

Meeting at Indianapolis on May 17, the Greenback convention renewed its earlier party demands for an "immediate and unconditional repeal of the specie resumption act," government issue of an "interconvertible bond" drawing a low yearly 3.65 percent interest rate, and the immediate halt to foreign sale of government bonds payable in gold. The Greenbackers also adopted a resolution condemning the section of the Resumption Act which substituted subsidiary silver coins for fractional greenbacks. The Indianapolis convention then denounced the practice of selling government securities in order to purchase silver bullion, a method stipulated under the 1875 act, as imposing additional taxation on "an already over-burdened people."[11]

9. "The two candidates are diametrically opposed to each other upon what is to-day the most vital issue of American finance." Ibid. See also McPherson, *Handbook of Politics,* pp. 222–23, for Hendricks' financial statement; also see Cincinnati *Commercial,* June 29, 1876. The Eastern hard-money wing of the Democratic Party felt particularly satisfied with the St. Louis platform and with Tilden's nomination (Unger, *Greenback Era,* pp. 309–10). See also Durbin Ward to David A. Wells, July 10, 1876; Henry Adams to Wells, July 15, 1876; Isaac Sherman to Wells, July 16, 1876, Wells MSS, LC.

10. Sherman to Wells. See also Adams to Wells, Wells MSS, LC.

11. For the Greenback Party platform and Peter Cooper's letter of acceptance, see McPherson, *Handbook of Politics,* pp. 224–25. The best description of the Greenback convention is in Unger, *Greenback Era,* pp. 306–08.

The platform called these bullion purchases "well calculated to enrich owners of silver mines," a charge also raised by gold standard Democrats like Abram Hewitt, who had denounced the purchases in similar terms during House debate.

With their convention already on record as opposed to issuing more subsidiary silver coins, the delegates were caught completely unprepared for a Michigan Greenbacker's proposal that the meeting endorse "the payment of . . . coin obligations in either gold or silver at the option of the government."[12] Although John Percival Jones and Lewis Bogy had raised the remonetization question in Congress weeks before its May 17 convention, few rank and file Greenbackers had considered carefully the response which their party should make toward the new financial movement. At the beginning of the silver drive in 1876, public support for restoration of the double standard came mainly from hard money expansionists who opposed additional issues of greenbacks and who, unlike the inflationists, favored a swift return to specie payments. After an initial period of confusion, the Greenback convention tabled the motion to support remonetization and returned to the subject only after completing its nominations for national office. "By this time, the delegates, or at least their leaders, had been briefed on the significance of the silver question, and the motion [making the old silver dollar a legal tender] carried."[13] Whether by accident or design, however, the official published text of the 1876 national Greenback party convention failed even to include the belatedly passed remonetization plank. Many of the delegates undoubtedly recognized the incongruity of condemning an increase in subsidiary silver coins while, at the same time, demanding full restoration of silver as a monetary standard!

Few Greenbackers developed an attachment to silver in subsequent years comparable to their devotion to paper money, and most of those who raised the issue of bimetallism during the

12. St. Paul (Minn.) *Anti-Monopolist,* Aug. 24, 1876, cited in Unger, *Greenback Era,* p. 307.

13. Ibid., McPherson, *Handbook of Politics,* p. 224.

1876 campaign did so for tactical reasons, having recognized the growing strength of public support for silver at a time when both major parties tried to avoid the question. "In the West, burdened with a sound money national platform [the Republicans], ran from the currency issue."[14] The Greenbackers were under no similar restraints, and throughout the summer of 1876, their local and state conventions in Indiana, Ohio, Missouri, and elsewhere denounced the demonetization of silver and demanded an immediate return to the double standard.[15]

Most Greenbackers recognized the shallowness of this sudden conversion to bimetallism and saw their stand on silver as a secondary issue, unimportant compared to their basic fight for a paper monetary standard geared to a commodity price index. Once adopted, the precious metals would become only two of many products in this index. Few third-party members expected to inflate the currency adequately through remonetizing silver, believing that only temporary relief from the existing shortage of currency was possible by this means. The Indianapolis *Sun,* for example, one of the leading midwestern Greenback dailies, ridiculed the "erroneous" idea "that we, in any sense, abandon the greenback by urging that full legal-tender powers be conferred upon the silver coins." The two currency movements "in no sense conflict," the *Sun* insisted, since the "people are compelled to use what they have and can get until they can get the better that they want."[16]

The remonetization issue remained a minor one, however, even for inflationists during the 1876 political campaign. Be-

14. Unger, *Greenback Era,* p. 316.

15. See, for example, the descriptions of Greenback conventions in all these states in the Cincinnati *Commercial,* which monitored the third party's financial arguments closely in order to distinguish its own hard-money silverite views from those of the Greenbackers. *Commercial* for the following 1876 dates: July 15, July 26, July 28, Aug. 18, Sept. 7.

16. Indianapolis *Sun,* Oct. 14, 1876. See also Ridge, *Ignatius Donnelly,* pp. 172–73. For a different interpretation of Greenback response to the silver movement, see Unger, *Greenback Era,* pp. 332–33.

fore the Indianapolis national convention, no state or local Greenback slate had proposed returning to bimetallism, and Peter Cooper's letter accepting the party's presidential nomination never mentioned the subject.[17] Although Samuel F. Cary, the party's vice-presidential choice, spoke repeatedly on the silver issue in the Midwest, where several state Greenback conventions eventually endorsed remonetization, inflationists in the Midwest and South directed most of their fire at the 1875 Resumption Act.[18] For every Greenback speaker demanding "restoration" of silver, there were hundreds who called for "repeal" of the Resumption Act and, as the movement's most recent historian observed, "to the end of the decade and beyond, third-party politics remained tied to greenbacks, with silver a mere adjunct."[19]

Only in California, Nevada, and Ohio did state conventions of either major party endorse remonetization during the 1876 campaign, and with the exception of the two mining states, both adversely affected by the existing market slump in world silver prices, only the inflationist Ohio Democratic party supported restoration of legal bimetallism in its 1876 platform. In the latter state, Democrats voted at their convention to accept a platform committee minority report that called both for restoration of the double standard and for repeal of the Resumption Act, although it is probable that supporters of repeal far outnumbered silverites at the meeting. A number of Democratic and Republican state parties endorsed resumption of specie payments "in coin," or called, in equally vague terms, for "gold and silver . . . the money of the Constitution." Such declarations were practically meaningless, however, as an index of the party's

17. See, for example, the Wisconsin Greenback convention, which met on May 10, a week before the Indianapolis national gathering. The Wisconsin Greenbackers called for immediate repeal of the Resumption Act without raising the silver question at all. *Appleton's Annual Cyclopedia for 1876* (New York, 1877), p. 808.

18. For Cary's role in the campaign, see Unger, *Greenback Era*, p. 344.

19. Ibid., p. 333.

later views on the monetary standard issue.[20] In Iowa, for example, the congressional delegation voted solidly for the Bland-Allison Act in 1878, even though both major parties had endorsed the gold standard in 1876.

Only in Ohio did the issue receive sustained and careful attention from politicians during the Hayes-Tilden contest. The state's Republicans, pressured first by Sam Cary's vigorous canvass for the Greenback ticket and next by the Buckeye Democratic convention's endorsement of remonetization, found themselves constantly forced to define and defend their party's future intentions toward silver.[21] "The [Republican] campaign orators all promised the silver dollar if Hayes was elected," wrote Benjamin F. Butler, who stumped the state for the Hayes-Wheeler ticket.[22] By July 1876, Republican county conventions in the state began demanding restoration of the double standard. "How palpably unjust it would be," remarked one Ohio Republican, "to insist upon *wheat* in payment for a debt contracted at a time when the currency of the country was *bi-cereal* . . . To say we mean *gold* when we say *coin*—as well say we mean *wheat* when we say *grain*."[23]

Among the Republican candidates and speakers who traveled through the state demanding either remonetization or, more ambiguously, who called for restoration of specie payments in

20. For the party platforms, see the state entries in *Appleton's Annual Cyclopedia for 1876,* passim. Among the Republican state parties supporting a return to "coin" or "gold and silver" payments were those in Indiana, Kentucky, Missouri, Nebraska and New Hampshire. Democratic parties adopting similarly vague and mild language on the issue included those from Connecticut, Kentucky, Maine, Delaware, Indiana, Minnesota, New Hampshire, Pennsylvania and Vermont.

21. For Cary's activities in Ohio, see the Cincinnati *Commercial,* July 15, 1876, and Unger, *Greenback Era,* p. 344.

22. Benjamin F. Butler to A. C. Story, Jan. 24, 1878, Butler MSS, LC.

23. Cincinnati *Commercial,* July 15, 1876. On the county conventions which endorsed silver, see Pittsburgh *Telegraph,* July 26, 1876. For Ohio hard-money Democratic silverite opinion, see Durbin Ward to David A. Wells, July 10, 1876, Wells MSS, LC.

"gold and silver" were James G. Blaine, Benjamin F. Butler, John Sherman's close political associate C. W. Moulton, Cincinnati businessman William S. Groesbeck, a member of the congressional Monetary Commission, and Hayes' old friend Stanley Matthews.[24] Jacob Dolson Cox, who later became the state's leading Republican supporter of the Bland bill, refused either to recommend or to denounce the double standard during his campaign for a House seat, while John Sherman enjoyed pointing out to Ohio voters that he had sponsored the first 1876 bill to restore the old domestic silver dollar. Sherman generally neglected to distinguish between his support for *limited* remonetization and demands by other Senators for a *complete* return to free coinage of gold and silver. "I was the first to propose its recoinage," he declared to a hometown Mansfield audience, adding a vague promise that the Republican party would make provision for "the silver dollar as an agency of resumption" following the election.[25]

On other occasions during the campaign, Sherman repeated his pledge that the silver question would be settled as soon as Congress convened after the election. Declaring himself a friend of silver coinage in a Marietta speech, he reminded his listeners that Senate Republicans themselves remained divided on the question: "We could have agreed upon recoining the old silver dollar; but whether it ought to be received for customs dues, now payable in gold, or paid out for interest on the public debt, we could not agree."[26] The cautious Sherman refused tactfully to state his own position on these disputed points until the congressional Monetary Commission had presented its report *after*

24. Cincinnati *Commercial* on the following 1876 dates: Aug. 4 (Groesbeck), Aug. 10 (Moulton), Aug. 31 (Butler), Sept. 27 (Matthews) and Oct. 1 (Blaine).

25. See, for example, Sherman's major speeches at Marietta (Ohio) on Aug. 12 and Mansfield (Ohio) on Aug. 16. Cincinnati *Commercial*, Aug. 14 and 29, 1876, where the texts of both speeches are reprinted.

26. Ibid., Aug. 14, 1876.

the election, and his fence-straddling posture on the question became popular among Republican orators during the campaign in Ohio.[27]

Of the state's leading politicians, only James A. Garfield was singled out for attack by silverites, both within his own Western Reserve district and elsewhere. The Cincinnati *Commercial* reminded its readers constantly that Garfield had led House Republican opposition to recoinage of the silver dollar at the recent session of Congress.[28] So virulent did Halstead's attacks on his fellow-Republican Garfield become that Hayes himself wrote a "short, decisive note" to the Cincinnati editor "suggesting that [he] should throw his force into the main issue, [the threat of] a united South to control the Country."[29] Halstead, however, persisted in denouncing the congressman. After Garfield won reelection handily, the *Commercial* acknowledged afterward that its assault on the legislator for his views on silver coinage had been doomed from the start "if for no other reason than no man in the present state of the case knew enough about it to make it an issue intelligently."[30]

In neighboring midwestern states silver received much less attention from campaign orators during the 1876 presidential contest than in Ohio. Only in Indiana did both Republican and Democratic speakers mention the issue, with the Democrats coming out squarely in favor of remonetization while Oliver P. Morton's soft money Republicans preferred expanding the

27. Stanley Matthews, for example, simply quoted Sherman's Marietta speech directly—without further comment—as representing his own views on finance. Ibid., Sept. 27, 1876.

28. See especially the *Commercial's* interview with Garfield, Aug, 25, 1876, and its Sept. 23 editorial. See also the Ashtabula (Ohio) *News,* Aug. 2, 1876, in Garfield Scrapbooks, Garfield Family MSS, LC.

29. Quoted in Garfield Diary, entry for Sept. 18, 1876.

30. Ashtabula (O.) *News,* Sept, 26, 1876, Garfield Scrapbooks. For a carefully argued defense of Garfield's views on remonetization, see James A. Garfield to J. A. Howells, Aug. 11, 1876, Garfield Letterbooks.

greenback supply to restoring the "dollar of the daddies." Both major parties in Indiana blamed each other for having demonetized silver in the first place, and almost all of the state's leading politicians promised swift action following the election to secure passage of a bill restoring legal bimetallism.[31] Other than the Greenbackers, most midwestern politicians tried to avoid discussing financial issues, and only in Ohio and Indiana did the silver question generate any significant amount of interest during the Hayes-Tilden contest.[32] This lack of concern may have stemmed partly from the fact that national party platforms had been written in June, before congressional debates over silver had filtered down into state and local political discussion. "The fact that [the people] do not yet fully understand the vast importance of the silver question," one silverite paper remarked, "sufficiently explains why the platforms are silent in regard to it."[33]

Yet had the platforms been written in August, probably neither major party would have ventured an opinion on remonetization even then, because of their unwillingness to stir up fresh intraparty conflict over disputed financial questions in the midst of the presidential canvass. Silverites, after all, held a comfortable majority in the House favorable to restoring bimetallism, and, as John Sherman himself acknowledged in August 1876,

31. On the Indiana campaign, see the Cincinnati *Commercial* on the following 1876 dates: Aug. 12, Aug. 25, Aug. 28 and Sept. 13. Republicans Carl Schurz and Oliver P. Morton hardly mentioned the issue in their Indiana speeches, while Democratic campaigners like gubernatorial candidate James D. ("Blue Jeans") Williams harped on Republican obstruction of Democratic efforts to pass the Bland bill at the previous session of Congress. See also Carl Schurz to R. B. Hayes, Oct. 6, 1876, typescript, Hayes MSS, Fremont.

32. R. B. Hayes to Charles E. Smith, Sept. 28, 1876, Hayes MSS, Fremont. See also D. Strange to David A. Wells, Oct. 4, 1876, Wells MSS, LC.

33. Unidentified pro-silver Ohio newspaper, n.d. (ca. Sept. 1876), in Garfield Scrapbooks.

"a decided majority of *both* Houses [at the session just ended] were in favor of this policy."[34] Agitating the issue during the 1876 campaign hardly appeared necessary to many supporters of remonetization given their apparent control of the national legislature. The only remaining uncertainty for a number of silverites involved the attitude of the new president toward their impending congressional victory; that is, "whether Mr. Hayes or Mr. Tilden would veto a bill for the restoration of the monetary *status quo ante bellum*."[35] Neither candidate was forced to make his decision during the presidential contest. Instead, Democrats stressed their long-standing charges of radical Republican misrule in the South and corruption in Washington, while Republicans in all sections waved the bloody shirt furiously and branded the Democrats once more as the party of rebellion. Remonetization attracted little public notice in any section during the election of 1876, since neither the program nor the symbolism associated with silver had yet produced a self-conscious movement, except among that small number of Americans with special knowledge or interest in the monetary standard question. A broader campaign to remonetize silver evolved only in 1877, since the intervening electoral crisis prevented final disposition of the question until after the new administration had taken office.

The lame duck session of the Forty-Fourth Congress, which stretched from November 1876 to the inauguration of Rutherford B. Hayes in March 1877, concerned itself almost exclusively with resolving the electoral crisis.[36] It seemed an unlikely setting in which to dispose of the silver question, and yet the monetary standard issue received a surprising amount of attention during the stormy legislative session, with silverites in the House passing another remonetization measure by an even larger majority than in the previous session. Richard Bland hoped to

34. Cincinnati *Commercial,* Aug. 14, 1876.
35. Ibid., Sept. 15, 1876.
36. Woodward, *Reunion and Reaction,* passim.

complete congressional action on remonetization before the new administration took office. He led an aggressive, predominantly Democratic, band of bimetallists in securing House agreement to his silver bill, restoring the old 412.5 grain silver dollar as a unit of account, only to watch the Senate again delay consideration of the measure until the new Forty-Fifth Congress met late in 1877.[37] Despite the dilatory tactics of Senate opponents, however, support for an amended version of the House silver bill began developing in the upper chamber even during the electoral crisis. Most of the major elements in the later Senate compromise measure emerged during this period, months before political agitation of the silver question during the fall 1877 elections alerted public opinion to the controversy. The new president's intentions regarding silver legislation remained unclear during the electoral crisis, but few politicians questioned the ability of bimetallists to pass another House version of the Bland bill in the approaching Forty-Fifth Congress and to commit the Senate to an acceptable compromise measure. A large majority in both houses of Congress clearly favored some form of remonetization by late 1876, if only to dispose of the issue. Ironically, months before a widespread silver movement had emerged in the country, the outlines of a settlement on the issue had emerged in Congress, and only the more pressing task of selecting a new chief executive prevented silver's being restored in the closing months of the Grant administration.

Soon after the House convened in December 1876, Bland resumed his earlier demand for immediate consideration of his remonetization measure, H. R. 3635, that had been shunted aside in the rush to adjourn before the presidential election. Bland introduced a substitute for this earlier bill on December 12, H. R. 4189, which eliminated its most inflationary provision, the system of silver notes to be issued in exchange for bullion deposited at the mints, a plan criticized widely by opponents

37. *Cong. Record,* 44th Cong., 2d sess., vol. 5, pt. 1, p. 172.

of remonetization because it provided mineowners with an artificially high mint price for their silver well above existing world market rates. The Missouri Democrat now called only for restoration of the 412.5 grain standard silver dollar as "a legal tender for all debts public and private, except where payment of gold coin is required by law."[38] This new December 1876 bill was substantially the same as "Pig-Iron" Kelley's earlier proposal, which had come close to receiving a two-thirds House majority in July.

House silverites revealed a desire for swift action on the question in December that they had lacked six months earlier. When a few eastern bimetallists like S. S. Cox of New York chided Bland for demanding immediate passage of the bill and suggested instead that the Missouri Democrat await the Monetary Commission's report before taking action, especially since Bland was a member of that group, Bland exploded. His outburst exposed the annoyance felt by many House silverites at the delaying tactics of their opponents. "To talk of a necessity for further discussion of a measure that has been discussed for nearly a year in the public press, and upon the hustings and everywhere else," Bland admonished Cox, "is simply a subterfuge and can be intended only to defeat this bill." As for the Monetary Commission, "I believe the only design of raising that commission was to defeat the passage of this bill. In my opinion that fact should not govern our action here." Bland then succeeded in placing his bill on the December 13 House calendar, at which time its advocates and opponents spoke for several hours on the subject, the longest House debate prior to passage of any remonetization measure during the entire silver drive.[39]

Both sides repeated arguments outlined in earlier House debates, although the silverites, aware of their numerical superiority, appeared almost indifferent during the discussion to any specific *economic* advantages that would flow from remonetiza-

38. Ibid., p. 142.
39. Ibid., pp. 150, 163–72.

tion. Instead, bipartisan supporters of the Bland bill—among them Republicans Kelley, Fort, and Cannon along with Democrats Durham and Holman—stressed the *moral* significance of their actions. "The absolute justice of this measure is too manifest for dispute," Holman exclaimed in words echoed by the other silverites. Opponents of the Bland bill also soft-pedaled their economic motives for opposing restoration of silver as a full monetary standard and requested only that the House postpone action until after the Monetary Commission's report had been received. "I plead for time, I plead for knowledge, I plead for information," cried Democrat Abram H. Hewitt, while James A. Garfield observed caustically of the silverite steamroller: "it is proposed, in the hot haste of a two hours' debate, under the tyranny of the previous question . . . in this Chamber that we settle this worldwide question and determine it today." Republican John A. Kasson of Iowa and Democrat Simeon B. Chittenden of New York vainly seconded Garfield's remarks, but after the two hour debate had run its predictable course, the House adopted Bland's substitute bill by a 167 to 53 margin (see Table 4).[40]

The electoral crisis itself had a significant impact on the tally, as party lines hardened still further on the issue. Fifty-six Democrats who now voted for their colleague Bland's silver bill had not supported William D. Kelley's identical measure in July. Included in their number were not only twenty-six southerners, from an area strongly favorable to restoring the double standard, but more significantly fourteen northeastern Democrats from New York, New Jersey, and Pennsylvania, five of whom had actually voted against the Kelley proposal. Only eight Democrats, half of them from the northeast, shifted from endorsement of remonetization in July 1876 to opposition by December. Silverites also picked up seventeen additional Republican votes from all sections, five from the northeast, indicating a probable

40. Ibid., pp. 167–72; Haswell, "The Public Life of Congressman R. P. Bland," pp. 65–66.

Table 4

Vote on the Bland Bill (Remonetizing Silver), House of Representatives, December 13, 1876

	Ayes			Nays		
	Rep.	Dem.	Ind.	Rep.	Dem.	Ind.
New England States						
Massachusetts				3	2	1
Maine				5		
New Hampshire				1	2	
Vermont				1		
Connecticut		1		1		
Rhode Island				2		
TOTALS		1		13	4	1
Middle Atlantic States						
New York	4	3		10	5	
Pennsylvania	2	11		5	1	
Maryland		4			1	
Delaware						
New Jersey		4		1		
TOTALS	6	22		16	7	
Midwestern States						
Ohio	4	10		1	1	
Illinois	5	8	1			
Indiana	4	7				
Wisconsin	5	2	1			
Minnesota	1					
Michigan	5				1	1
Iowa	6		1	1		
Kansas	2					
Nebraska	1					
TOTALS	33	27	3	2	2	1
Border States						
Kentucky	1	7				
Tennessee	1	8				
West Virginia		3				
Missouri		10			1	
TOTALS	2	28			1	

Table 4—Continued

	Ayes			Nays		
	Rep.	Dem.	Ind.	Rep.	Dem.	Ind.
Southern States						
Virginia	1	6				
North Carolina		7				
South Carolina						
Georgia		6			1	
Alabama		6		1		
Mississippi	1	4		1		
Florida		1				
Louisiana		2		1	2	
Texas		5				
Arkansas		2				
TOTALS	2	39		3	3	
Far Western States						
California	1	2				
Nevada						
Colorado						
Oregon		1				
TOTALS	1	3				
GRAND TOTALS	44	120	3	34	17	2

TOTAL AYES: 167

TOTAL NAYS: 53

increase in public support for remonetization during the intervening months, since eight of the seventeen had opposed the Kelley bill. Finally, of the eleven Republicans who had voted for the earlier measure but now opposed the Bland bill, eight came from northeastern constituencies where gold standard sentiment had begun to dominate public discussion. Despite a substantial degree of support from House Republicans, therefore, the Bland bill passed easily in December 1876 because it received overwhelming support from the lower chamber's Democratic majority, and the measure sent to the Senate bore the decided stamp of Democratic party endorsement.[41] Although Republicans narrowly approved the Bland bill by a 44 to 34 tally, Democrats piled up a remarkable 120 to 17 majority for the legislation.

House passage of the silver bill left the supporters of remonetization understandably elated and its opponents equally dispirited. Halstead's *Commercial*, for example, called the measure "imperfect" only because it did not contain a provision for redeeming greenbacks in exchange for silver issued, since "the silver dollar will not float on a sea of legal-tender paper." Otherwise, Halstead considered the House bill "precisely right," and agreed with Bland that "the country need not wait for the silver commission to understand the leading and controlling facts in the silver question."[42] The Baltimore *Sun*, on the other hand, voiced the sentiments of many gold standard advocates when it criticized the House for not having delayed considering the measure until after the commission had submitted its findings. The *Sun* denounced the Bland bill for its possibly harmful effect on government credit, especially its impact on "the successful negotiation hereafter of United States bonds abroad."[43]

Unlike the House, the Senate showed little disposition to tackle the monetary standard problem at a time when it was still struggling with the question of presidential succession. Even

41. A breakdown by section of those voting for or against the Bland bill in December 1876 who either refrained from voting on the Kelley measure in July or changed their votes in December reveals the following:

Democrats favorable: South—26; Middle West—16; Northeast—14; total—56.

Democrats opposed: South—3; Middle West—1; Northeast—4; total—8.

Republicans favorable: South—2; Middle West—10; Northeast—5; total—17.

Republicans opposed: South—2; Middle West—1; Northeast—8; total—11.

42. Cincinnati *Commercial*, Dec. 15 and Dec. 19, 1876.

43. Baltimore *Sun*, Dec. 19, 1876.

silverite senators preferred to delay action on remonetization until the next Congress met in the fall of 1877, by which time the new President would be established in office and the Monetary Commission's report available. When the Bland bill, H. R. 4189, reached the Senate on December 14 after House passage the previous day, the measure was referred to the Committee on Finance, whose chairman John Sherman reported it back in January 1877 without recommendation. Sherman suggested that the Senate delay debate on the entire question, but observed that if the upper chamber insisted on immediate consideration, he had prepared a substitute bill that provided for limited rather than complete remonetization, something he had urged earlier in the year. The Senate shelved the Bland bill for the remainder of its session, however, without further discussion.[44]

John Logan led one final attempt to force Senate consideration of the silver question at this session in February 1877. Logan, by then a lameduck Illinois Republican, had introduced a remonetization measure in August 1876 that was buried in the Finance Committee.[45] Logan's measure, S. 1026, provided like the Bland bill for full restoration of the 412.5 grain silver dollar as a monetary unit of account. On February 17, he moved to call the bill up for immediate floor debate without prior committee approval, at a time when Finance Committee Chairman John Sherman was absent from the Senate. Opponents of remonetization objected to this deliberate breach of senatorial courtesy, but Logan pressed the issue and rebuked the upper chamber's Republican leadership for its stalling maneuvers. "I am very well aware that neither this bill nor any other bill remonetizing the silver dollar will ever get a hearing unless it is pressed," Logan informed his reluctant colleagues. "The House has passed two bills, or probably three bills on this subject, which have been referred to the Committee on Finance," he reminded the Senate "[and] none of these bills has been re-

44. *Cong. Record,* 44th Cong., 2d sess., vol. 5, pt. 1, pp. 196, 647.
45. Ibid., 1st sess., vol. 4, pt. 6, p. 5096; 2d sess., vol. 5, pt. 1, p. 96.

ported back . . . the time seems never to come when we can take a vote on a bill of this kind."

Hoping to force Senate consideration of the silver question before his term of office ended in March, Logan brushed aside complaints about Sherman's absence and scoffed at the demands of Justin Morrill and other monometallists that the Senate await the silver commission report before proceeding: "I do not think the report of the commission will change the judgment of a solitary man in this Senate in reference to the remonetization of the silver dollar."[46] Although the Senate agreed to consider the measure the following week, perhaps merely to get the insistent Logan back into his seat, the upper chamber avoided further discussion of silver for the remainder of the session. Both the Bland Act and Logan's measure remained bottled up in the Finance Committee, although even opponents of remonetization expected swift and favorable Senate attention to the question at the next Congress.[47]

If advocates of the double standard could not force Senate consideration of the Bland bill, supporters of a Senate resolution that called for an international monetary conference were equally unsuccessful during the electoral crisis in securing House approval of their proposal. "The people . . . have spoken on this question," cried Franklin Landers of Indiana as the lower chamber discussed the resolution. "In my State, in Indiana, there is no party today that raises its voice against silver as money . . . It is no party question . . . It is a settled question there." Other legislators also pointed to the bipartisan support for immediate remonetization in their own states.[48] Despite this congressional impasse, two of the three basic elements in the 1878 congres-

46. Ibid., vol. 5, pt. 2, pp. 1624–25.

47. "Action on Silver Bills at this session," Mint Director Linderman telegraphed Samuel Ruggles in Feb. 1877, "not probably for want of time." Linderman to Ruggles, Feb. 28, 1877, Letterbooks, Director of the Mint, NA, RG 104.

48. *Cong. Record,* 44th Cong., 2d sess., vol. 5, pt. 1, p. 552; pt. 2, p. 1625.

sional compromise on silver—Senate agreement to restore silver as a full legal tender and House acceptance of an international monetary conference—were first thrashed out at the electoral crisis session. Had the disputed presidential contest not preoccupied Congress between December 1876 and March 1877, a compromise bill similar to the Bland-Allison Act would probably have been enacted at this time after negotiation between the two houses.

As early as June 1876 the Senate had passed without debate a resolution that authorized the President to send American delegates to any conference called by the European nations "to consider the important change which has recently occurred in the relative values of gold and silver, and the adoption of international measures for the removal of embarrassments arising therefrom."[49] When the chairman of the Committee on Coinage, Weights, and Measures, Democrat William J. O'Brien of Maryland, finally reported this Senate resolution to the House in January 1877, the lower chamber had already dispatched the Bland bill to its Senate grave. Under such circumstances, House silverites were keenly suspicious of any moves by the upper chamber to delay final approval of remonetization. They treated the international conference proposal as such a dilatory tactic.

In a peppery display of flag-waving Fourth of July oratory, House bimetallists wrapped Old Glory firmly around their arguments against any foreign efforts to interfere with restoration of the "dollar of the daddies." The mainstays of the lower chamber's Democratic-led silver drive—Bland, Bright, Reagen, Landers, and Holman—all opposed the Senate plan "to appoint a commission to ramble over the world and hobnob with the bullionists of Europe to ascertain what silver is worth," as one silverite phrased it. "All these schemes, all these projects have in view the continued demonetization of silver." The only House bimetallists to endorse the international conference were

49. Ibid., 44th Cong., 1st sess., vol. 4, pt. 4, pp. 3879, 3945; Senate Resolution No. 16.

moderate Republicans like George Willard of Michigan, himself a member of the silver commission, and James Monroe, Jr. of Ohio. Even the Republicans, however, insisted that the United States first remonetize silver and then seek a meeting on the question with European states.

Most supporters of the conference idea, however, opposed unilateral restoration of the double standard and believed that only "united action of the commercial nations" could insure the success of American bimetallism. Congressmen such as O'Brien, Hewitt, Chittenden, Garfield, and Kasson, all of whom had voted against the Bland bill, argued that remonetization would drive American gold out of circulation unless an international agreement established a common legal ratio in value between the two metals. A letter from Mint Director Linderman, introduced into the House debate, lent the Treasury Department's sanction to this argument.[50]

Few supporters of the monetary conference resolution, in fact, actually favored the success of such a meeting. O'Brien, for example, admitted that he "would like a conference of this kind to assemble in order that those men who are in favor of the silver standard may be convinced of the impropriety and error of their way." He grew even more candid as the debate intensified and talked at one point about "an irrepressible conflict between the two metals [in which] one or the other . . . must survive as the only acknowledged legal tender." With House silverites divided on the Senate resolution, the lower chamber rejected the international conference proposal by a voice vote and then turned down a motion to reconsider by a close 127 to 104 roll-call margin. Seventeen Republican and twenty-four Democratic bimetallists, almost all from eastern or midwestern states, joined opponents of remonetization in voting to reconsider, while a majority of midwestern and southern silverites

50. Ibid., 2d sess., vol. 5, pt. 1, pp. 548–59, 584, 663–64. See also Linderman to Samuel B. Ruggles, Dec. 27, 1876, Letterbooks, Director of the Mint, NA, RG 104.

opposed the move.[51] This inconspicuous ballot suggested clearly that the key to future congressional compromise on the silver question rested with the pivotal group of moderate House bimetallists who favored an eventual international solution. Although small in numbers, they had sufficient votes to force House approval for an amended Senate version of the Bland bill or, on the other hand, to stalemate the issue once the new Congress resumed debate.

During the electoral crisis itself, the incoming president's attitude toward remonetization remained unclear. Hayes had fought his Ohio gubernatorial canvass of 1875 on a hard money, anti-inflation platform, but this offered little basis for deciding whether he would oppose the Bland bill. Many congressmen wondered if Hayes would accept a modified Senate version of the measure without exercising his veto? The new chief executive had remained deliberately silent on currency policy since his presidential nomination, and although voters knew of his firm commitment to resumption, Hayes seldom spoke during the 1876 campaign about his belief in sound money.[52]

This diffidence arose partly because of the deep divisions within his own party over financial policy, but it stemmed also from a painful recognition that he lacked competence when discussing money questions. On this score, Tilden's nomination produced a curious sense of complacency in Hayes. As the Ohioan acknowledged in his *Diary* during those gloomy No-

51. For the entire House debate, see 44th Cong., 2d sess., vol. 5, pt. 1, pp. 521–22, 547–52, 663–65. Congress still awaited receipt of the Monetary Commission's report. The report had been promised by the Commission's chairman, John Percival Jones, for the beginning of the new session, but on January 15, 1877, he requested a month's extension. On February 15, a concurrent resolution passed both Houses granting this extension and, on March 2, the preliminary majority and minority reports of the Commission were finally submitted. By then, however, the session itself was about to end. Ibid., p. 620; pt. 2, pp. 1589 and 1618; pt. 3, p. 2079.

52. Unger, *Greenback Era, pp.* 269–81, 322.

vember 1876 days when it appeared that the Democrats might have won the presidency, he did not "apprehend any great or permanent injury to the [country's] financial affairs" by this turn of events. "The hard-money wing of the (Democratic) party is at the helm. Supported, as they should be and will be, in all wise measures by the great body of the Republican party, nothing can be done to impair the national credit or debase the national currency."[53]

Hayes did not possess similar confidence in his own command of economic questions or in his own ability to lead the country out of the existing depression and back to specie payments. Six months after passage of the 1875 Resumption Act, Hayes confessed to his friend, John Sherman, that he was not yet familiar with its provisions, and during his 1875 and 1876 campaigns, he leaned heavily on the Ohio senator for advice on economic policy questions.[54] As a novice, temperamentally indifferent to such issues, Hayes deliberately sought the counsel of politicians like Sherman who were adept at adjusting the conflicting demands of national finance and local politics. Thus, the president-elect heard all shades of advice on the silver question after his November 1876 election, but responded to almost none of it. Letters from friends and Republican political associates poured into his Fremont residence during the following months; some demanded immediate restoration of the double standard, a few counseled an international conference, while still others urged retention of the gold standard. Murat Halstead described the silver issue to Hayes in one letter as "the great question" of his administration and advised careful study before deciding on a policy.[55] Halstead's suggestion was timely, for

53. Charles Richard Williams, ed., *Diary and Letters of Rutherford Birchard Hayes,* vol. III, p. 377, Nov. 12, 1876.

54. Hayes to Sherman, June 29, 1875, Hayes MSS, Fremont.

55. See, for example, Samuel Ruggles to Hayes, Feb. 24, 1877; M. B. Force to Hayes, Feb. 16, 1877; Murat Halstead to Hayes, Dec. (n.d.), 1876. See also Carl Schurz to Hayes, Jan. 25, 1877, Hayes MSS. LC.

the new chief executive had not yet determined on any course of action regarding remonetization. Shortly before his inauguration, Hayes admitted to an Ohio friend, Manning Force, who wrote urging restoration of the double standard, that he still considered himself "a pupil in all that great topic."[56]

Hayes' choice as secretary of the Treasury, John Sherman, was a more advanced student than the President, after having struggled to resolve the silver issue in Congress for almost a year before he assumed his new post in March 1877. Sherman's appointment came as "a distinct shock to the hard money purists," unfamiliar with the teacher-pupil relationship that had existed between the two men on economic policy matters since the successful Ohio campaign of 1875, when the Republican candidate for governor first solicited Sherman's assistance. "You can deal with [the tariff and finance] better than any other man," Hayes had written the senator in 1875, and his close dependence on Sherman for sound, politically practicable advice on currency questions dated from that time.[57]

Monetary contractionists still considered the Ohio senator a hopeless "trimmer" as well as "trickster by birth and habit" who in 1868 had even briefly endorsed the interconvertible bond, the Greenbackers' favorite currency scheme, "believing the principle wise and the theory popular."[58] Sherman had also offended many gold standard advocates by his recent support for expanded silver coinage, especially after he sponsored the first important remonetization measure during the spring of 1876 aimed at restoring the domestic silver dollar as a subsidiary coin with its legal tender power limited to twenty dollars. This recent concern for silver contrasted sharply with Sherman's

56. Hayes to M[anning] L. Force, Feb. 14, 1876, ibid.

57. Hayes to Sherman, June 29, 1875, Hayes MSS, Fremont.

58. Jacob Heaton to James A. Garfield, Mar. 4, 1877, Garfield MSS, LC; Burke A. Hinsdale to Garfield, Feb. 18, 1877, in Mary L. Hinsdale, ed., *Garfield-Hinsdale Letters: Correspondence Between James Abram Garfield and Burke Aaron Hinsdale* (Ann Arbor, Mich., 1949), pp. 364–65; Unger, *Greenback Era,* pp. 322–23.

earlier role in helping to demonetize the metal, but as the shrewdest Republican in Ohio, many of whose voters sympathize strongly with remonetization and most other forms of currency expansion, Sherman had learned to bend with the prevailing political headwinds.[59]

Sherman's gold standard critics would have been pleasantly surprised to learn that the new Treasury Secretary had already outlined views similar to theirs on government silver policy in a detailed letter to Hugh McCulloch, Andrew Johnson's Secretary of the Treasury.[60] McCulloch had written Sherman in December 1876 to express concern that the Bland bill might slip through the Senate before Hayes' inauguration, and Sherman responded with a candid if private statement on the issue that foreshadowed the new administration's eventual response to silver legislation:

> I agree with you [he informed McCulloch] that the attempt to issue silver dollars and make them a legal tender for all debts public and private would not only impair the public credit but would lead to great derangement of business and practically establish the single standard of silver. Nor do I anticipate the adoption of such an extreme

59. Ibid. Sherman had alienated the hard money men even further during the electoral crisis, when he introduced a Senate substitute for John A. Logan's remonetization measure. Sherman's bill provided for restoration of the silver dollar as a legal tender on the same basis as the greenbacks. In other words, it would be accepted for all purposes except payment of customs duties, the interest and principal of the public debt, and the discharge of contracts specifically payable in gold coin. Sherman's substitute was not inflationary, since it provided that silver dollars would be issued only to redeem greenbacks at the request of their holders. However, Sherman's measure was attacked by some contractionists for proposing even limited remonetization. *Cong. Record,* 44th Cong., 2d sess., vol. 5, pt. 1, p. 647, Jan. 16, 1877; ibid., vol. 5, pt. 3, pp. 2163–66, Mar. 3, 1877; Cincinnati *Commercial* on the following 1877 dates: Jan. 16, Feb. 23 and Feb. 26; Murat Halstead to John Sherman, Feb. 22, 1877, Sherman MSS, LC.

60. Hugh McCulloch to Sherman, Dec. 18, 1876, ibid.

> measure. The use of silver ought to be largely encouraged and the silver dollar might well be restored to the coinage of the country. I am in favor of issuing it and a very large sum of subsidiary coins and with them reducing the greenback circulation, making the silver dollar a legal tender to the same extent that U.S. notes are now a legal tender, but excepting expressly customs duties and the public debt. I think by a pretty rapid dissemination of silver coin, it being issued only by the Gov't to a limited extent, it will like silver change in England be kept at the standard of gold when we come to specie payments. This letter is written for yourself and not for public use . . .[61]

Hayes, on the other hand, said nothing concerning the silver question in his inaugural address but instead restated the passages from his earlier letter of acceptance in which he expressed opposition to an "irredeemable paper currency." He avowed in orthodox fashion that "the only safe paper money is one which rests upon a coin basis, and is at all times and promptly convertible into coin."[62] The President did not define further the critical word "coin," suggesting that his own views on the monetary standard question had not yet become clear. But while the Hayes administration groped a policy on remonetization, silverites began marshalling political and public support for the legislative battle over bimetallism that was expected when the new Congress convened in the fall of 1877.

61. Sherman to McCulloch, Dec. 21, 1876, McCulloch MSS, LC.

62. Quoted in Edward McPherson, *Tribune Almanac for 1877* (New York, 1877), pp. 28–30. See also the interview with Carl Schurz, Chicago *Inter-Ocean,* Jan. 2, 1877.

8

Good as Gold? Hayes, Sherman, and Government Monetary Policy

During the six months following Hayes' inauguration, bimetallists and gold standard partisans alike waited for some expression of the administration's views on the silver question. Since the Forty-Fifth Congress had adjourned on March 17 after a brief session until November 1877, silverites had months in which to speculate on the opinions of the chief executive and Secretary of the Treasury Sherman. Hayes declined to speak publicly on the issue, however, before Congress had disposed of it at its November session or before the local and state elections later in the year. Because of the President's silence, a furious debate began among politicians and in the press over his probable course of action on the silver question.

"The correspondents say Pres. Hayes is in favor of 're-monetizing' the silver dollar," Justin Morrill wrote Secretary of the Interior Carl Schurz in June 1877. Morrill had recently visited the White House and emerged from a talk with Hayes on the problem uncertain whether he would use his veto power. The Vermont Republican feared the influence of such Ohio silverites as Congressman Charles "Calico Charley" Foster, a small-town banker and friend of the President's, who advised Morrill that Hayes favored restoration of the double standard.[1] Schurz, the most aggressive opponent of remonetization in Hayes' cabinet, chided his Vermont friend against undue pessi-

1. Morrill to Schurz, June 4, 1877, Morrill MSS, LC.

mism concerning the outcome and referred to the chief executive as "too cautious a man to [endorse the silver drive] contrary to the policy followed by the Secretary of the Treasury."[2] Schurz's confidence that the President would eventually block the Bland bill did not extend to the gold standard New York commercial press and banking community, however, especially after influential western silverite journals began treating Hayes' silence as tantamount to assent. "Colorado can take comfort in the fact that President Hayes is in full accord with them on the silver question," crowed the *Rocky Mountain Daily News.* He "is definitely in favor of restoring it to place and power as a legal tender."[3]

Something approaching panic seized the New York banking community at the thought that the President, if not actually in favor of remonetization, had decided not to place an executive veto in its path. "We call upon the President to refute at once the report (if unfounded) that he approves of a double metallic standard," demanded the New York *Journal of Commerce.* "He is being quoted all over the country as a 'silver man' . . . Let us know the President's real views on this question!"[4] E. L. Godkin's *Nation* also feared that Hayes lacked sufficient integrity to resist the appeals of trusted Ohio friends who were silverites, men like Stanley Matthews, Charles Foster, and Jacob Cox. At the very least, Godkin was convinced that Sherman, whom he regarded as untrustworthy because of his support for limited remonetization, would determine the President's response to silver legislation. Other gold standard advocates shared this

2. Schurz to Morrill, June 5, 1877, ibid.

3. *Rocky Mountain Daily News* (Denver), June 13, 1877. The source for most of the rumors concerning Hayes' silverite convictions was the New York *Times,* whose Republican Stalwart editor, George Jones, bitterly opposed the new directions being taken by the Administration on civil service and Southern policies. See, for example, New York *Times,* June 12 and 13, 1877.

4. New York *Weekly Journal of Commerce,* June 14, 1877; ibid., June 21, 1877.

assessment of the Treasury secretary as an inveterate trimmer.[5]

Sherman, himself, his attention preoccupied for several months after taking office with renegotiating resumption bond sale contracts, preferred, like the President, to avoid comment on the silver question. He responded to all inquiries concerning his views with vague generalities. "I have had to suffer in silence all sorts of false statements and garbled opinions attributed to me about financial matters," Sherman lamented to Senator Oliver P. Morton in May 1877. "I think any attempt, however, to satisfy the newspapers would only lead to further agitation and do no good."[6] Thus Sherman offered restorationists like J. Watson Webb, a former congressional colleague, hearty but intangible assurances that he supported continued use of silver in some form as legal-tender currency, if "properly regulated." At the same time the secretary endorsed international bimetallism even more heartily to its proponents, stipulating only that Congress first sanction a conference so that the United States was not put "in the position of negotiating a treaty, which Congress would not approve."[7] To monometallists like the New York editor Whitelaw Reid, who wrote Sherman expressing his impatience with the administration's inaction on the silver question but agreeing "in view of the greater issues [of specie resumption and southern policy] to put off quarreling with your shrewd compromises on [silver] as long as possible," the Ohioan responded warmly and with gratitude for the *Tribune's* fore-

5. *The Nation,* June 28, 1877. Hayes himself contributed to the rumors by carelessness in expressing his general views on the monetary standard question in private conversation. Thus, despite his praise for Governor Shelby Cullom's veto of the Illinois legislature's measure remonetizing silver in the state, Hayes confided to Cullom in their White House chat that "he was a good deal of a silver man." New York *Times,* June 12, 1877. See also, Morrill to Schurz, June 4, 1877, Morrill MSS, LC.

6. Sherman to Oliver P. Morton, May 28, 1877, Sherman MSS, LC. See also Linderman to Sherman, Apr. 9, 1877, Letterbooks, Director of the Mint.

7. Sherman to General J. Watson Webb, June 20, 1877; Sherman to B. F. Nourse, June 13, 1877; Sherman MSS, LC.

bearance. Still he remained adamant about deferring further public statements on remonetization and replied to Reid cryptically: "I note what you say about the silver question, but 'sufficient for the day is the evil thereof'."[8]

Unfortunately for the Treasury secretary, he could not deflect the persistent inquiries of New York bankers as skillfully or as easily as he could those that came from correspondents with less economic power. Financiers engaged in funding government loans demanded to know the precise nature of the Hayes administration's obligations toward these securities, particularly whether they would be considered payable, either principal or interest, in anything but gold. Shortly after taking office, Sherman had assured H. C. Fahnestock of the National City Bank of New York that although "the terms of the new [four percent] bonds will have to conform to the words of the law, 'payable in coin,' etc . . . they will be of the present date when only one kind of coin [gold] is a legal tender for all debts."[9]

Fahnestock remained skeptical and reminded Sherman that his predecessors as Secretary of the Treasury had construed the phrase "payable in coin of the present standard value" to relate to the original 1869 Funding Bill which authorized bond sales for resumption purposes, thus making them redeemable in *either* gold or silver, both of which were full legal tenders in 1869. This crucially disputed point remained unsettled for several months after Sherman took office, yet bond sales had progressed so well by May 1877 that the secretary wrote confidently to his London Treasury agent, Charles F. Conant, "I consider myself strong enough to undertake the placing the bonds even without [the banking syndicate's] aid if they will not agree to reasonable terms."[10]

Sherman had just signed a contract for the sale of new four

8. Whitelaw Reid to Sherman, June 13, 1877; Sherman to Reid, June 14, 1877, ibid.

9. Sherman to H. C. Fahnestock, Apr. 16, 1877, ibid.

10. Fahnestock to Sherman, Apr. 17, 1877; Sherman to Charles F. Conant, May 3, 1877, ibid.

percent government bonds—part of its proceeds to be set aside by the Treasury as a coin reserve to sustain resumption—with a syndicate of domestic and international bankers composed of the First National Bank of New York; August Belmont and Company, acting on behalf of the English Rothschilds; the Seligman Brothers; Morton, Bliss, and Company; and Drexel, Morgan, and Company, representing Junius Spencer Morgan of London.[11] Despite Sherman's optimistic May pronouncement, by the following month the Treasury faced losing a substantial amount of revenue because of a threatened decline in bond sales, for which the syndicate blamed the banking community's anxieties over government silver policy. Sherman quickly forgot his earlier dismissal of the syndicate's importance when New York and London financiers, fearful that the four percents would eventually be repaid in depreciated silver coin instead of gold, considered washing their hands of American public securities unless the Hayes administration assured them immediately that the bonds would be redeemed in gold alone. This imminent break between the banking community and the Treasury probably would have crippled Sherman's plan to accumulate a multimillion dollar resumption coin reserve and would therefore have delayed indefinitely hopes for an early return to specie payments.

Sherman had managed to avoid, until then, an open declaration of administration silver policy hoping to postpone a public stand until after the fall elections. The secretary's hand was forced, however, by the constant stream of rumors from Washington which linked the President to the silver movement, including "assurances" by Hayes' intimate friends like Matthews, Cox, and Foster that the chief executive would sign a silver bill. These reports, which stirred the anxieties of syndicate bankers, gained credibility from a June 12 article in the New York *Times*. George Jones, Republican editor of the *Times,* had previously opposed bitterly Hayes' policy of conciliating the South

11. Unger, *Greenback Era,* p. 351.

and had questioned the President's capacity for national leadership.[12] On June 12, he ran a dispatch from Washington quoting unidentified officials who insisted that, if remonetization succeeded, the new bond issue "would be payable, principal and interest, in that coin."[13] The *Times* article cautioned prospective purchasers against acquiring the new four percent securities, a warning that alarmed leading New York bankers responsible for their sale. J. and W. Seligman and Company, on behalf of its syndicate partners, promptly wrote Sherman in June 1877 suggesting that the secretary and President Hayes issue a statement denying categorically that either man favored restoration of silver or that government bonds would be repaid in the metal.[14]

Hoping not only to placate the bankers but at the same time to temper expectations by Republican silverites that the administration would eventually endorse a modified Bland bill, Sherman used both a series of private letters and carefully planted newspaper interviews to explain his opinions on the question. Thus he assured J. and W. Seligman and Company on June 13 that the New York *Times* had "grossly perverted the opinion of the President and myself, for neither of us ever conceived of and never assented to the absurd idea of an unlimited issue of legal silver dollars."[15] At the same time, silverite dailies like the Chicago *Tribune* and Cincinnati *Commercial* quoted

12. See, for example New York *Times,* June 9, 1877, "The Treasury Policy." Also see New York *Times,* June 13, 1877. Sherman attempted to pressure Jones into dropping his criticism of the Hayes Administration by calling for help from mutual friends in the New York banking community. See especially Sherman to J. and W. Seligman and Company, June 13, 1877, and Levi P. Morton to Sherman, June 27, 1877. Sherman MSS, LC.

13. New York *Times,* June 12, 1877. See also June 9, 1877 edition, and Sherman, *Recollections,* pp. 469–70.

14. J. and W. Seligman and Company to John Sherman, June 12, 1877, cited in Sherman, *Recollections,* p. 469.

15. John Sherman to J. and W. Seligman and Company, Sherman MSS, LC.

Sherman as endorsing *limited* recoinage of the 412.5 grain silver dollar on the same legal tender basis as the greenback, following the outlines of his earlier Senate bill.[16] In effect, the Treasury Secretary favored the widest possible expansion of silver coinage without abandoning the gold standard and viewed the silver dollar as one more *subsidiary* coin: "practically silver and paper will be the current money and gold the ultimate standard."[17]

The New York banking community expressed relief at Sherman's open repudiation of complete remonetization and at his private guarantees of bond payment in gold. But it still considered the secretary a trimmer on problems of sound finance, especially after he expressed the desire to expand greatly the amount of subsidiary silver coinage in circulation as a political gesture to midwestern Republican silverites. "He appears to have arrived at the conclusion," commented *The Nation* on Sherman's proposal, "that the Ohio election can be carried and the silver agitators satisfied by conceding to them a recoinage of a limited amount of silver dollars . . . and that both parties to the question can be harmonized on this compromise."[18]

More important to Sherman than continued criticism from diehard contractionists like Godkin, Schurz, and Morrill, however, was the syndicate's stubborn refusal to accept anything less than an open declaration from the administration stating the precise mode of repayment for the new four percent bonds. Near panic gripped some of the world's leading banking houses at the prospect of United States government securities being redeemed in depreciated legal tender silver, and financiers as sophisticated as the Seligmans, August Belmont, and Levi P.

16. See especially Chicago *Tribune,* June 13, 1877; Cincinnati *Commercial,* June 12 and 13, 1877. For a different analysis of Sherman's actions during this period, see Unger, *Greenback Era,* pp. 351–52, or Nichols, "John Sherman and the Silver Drive," pp. 152–53.

17. Unidentified newspaper clipping, dated June 13, 1877, Sherman MSS, LC.

18. *The Nation,* June 21, 1877. See also New York *Weekly Journal of Commerce,* June 14, 1877.

Morton all believed that large sales of American bonds to foreign investors would become impossible without an immediate guarantee of eventual payment in gold.[19] Their opinions were well founded, for as one of Morton's London partners wrote him shortly after rumors began reaching England in June 1877 that the Hayes regime would allow remonetization:

> I have been to see Mr. Conant [the Treasury's bond sale agent] today . . . to see if he cannot make some authorized statement as to the vexed question of authorization of payment in silver. It is astonishing how sensible people go on about and are deterred from going into United states securities in consequence. We expected to have sold the London Westminster Bank half a million this week, but after full debate, the Directors decided against the investment on the uncertainty of payment in gold and silver. When a body of men representing some of the leading firms in London are influenced by this doubt, you may be sure many other people of less intelligence have the same fears.[20]

At first Sherman refused to satisfy these syndicate demands for a public statement. Despite impassioned pleas from Belmont and other major bankers, Sherman feared the political repercussions among Republican silverites, whose support in Congress the secretary needed to protect the Treasury's resumption program.[21] In the end, however, Sherman's anxiety over the possible failure of the resumption bond issue outweighed his fear of antagonizing Republican bimetallists, and the syndicate exacted from him a strong declaration of government policy.[22]

19. See, for example, August Belmont to Sherman, June 14, 1877, Sherman MSS, LC. Also see J. and W. Seligman and Company to Sherman, Sherman, *Recollections*.

20. Cited in Morton to Sherman, June 27, 1877, ibid. See also Unger, *Greenback Era*, p. 352.

21. Sherman to Belmont, June 16, 1877, Sherman MSS, LC.

22. Sherman to Belmont, June 18, 1877, ibid.

The national banker F. O. French wrote the secretary on June 19 requesting such a statement and mentioned Congressman Stanley Matthews' reported comment that the bonds were legally payable in silver. Pointing to Matthews' close friendship with the President, French observed that "while [Matthews'] opinions always command respect, it is because he is thought to shine with reflected light, that his remark causes uneasiness." Sherman responded the same day, assuring French and his syndicate associates that "under laws now in force, there is no coin issued or issuable in which the principal of the four percent bonds is redeemable or the interest payable except the gold coins of the United States . . . "[23] Sherman's letter to French, circulated widely among bankers and investors, both in the United States and abroad, served to quiet any remaining doubts concerning the administration's intention to redeem securities with anything but gold.

Once the syndicate's confidence in the bonds had been restored, sales proceeded briskly, and within a month, over $77 million worth of the four percents had been sold. A major crisis in the Treasury's resumption program had been hurled without noticeably damaging the administration's popularity among moderate Republican silverites. Sherman's sincere belief in *limited* remonetization—"the substitution of silver money to the full extent that it can be maintained at par with gold"—satisfied most bimetallists for the moment, while his pronouncement on gold repayment of government obligations placated monometallists in the eastern investment community.[24]

Republican supporters of the Bland bill were certain enough of Sherman's private sympathies to consider him a borderline silverite, and most political observers continued to view the

23. F. O. French to Sherman, June 19, 1877; Sherman to F. O. French, June 19, 1877, ibid.

24. Unger, *Greenback Era,* p. 353; French to Sherman, June 20, 1877. Sherman MSS, LC. See also Sherman to Charles F. Conant, June 27, 1877, and Sherman to Charles Nordhoff, June 18, 1877, Sherman MSS, LC.

President's position as "a subject of public doubt and debate."[25] Sherman recognized, of course, that although Hayes' silence on the issue would help Republican chances in states like Ohio and Indiana during the fall elections, the chief executive's period of grace would expire once Congress reconvened in November. At that time, silverites would ask the administration either for assistance or at least for its neutrality in the remonetization drive, and Hayes would finally have to declare his views on the monetary standard question. Until then, both the President and his cabinet could crouch comfortably behind Sherman's June 1877 bond payment statement, although the Treasury secretary admitted privately to James Garfield in July that "as to the silver question, there is no definite administration policy."[26]

25. J. Watson Webb to Thurlow Weed, July 1, 1877, Weed MSS, New York Historical Society; Warner M. Bateman to Sherman, June 13, 1877, Sherman MSS, LC. See also Samuel Bowles to Murat Halstead, June 12, 1877, Halstead MSS, Cincinnati Historical Society; J. Watson Webb to Sherman, June 15, 1877, and Henry L. Johnson to Sherman, June 22, 1877, Sherman MSS, LC.

26. Sherman to Garfield, July 24, 1877, Sherman MSS, LC.

9

The Second Battle: The Politics of Silver, 1877

Although Sherman and Hayes attempted to divert national attention from the silver issue, it had intruded into local political debate in some areas by the spring and summer of 1877. Even earlier, during the electoral crisis, state legislatures in Minnesota, Illinois, and Wisconsin petitioned Congress demanding restoration of the double standard, and bipartisan support for bimetallism characterized midwestern state politics during the congressional struggle over the Bland bill.[1] Curiously, however, the silver question became an important issue mainly in the Midwest during the 1877 fall campaigns.

In the South, despite both the overwhelming endorsement of the Bland bill by the region's congressional delegation and silver's evident popularity among Southerners, the issue received scant political attention. This neglect resulted partly from the general approval of silver but also because of two other factors: the absence of major statewide contests in 1877 in the area and the continuing obsession of the region's dominant Democratic state parties with the problem of eliminating the remaining traces of Radical Reconstruction. Thus, almost all Democratic state party platforms in the South that year lacked detailed statements on financial policy, concentrating almost exclusively on the home rule question. Few Republican or Democratic parties south of Maryland even bothered taking an official position on

1. "Petitions," Senate Finance Committee Records, 44th Cong., 2d sess., NA. See also Cincinnati *Commercial,* Feb. 10, 1877.

remonetization throughout the months of political controversy in 1877 and 1878.[2] A recent historian's assertion that "silver's allure for the farmer raised the South for the first time [since the Civil War] to a prominent place in the postwar financial discussion" seems incongruous, considering the almost complete absence of agitation on the question during the silver drive.[3] Only in Mississippi, where L. Q. C. Lamar defied his state legislature's explicit mandate by voting against the Bland-Allison Act in the Senate, did the monetary standard question catch fire briefly as a dramatic local issue in the South.[4]

The Northeast also produced only a scattering of vague state platform pronouncements, with clear-cut declarations on the silver question made only by the Republican parties of Pennsylvania and Massachusetts, with the former strong for silver while the latter endorsed the gold standard. Although both major parties in California and Nevada also supported remonetization, the issue during the campaign of 1877 had significant political impact only in five midwestern states—Illinois, Iowa, Minnesota, Ohio, and Wisconsin. Despite the fact that Democratic, Republican, and Greenback-Independent organizations in all five states favored remonetization, silver policy was debated widely there during the campaign because of differences among the parties over bimetallism's relation to the more urgent financial question of resumption.[5] Once more, as during the 1876 canvass, silver politics involved largely partisan rather than sectional considerations. Thus in the Midwest, although

2. *Appleton's Annual Cyclopedia for 1877* (New York, 1878), passim. See also Edward McPherson, *Handbook of Politics for 1878* (New York, 1878), passim.

3. Unger, *Greenback Era,* p. 340. Unger himself points only to scattered letters written by individual southerners during the agitation to support his thesis. He fails to mention any organized pro-silver campaigns among southern political parties during the 1870s. There were none (p. 342ff).

4. Woodward, *Reunion and Reaction,* p. 250.

5. *Appleton's for 1877,* passim.

both Republican and Democratic state parties supported the Bland bill, they did so for different reasons, which reflected different policies designed to resolve the vexing problems of business depression and specie resumption.

"The Democrats will call for the remonetization of silver as a step for [monetary] inflation," Stanley Matthews informed a New York *Sun* correspondent in June 1877, "while the Republicans will ask it as a step in the aid of the resumption of specie payments."[6] The Democrats did join their demands for restoration of legal bimetallism, especially in the Midwest, to planks that called for repeal of the 1875 Resumption Act, while Republican state platforms invariably endorsed that measure and defended remonetization "as a great aid in resumption."[7] This distinction between Democratic and Republican interpretations of the silver issue was recognized and stressed by both parties, and agitation of the silver question during the 1877 midwestern state campaigns can best be understood in this light, as a new dimension in the older, continuing political debate over resumption policy.

Most Republican resumptionist-silverites, for example, would have agreed with the explanation Jacob D. Cox gave of his position to David A. Wells shortly after Cox entered Congress in March 1877. Although he had been a bimetallist during the campaign of 1876, Cox informed Wells, he had previously "said little about it so long as it seemed to play into the hands of inflationists of any kind."[8] When the Democrats and Greenbackers began attacking the unpopular Resumption Act to responsive audiences throughout the Midwest during the 1877 fall campaigns, however, Republicans in the region coupled defense of their party's resumption policies with strident de-

6. Cited in San Francisco *Chronicle*, June 14, 1877.

7. John Sherman to W. G. Deshler, Sept. 24, 1877, Sherman MSS, LC.

8. Jacob D. Cox to David A. Wells, March 22, 1877, Wells MSS, LC.

mands for the more popular remonetization of silver.[9] Republican politicians, having sensed widespread enthusiasm for silver, tried to capitalize on it. "Drifting about the country lecturing from New England to Nebraska," Schuyler Colfax wrote Halstead in September 1877, ". . . I have never seen such unanimity among *the people* on any disputed question as on the Silver matter."[10]

Little organized opposition to remonetization had yet emerged among businessmen and economic publicists by mid-1877, and, of all the state parties, only the Massachusetts Republicans called for retaining the gold standard in the period from the election of 1876 to passage of the Bland-Allison Act.[11] Monometallist eastern Republicans in Maine, Maryland, New Jersey, and New York adopted, instead, financial resolutions during the 1877 campaign that skirted the issue with ambiguous phrases that talked of redeeming government obligations either in a currency "based on coin and redeemable in coin" (Maine) or in a "sound currency of coin" (New York).[12] Don Cameron's Pennsylvania Republican party actually endorsed remonetization in 1877 with a ringing denunciation of the "Crime of 1873," "a clear and emphatic demand," wrote the Philadelphia *Inquirer,* "[that] will surprise a good many monometallists, who have assumed that this demand was confined to the west and South."[13]

Silver, then, became a local issue of any political consequence in 1877 only in the Midwest, where it fit comfortably into the framework of earlier partisan disputes over resumption policy. Because of the Resumption Act's apparent unpopularity among voters, Republicans in that section found themselves on the

9. Unger, *Greenback Era,* pp. 345–47.

10. Schuyler Colfax to Murat Halstead, Sept. 2, 1877, Halstead MSS, Cincinnati Historical Society. See also Charles Case to Sherman, Sept. 2, 1877, Sherman MSS, LC.

11. McPherson, *Handbook of Politics,* p. 24, adopted Sept. 19, 1877.

12. *Appleton's for 1877,* passim.

13. Philadelphia *Inquirer,* Sept. 6, 1877.

defensive during the 1877 canvass and "seized the 'dollar of the daddies' as a drowning man clutches his rescuer."[14]

Although midwestern Republicans, Democrats, and Greenbackers all endorsed remonetization during the fall campaign, the three parties held different opinions regarding both its economic value and political importance. The Greenbackers continued to emphasize repeal of the Resumption Act and demanded additional large issues of paper money in their platforms, while the Democrats devoted most of their financial discussions to resumption repeal alone. Only the Republicans, saddled with the Hayes administration's unpopular efforts to make the 1875 statute work, concentrated on the need for restoring silver at the approaching session of Congress.[15]

In the Ohio and Illinois legislatures, for example, Republicans sponsored and helped pass resolutions declaring silver coin full legal tender within each state, although in Illinois, Governor Shelby Cullom vetoed his party's attempt to champion remonetization.[16] From Iowa William Boyd Allison wrote John Sherman shortly before the state party's June meeting, warning that any administration attempt to contract the currency before the fall harvest would result in political disaster for midwestern Republicans:

> not only in the N.W. but in your own state and in Indiana, the close money market will greatly hinder [the autumn crops] reaching a market. The pinch will come by agitation

14. Unger, *Greenback Era,* p. 345.

15. Ibid., pp. 344–49. Unger's study contains the best discussion of Midwestern financial politics in the elections of 1877.

16. *Appleton's for 1877,* p. 384. *The Nation,* May 10, 1877. Both measures, apparently aimed at influencing swift action on the Bland bill once Congress convened in the fall, were supported in their respective states by Halstead's Cincinnati *Commercial* and Medill's Chicago *Tribune.* Joseph Medill to David A. Wells, July 19, 1877, Wells MSS, LC; New York *Times,* June 12, 1877; Cincinnati *Commercial* for 1877, passim.

> and appeal to Congress. This is why I make an appeal to you for moderation in your movements.[17]

Sherman responded immediately, assuring the Iowan that the Treasury Department had no intention of contracting the supply of greenbacks during the harvest months, but the Iowa Republican convention still linked its demand for remonetization to the problem of currency contraction in a resolution that demanded "the silver dollar [be] made with gold a legal tender for the payment of all debts, both public and private . . . [and] the present volume of currency [maintained] until the wants of trade and commerce demand its further contraction."[18]

In Wisconsin, gold standard Republicans controlled the party's September 1877 convention, which adopted a comparatively mild plank endorsing bimetallism only because of the threat posed by a popular gubernatorial candidate, Independent-Greenbacker E. P. Allis. Republican party leaders included the silver plank as a sop to the party's bimetallists, fearing that without it, Milwaukee iron manufacturer Allis would draw enough votes from soft money Republicans to help elect the Democratic candidate for governor. Senator Timothy Howe, an early congressional supporter of remonetization, explicitly warned the Republican monometallist state chairman, Horace Rublee, that there was "no better antidote to Allis than Silver."[19] The pronouncement eventually adopted by the party's Madison convention, however, differed little from John Sherman's moderate views. Proud of his efforts in diluting a stronger pro-silver statement, Rublee wrote Carl Schurz that the "lunacy about the silver dollar is ostensibly" in the platform "but in such a form as to

17. William Boyd Allison to Sherman, June 21, 1877, Sherman MSS, LC.

18. Sherman to Allison, June 25, 1877, ibid.; McPherson, *Handbook of Politics,* p. 22, adopted June 27, 1877.

19. Unger, *Greenback Era,* pp. 346–47.

be empty of any signification; one end of the resolution swallows up and neutralizes the other."[20]

Supported by the Honest Money League of the Northwest, a pro-resumption, gold standard businessmen's organization headquartered at Milwaukee, the Wisconsin Republicans under Rublee's direction conducted the most unabashed sound money campaign of any state party in the country in 1877. Rublee's forces even abandoned the compromise pro-silver plank adopted at Madison for a solid endorsement of the gold standard at a later Milwaukee conference of conservative Republican businessmen and politicians. At this meeting, greenbackers, silverites, and other financial heretics were excluded and read out of the party. For its efforts, Wisconsin's monometallist Republicans squeaked through to a narrow November victory over the Democrats and Independents by a margin well below their usual electoral majority.[21]

Although the Wisconsin party rejected any compromise with bimetallism, Ohio Republicans struggled feverishly to construct a monetary standard plank upon which all the faithful could stand agreeably. Deeply split over remonetization, Hayes' state party divided into at least three acknowledged positions on the issue, discounting for the moment the President's still unspoken opinions. Many of the silver forces' national leaders were Ohioans, including Murat Halstead of the Cincinnati *Commercial,* Hayes' close friend Stanley Matthews and the Toledo Congressman-elect Jacob Cox. On the other hand, James A.

20. "We hold that the silver dollar should be restored to its former place as money, and made legal tender for the payment of debts, except where otherwise distinctly provided by law, with the coinage so regulated as to maintain equality of value, and the harmonious circulation of gold, silver and legal tender notes in money . . . " Cited in Philadelphia *Inquirer,* Sept. 12, 1877. Horace Rublee to Carl Schurz, Sept. 14, 1877, Schurz MSS, LC.

21. Ibid.; Unger, *Greenback Era,* pp. 346–47; Ellis B. Usher, *The Greenback Movement of 1875–1884 and Wisconsin's Part in It* (Milwaukee, 1911), pp. 32–34.

Garfield stood alone among the state's congressional delegation in opposing remonetization, but he represented the sentiments of a large number of the state's Republicans, especially in the Cleveland area. Somewhere between these two extremes stood men like John Sherman, willing to expand subsidiary silver coinage by limited restoration of the 412.5 grain dollar but fearful that a complete return to the double standard would drive gold coinage from circulation. Only the rare optimist among Ohio Republicans could assert, as J. M. Dalzell did, that "there will be no trouble at all, I think, to harminize [sic] on the Money question" in the campaign of 1877."[22] Most party stalwarts feared the forthcoming campaign against an inflationist state Democratic party. The national administration provided no useful guidelines for its own Ohio party, since Hayes refused to break his silence on the question when state Republicans gathered at Cleveland in late July to nominate a candidate for governor.[23]

Most delegates recognized that a strong endorsement of remonetization was needed if Republicans were to compete with the attractive soft-money financial planks that the Democrats would offer voters in that depression year. "I see it is quite evident that the Republican party is going to have to go in for silver," an Ashtabula newspaper editor wrote Garfield, "or the cry will be raised that we legislate for the wealthy class to the loss of the poor."[24] Politicians on the scene warned Sherman and Garfield repeatedly that public opinion in the state insisted upon immediate restoration of the double standard. More importantly, state party unity would crumble if the Cleveland convention did not sanction this demand. "It may occur to you,"

22. D. W. McClung to John Sherman, Feb. 20, 1877; J. M. Dalzell to Sherman, July 18, 1877; Sherman MSS.

23. Unger, *Greenback Era,* p. 345; Warner Bateman to John Sherman, June 13, 1877, Sherman MSS, LC; Samuel Bowles to Murat Halstead, June 12, 1877, Halstead MSS, Cincinnati Historical Society.

24. J. A. Howells to James A. Garfield, July 26, 1877, Garfield MSS, LC.

one gold standard Republican informed Garfield, "that we might as well declare the true doctrine at once and fight for it. But if we do, we divide our hard-money forces, and will probably lose the state this fall."[25]

To avoid a disastrous schism on the silver question, Ohio Republicans worked during the weeks preceding the state convention to draft a statement acceptable to all party factions. A flurry of trial resolutions emerged from correspondence between local leaders and the party's phalanx of Washington officeholders. Only when the Democratic convention had adopted its expected inflationist platform, which called for remonetization, resumption repeal, and greenback expansion did quarreling Republicans bury their differences and begin moving toward a compromise on silver policy. This would allow the party to conduct a unified campaign, one that would stress, in Stanley Matthews' words, "Resumption of Specie payment and the Restoration of the Silver Dollar to the coinage, the latter first."[26]

Garfield himself rushed to Cleveland to direct the efforts toward achieving a compromise. After consulting with Matthews, Cox, Foster, and other silverites, Garfield was appointed permanent chairman of the convention and helped draft a conciliatory resolution closer to Wisconsin's mild remonetization plank than to the militant declarations of the Iowa, Pensylvania, and Illinois Republicans. The second half of the Ohio resolution, like Rublee's Wisconsin statement, swallowed up and neutralized the first part:

25. D. W. McClung to James A. Garfield, July 2, 1877, ibid. See also C. W. Moulton to John Sherman, June 17, 1877, Sherman MSS, LC.

26. D. W. McClung to James A. Garfield, July 2 and July 21, 1877, Garfield MSS, LC; Charles Foster to Warner M. Bateman, July 14, 1877, Bateman MSS, Western Reserve Historical Society (Cleveland, Ohio); Warner Bateman to John Sherman, July 4, 1877, Sherman MSS, LC; McPherson, *Handbook of Politics,* p. 17; Stanley Matthews to James Monroe, July 21, 1877, Matthews MSS, Hayes Library, Fremont.

> We are in favor of both silver and gold as money; that both shall be a legal tender for the payment of all debts, except those specifically provided for by law, with coinage and valuation so regulated that our people shall not be placed at a disadvantage in our trade with foreign nations; and that both metals shall be kept in circulation as the money of the nation, as contemplated by the Constitution; and we therefore demand the remonetization of silver.[27]

Those Republicans who opposed full remonetization, having expected the worst from the Cleveland meeting, were plainly delighted with its outcome. "If you had seen how much evil we avoided, you would praise the Platform for what it does not contain," Garfield wrote one gold standard correspondent. Sherman, also pleased with the compromise, boasted that Ohio's action had decreased "the danger from a wrong settlement of the silver question [by Congress]."[28] Even implacable Justin Morrill congratulated Garfield for having extracted "more sound sense than was to be expected where the silver epidemic rages so fiercely."[29] Despite all of this high praise from hard money men, Garfield's outspoken opposition to bimetallism probably cost him a Senate seat. Later in the year the Ohio legislature sent

27. James A. Garfield to D. W. McClung, July 23, 1877, Garfield MSS, LC; John Sherman to Warner Bateman, July 23, 1877, Sherman MSS, LC; Unger, *Greenback Era,* pp. 345–46; Theodore Clarke Smith, *The Life and Letters of James Abram Garfield* (New Haven, Conn., 1925), 2, 655–56. Garfield claimed at this time to have abandoned his earlier gold standard position and become "a probationary convert to [international] bimetallism," although he remained an unrelenting opponent of *unilateral* remonetization. Garfield to Burke A. Hinsdale, Sept. 10, 1877, in Mary L. Hinsdale, ed., *Garfield-Hinsdale Letters,* pp. 376–77. See also McPherson, *Handbook for Politics,* p. 26.

28. Garfield to Henry W. Elliot, Aug. (n.d.) 1877, Garfield MSS, LC; Sherman to Francis Bowen, Aug. 4, 1877, Sherman MSS, LC. See also Garfield to A. G. Riddle, Aug. (n.d.), 1877; Henry W. Elliot to Garfield, Aug. 12, 1877; A. G. Riddle to Garfield, Aug. 3, 1877, Garfield MSS, LC.

29. Justin S. Morrill to Garfield, Aug. 6, 1877, Garfield MSS, LC.

Stanley Matthews to Washington to fill John Sherman's unoccupied chair, partly because of Matthews' popularity as a vociferous advocate of the Bland bill. Prior to Matthews' appointment, Halstead's *Commercial* had thundered repeatedly against Garfield's selection on the grounds that he could not harm the chances for remonetization in the House, where silverites held an overwhelming majority, but that his appointment to the upper chamber might endanger passage of a silver bill in the more closely divided Senate.[30]

The Ohio Republican convention's endorsement of remonetization, however, contributed more to the success of the silver drive than a personal triumph of Matthews over Garfield. Throughout the Midwest, even in the divided Ohio and Wisconsin parties, Republican politicians found themselves compelled by political pressure from inflationist Democratic and Greenback organizations in the fall campaigns to endorse formally the silver movement. Democratic conventions in Illinois, Iowa, Ohio, Minnesota, and Wisconsin demanded repeal of the Resumption Act along with remonetization, and "sound strategy called for the Democrats to emphasize repeal." Conversely, Republican conventions in all six states coupled every appeal for restoration of the double standard with a strong defense both of the Resumption Act and of Sherman's attempt to implement the measure by accumulating a Treasury gold reserve through the sale of four percent bonds.[31]

Republicans, thus, supported remonetization in 1877 so that the additional legal tender silver coinage would assist the Treasury's resumption efforts, while Democrats generally viewed bimetallism either as a disruptive or an inflationary proposal which, like their earlier demands for resumption repeal and greenback expansion, would impede Republican resumption

30. See, for example, the Cincinnati *Commercial* on the following 1877 dates: March 8, March 11 and March 12; also H. R. McCalmont to James A. Garfield, Aug. 20, 1877, Garfield MSS, LC.

31. Unger, *Greenback Era*, p. 345; *Appleton's for 1877*, passim.

plans. In the argument over the role that silver would play in subsequent government economic policy, the most significant quarrels were partisan, not sectional, ones.

Outside the Midwest remonetization never became a major campaign theme in 1877. Silver never entered southern political debate that year other than in Mississippi, and, in the East most Republican platforms remained ambiguous on the issue. Most eastern Democratic parties also remained silent on the question, except for the New York organization, which had both a powerful monometallist wing led by Samuel J. Tilden, Abram Hewitt, and August Belmont as well as a vocal silverite minority that rallied behind Congressman S. S. Cox. At its October 1877 convention the New York Democracy deftly sidestepped the entire problem, referring ambiguously to "gold and silver [as] the only legal tender."[32] In the mining states of the Far West, support for remonetization had become axiomatic for all politicians, and the question rarely entered political discussion in the fall elections. Only in the Midwest, then, did Republicans, Democrats, and Greenbackers battle furiously over the issue and its meaning that year, all agreeing on the need for remonetization but differing over its purpose. Why was it important? To insure the success of the Republicans' resumption program or, as Democrats and Greenbackers insisted, to provide the country with new inflationary legal tender currency and thereby destroy the chances for an early return to specie payments under Republican auspices?

Although most Greenback-Independent state organizations also supported the silver drive during the seventies, third-party adherents continued to harbor grave doubts concerning remonetization. Greenback conventions in Iowa, Massachusetts, Minnesota, New Jersey, New York, Ohio, and Pennsylvania all passed resolutions during the 1877 campaign demanding recoinage of the legal tender 412.5 grain silver dollar but, in almost every case, this plank remained a secondary one compared

32. *Appleton's for 1877*.

to the party's earlier demands for repeal of the Resumption Act, abolition of the national banking system and expansion of the paper currency.[33]

Greenbackers supported silver for a variety of motives. It seemed to offer for some simply a chance to supplement immediately the supply of circulating paper money which they considered inadequate. Still others viewed remonetization as the opening wedge in eventual legislative enactment of the party's entire financial program. Many rag-baby enthusiasts believed that the congressional majority that secured passage of the Bland bill would also repeal the hated Resumption Act and expand the paper money supply. Once "get silver . . . made applicable to payment of the national debt," Alexander Cambell acknowledged to Thomas Ewing, "and you will see the 'rag baby' stepping out in its holiday dress."[34] In no state, however, did Greenbackers assume a major role in stirring public sentiment for remonetization, and the paper money advocates remained clearly uncomfortable with the rhetoric and imagery of the silver movement.

Few bedrock paper money advocates could discourse easily on their adopted cousin, the 'dollar of the daddies,' especially since, until recently, they had dismissed both gold standard advocates and bimetallists as "bullionists," a term of contempt Greenbackers reserved for all believers in a coin standard of monetary value. For the third-party forces, the real financial "crime" had not taken place in 1873 with the demonetization of silver but first in 1869, when passage of the Public Credit Act pledged payment of government debt in coin, and later in 1875, when Congress approved the Resumption Act.

33. Ibid.; Unger, *Greenback Era,* pp. 332–33.

34. Unger, *Greenback Era,* pp. 332–33. Thomas Ballinger to W. B. Allison, Apr. 9, 1878, Allison MSS, Iowa State Department of History and Archives (Des Moines, Ia.); Fred J. L. Blandy to Thomas Ewing, Mar. 13, 1878, and A. Ellis to Thomas Ewing, Jan. 20, 1878, in Salmon P. Chase MSS, Pennsylvania Historical Society (Philadelphia); Horace Samuel Merrill, *Bourbon Democracy of the Middle West, 1865–1896* (Baton Rouge, La., 1953), p. 123; Alexander Cambell to Thomas Ewing, Jan. 30, 1878, Ewing MSS, LC.

This inherent and long-standing antagonism toward a metallic standard of values did not prepare most third-party men for easy acceptance of bimetallist ideas, and most Greenbackers-Independent state platforms made no effort to relate the politically popular demand for remonetization to the party's basic paper money dogmas. The Pennsylvania Greenbackers, for example, after endorsing the silver drive in its 1877 platform, went on to insist that "gold and silver [be] supplemented [before resumption] by full legal-tender paper." The United Labor Party of Pennsylvania, meeting separately in September 1877 before its fusion with the Greenbackers, failed even to mention silver, and its declaration simply restated the usual demands for resumption repeal, destruction of the national banking system and paper money expansion. The West Virginia Greenback organization also failed to endorse remonetization, observing instead that "resumption in the existing supply of the precious metals [i.e., under legal bimetallism] will entail national disgrace." Only in the Midwest did the Greenbackers chafe less openly about linking their political fortunes to the silver issue, and third-party platforms in Indiana, Ohio, and elsewhere in the region contained fewer reservations regarding the importance of remonetization. Elsewhere, however, many Greenbackers refused to accept their party's expedient decision to endorse the Bland bill and openly opposed its passage, believing that if silver agitation failed, voters would become more sympathetic toward increasing the supply of paper currency.[35]

Greenback hostility or skepticism regarding remonetization intensified in areas distant from the silver movement's midwestern political center. In New York, for example, the third party did not even bother mentioning the monetary standard issue in its 1877 platform except to oppose the continued substitution of subsidiary silver for fractional notes![36] The paper-

35. *Appleton's for 1877*, pp. 635, 765–66 and passim. See also Cincinnati *Commercial*, Feb. 9, 1877; N. W. C. Jameson to R. B. Hayes, Feb. 23, 1878, Hayes MSS, Fremont.

36. *Appleton's for 1877*, p. 566.

money candidate for governor of Pennsylvania in 1877, F. W. Hughes, later chairman of the Greenback National Convention at Toledo in February 1878, managed only a humorously ambiguous endorsement of the Bland bill during his campaign. "I am opposed to a double standard," Hughes insisted, "yet it by no means follows that the remonetization of silver implies necessarily a double standard."[37] Among Pennsylvania's political parties only Don Cameron's Republican organization *actively* supported the Bland bill, although most of the state's Democratic congressmen voted for the measure. Nor was Pennsylvania the only state in which rag-baby enthusiasts repudiated the silver drive. In Colorado, itself a large silver-producing state, the Greenback party's state chairman, Joseph Wolff, informed Senator Henry Teller that a stable monetary system could not be restored without substantial expansion of the greenback supply, and that "resumption in either one or both metals [alone on] a specie basis . . . is an absolute impossibility."[38]

The programs of silverites and greenbackers clashed head-on concerning the basic question of specie resumption. Congressman Benjamin Butler acknowledged to one New York City silverite that he supported the Bland bill only as "a step in the direction of the establishment of an American [i.e., non-specie] system of finance."[39] The Massachusetts Greenbacker's response to the silver drive underscored the reservations held by most rag-baby supporters concerning restoration of the legal tender silver dollar. Butler, although a supporter of the Bland

37. Philadelphia *Inquirer,* Jan. 21, 1878. See also *Appleton's for 1877,* Nov. 8. One Greenback-Labor campaigner in the Keystone state was more candid than Hughes and called remonetization "a national extravagance, a tax upon the people for the benefit of the producers of silver." *Appleton's for 1877,* Nov. 5.

38. Joseph Wolff to Henry Teller, Jan. 5, 1878, Teller MSS, Denver (Colo.) Public Library.

39. Benjamin F. Butler to Marcus Hanlon, Jan. 30, 1878, typescript, Butler MSS, LC.

bill, ironically remained an equally bitter opponent of *subsidiary* silver coinage, and he saw establishment of the double standard as merely an intermediate step toward creating a non-specie financial system based largely on legal tender paper money. "I am not in love with silver as a currency," Butler acknowledged privately, and his role during the congressional campaign to remonetize the metal was an important but devious one.[40] Although he endorsed the silver bill along with other House inflationists, Butler managed somehow to convert the measure's major Senate sponsor, John Percival Jones, to temporary belief in a greenback standard![41] At the same time, he assured his Massachusetts textile town constituents, many of whom opposed bimetallism, that his support for silver was an expedient, meant "to so far get in accord with my Western colleagues as to get a hearing with them upon the [tariff] interests of the Eastern manufacturers."[42] Finally, in the brief period between initial congressional passage of the Bland-Allison Act and the President's veto, Butler secretly urged the Greenback party's national convention meeting in Toledo to approve a resolution denouncing the measure.[43]

Greenbackers did not require Butler's suggestions, however,

40. Butler to T. J. Moore, Apr. 6, 1877; Butler to R. S. Fay, Nov. 25, 1877; Butler to O. J. Smith, May 14, 1877; Butler to Robert Patterson, July 18, 1877; Butler to E. J. Sherman, Mar. 25, 1878; typescripts, Butler MSS, LC.

41. Butler to R. S. Fay, ibid.; San Francisco *Chronicle,* June 14, 1877; Henry Linderman to Justin Morrill, June 5, 1877, Morrill MSS, LC; Interview with John Percival Jones, Washington *National Republican,* Jan. 10, 1878.

42. Butler to A. W. Stearns, Feb. 27, 1878; Butler to George A. Marden, Feb. 11, 1878, Butler MSS, LC.

43. "Bill a delusion and a snare," Butler wired his representative at Toledo. "Have resolution denouncing it passed by the convention." Butler to Thomas J. Durant, Feb. 21, 1878. Within days, however, Butler began denying that he had exercised any influence on the Greenback convention or that he had any association with it! Butler to S. G. Rice, Feb. 26, 1878, ibid.

to demonstrate their basic detachment from the silver drive. The Toledo convention, although it met before congressional repassage of the silver bill, did not bother mentioning the monetary standard question in its lengthy platform, except for a general demand that "the coinage of silver be placed on the same footing as that of gold." Presided over by anti-silverite Francis W. Hughes of Pennsylvania, the convention adopted Butler's resolution denouncing the amended Bland bill and then adjourned.[44] This ended the brief unrequited effort by paper money advocates to exploit popular enthusiasm for remonetization. The Greenbackers never became an influential factor in the campaign to restore legal bimetallism, since their basic commitment to a non-specie system of finance precluded anything more than superficial and temporary alliance with the silverites. By the time Congress repassed the Bland-Allison Act in February 1878, this shallow alliance of paper money advocates and bimetallists had already crumbled.

Four years of business depression climaxed during the summer of 1877 with a series of violent industrial strikes and riots.[45] Although Greenback and Independent-Labor parties canvassed actively in almost every state proposing drastic remedies for the economic distress, most major party stalwarts continued to assess their problems in traditional political terms, James Garfield thus credited the defeat of Ohio's Republican gubernatorial candidate to the following factors, without ever mentioning the hard times:

> First. Usual apathy of the off year. Second. Effects of [Hayes'] Civil Service policy. Third. Dissatisfaction with his Southern Policy. Fourth. Judge West's [Republican candidate] speech on the evening of his nomination. Fifth. The greenback and labor craze.[46]

44. McPherson, *Handbook of Politics,* p. 168.

45. Robert V. Bruce, *1877: Year of Violence* (Indianapolis, 1959), passim.

46. Garfield Diary, Oct. 9, 1877, Garfield MSS, LC.

Not surprisingly, Garfield evaluated "the greenback and labor craze" as the least important factor in the Republicans' electoral loss.

Politicians of both major parties found it convenient to neglect the impact of social and economic distress on the electorate. They continued to think in terms of their skillfullness at handling manageable issues during the autumn campaign rather than recognize the effect of widespread unemployment and hunger upon voting behavior.[47] Only rarely did they acknowledge, as Warner Bateman did to John Sherman, that "hard times and the labor movement" constituted an important factor in the Republican defeat. Even Bateman insisted that these could have been overcome, if his party had defended its resumption policies more vigorously or had nominated a more attractive gubernatorial candidate.[48] Despite the indifference of the professionals, the election results in 1877 indicated that economic and social discontent had taken a heavy toll on traditional political voting patterns, and the new parties—whether Greenback, Greenback-Labor, or Independent-Labor—more than doubled their national following in less than a year, from an estimated 80,000 votes in 1876 to over 185,000 in the 1877 polls.[49]

The marked increase in political revolt among the electorate reflected widespread agrarian and industrial protest against the depression. It centered around popular demands for some form

47. For a sampling of traditional political analysis of the election campaign and results, see the following: Beman Wells to Garfield, Aug. 19, 1877; John A. Gand to Garfield, Sept. 30, 1877; E. N. Stoughton to Garfield, Oct. 13, 1877; Garfield MSS, LC. See also T. C. Reynolds to John Sherman, Aug. 13, 1877; L. T. Hunt to Sherman, Aug. 22, 1877; Sherman MSS, LC. Also M. F. Force to J. D. Cox, Sept. 28, 1877, Cox MSS, Oberlin College Library.

48. Warner L. Bateman to John Sherman, Oct. 11, 1877, Sherman MSS, LC.

49. Fred E. Haynes estimated that 82,640 votes were cast for third-party tickets in 1876 compared with 187,095 votes in 1877. Fred E. Haynes, *Third Party Movements Since the Civil War, With Special Reference to Iowa: A Study in Social Politics* (Iowa City, 1916), p. 124.

of government economic relief through currency expansion, either by increasing the greenback supply, repealing the Resumption Act or remonetizing silver. Although the Greenback-Independent third parties gained significant strength, the Democrats were the major political beneficiaries of voter dissatisfaction in 1877, especially in the Midwest. They ran best in states like Ohio and Wisconsin, where hard money anti-greenback Republicans fashioned moderate planks on the silver issue. They gained less in states like Iowa, where the Republican organization attempted to channel the electorate's discontent into an enthusiastic campaign for restoration of the "dollar of the daddies." Elsewhere, the Democrats not only won the Ohio state house but came within eight thousand votes of upsetting the traditionally dominant Wisconsin Republicans. Both elections were decided by pluralities, with third-party candidates receiving the balance of votes. In Iowa, however, the Republican gubernatorial candidate, John H. Gear, ran up a forty thousand vote plurality over his Democratic opponent and came within a few thousand ballots of an absolute majority. The vehemently pro-silver Iowa Republicans also retained control of both houses of the legislature, despite substantial Greenback strength in the state.[50]

For most politicians, silver still remained peripheral to the more pressing financial question of resumption. With both Democrats and Greenbackers denouncing Sherman's efforts to accumulate a Treasury gold reserve through syndicate bond sales, most Republicans had become resigned to the fact that, whatever stand they took on remonetization, "the party would find peace from the money problem only after resumption."[51]

Hardly had the Ohio tallies been published in the East than speculation resumed over Hayes' attitude toward any future congressional silver bill. "No doubt is entertained that Presi-

50. *Appleton's for 1877*, pp. 621, 679.
51. Unger, *Greenback Era*, p. 349.

dent Hayes would promptly veto any bill repealing the existing Resumption law," remarked the New York *Journal of Commerce* in mid-October, "but many do doubt whether he would veto a bill 'restoring' the silver dollar and this doubt lends much encouragement to the silver movement among Congressmen."[52] Renewed declarations by Ohio silverite Stanley Matthews that the President would sign the Bland bill fed the anxieties of gold standard advocates, despite increasing signs that Hayes would veto. "Calico Charley" Foster, another of the chief executive's Ohio associates who supported restoration, reversed an earlier estimate and predicted in November that the President would oppose the Bland bill. Even Matthews began acknowledging that he had no personal assurances from Hayes but believed simply that he would not stand in the way of the "public will" as expressed by large majorities in both houses of Congress.[53]

Rumors that the President would not stand firm against the silverite tide continued to disturb syndicate bankers, who again pressed Sherman for a forthright statement of Hayes' intentions.[54] Sherman assured Belmont, Fahnestock and other syndicate members that Senate amendments would remove any threat posed to the public credit by the silver bill through guaranteeing repayment of all government bonds in gold alone, although privately, the Treasury official felt less certain of this point. "I only fear that the premature action of Congress . . . will defeat all our plans for resumption," Sherman wrote Horace White shortly after House passage of the Bland bill. "Already the agitation in Congress has crippled this Department very much."[55]

52. New York *Journal of Commerce,* Oct. 18, 1877; Nichols, "John Sherman and the Silver Drive of 1877–78," p. 151.

53. New York *Journal of Commerce,* Nov. 15, 1877; Philadelphia *Inquirer,* Nov. 9, 1877.

54. H. C. Fahnestock, to John Sherman, Nov. 7, 1877, Sherman MSS, LC; Unger. *Greenback Era,* p. 356.

55. John Sherman to August Belmont, Dec. 1, 1877; John Sherman to Horace White, Nov. 5, 1877, Sherman MSS, LC.

Meanwhile, events connected with the sale of government bonds moved swiftly. On November 5 the House repassed the silver bill by more than a two-thirds majority. August Belmont warned Sherman two days later, on behalf of the syndicate, that the threat of remonetization would soon completely halt sales of the four percents both in this country and abroad, a fear realized within forty-eight hours when the securities fell below par in New York bond markets. The syndicate, after purchasing $750,000 worth of the bonds themselves in an unsuccessful effort to bolster their market price, suspended sales entirely.[56]

European investors also became alarmed at the possibility of repayment in silver, and in a few days the purchase of American resumption bonds ground to a halt both in England and on the continent. The Treasury Department's London bond sale agent, Charles F. Conant, telegraphed repeatedly for some statement either from the Treasury secretary or the President on the repayment question, but Sherman refused to issue one on the grounds that the silver bill was still before Congress. Acknowledging that the silver agitation had completely "arrested refunding and the sale of four percent bonds," he advised Conant simply to assure prospective purchasers that no congressional measure would be allowed to interfere with the government's obligations to its creditors. Sherman was determined to pay the principal and interest of the bonds in gold alone, whether or not Congress remonetized silver.[57]

Syndicate bankers and European investors, however, did not breathe easily on this point until the appearance of the President's *Annual Message* and the Treasury Secretary's *Annual Report* in December, both of which expressed opposition to full

56. August Belmont to John Sherman, Nov. 7, 1877, ibid., reprinted in *Specie Resumption and Funding of National Debt* (Washington, 1879), p. 183; Unger, *Greenback Era,* pp. 355–56; Nichols, "John Sherman and the Silver Drive," p. 159.

57. Andrew D. White [Stuttgart, Germany] to R. B. Hayes, Dec. 18, 1877, Hayes MSS, Fremont; John Sherman to Charles F. Conant, Nov. 24, 1877, Sherman MSS, LC.

remonetization in unmistakable terms. These fears might have been put to rest even sooner had the President's November 5 diary entry been known:

> Silver was demonetized by the act of 1873 [Hayes wrote]. When was the first movement in Congress to remonetize it? Was there any until silver had lost its value?
>
> To attempt to pay the public debt in depreciated silver coin is a violation of public credit and public faith and thereby [would] add to the burden of the debt.

Hayes felt sympathy, nevertheless, toward regulated expansion of subsidiary silver coinage. The same entry endorsed "a 'full' and not 'a scanty circulation' . . . all to be coin, or redeemable in coin" but "without injustice to creditors, either public or private, and without impairing the public or private credit."[58] From this point in November 1877 Hayes never wavered in his belated determination to oppose full restoration of the double standard.

The President's diary comments were provoked by House passage of the Bland bill earlier in the day. A special session of the Forty-Fifth Congress had convened in October to vote military appropriations left unpaid by the previous Congress.[59] Within two weeks after assembling, twenty bills "authorizing the free coinage of and remonetization of the silver dollar" had been introduced into the House by both Republicans and Democrats from all sections of the country. Democratic control of the lower chamber gave the chairmanship of the important Banking and Currency Committee to Missouri inflationist Aylett Buckner, and a majority of Buckner's committee favored both repeal of the Resumption Act and immediate remonetization. After considerable maneuvering for legislative priority between hard money Republicans working for restoration of the double standard and soft money Democrats whose major object was re-

58. Charles R. Williams, ed., *Diary and Letters of R. B. Hayes, 3,* 451, Nov. 5, 1877.

59. Unger, *Greenback Era,* p. 353.

sumption repeal, the two partisan groups arrived at a timetable for taking up the proposals.[60]

Democratic opponents of resumption agreed to allow their colleague, Richard Bland, Chairman of the Committee on Mines and Mining, to report his silver bill first and to request an immediate vote by suspending House rules. In return, pro-resumption Republican silverites agreed to allow Democrat Thomas Ewing of Ohio, chief strategist of the repeal forces, to bring his measure up for debate under a special order. Both motions required a two-thirds majority. Ewing hoped to force a quick vote on resumption repeal, but, as it turned out, he succeeded only in opening a bitter two-week debate that ended finally in passage of the measure by a strict party vote, with both silverite and gold standard Republicans opposing repeal. Under the original informal November 5 agreement, however, a small group of midwestern Republican bimetallists kept their part of the bargain and joined the Democrats in voting for the special order that called Ewing's bill up for debate by a 143 to 47 margin. This occurred only after silverites from both parties had passed the Bland bill, H. R. 1093, by a lopsided 163 to 34 majority[61] (see Table 5).

Although its margin of victory in November 1877 compared favorably with the December 1876 House tally of 167 to 53 on the same measure, the bimetallist coalition in the lower chamber had changed in some important respects. Southern, border-state, and midwestern Democrats remained overwhelmingly committed to the legislation, but only six northwestern Democrats now endorsed the proposal compared with twenty-three in December 1876. Throughout the Northeast, in the New England and middle atlantic states, congressmen of both parties

60. *Cong. Record,* 45th Cong., 1st sess., vol. 6, Index, p. 159; Philadelphia *Inquirer,* Oct. 30, 1877; Unger, *Greenback Era,* pp. 353–54; Nichols, "John Sherman and the Silver Drive," p. 156.

61. Nichols, "John Sherman and The Silver Drive"; *Cong. Record,* 45th Cong., 1st sess., vol. 1, pp. 241–42.

tried to avoid committing themselves on the Bland bill, and only half the number of legislators from these areas voted on the November 1877 measure compared with the earlier balloting.

The new vote also revealed a notable upsurge in silverite strength among Midwestern and Far Western Republicans. Eighteen additional Republican representatives supported the legislation from the Midwest alone, with the total number of party votes for silver from the area increasing from 33 to 51 during the intervening year. The overall silverite majority now reflected an increasing degree of bipartisanship, distinctly different from the predominantly Democratic vote for the Bland bill during the electoral crisis session. In November 1877, the measure received 66 Republican and 97 Democratic ballots, compared to a 44 to 120 ratio the previous December. The silver issue's political impact on Republicans in local and state races, especially in the Midwest, clearly influenced this major shift in congressional voting patterns.

The House did not debate the Bland bill prior to its passage in November 1877, nor would its sponsor allow any alterations to be proposed from the floor. John A. Reagen, for example, who had introduced the first remonetization measure in 1876, tried unsuccessfully to offer an amendment changing the 412.5 grain dollar to a 399.9 grain coin, in order to make the American silver dollar equal to the standard silver coin of Europe's Latin Monetary Union. Reagen's amendment implemented a recommendation contained in the Monetary Commission's majority report, a report that Bland had signed as a commission member, but the Missourian still refused to accept any changes in his bill and steered it quickly to a vote. Still, even most inflationist Democrats expected the Senate to amend the measure substantially before its final passage. Chairman Buckner, for example, confessed to one interviewer that he did not believe the Senate would agree completely to House measures on remonetization or on resumption repeal, and "hence it is the policy of the silver advocates of the House to make as large a

Table 5

Vote on the Bland Bill (Remonetizing Silver), House of Representatives, November 5, 1877

	Ayes			Nays		
	Rep.	Dem.	Ind.	Rep.	Dem.	Ind.
New England States						
Massachusetts				4	1	
Maine				4		
New Hampshire				2		
Vermont				3		
Connecticut						
Rhode Island				2		
TOTALS				15	1	
Middle Atlantic States						
New York	2	1		3	5	
Pennsylvania	1	5		1		
Maryland					1	
Delaware						
New Jersey						
TOTALS	3	6		4	6	
Midwestern States						
Ohio	11	8				
Illinois	8	7				
Indiana	7	3				
Wisconsin	5	2				
Minnesota	3					
Michigan	6			2		
Iowa	8					
Kansas	2					
Nebraska	1					
TOTALS	51	20		2		
Border States						
Kentucky		9				
Tennessee	2	6				
West Virginia		2				
Missouri	2	9		1		
TOTALS	4	26		1		

Table 5—Continued

	Ayes			Nays		
	Rep.	Dem.	Ind.	Rep.	Dem.	Ind.
Southern States						
Virginia		4				
North Carolina	1	7				
South Carolina	2	3				
Georgia		6			1	
Alabama		8				
Mississippi		6				
Florida						
Louisiana	1	3		1	1	
Texas		5			1	
Arkansas		2				
TOTALS	4	44		1	3	
Far Western States						
California	2	1		1		
Nevada	1					
Colorado						
Oregon	1					
TOTALS	4	1		1		
GRAND TOTALS	66	97		24	10	

TOTAL AYES: 163

TOTAL NAYS: 34

demand as they can, so as to influence the Senate and President to yield more than they otherwise would. This is the silver programme." The Bland bill itself was quickly referred to William Boyd Allison's Senate Finance Committee, which reported it on November 21 with amendments that altered its content significantly.[62]

Only days later, Hayes, who had previously resisted the cross-

62. New York *Journal of Commerce,* Nov. 1, 1877; *Cong. Record,* 45th Cong., 1st sess., vol. 1, pp. 241, 247, 581.

current of pressures for a statement on silver, from the eastern banking community and from his Ohio bimetallist friends, issued on December 3 his first Annual Message to Congress.[63] Here, the President finally indicated his growing concern over the threat posed by remonetization to the successful resumption of specie payments. "The obligation of the public faith transcends all questions of profit or public advantage," he commented, and "any attempt to pay the national indebtedness in any coinage of less commercial value than the money of the world would . . . . do irreparable injury to the public credit." Hayes' anxiety over the sharp decline in syndicate bond sales that followed House passage of the Bland bill, more than any other factor, provoked his decision to oppose remonetization openly. Thus, the Chief Executive noted in his message that he would approve a silver bill only if it provided for a dollar heavier than 412.5 grains. He proposed a silver dollar that would approximate the existing commercial value of the gold dollar, and he felt that even this coin would have to remain limited in its legal tender. The President implied broadly in his annual message that he would veto any measure that did not meet these specifications or that provided for repayment of the public debt, either principal or interest, in silver coins "of less commercial value than the present gold coinage of the country."[64]

Sherman's first annual Treasury Department report, also issued on December 3, echoed the President's recommendations, although it called in more enthusiastic terms than had Hayes for limited remonetization. Hoping to arrive at some compromise with moderate silverites, the secretary proposed substantial enlargement of the subsidiary coinage, supported an international monetary conference and approved restoration of the 412.5 grain silver dollar on the same limited legal tender basis as the

63. On the Ohio bimetallists and Hayes, see S. Dana Horton to R. B. Hayes, Nov. 21, 1877, and M. F. Force to Hayes, Dec. 14, 1877, Hayes MSS, Fremont. On banking community pressures, see Chap. 8, passim.

64. Richardson, ed., *Messages and Papers,* 9, 4415–17. See also Philadelphia *Inquirer,* Dec. 7, 1877; New York *Tribune,* Dec. 4, 1877.

greenbacks.[65] Sherman, unlike Hayes, did not denounce supporters of the Bland bill as inflationists bent upon repudiating the nation's legitimate obligations to foreign and domestic creditors. Even Hugh McCulloch, the banker and ex-Secretary of the Treasury who disliked Sherman personally and opposed many features of his resumption plan, praised the secretary for his skillful defense of the gold standard, calling it "singularly able and adroit."[66] Hayes' blunt condemnation of bimetallists as dangerous economic radicals may have led the chief executive's close friend, Stanley Matthews, to introduce his December 1877 Senate resolution declaring that all securities issued by the government prior to demonetization were payable either in gold *or* silver.[67]

Sherman had keener and more adroit political instincts than the President, and even while preparing his December 1877 recommendations opposing the Bland bill, the Treasury Secretary began exploring the possibility of a Senate compromise measure acceptable to the Administration. "As you have seen, the Senate [Finance Committee will] strike out the free coinage of silver and make it issuable by the United States from bullion purchased in the market, at the rate of $2,000,000 a month," he wrote Conant in London late in November 1877. "While grave objections exist to this proposition, it is very different from the one contained in the House bill."[68]

Shortly before issuing his December *Report* Sherman also tried once again to soothe the anxieties of syndicate bankers.[69] He assured them that unless the Senate incorporated three

65. *Annual Report of the Secretary of the Treasury for 1877* (Washington, 1877), pp. xix–xxv.

66. Hugh McCulloch to John Sherman, Dec. 5, 1877, McCulloch MSS, LC.

67. Nichols, "John Sherman and the Silver Drive," pp. 157–58. For debate on the Matthews Resolution, see *Cong. Record,* 45th Cong., 2d sess., vol. 7, pt. 1, pp. 47, 87–94, 549–64, 627–28.

68. John Sherman to Charles F. Conant, Nov. 24, 1877, Sherman MSS, LC.

69. John Sherman to August Belmont, Dec. 1, 1877, ibid.

"necessary amendments"—a limitation on the amount of coinage, a provision giving the profits of coinage to the government and not bullion sellers, and specific exemption of the public debt from repayment in silver—Hayes would veto the measure. Sherman believed that silverites lacked the two-thirds majority in both houses required for repassage. To avoid the necessity of a veto, however, Sherman urged Allison, Senate manager of the measure, to draft the appropriate changes in the House bill.[70]

The administration felt particularly disappointed with Allison's refusal to include provisions limiting silver's legal tender power or excluding payment of the public debt in silver among the amendments that the Iowan submitted to the Senate in November 1877. Sherman's request for additional changes, not accidentally, reached Allison on the same day that Senate debate began on the Matthews resolution which declared government securities payable in both gold and silver.[71] News of the resolution led to a further European decline in sales of American resumption bonds, according to most reports, and both the President and Sherman feared that even a greatly modified Senate bill would no longer quiet fears of investors unless government debts were exempted explicitly from repayment in silver.[72]

Allison, on the other hand, considered Senate passage of the revised Bland bill impossible with such a provision, and he refused to jeopardize the success of his other amendments by yielding to Sherman's request. In late December the Secretary

70. John Sherman to Charles F. Conant, Dec. 15, 1877 and Jan. 15, 1878; Sherman to John Rose, Jan. 7, 1878, Sherman MSS, LC. See also Sherman to R. B. Hayes, Jan. 30, 1878, enclosing Conant to Sherman, Jan. 30, 1878, Hayes Library, Fremont. "I know that upon you must mainly rest the responsibility for this measure," Sherman wrote Allison in December 1877, appealing for the Finance Committee chairman "to so amend the silver bill that it will not arrest the refunding of our debt or prevent the sale of our four per cent bonds." John Sherman to W. B. Allison, Dec. 10, 1877, Sherman MSS, LC.

71. *Cong. Record,* 45th Cong., 2d sess., vol. 7, pt. 1, pp. 47, 87–94.

72. Unger, *Greenback Era,* pp. 357–58.

informed Conant that he had "almost lost hope of getting the public debt excepted from the operation of the bill."[73] From this point until passage of the compromise Bland-Allison Act in February 1878, the Hayes administration played only a minor role in the congressional struggle for remonetization, although these were precisely the months when the issue dominated public and congressional discussion. The climax of the first silver drive lasted only three months, but this brief campaign to return the "dollar of the daddies" to the coinage generated the first important national bimetallist movement, and it opened two decades of agitation aimed at completely restoring silver as a monetary standard.

73. John Sherman to Charles F. Conant, Dec. 31, 1877, Sherman MSS, LC. See also Henry Arnitt Smith to Benjamin H. Bristow, Jan. 7, 1878, Bristow MSS, LC.

10

First Principles: Theorists and Theories of American Coinage

In the House the day was spent in the usual manner of Mondays, and at three o'clock the death of poor Mr. Mellish [Republican congressman from New York] was noticed. He died Saturday in the Insane Asylum. At half-past-three o'clock the House adjourned. He devoted himself almost exclusively to the study of the currency, became fully entangled with the theories of the subject and became insane. His public life was a terrible strain upon his nervous system.

The Diary of James A. Garfield, May 25, 1874.

The congressional Monetary Commission report, once published, became the bible of American bimetallists. John Percival Jones, Chairman of the Commission, began circulating the final printed document among his colleagues in October 1877, although an earlier draft had been submitted to Congress in March.[1] The majority report, which recommended immediate restoration of the double standard, was largely Jones' handiwork, and its conclusions reflected the prior convictions of Commission members. Jones, Richard Parks Bland, and Lewis Bogy had led the silver drive from its inception, and two other Commission members, Republican Congressman George Willard of Michigan and William S. Groesbeck of Ohio, had also been early bimetallists. Minority members included Republican Senator George

1. Unger, *Greenback Era*, p. 357.

S. Boutwell of Massachusetts, who had helped demonetize silver while serving as Grant's Secretary of the Treasury; the reformer and Harvard economist, Francis Bowen; and Democratic Congressman Randall Gibson of Louisiana.[2] The majority's endorsement of remonetization was never in question after George Melville Weston, original publicist of the "Crime of 1873," became the Monetary Commission's Recording Secretary.[3] Despite this, the group heard testimony from a score of bankers, merchants, government officials, economists, and monetary experts during the fall and winter of 1876–77.[4] It completed its inquiries in January 1877 and submitted its preliminary report to Congress in March.[5]

Critics of the silverite majority complained that, during the investigation, Jones and his associates sought "to color all the testimony given, suppress all that might be adverse, and direct it all to secure the verdict desired"—objections that appear justified.[6] Weeks before the group began compiling its findings, for example, George Weston wrote to Thurlow Weed soliciting the New Yorker's advice on using an 1868 Senate report by E. D. Morgan in which Morgan had defended the double standard. Weston's inquiry reveals the extent to which Jones and his recording secretary had prepared their recommendations even before public testimony had ended:

2. *Report of the United States Monetary Commission* (1877), passim.

3. *Commercial and Financial Chronicle,* Oct. 18, 1876.

4. For testimony taken before the Monetary Commission, see *Report,* vol. 2, passim. Among those advocating remonetization in their writings to or testimony before the commission were Henry Carey Baird, Thurlow Weed, I. S. Homans, Editor of *Banker's Magazine,* and John A. Dix. Opponents of the double standard included August Belmont, Director of the Mint Linderman, and Edward Atkinson. A third group of witnesses who favored an international bimetallic agreement included Henri Cernuschi, Ernest Seyd, and William Graham Sumner.

5. See Chap. 7, n. 51.

6. New York *Weekly Journal of Commerce,* Mar. 1, 1877.

> Gov. Morgan's report of 1868 in U.S. Senate, is full of matter which could be most advantageously quoted and used by the Silver Commission [Weston wrote Weed]. But the danger is that Gov. M. may *go back on us*. How much of a danger is this? You know him. Can he be influenced to say that he has changed his mind, and *now* thinks that Silver must be given up?
>
> He certainly dodged coming before the Commission in New York . . . although two or three invitations were sent him.
>
> It will hurt us, if we quote him, and he then goes back. If he could be relied on to keep silent, it would answer all purposes.
>
> Is it safe to quote him?[7]

Having submitted a first draft in March 1877, Jones and Weston remained in Washington throughout the spring and summer after Congress adjourned, working on the final text of the silver report. Lewis Bogy returned to Missouri where he died later in the year, and Groesbeck and Willard, the other two bimetallists on the commission, played only minor roles in composing the document. Several factors contributed to the long delay between submission of an early draft in March and publication in the fall. Jones wished to present the most credible economic arguments possible for remonetization, and Weston used the extra months to compile additional information and statistics on the monetary systems of other commercial nations.[8] Furthermore, the Nevada Republican wished to have the report widely read and rewrote the text several times, striving for plain and concise language.[9] Finally, Jones' conversion to greenback-

7. George Weston to Thurlow Weed, Dec. 13, 1876, Weed MSS, New York Historical Society. See also J. Barr Robertson to John C. Macdonald, Jan. 12, 1877, Robertson Letterbooks, Bancroft Library (Berkeley).

8. *Report,* vol. 1, passim.

9. John Percival Jones to Georgina Jones, July 21, 1877, Jones MSS, Huntington Library. See also J. P. Jones to Georgina Jones on the

ism in the spring of 1877, under the tutelage of his Washington neighbor and friend Benjamin F. Butler, meant that the westerner had to write the classic document defending restoration of bimetallism at a time when he believed this policy an inadequate solution for the country's monetary problems.

Jones' new paper money convictions quickly became known in Washington, and the dilemma of being a mining-state senator and Chairman of the silver commission while advocating the rag-baby became unnerving. In a September 1877 letter to his wife he complained bitterly "at being obliged [in the report] to leave these [new] fields untrodden," and the previous month, he informed one Ohio politician who had asked about the Monetary Commission report that "in his opinion it would not be of much service.[10] Committed to the silver bill for political reasons, however, Jones kept his new convictions to himself and completed the final report in time for distribution at the opening of Congress in October 1877.

The commission's majority argued that silver's current decline in market value was only temporary and caused primarily by legislative interference with "natural" monetary laws: specifically, by the metal's recent demonetization by the United States, Germany, and the Scandinavian states, and by the closing of Latin Union mints to further silver coinage. Jones and his

---

following 1877 dates: Feb. 13, Mar. 24, July 14, Aug. 28 and Sept. 4; Jones MSS. See also article by an anonymous "Observer," Washington (D.C.) newspaper column (n.p.), ca. July 1877 (n.d.) in Hayes Library, Fremont.

10. John Percival Jones to Georgina Jones, Sept. 2, 1877, Jones MSS, Huntington Library; A. F. Childs to James A. Garfield, Aug. 3, 1877, Garfield MSS, LC; Henry Linderman to Justin S. Morrill, June 5, 1877, Morrill MSS, LC; San Francisco *Chronicle,* June 14, 1877. Jones, an avowed opponent of the Hayes Administration and supporter of Roscoe Conkling's Stalwart wing of the party, also enjoyed the fact that the silver question embarrassed Midwestern Republican supporters of the President during the fall 1877 campaigns. John Percival Jones to Georgina Jones, Sept. 24, 1877, Jones MSS; John Percival Jones to William Boyd Allison, Aug. 13, 1877, Allison MSS.

colleagues denied that increased American production of silver had influenced the market slump substantially but acknowledged that a temporary decrease in Asian demand for western bullion, along with exaggerated estimates of Comstock silver mine yields, might have contributed to the decline. Above all, the silverites argued that unilateral American action to restore legal bimetallism could reverse, by itself, the downward movement of world silver prices.[11]

All five members of the majority—Jones, Bogy, Willard, Bland, and Groesbeck—agreed that legislative demonetization, more than any other factor, had been responsible for the metal's market decline. They unanimously recommended restoring the double standard and the "unrestricted coinage of both metals." The majority could not agree, however, on the legal relation to be established between gold and silver and filed separate reports on that question. They also skirted the controversial issue of the relationship between remonetization and resumption, although they argued that resumption was impossible under a single gold standard and that restoration of the silver dollar was "a measure essential to specie payments and *may* make such payments practicable." Jones and his associates concluded that returning silver, "one-half of [our] ancient and constitutionel money," to full legal-tender status would also help stimulate commerce and assist recovery from the protracted depression.[12]

Several witnesses before the commission influenced the conclusions of at least three silverites—Jones, Bogy, and Willard. The Yale economist William Graham Sumner, B. F. Nourse of the National Board of Trade, and Henri Cernuschi, the most prominent European advocate of the double standard, all testified in favor of establishing by treaty a worldwide valuation of the legal mint ratio between gold and silver. These "international bimetallists," a term then becoming fashionable to describe proponents of a negotiated solution to the monetary standard

11. *Report, I,* 125.
12. Ibid., pp. 126–28. Italics mine.

question, generally held the Latin Union silver-gold ratio of 15.5 to 1 to be the most acceptable world measurement. Jones, Bogy, and Willard followed their recommendation, calling the Latin Union ratio "most likely to assure stability and permanency" after remonetization. To adopt the 15.5 to 1 proportion would have involved either reducing the American silver dollar's weight from 412.5 to 399.9 grains or increasing the weight of the gold dollar from 25.8 to 26.6 grains, a drastic revision in American coinage which the three legislators recommended be placed on the agenda of an international conference only after the restoration of American bimetallism at the old 16 to 1 ratio. They stressed that the precise legal relation between silver and gold was "of far less importance" than immediate remonetization, and that their support for the eventual adoption of a 15.5 to 1 measurement did not imply opposition to the Bland bill, which authorized a return to the old ratio.[13]

Bland and Groesbeck, the two remaining silverite members, filed individual dissents defending the 16 to 1 American ratio. Groesbeck argued on nationalistic grounds while Bland feared that any suggested change in the current ratio would jeopardize swift congressional approval of his silver bill. But neither Groesbeck, an Ohio politician whose views on the monetary standard issue closely resembled Murat Halstead's, nor Bland greatly influenced the work of the Commission. The Missouri Democrat thought so little of its deliberations that he pressed for House approval of the silver bill in December 1876 without even bothering to wait until Jones had written his report.[14]

Three members of the commission dissented from the majority recommendations. Senator George S. Boutwell filed a brief statement calling for an international conference and postponement of congressional action on the question until an attempt to secure world cooperation had been made. Boutwell, although

13. Ibid., *1*, 128–31; vol. 2, passim.

14. Ibid., *1*, 131–33. See also W. S. Groesbeck to John Sherman, Jan 3, 1877, Sherman MSS, LC.

a gold monometallist, hoped to deflect the silver drive through the promise of eventual international bimetallism.[15]

Francis Bowen, on the other hand, rejected even the pretense of seeking a negotiated agreement and termed the "so-called double standard . . . an illusion and an impossibility." Bowen's recommendations, in which Randall Gibson concurred, urged retaining the gold standard on the grounds that recent fluctuations in the market price of silver made that metal "entirely unfit for use as a standard of value." The Harvard economist believed that silver should be employed only to supplement gold coinage through withdrawing an equivalent amount of paper money for each subsidiary silver piece placed in circulation. He suggested minting a subsidiary 345.6 grain silver dollar, equivalent in bullion content to two existing half-dollars, which would be legal tender for only twenty dollars. In Bowen's plan, these new dollars would be issued in exchange for greenbacks that would be destroyed immediately, thereby preventing further inflation of the currency while preparing for eventual resumption of specie payments. Bowen's forthright endorsement of greenback contraction as a prelude to resumption found few defenders except for a segment of the academic-reform community and a few northeastern politicians like Morrill.[16]

Despite its wide publicity, the Monetary Commission's report added little to previous arguments on the monetary standard question, and one monometallist newspaper termed it largely "a rehash of Senator JONES' speech upon silver made in the last Congress."[17] Disagreements among commission members corresponded remarkably well to the existing political divisions on the question in Washington. Jones and his four colleagues who advocated immediate remonetization spoke not

15. *Report, I,* 134–38. See also George S. Boutwell to Justin S. Morrill, Oct. 22, 1877, Morrill MSS, LC.

16. *Report, I,* 159–60. See also George S. Boutwell to Justin S. Morrill and Morrill to Francis Bowen, n.d., c. July 1877, Morrill MSS, LC; Bowen to John Sherman, July 21, 1877, Sherman MSS, LC.

17. San Francisco *Chronicle,* Oct. 21, 1877.

only for a majority of the commission but for a majority in both houses of Congress, while Boutwell's call for an international conference reflected the delaying tactics favored by moderates like John Sherman and hard-pressed congressmen like James Garfield, caught between his own belief in the gold standard and his constituents' enthusiasm for silver. Francis Bowen, on the other hand, opposed all varieties of bimetallism as did an embattled congressional minority, strongest perhaps among northeastern legislators but with some support in other sections of the country, as Louisiana Democrat Gibson's concurrence with Bowen's recommendations indicated. Although the majority and minority reports of the Monetary Commission probably made few converts, either in Washington or elsewhere, they provided ammunition for subsequent legislative and public debate on the silver issue.

Publication of the commission's report clearly failed to influence existing divisions among American intellectuals over the merits of remonetization, and no consensus on the question emerged from the correspondence exchanged among academics and reformers during the closing months of the silver drive. Thus, although gold-standard advocates remained prominent in groups such as the American Social Science Association, strong support for an international bimetallic standard also existed within this informal league of professional and amateur social theorists. In 1877, for example, the Association's executive committee chose a bimetallist tract, S. Dana Horton's *Silver and Gold,* as its semiofficial manual of information, and Henri Cernuschi's well-publicized visit to the United States to testify before the Monetary Commission had, according to the Association's Secretary, F. B. Sanborn, "made many converts to his theory of international bimetallism," although few reformers advocated immediate remonetization.[18] Testimony taken by the

18. *Transactions of the American* [*Social Science*] *Association,* 9, January 1878, 8–9.

Monetary Commission exposed this schism among American economists over proper disposition of the silver issue. Respected hard-money advocates like William Graham Sumner and B. F. Nourse argued the bimetallist case forcefully while Edward Atkinson and Horace White urged retention of the gold standard with equal vigor.[19]

Four basic positions on the question emerged among publicists. Amateur and professional economists, despite an abundance of variations and individual refinements in argument, divided into one of four basic groups: gold monometallists, international bimetallists, tactical bimetallists, and advocates of immediate remonetization. Furthermore, although these four major lines of argument dominated the controversy, none of the intellectual camps had either acknowledged leaders or organizational identity. They represented informal ideological clusters of men who held similar ideas on the silver question and who corresponded frequently while working independently to publicize their beliefs. Personal contacts within each group remained haphazard and irregular, and there was no systematic effort to promote or to oppose remonetization made by the intellectual community during the brief silver drive of the seventies.

Three writers became particularly prominent among defenders of the gold standard in the 1870s, Henry Richard Linderman, Henry Varnum Poor, and David A. Wells, who all published widely distributed treatises on the monetary standard question during the controversy. Wells, by common agreement, was American monometallism's leading polemicist.[20] Linderman, because of his official duties as Director of the Mint, attempted primarily to influence congressional and executive opinion

19. *Report,* vol. 2, passim.

20. Linderman, *Money and Legal Tender;* Henry Varnum Poor, *Resumption and the Silver Question* (New York, 1878); David A. Wells, *The Silver Question. The Dollar of the Fathers versus the Dollar of the Sons* (New York, 1877).

against remonetization, although he also wrote a popular gold standard tract on *Money and Legal Tender in the United States.*[21] Poor, a business editor and railroad expert who published several volumes on the silver issue, drafted the long petition sent to Congress in January 1878 by a hastily organized committee of eastern national bankers and businessmen opposed to passage of the Bland bill.[22]

Wells corresponded regularly with anti-silver public officials and reformers, and his published articles attacking the double standard were widely reprinted and quoted by the gold standard forces. The Connecticut Democrat, an intimate friend of both silverite leaders like Jacob D. Cox and of anti-silverites like James Garfield, had built his public reputation in previous service as a reforming government civil servant and through strenuous pamphleteering on behalf of tariff reduction. Wells, more than any other single individual, served as a clearing house for economists and reformers anxious to express opposition to bimetallism.[23] His gold standard pamphlet on "The Dollar of the Fathers and the Dollar of the Sons," originally published in Halstead's Cincinnati *Commercial,* was reprinted in monometallist newspapers throughout the country and became the most popular presentation of arguments for retaining the single standard.[24]

21. Henry Linderman to Justin S. Morrill, June 5, 1877. See also Morrill to Carl Schurz, June 4, 1877, and Schurz to Morrill, June 5, 1877, Morrill MSS, LC.

22. Alfred D. Chandler, Jr., *Henry Varnum Poor: Business Editor, Analyst, and Reformer* (Cambridge, Mass., 1956), pp. 274–76.

23. David A. Wells to Carl Schurz, July 2, 1877, Schurz MSS, LC; Hoogenboom, *Outlawing the Spoils,* pp. 17–18, 26–27, 78, 112, 127, 144, 161. For a sampling of the large number of letters received by Wells from anti-silver reformers, see the following: Allan Laquihar to Wells, May 31, 1877; Henry Kemp to Wells, July 26, 1877; A. Thorndike Rice to Wells, Oct. 8, 1877; and Isaac Sherman to Wells, Jan. 11, 1878; Wells MSS, LC.

24. Wells to Schurz, July 2, 1877, Wells MSS, LC; Wells to Garfield, Nov. 26, 1877, Garfield MSS, LC. Wells, *The Silver Question.*

Few monometallist writers had Wells' rare ability to maintain amicable personal ties with silverite friends despite their differences over monetary policy. Many gold standard advocates, while haranguing constantly against the "silver lunacy," hardly bothered to disguise a personal contempt and moral outrage toward bimetallists that matched their earlier distaste for Greenbackers and other financial "repudiators."[25] This particular segment of the academic-reform community saw remonetization as a threat to social stability as well as an economic policy question. In a typical expression of elitest hostility towards "bimetallist Jacobinism," Harvard's Charles W. Eliot wrote President Hayes in December 1877 "that all respectable people in this part of the country (of both parties) are on your side upon the silver question, and are relying upon your resoluteness to protect the nation from the shame and loss with which Congress threatens it."[26] Sometimes the aversion felt by self-professed "respectable" monometallists toward the silverite cause provoked piquant reactions, such as the novelist William Dean Howell's confession to James Garfield that, as editor of Boston's *Atlantic Monthly,* he would first have to "conquer [his] repugnance to silverism" before soliciting an article from an advocate of the double standard for inclusion in a symposium on the monetary issue planned by the magazine.[27]

Patrician hostility toward "the Silver madness and wickedness" stressed the gold standard views of "the better classes of our people in both parties." Close political ties existed among a number of monometallist reformers and their legislative counterparts in Washington who opposed the Bland bill, ties that had been developed in earlier struggles for resumption and against

25. Unger, *Greenback Era,* pp. 337–38.

26. Charles W. Eliot to R. B. Hayes, Jan. 8, 1878, Hayes MSS, Fremont.

27. William Dean Howells to James A. Garfield, Dec. 1, 1877, Garfield MSS, LC.

the rag-baby.[28] These friendships and informal associations often crossed partisan and sectional lines. Wells, himself a Democrat, corresponded regularly with Republican friends like Garfield and Schurz on the silver issue as well as with Democratic opponents of restoration.[29] Another important monometallist writer, Edward Atkinson, commented on this ideological camaraderie among "the better classes . . . in both parties" in an 1878 letter to Garfield, inviting him to visit Boston "with [Democrats] Bayard—Lamar, Hill, Gibson, etc., etc.," all vocal opponents of the Bland bill. Almost as an afterthought, Atkinson quipped: "Let Allison in . . . if he will behave well."[30]

Opposition to immediate remonetization came not only from gold standard economists and publicists, however, but also from most leading American advocates of international bimetallism. The three major figures in the new movement were S. Dana Horton, an enthusiastic young Ohio friend of the President's; the New York banker and businessman, George Walker; and the Harvard economist Francis Amasa Walker. Of the three, Dana Horton and George Walker were most active and influential during the struggle over the Bland bill. The intellectual godfather of these American "agreement silverites," as they sometimes called themselves, was Henri Cernuschi, "the chief bimetallist missionary of Europe." Cernuschi retired from a French banking firm in the seventies to publicize his belief in a dual world monetary standard.[31]

28. Burke Hinsdale to James A. Garfield, Dec. 31, 1877, *Garfield-Hinsdale Letters,* pp. 384–86; I. N. Demmon to Garfield, Dec. 8, 1877; and Lemuel Moss to Garfield, Sept. 3, 1877, both Garfield MSS, LC; Unger, *Greenback Era.*

29. Wells to Schurz and Wells to Garfield, Schurz and Wells MSS, LC. See also Wells to Thomas F. Bayard, Mar. 27, 1878, Wells MSS, LC.

30. Edward Atkinson to James A. Garfield, Apr. 19, 1878, Garfield MSS, LC.

31. Cincinnati *Commercial,* Dec. 9, 1876; New York *Graphic,* Sept. 7, 1876. See also *Graphic,* Jan. 11 and Jan. 12, 1877.

The French bimetallist, formerly an Italian associate of Garibaldi's, arrived in the United States in December 1876, where he spent several months. He met with sympathetic businessmen and economists, testified before the Monetary Commission and gave numerous newspapers interviews in order to stimulate American support for his ideas. Believing that the amount of gold coin available in the United States to support specie resumption was inadequate, Cernuschi hoped to arouse public enthusiasm on both sides of the Atlantic for an agreement among all western nations to restore legal bimetallism. The United States, he believed, found itself trapped within a simple yet vicious monetary cycle:

> For the United States to resume specie payments, M. Cernuschi says they must give the silver dollar the same value as the gold, accept silver at custom-houses and be able to pay European bond-holders in silver dollars. But first Europe must become bi-metallic, else European creditors would suffer serious losses by receiving inconvertible dollars.[32]

American supporters of an international conference invariably accepted Cernuschi's argument that a European treaty on the monetary standard question must *precede* domestic remonetization in order to make bimetallism work. These "agreement silverites" also disassociated themselves from supporters of the Bland bill because of the suspicion that congressional silverites mingled with "inflationists and repudiationists."

"'The object of the Bi-metallists . . . is not so much to favor the debtor class by diminishing the weight of debts," Francis Amasa Walker concluded in the 1878 first edition of his famous study of *Money*, "as to prevent those debts being artificially increased by a diminution in the stock of money, through the demonetization of one of the precious metals."[33] Francis Walker

32. *Graphic.* See also *Report of the Monetary Commission*, 2, 473–511, for Cernuschi's testimony.

33. Francis Amasa Walker, *Money* (New York, 1878), p. 268.

took little part in the struggle against immediate remonetization, but his namesake, George Walker, published a number of letters in the New York *Tribune* denouncing the Bland Act. Once passage of a congressional silver bill appeared certain, however, George Walker worked closely with William Boyd Allison to modify the House measure's more inflationary aspects.[34]

Dana Horton also opposed domestic action on silver prior to calling an international conference, on the paradoxical grounds that once the United States had restored legal bimetallism, the market price of silver would inevitably rise, the metal would cease to depreciate and, therefore, European states would lose interest in negotiating a worldwide monetary agreement.[35] The young Ohioan bombarded Hayes and other officials with a series of interminably long letters outlining his monetary notions and, unlike the two Walkers, politicians considered Horton a pedantic nuisance. Later in the century, President Benjamin Harrison paused after examining one of Horton's periodic epistles and referred to him derisively as "an encyclopedia to which a more practical man might refer."[36] Horton later served as an unofficial American diplomatic agent and as an official representative to European monetary conferences, but he played no major role in shaping government policy or public opinion during the silver drive itself. His major contribution was an ebullient probimetallist tract, *Silver and Gold,* first published in 1876 and circulated subsequently by the American Social Science Association.[37]

Although Francis Walker wrote the decade's most intelligent

34. George Walker to Whitelaw Reid, Dec. 26, 1876, and Walker to Reid, Dec. 24, 1877, Reid MSS, LC; Walker to W. B. Allison, Mar. 2, 1878, Allison MSS.

35. S. Dana Horton to R. B. Hayes, Feb. 29, 1877, Hayes MSS, LC.

36. Benjamin Harrison to T. Jefferson Coolidge, Aug. 14, 1891, Harrison MSS, LC. On Horton's role as a diplomatic agent, see Jeanette P. Nichols, "Silver Diplomacy," *Political Sciences Quarterly, 48,* 1933, 565–88.

37. Horton, *Silver and Gold.*

American defense of international bimetallism and Dana Horton was the policy's most passionate advocate, George Walker became the group's ablest political strategist. Of all the "agreement silverites," only this New York businessman remained close to government policymakers during the 1870s. Having served as Assistant Secretary of the Treasury under Salmon P. Chase during the Lincoln administration, and as an active liberal Republican and banker during the Reconstruction years, Walker had developed a number of close friendships with congressmen, cabinet members, and other leading public officials. During the silver drive he exploited his earlier associations with Schurz, Sherman, Garfield, Allison, and other important figures in the controversy to promote his views and serve as an important intermediary between the advocates of international bimetallism and the political community, a role similar to the one David A. Wells performed for gold monometallists. For example, during James A. Garfield's brief 1877 phase as a "probationary" convert to bimetallism, Walker tutored the Ohio congressman, introducing him to domestic and European literature on the subject.[38]

When William Boyd Allison began to amend the Bland bill to blunt its inflationary potential, therefore, the Iowa Republican turned naturally to Walker for advice and leaned heavily on his counsel during the closing months of the silver drive. Walker helped Allison prepare his amendments, but he continued to oppose the silver bill itself. Like most American "agreement silverites," he considered its passage harmful to the chances for eventual international solution. He believed that the 16 to 1 legal ration of the remonetized 412.5 grain silver dollar to gold, once restored, would probably endanger chances for negotiating successfully with Latin Union nations that maintained a 15.5 to 1 ratio. "There are different ways of fighting the Bland bill," Walker wrote Whitelaw Reid in December 1877, "mine as you

38. George Walker to James A. Garfield, Dec. 3, 1877 and Jan. 18, 1878, Garfield MSS, LC.

know is from the side of international bimettalism [*sic*] . . . Now if you think I can do any good by writing one two or three more letters for the Tribune all to be published within the next fortnight, I will go to work and write the first tomorrow."[39] Working with government officials and through the press, George Walker played a significant if unrecognized role in preventing a complete victory for silver in Congress.

Although men such as Walker and Horton believed sincerely in international bimetallism, others supported this policy in order to delay congressional action on the silver question. Honest "agreement silverites" like J. S. Moore of New York, for example, complained bitterly when the House failed to approve the Senate's international conference resolution in January 1877, but support for such a meeting came also from more surprising quarters.[40] Thus, Samuel B. Ruggles, the earliest post-Civil War American gold standard advocate, endorsed the Senate resolution in a November 1876 letter to Director of the Mint Linderman. Writing on behalf of the New York Chamber of Commerce, which had lobbied for demonetization from 1867 on, Ruggles recommended convening a conference with the European states although, in the same letter, the New York merchant referred to Henri Cernuschi's recently developed phrase "international bimetallism" as "an imposing polysyllable used to cloak the naked and inherent logical absurdity of a DOUBLE *standard*."[41] Reluctant "agreement silverites" like Ruggles hoped that convening an international conference would forestall congressional action on silver legislation. Pronounced congressional goldbugs such as Garfield and Justin Morrill, monometallist newspapers like Boston's *Commercial Bulletin* and leading syn-

39. George Walker to Whitelaw Reid, Dec. 24, 1877, Reid MSS, LC.

40. New York *Evening Post*, cited in Cincinnati *Commercial*, Jan. 21, 1877.

41. "Letter from Samuel B. Ruggles in behalf of the N.Y. Chamber of Commerce to the Director of the Mint of the U.S.," Nov. 18, 1876; reprinted (New York, 1877), p. 5.

dicate bankers like August Belmont all joined Ruggles in 1877 to support a world conference that would resolve what the English economist Stanley Jevons called "the battle of the standards."[42]

Other gold monometallists scoffed at this rush of unexpected conversions to international bimetallism even while recognizing its tactical importance. The New York reformer Isaac Sherman bubbled with delight in a July 1877 note to David A. Wells at Hayes' rumored endorsement of such a conference, since Sherman felt that the change symbolized the President's repudiation of his Ohio silverite friends, "for it is simply chimerical to suppose that the great commercial nations will adopt the bimetallic standard. This is the domain of dream land."[43] Even many sincere "agreement silverites" understood the strategic importance of their policy in fighting the Bland bill. "If we are to defeat the establishment of bi-metallism in this country, acting by itself," B. F. Nourse wrote Wells in July 1877, "it *must be* by and through the hope of international bi-metallism." The Boston merchant cautioned Wells that "if that hope be destroyed, or put aside as unworthy of effort, I fear we cannot defeat the local adoption of bimetallism even over the executive veto."[44]

Debate over the monetary standard question among American intellectuals lacked, for the most part, that clear division evident in earlier Reconstruction quarrels over inflation, specie resumption, and other public credit issues. Instead of splitting into easily distinguishable soft money and hard money camps, all factions in the struggle over remonetization except for the Greenbackers claimed to represent sound, hard-money beliefs. In such ideological confusion, gold standard advocates like Wells and inter-

42. Henry B. Russell, *International Monetary Conferences* (New York and London, 1898), pp. 183–87; Boston *Commercial Bulletin,* cited in *The Iron Age,* Aug. 23, 1877; August Belmont to John Sherman, Nov. 29, 1877, Sherman MSS, LC. The Jevons phrase is quoted in Horton, *Silver and Gold.*

43. Isaac Sherman to David A. Wells, July 10, 1877, Wells MSS, LC.

44. B. F. Nourse to David A. Wells, July 3, 1877, ibid.

national bimetallists like Nourse battled strenuously, but not jointly, against the Bland bill. "Agreement silverites," in turn, included some who took international negotiation seriously and others who wished mainly to prevent restoration of the "dollar of the daddies" under any circumstances. Believers in the Bland bill, of course, insisted that American silver first be restored as a full legal tender before embarking on a world conference, but suport for *immediate* remonetization rarely came from academics or reformers.

Only a handful of intellectuals and publicists, notably Thomas Balch, a Philadelphia member of the Social Science Association, and New York City's Union League Club President, W. S. Palmer, favored swift passage of the House silver bill.[45] Except for the Monetary Commission report, no systematic treatise appeared defending unilateral restoration of the double standard that was even roughly comparable either to Francis Amasa Walker's writings on international bimetallism or to the gold standard tracts of Linderman, Poor, and Wells. Almost two decades were to pass before young Master "Coin" emerged to confound the arguments of scheming financiers, and the most influential publicist among silverites in the seventies was the Cincinnati *Commercial's* acerbic editor, Murat Halstead.

The curriculum in *Halstead's* financial school consisted of a daily editorial litany demanding immediate restoration of the double standard. Halstead dismissed international bimetallism as a snare skillfully set by gold monometallists to delay action on the Bland bill: "[It] has to recommend it to the gold men, the sweetness of doing nothing." Restore the old silver dollar, the *Commercial's* liberal Republican editor intoned repeatedly, and thereby insure the success of resumption. Halstead disputed the suggestion advanced by Cernuschi and other "agreement silverites" that only American acceptance of the Latin Union's 15.5 to 1 silver-gold ratio would halt fluctuations in the metal's

45. Cincinnati *Commercial,* Sept. 15, 1876; W. S. Palmer to John Sherman, Nov. 12, 1877, Sherman MSS, LC.

world market value. Although he did not oppose an international conference after domestic remonetization, Halstead, like most other late-nineteenth-century monetary "theorists," approached the silver question as a moral problem as well as a strictly economic one: "We wish not so much to attain the nicety of moneyed righteousness at once, as to do ourselves an act of justice, and to make the American contracts that which they were before the change [in 1873] that we denounce as illegal, unconstitutional, impolitic and vicious.[46]

Few advocates of immediate restoration in the 1870s concerned themselves primarily with the economic implications of returning to a dual monetary standard, and Halstead's preachments stand as a valid barometer of the first silver movement's temper. Men like Halstead, Jones, Weed, and Medill all insisted on remonetization as much for the justice of this demand as for its effectiveness. John Sherman recognized this more clearly than most opponents of restoration when, soon after final congressional approval of the silver bill, he explained to an English friend that the movement's success was "unavoidable, growing out of the impression that prevailed that the old dollar had been dropped from the coinage . . . under circumstances which led to suspicion that it was done to add to the burden of private debts . . . it was the feeling of resentment that caused the passage of the silver bill."[47] On all sides of the quarrel, this "feeling of resentment" inspired most of the prominent theorists and theories of American coinage during the first silver drive.

46. Cincinnati *Commercial,* Jan. 18 and 21, 1877.

47. John Sherman to J. H. Tuleston, Mar. 1, 1878, Sherman MSS, LC.

11

Money and Party: Business, Politics, and the Silver Movement

Matters of currency are accepted by the masses of people as quasi *matters of fate.*

Ernest Seyd, *Suggestions in Reference to the Metallic Coinage of the United States of America* (London, 1871)

House passage of the Bland bill in November 1877 stirred significant public interest in the silver issue for the first time, and within months the business community and the American electorate had polarized dramatically in their response to remonetization. The first silver movement emerged at this time, and its composition differed significantly from the later, more prominent, bimetallist crusade during the 1890s. The major components in this early "free-silver" coalition mirrored the economic and social tensions of an America then still reeling from four unrelieved years of business depression.

The ease and swiftness with which the House disposed of the silver bill horrified the country's monometallists and helped galvanize opposition to remonetization, especially from members of the eastern banking community who held substantial amounts in government securities. A hastily organized delegation of syndicate bankers, merchants, insurance underwriters, savings bank and trust company officials from New York and Philadelphia descended upon Washington on November 13 to lobby against

Senate approval of the Bland bill.[1] They appeared before the Senate Finance Committee and at the Treasury Department to remonstrate against the silver bill, marking the opening of a well-financed effort led by the New York banking community aimed at defeating the legislation.[2] The organizer of this campaign was George S. Coe of the American Exchange Bank of New York, who had previously helped develop that city's National Bank Clearing House Association, had assisted in founding the American Bankers' Association in 1875 and tirelessly advocated cooperation among financiers on common economic and political problems.[3]

National bankers like Coe, in order to develop a meaningful alliance among anti-silver businessmen, had to restrain their long-standing hostility toward the great independent banking houses—firms such as August Belmont and Company; Drexel, Morgan, and Company; J. and W. Seligman, and Company; and Morton, Bliss, and Company—that enjoyed the benefits of exclusive participation in profitable government funding syndicates. Secretary Sherman had rejected an earlier 1877 bid by a group of New York national banks for control of his new four percent resumption bond sale because of a more favorable pro-

1. New York *Tribune,* Nov. 18, 1877; Philadelphia *Inquirer,* Nov. 14, 1877; Chicago *Tribune,* Nov. 14, 1877; New York *Graphic,* Nov. 14, 1877; Unger, *Greenback Era,* p. 356; Nichols, "John Sherman and the Silver Drive," p. 157.

2. Syndicate member F. O. French opened this campaign in a November letter to John Sherman, announcing the imminent arrival in Washington of the "Committee of gentlemen connected with insurance and trust companies as well as with the Banks." French to Sherman, Nov. 12, 1877. See also Belmont to Sherman, Nov. 7 and Nov. 29, 1877, Sherman MSS, LC.

3. The best account of Coe's contribution to American banking can be found in Fritz Redlich's *The Molding of American Banking, Men and Ideas, Part II, 1840–1910* (New York, 1951), Appendix, pp. 424–38.

posal by the older syndicate of private bankers.[4] Furthermore, many eastern financiers still resented the Treasury's decision to prepare for resumption not by cooperating with the national banks but by accumulating a gold reserve through those private bond sales which would be held separately from government bank deposits.[5]

Despite reservations concerning the Treasury's resumption policy, however, national banks and eastern insurance companies owned an amount in government securities estimated by some at over $600 million dollars, and they had no wish to be repaid in depreciated silver coin.[6] During the Christmas congressional recess, therefore, petitions against the silver bill poured into Washington from Boston, Philadelphia, and New York financial institutions.[7] In New York City syndicate bankers explored the possibility of financing a "nonpartisan" political drive on behalf of sound money in the midwestern strongholds of greenback and silverite heresies, a campaign later conducted during the state elections of 1878 under auspices of a newly created "Honest Money League of the Northwest."[8]

Opponents of remonetization made haste to organize in January 1878 at a special meeting of "representatives of about all the national and State banks in [New York] city."[9] To coordinate

4. Sherman forced the old syndicate led by August Belmont and Company to make room for the First National Bank of New York in order to placate that city's national banking fraternity. Ibid., p. 368. See also Chap. 6, n. 41.

5. New York *Journal of Commerce,* Nov. 22, 1877. See also Horace White to Carl Schurz, Aug. 17, 1877, Schurz MSS, LC.

6. Unger, *Greenback Era,* p. 360.

7. Philadelphia *Inquirer,* Dec. 1, 1877; New York *Graphic,* Dec. 7, 1877 and Jan. 8, 1878; "Uncle Sam" [Riggs and Company] to T. F. Bayard, Dec. 15, 1877, Bayard MSS, LC.

8. Levi P. Morton to Whitelaw Reid, Dec. 27, 1877 and Jan. 14, 1878; H. C. Fahnestock to Reid, Dec. 7, 1877, Reid MSS, LC; Unger, *Greenback Era,* p. 388.

9. New York *Weekly Journal of Commerce,* Jan. 17, 1878.

their anti-silver activities, the assemblage appointed a committee composed of bankers, merchants, trust company, insurance company and savings bank officials from New York, Boston, Philadelphia, and Baltimore.[10] Such united action by the eastern financial community on political issues was still comparatively new and not entirely effective. The president of one Philadelphia bank, for example, agreed to support the campaign personally but declined to commit his institution. Also, at the same meeting, the head of the Bowery Savings Bank, then the country's largest savings enterprise, endorsed the circulation of up to $150,000,000 worth of subsidiary silver coins, a proposal promptly ridiculed by his counterpart at the Emigrant Industrial Savings Bank, who told the amused throng of bankers and businessmen that it would require "trucks for the loading of sufficient [silver] with which to go to market."[11] Before the meeting broke up, however, it appointed George S. Coe to organize national business opposition to the Bland bill and to solicit banks and other financial groups as well as merchants and manufacturers for their cooperation. Those contacted would be urged to petition Congress against passage of the silver bill, a task that Coe began immediately on behalf of his newly formed ad hoc committee representing the eastern banks.[12]

Coe asked his friend, Henry Varnum Poor, the railroad economist, to draft the group's memorial to Congress and Poor's long remonstrance, published and widely circulated among gold standard advocates, was an extremely able defense of monometallism. Poor stressed the argument that silver, once recoined at the now overvalued ratio of sixteen to one, would not only drive gold coinage from circulation. It would also interfere with

10. Ibid.; Redlich, *The Molding of American Banking*, pp. 430–32; Unger, *Greenback Era*, p. 360.

11. New York *Weekly Journal of Commerce.*

12. Ibid.; Redlich, *The Molding of American Banking;* Unger, *Greenback Era.*

foreign trade and with the sale of resumption bonds abroad, cause inflation and aggravate economic distress at home.[13] The eastern bankers appeared pessimistic about their ability to delay or defeat remonetization in Congress, and Coe's committee also urged the country's financial institutions, mercantile groups and manufacturers to place their business affairs completely on a gold basis as quickly as possible to prepare for the onslaught of possible "silver inflation" following passage of the Bland bill.[14]

By February 1878 Hayes had received memorials opposing the Bland bill not only from the eastern bankers but also from financial Clearing House Associations in Chicago, Milwaukee, New Orleans, and elsewhere.[15] Coe's coordinating group made little effort to contact the majority of legislators who either supported restoration or wavered on the question. Fearing imminent Senate passage of the Bland bill, most bankers saw their only hope in a presidential veto, believing that the silverites would find it difficult to muster the two-thirds majority in both houses needed for repassage. Coe and his associates directed their energies, therefore, primarily toward impressing upon Hayes and his advisers the danger that remonetization presented to successful resumption of specie payments. In one letter to the President, Coe called the silver agitation an "imminent danger . . . greater in fact than the darkest moment of the war," and acknowledged that the banking community's object was "frankly . . . to possess your mind with some of the views entertained by

13. Chandler, *Henry Varnum Poor,* pp. 275–76; Committee of the Banks of New York, Boston, Philadelphia and Baltimore, *The Silver Question: Memorial to Congress* (New York, 1878).

14. Redlich, *The Molding of American Banking.* See also George S. Coe to R. B. Hayes, Jan. 31, 1878; Hayes MSS, Fremont; George S. Coe to Thomas F. Bayard, Feb. 9, 1878 and Feb. 12, 1878; August Belmont to Bayard, Nov. 18, 1877 and Feb. 12, 1878; A. F. Drexel to Bayard, Feb. 14, 1878; Bayard MSS, LC; August Belmont to James A. Garfield, Feb. 1, 1878 and Mar. 2, 1878, Garfield MSS, LC.

15. Unger, *Greenback Era,* p. 260.

the best men in our profession, in order to strengthen if possible your own deep convictions."[16]

The hue and cry against silver raised in eastern banking circles on the whole had little significant impact on congressional or executive response to the silver question. The bankers, fighting a strong public tide favorable to restoration, showed no disposition to assist moderate senators like Allison or Wallace of Pennsylvania in preparing amendments to the Bland bill that might remove its most objectionable features. Instead, they devoted themselves to lobbying the President, who already agreed with them. In some cases the eastern financiers even opposed attempts in the Senate to restrict the inflationary potential of remonetization. "My feeling was that if the Bland bill passed, the country would get so sick of it in a short time that there would be an equal hue and cry to repeal it as there is to pass it," Morris K. Jesup of the New York investment house of Jesup, Paton, and Company wrote his friend Allison in February 1878. "On the other hand, if it was loaded down with amendments (as you have done) . . . it would take a longer time to know the mischief it was doing, than if we had the Bill pure and simple."[17]

Less important figures in the banking community from New England to New Orleans responded to the threat posed by remonetization with similarly fearful estimates of its economic impact. "It must be considered a *warfare* on the resumption act," one upstate New York banker wrote Sherman, while from his Wall Street office another frenzied financier exclaimed that he could "compare the 'silver craze' only to the Crusades, especially that one in which the school-children took the lead and perished by tens of thousands."[18]

16. George S. Coe to R. B. Hayes, Hayes MSS, Fremont; August Belmont to David A. Wells, Jan. 19, 1878, Wells MSS, LC.

17. Morris K. Jesup to W. B. Allison, Feb. 20, 1878. On Jesup's anxieties concerning remonetization, see also Jesup to Allison, Jan. 30, 1878 and Feb. 4, 1878, Allison MSS, Des Moines.

18. Isaac Sherman to John Sherman, Nov. 23, 1877, Sherman MSS, LC; James B. Hodgskin to David A. Wells, Mar. 6, 1878, Wells MSS,

Despite public enthusiasm for silver in the region, a number of midwestern bankers joined their eastern colleagues in vehemently opposing the Bland bill. The Milwaukee Clearing House Association announced its hostility to the double standard early in the silver drive, and monometallist sentiment permeated Chicago's influential banking community. In Ohio a number of individual bankers denounced the silver agitation, while in Chicago and Milwaukee several hundred bankers and businessmen signed petitions in December 1877 endorsing the administration's financial policy, although the move may have been only a gesture of sympathy by friends of Hayes and Sherman rather than an anti-silver statement.[19]

More surprisingly the financial and business leaders of San Francisco almost unanimously opposed remonetization. Despite close economic ties between the city's leading banks and the major silver mines on Nevada's Comstock Lode—every major San Francisco bank held a controlling interest in various mines on the Lode—the Pacific coast bankers remained as hostile to restoring bimetallism as Coe and his eastern associates. California Governor F. F. Low, a Republican stalwart and manager of the

---

LC. For other evidence of Eastern banking opposition to silver, see also W. H. Y. Hackett (Portsmouth, New Hampshire) to Thomas Bayard, Feb. 6, 1878, and Elliot, Johnson & Company (Wilmington, Del.) to Bayard, Feb. 8, 1878; Bayard MSS, LC; C. P. Williams (Albany, N.Y.) to Garfield, Dec. 12, 1877, Garfield MSS, LC; W. H. Hayes to Sherman, June 15, 1877, Sherman MSS, LC; Unger, *Greenback Era,* pp. 355–56; Philadelphia *Inquirer,* Feb. 21, 1878; G. L. Foote to H. C. Fahnestock, in Fahnestock to Sherman, Nov. 8, 1877, Sherman MSS, LC.

19. Unger, *Greenback Era,* p. 360; Frank C. James, *The Growth of Chicago Banks* (New York, 1938), *1,* 478; *Cong. Record,* 45th Cong., 2d sess., vol. 7, pt. 2, p. 765; S. Hayward to Garfield, Nov. 15, 1877. See also A. S. Stratton to Garfield, Dec. 11, 1877, Garfield MSS, LC; C. F. Adae to Sherman, Oct. 10, 1877, and Pitt Cooke to Sherman, Jan. 10, 1878, Sherman MSS, LC; William Henry Smith to John Sherman, Dec. 22, 1877; William Henry Smith to R. B. Hayes, Jan. 10, 1878, both Smith MSS, typescript, Hayes Library, Fremont.

Bay City's powerful Anglo-Californian Bank, praised "the tendency in all the leading commercial nations . . . toward a single-standard" as he denounced congressional silver legislation.[20] The leaders of the Bank of California, the Anglo-Californian Bank, and other financial institutions in the city openly attacked the Bland bill as a threat to resumption in terms similar to those used by bankers in eastern seaboard cities. Despite the importance of silver to San Francisco as a local product, the drive to restore legal bimetallism received no personal or financial encouragement from the banking or mining kings of the Pacific coast. Even the city's Chamber of Commerce petitioned Congress against passage of the silver bill "as a killing blow at private and national faith." The major West coast business community was even more implacably opposed to remonetization than its eastern counterparts.[21]

Anti-silver sentiment also arose forcefully among many southern businessmen, whose sentiments on the question have generally been neglected by historians. Quarrels between hard money and paper money advocates in the South extended back to the antebellum period struggles of Jacksonians and Whigs, and no single sectional position on remonetization existed in the South anymore than elsewhere in the country.[22] Despite the preponderance of southern congressional votes favorable to the Bland bill, many of the section's businessmen remained hostile to silver legislation and managed to generate considerable local opposition to the measure. Resolutions denouncing the bill passed the Clearing House Association of New Orleans banks unanimously in January 1878, stimulating a flurry of similar

20. San Francisco *Chronicle,* Oct. 20, 1877; also Chap. 6, passim.

21. Philadelphia *Inquirer,* Feb. 7, 1878.

22. New York *Weekly Journal of Commerce,* Jan. 17 and Jan. 24, 1878. For a qualified statement of the sectional alliance thesis, see C. Vann Woodward, *Origins of the New South, 1877–1913* (Baton Rouge, 1951), pp. 47–50.

activity among other southern business groups.[23] Within two weeks the New Orleans Chamber of Commerce and the city's Cotton Exchange, the Charleston (S.C.) Chamber of Commerce, the Savannah Chamber of Commerce, and that city's Cotton Exchange had all denounced remonetization. With the commercial interests of the South solidly opposed to restoring legal bimetallism, New York City's financial press rejoiced that "the Southern cities hitherto regarded as strongholds of silver are wheeling into line with the defenders of the national honor and good faith."[24]

Leading southern railroad companies like Tom Scott's Texas and Pacific also wheeled into line. Some of the region's railroad men genuinely favored the gold standard, but the Texas and Pacific's response was more opportunistic, as Scott's associates attempted unsuccessfully to stimulate presidential interest in a government subsidy by supporting Hayes on the silver question. At a time when most American railroad executives, unlike the banking and mercantile communities, remained silent on the issue, Scott's colleagues plunged eagerly into the controversy. The link between railroad subsidies and sound finance was drawn in a somewhat garbled January 1878 letter to Hayes by the Texas and Pacific's Washington agent and lawyer, Pennsylvania Republican W. Cornell Jewett:

> Since our interview [Jewett informed the Chief Executive] I have submitted to Col Scott the proposed Texas "Bill" & . . . he also applauds my views as addressed to you on resumption . . . He believes with me [that] . . . the silver [movement is] a political movement to destroy your administration . . . I sincerely believe a special message urging aid

23. Edward C. Palmer to Thomas F. Bayard, Jan. 8, 1878, Bayard MSS, LC. See also Palmer to Bayard, Feb. 5, 1878, enclosing a copy of the resolution.

24. New York *Weekly Journal of Commerce,* Jan. 17 and Jan. 24, 1878.

> to complete the Texas & Pacific R.R. Co. . . . as especially due to the South . . . would renew general confidence.[25]

Scott, himself, opposed remonetization but favored a controlled expansion of the greenback supply! However, Jewett and O. H. Booth, superintendent of the Pennsylvania Railroad and another Scott cohort, both urged the President to veto the Bland bill to save the country from "the tide of silver lunacy that is now sweeping over [it]," while returning whenever possible in their letters to the subject of the stalled Texas and Pacific federal grant.[26] Other southern opponents of remonetization—especially chambers of commerce, cotton exchanges, and banking houses in the major cities—voiced honest gold standard convictions despite strong local political pressures to remain silent. The militant hostility of southern businessmen toward the Bland bill exposed the continuing schism in the section between monetary expansionists and financial conservatives, the roots of which extended deep into the antebellum period.

Most eastern mercantile organizations opposed restoration of silver as a monetary standard, although several professed an admiration of bimetallism for tactical reasons. The influential New York Chamber of Commerce and Boston Board of Trade, for example, both supported an immediate international monetary conference. The merchant associations, led by John C. Ropes and B. F. Nourse in Boston and by Samuel Ruggles in New York, demanded that congressional action be delayed until after the conference.[27] After House passage of the Bland bill, how-

25. W. Cornell Jewett to R. B. Hayes, Jan. 3, 1878, Hayes MSS, Fremont. For a more straightforward statement of opposition to the Bland bill by a Southern railroad executive, see H. S. M. Comle to Thomas F. Bayard, Feb. 5, 1878, Bayard MSS, LC.

26. O. H. Booth to John Sherman, Jan. 30, 1878, Sherman MSS, LC; W. Cornell Jewett to R. B. Hayes, Feb. 22, 1878, Hayes MSS, Fremont; Tom Scott to W. B. Allison, Feb. 1, 1878, Allison MSS, Des Moines.

27. "Resolution of the Chamber of Commerce of the State of New York in respect to an International Money Conference," Jan. 4, 1877, records of the Senate Finance Committee, 44th Cong., 2d sess., NA;

ever, eastern commercial groups shed this strategy completely and demanded instead defeat of the Bland bill and retention of the gold standard. Resolutions opposing remonetization passed not only the New York Chamber of Commerce and the Boston Board of Trade but also the Boston Commercial Club, the New York Cotton Exchange, and the New York Maritime Exchange.[28] Up and down the East coast, merchant organizations vied with each other in denouncing the Bland bill. Chambers of Commerce and Boards of Trade in Providence, Philadelphia, Baltimore, and New Orleans, along with smaller groups both North and South, joined their San Francisco compatriots in warning of the economic disaster that would befall American commerce following passage of a silver bill.[29]

The hardening of eastern mercantile attitudes toward remonetization can be seen in the deliberations of a typical association, the Philadelphia Board of Trade. Prior to House passage of the Bland bill, its executive committee in October 1877 postponed action until its next meeting on a pending resolution that requested an international monetary conference. No further mention was made of the international coinage resolution at the following meeting, however, held only days after House passage

---

Boston *Daily Advertiser,* Jan. 6, 1877; Samuel B. Ruggles to John Sherman, Feb. 17, 1877, and B. F. Nourse to Sherman, Jan. 25, 1877, Sherman MSS, LC.

28. New York *Weekly Journal of Commerce,* Jan. 14, and Jan. 31, 1878; New York *Graphic,* Jan. 8, 1878; C. H. Hamilton to James A. Garfield, Feb. 25, 1878, Garfield MSS, LC.

29. Joseph C. Grubb to Thomas F. Bayard, Dec. 9, 1877, Bayard MSS, LC. Grubb was an official of the Philadelphia Board of Trade. See also *The Financial Situation Considered . . . by a Merchant of Philadelphia* (n.d.) ca. 1877, Hayes pamphlet collection, Hayes Library, Fremont; H. K. Slayton (Manchester, New Hampshire Board of Trade) to James A. Garfield, Nov. 19, 1877, Garfield MSS, LC; New York *Graphic,* Jan. 4, 1877; Minutes of the Executive Committee of the Philadelphia Board of Trade for 1877 (Sept. 17, Oct. 15, Nov. 19, Dec. 17). Historical Society of Pennsylvania (Philadelphia).

of the Bland bill, except by one member of the executive committee who now opposed the motion because "the attempt to maintain a given ratio between the two metals has been tried already and has failed [and a] Convention would have the tendency to hinder and embarrass Resumption." At its December meeting, the executive committee again shelved the international conference proposal and adopted instead a strong resolution opposing passage of the Bland bill.[30] For most mercantile associations in major port cities throughout the country—whether Providence, Boston, New York, Philadelphia, Baltimore, New Orleans, or San Francisco—protection of their gold-based foreign commerce outweighed the possibility of expanding the hard coin in circulation by remonetizing silver. Gold remained the basic medium of exchange in American foreign trade, and most export merchants were convinced that restoring the depreciated silver dollar as legal tender would seriously disrupt overseas commerce.[31]

Like the national bankers, however, mercantile opponents of the Bland bill did little except petition Congress. Some of the larger associations in New York and Boston joined with local bankers in coordinating memorials to the national legislature, but efforts to organize mass meetings and stir public sentiment against remonetization were generally unsuccessful. At a special meeting called by the New York Board of Trade and Transportation in February 1878, for example, some of the city's wholesale merchants adopted a stern anti-Bland bill remonstrance that was promptly signed by the dozen or two board officers in attendance.[32] Although the board's petition claimed to represent three hundred firms with annual receipts of over six hundred million dollars, the silverite New York *Graphic* observed merrily that "the meeting which issued it was attended by only fourteen

30. *The Financial Situation Considered,* for the following 1877 meetings; Oct. 15, Nov. 19 and Dec. 17.

31. Unger, *Greenback Era,* p. 334.

32. New York *Weekly Journal of Commerce,* Feb. 7, 1878.

men, of whom six voted to adjourn without any action, and several were directly opposed to the views expressed."[33] In Baltimore, that same month, a rally by "prominent citizens, professional gentlemen, merchants and capitalists of the city" to organize an anti-greenback and anti-silver "honest money league" broke up in "considerable confusion" after a pro-Bland bill speaker gained the floor and began haranguing the crowd.[34]

Even the commercial groups most vehemently opposed to remonetization displayed a singular lack of enthusiasm and initiative in their campaign against the silver bill. Most merchants seemed torn between their traditional reverence for hard coin, whether gold or silver, and their fear that recoining the "dollar of the daddies" would force gold from circulation in the export trade. These tensions erupted forcefully at the 1877 meeting of the National Board of Trade during an inconclusive debate over remonetization. A resolution by the Chicago Board of Trade calling for an international monetary conference was accepted with only one dissenting vote. The Cincinnati Chamber of Commerce then proposed that the National Board of Trade follow its lead and endorse the Bland bill, a suggestion that provoked lively opposition from representatives of trade bodies in the eastern port cities. The resolution finally passed in amended form, 16 to 11, although it now recommended that recoinage of the restored 412.5 grain silver dollar be restricted to a maximum of fifty million dollars.[35] Since the motion failed to receive the two-thirds majority required under the National Board's rules of procedure, however, it was not included in the group's annual memorial to Congress.

The composition of the board's silverite majority was particularly interesting. Voting in favor of the resolution were delegates from eastern mercantile groups as well as from midwestern

33. New York *Graphic,* Feb. 11, 1878.

34. Philadelphia *Inquirer,* Feb. 15, 1878.

35. *Proceedings of the National Board of Trade, August 1877* (Chicago, 1877), pp. 174–77, 188–218.

ones. The Baltimore Corn and Flour Exchange, the Philadelphia Commercial Exchange, and the Trenton (New Jersey) Board of Trade joined Cincinnati and Milwaukee commercial groups in supporting the motion. The Milwaukee and Chicago Boards of Trade split their votes on the question, while Detroit's trade association joined the Boston, Philadelphia, and New York Boards of Trade in opposing the move. In other words, solid sectional divisions on the silver issue did not emerge among the merchants, and any attempt to portray a clear cut split between eastern and western commercial groups on the question distorts the actual diversity and confusion that characterized business response to the Bland bill in every section.[36]

A similar absence of cohesion beset the scattered opposition to remonetization among American manufacturers. Industrialists made no attempt to organize behind the gold standard similar to George S. Coe's efforts in the financial community. Nor did major trade associations like the National Wool Growers Association, the American Iron and Steel Association, or the National Association of Wool Manufacturers follow the lead of mercantile groups in denouncing the silver bill. The trade associations remained generally silent or cautious on the question, with opposition to the "dollar of the daddies" coming largely from individual manufacturers.[37]

Anti-Bland bill congressmen received a number of letters from producers of farm machinery, ship builders, mill owners, patent medicine makers, and other gold standard businessmen denounc-

36. Ibid., pp. 9–10, 217–18; Unger, *Greenback Era,* p. 334. The Portland (Oregon) delegate, for example, voted *for* remonetization, while San Francisco's mining-state Chamber of Commerce opposed the policy.

37. The Secretary of the National Wool Growers Association did call James Garfield "eminently sound on the currency question" but without referring specifically to Garfield's position either on silver or on resumption. William G. Markham to Garfield, Nov. 26, 1877, Garfield MSS, LC.

ing "restoration."[38] A sizable number of railroad executives and railroad supply companies also expressed their hostility to the silver drive.[39] Only in rare instances, however, did these businessmen and their firms engage in organized opposition to silver, most notably in a mild letter signed by one hundred and twenty Cleveland entrepreneurs *after* final passage of the Bland-Allison Act in which they commended James Garfield's vote against the measure.[40] During the silver drive itself, however, these same Cleveland merchants and manufacturers refrained from any attempt to mobilize public opinion against the bill!

The disorganized character of business opposition to the Bland bill helps explain the ease with which silver legislation moved through both houses of Congress. Only eastern banking and financial interests united to oppose the bill, and the efforts of Coe and his colleagues concentrated upon insuring a presidential veto rather than attempting to block the measure prior to passage. Most American merchants, manufacturers, and other business groups, unlike the eastern bankers, were more closely divided on the merits of remonetization. They did little to influence congressional or executive action on the question.

A significant number of trade associations, manufacturers, and

38. See, for example, the following sample of anti-silver letters from individual manufacturers: W. Hastings to Bayard, Feb. 6, 1878; Wilbur H. Burnite to Bayard, Feb. 9, 1878; B. A. Moore to Bayard, Feb. 21, 1878; Bayard MSS, LC; C. B. Lockwood to Garfield, Dec. 26, 1877; John Tod to Garfield, Mar. 9, 1878, Garfield MSS, LC; William H. Henry to Morrill, Feb. 2, 1878, Morrill MSS, LC; John Osborne to Sherman, Feb. 28, 1878, Sherman MSS, LC; George W. Allen to Allison, Mar. 5, 1878, Allison MSS, Des Moines.

39. George W. Stone to Bayard, Feb. 9, 1878; Samuel Wilkeson to Bayard, Feb. 14, 1878; William Manby to Bayard, Feb. 18, 1878; Bayard MSS, LC; H. C. Hubbell to Garfield, Jan. 22, 1878, Garfield MSS, LC; D. M. H. Howard to Sherman, Nov. 28, 1877, Sherman MSS, LC.

40. John Tod to Garfield, Mar. 9, 1878, Garfield MSS, enclosing a "Petition from Cleveland Honest Money Men to . . . Garfield," dated Mar. 6, 1878.

bankers actually favored a return to legal bimetallism. Even in New York several leading financiers dissented from the views of the city's Clearing House Association. John Thompson of the Chase National Bank, for example, argued that "only the importer and foreign banker . . . have a direct interest in establishing the gold standard," and he estimated that three quarters of the businessmen in lower Manhattan and one quarter of its bankers favored remonetization.[41] The Wall Street silverites, if they existed at all, remained surprisingly silent, but even within the syndicate's own precincts, a strong undercurrent of support existed for an *international* monetary agreement if not for immediate restoration of the double standard.

August Belmont, who supervised the American investments of the bimetallist Rothschild family, for example, urged Secretary Sherman to press for an immediate international conference. J. and W. Seligman and Company, which joined Belmont's company in selling substantial amounts of silver bullion to the government under the subsidiary coinage provision of the Resumption Act, wrote Hayes in August 1877 reminding the President that the monetary agreement among the Latin Union states would soon expire. This afforded "our Government desirable opportunity to join the latter, and, other powers, with a view to obtain a universal adoption of a Silver standard."[42] New York bullion dealers like J. B. Colgate generally supported the Bland bill, and the president of the New York Mining Stock Exchange, George B. Satterlee, suggested abandoning gold entirely in favor of a single silver standard! Several Wall Street stockbrokers also declared publicly for the double standard, and one banker who opposed the Bland bill insisted that most of his colleagues remained indifferent to the measure, informing a New York *Graphic* reporter that "he did not believe, if a ballot box were

41. New York *Graphic,* Dec. 1, 1877; John Thompson to Thurlow Weed, Aug. 23, 1877, Weed MSS, New York Historical Society.

42. August Belmont to John Sherman, Nov. 29, 1877, Sherman MSS, LC; J. and W. Seligman and Company to R. B. Hayes, Aug. 24, 1877, Hayes MSS, Fremont.

placed on the corner of Broad and Wall streets, with the request that all those who opposed or favored the bill should vote, that one-third of the businessmen passing would take the pains to do so."[43]

Although silverites remained a minority among New York City bankers and businessmen, their ranks included the two ablest local pamphleteers in the controversy, Thurlow Weed, who favored immediate remonetization, and the international bimetallist George Walker.[44] Silver advocates also benefited from support given by the city's popular tabloid daily, the *Graphic,* which had been among the earliest advocates of the "dollar of the daddies." Several important Albany bankers also endorsed the silver bill, including J. H. Van Antwerp of the State Bank and Thomas Olcott, the aging president of the Mechanics and Farmers' Bank and a leading old Jacksonian figure. Olcott, like other resumptionist-silverites, believed that restoring the double standard would raise the market price of silver to its former level equivalent to gold, thereby more than doubling the supply of coin available for supporting the Treasury's resumption program. Along with Halstead and Jones, Olcott urged that the supply of circulating greenbacks be reduced after remonetization by exchanging silver dollars for the paper notes. With an ardor developed over decades of political battles for hard money against paper note inflation, the old Jacksonian viewed the silver movement as another incarnation of the perennial "contest between paper and coin [gold and silver separately or together]."[45]

43. New York *Graphic* for the following 1877 dates: Nov. 17, Nov. 23, Dec. 27, and Dec. 28. See also August Belmont to Thomas Bayard, Nov. 26, 1877, copy in Sherman MSS, LC.

44. Thurlow Weed "To the Editor of the New York *Tribune,*" Nov. 23, 1877, enclosed in Governor William Dennison to W. K. Rogers (Personal Secretary to President Hayes), Nov. 30, 1877, Hayes MSS, Fremont.

45. Weed described Olcott as "widely known as a uniform, earnest, and enlightened hard-money man." Ibid., also Thomas Olcott to David A. Wells, July 5 and July 20, 1877, Wells MSS, LC; Olcott to

Many midwestern bankers also favored remonetization, including some close associates of Sherman and Hayes. One Ohio financier urged the President in a personal talk shortly after his 1876 nomination to see "that *our party* would not, as a party, oppose the bringing back again the silver dollar of our fathers [that] has secured such a hold on the American people as to admonish all prudent persons to stand out of the way of its accomplishment."[46] Hayes' intimate friend, the editor William Henry Smith, wrote the chief executive in 1877 that he had found the silverite president of one bank "so wrought up on the subject that he wishes for the success of the Democratic party in Ohio, unless you indicate your approval of the remonetization of silver." Smith also confided to Hayes that "the most prominent business man in the Northwest," unnamed but apparently familiar to the President, also favored remonetization, not on economic grounds but simply because "the law of 1873 which demonetized silver . . . was wrong."[47]

One group of Pennsylvania bankers followed George Coe's example by drafting a joint petition to Congress, in their case endorsing the Bland bill. Even Jay Cooke, the government's original Civil War bond sale agent and himself a monometallist, told one interviewer in March 1878 that "all agree, both East and West, as to the desirability of the remonetization of silver." The financial community had attacked the silver bill, Cooke

---

John Sherman, Oct. 5, 1878, in *Specie Resumption and Refunding of National Debt,* p. 387. For a similar pro-silverite position taken by the Cashier of Albany's important State Bank, see J. H. Van Antwerp to Thurlow Weed, Nov. 10, 1877, included in Weed, "To the Editor of the New York *Tribune,*" Hayes MSS, Fremont. Also see New York *Times,* Sept. 14, 1877, for the remarks of Eastern pro-silver bankers at the 1877 meeting of the American Bankers Association.

46. John D. Martin to W. K. Rogers, June 12, 1877, Hayes MSS, Fremont.

47. William Henry Smith to R. B. Hayes, August (n.d.), 1877, typescript, Smith MSS, ibid.

insisted, not because of hostility toward bimetallism but as a result of their overriding fear that government securities would be redeemed in depreciated silver rather than gold. If adequate assurances had been given to the contrary, Cooke insisted, then most American bankers would not have opposed remonetization.[48]

Widespread support for the "dollar of the daddies" existed also among mercantile groups in every section of the country. The Cincinnati and St. Paul Chambers of Commerce endorsed remonetization soon after the silver agitation began in 1876 and were joined the following year by other midwestern trade associations in Iowa and Illinois. The important Nashville Merchants' Exchange supported the Bland bill, although other southern commercial groups denounced the measure. Even in the eastern strongholds of gold monometallism, the Baltimore Corn and Flour Exchange, the Philadelphia Commercial Exchange, and the Trenton Board of Trade bucked prevailing commercial

48. Haswell, "The Public Life of Congressman R. P. Bland," pp. 73–74; New York *Weekly Journal of Commerce,* Feb. 18, 1878; Chicago *Post,* n.d., included in Jay Cooke to John Sherman, Mar. 29, 1878, Sherman MSS, LC. For other expressions of support for the Bland bill by Midwestern bankers, see Henry B. Curtis to John Sherman, Mar. 27, 1878, Sherman MSS, LC; E. Johnson to W. B. Allison, Mar. 14, and Apr. 10, 1878, Allison MSS, Des Moines; New York *Times,* Sept. 14, 1877. The clearest indication of the widespread support for the silver movement, even among the bankers of the Middle West and Northeast, came at the September 1877 meeting of the American Bankers Association, attended by 200 to 300 financiers. Speeches endorsing remonetization were made by bankers from all sections of the country, along with a number of gold standard orations. The convention finally adopted an ambiguous resolution prepared by George S. Coe and an unknown Ohio banker which stated simply "that the general use of coin, the measure of value as formerly, will alone secure [prompt resumption of specie payments.]" New York *Times,* Sept. 14, 1877. See also New York *Tribune,* Sept. 14, 1877. Whether or not "the measure of value as formerly" referred to the bimetallic standard that existed before 1873 was left unspecified, so that both goldbug and silverite bankers could stand comfortably on a compromise plank.

opinion by voting for the pro-silver resolution passed by the National Board of Trade in August 1877.[49]

The National Board of Trade's response, mentioned earlier, contradicts the notion of a "traditional rift" on the silver question between eastern and western merchants during the 1870s.[50] At its June 1876 convention in New York City the Board had approved a declaration requesting that Congress retain the current five dollar legal tender limitation on silver.[51] Delegates from leading midwestern and eastern merchant associations along with several southern trade groups attended the 1876 meeting, and the anti-silver resolution passed unanimously without debate or a roll call vote. At the board's 1877 Milwaukee meeting, however, three eastern groups which had opposed remonetization the previous year—the Baltimore, Philadelphia, and Trenton bodies—now voted in favor of the pro-silver memorial to Congress.[52] One Boston merchant acknowledged in February 1878 that "the silver as well as the greenback heresy has made an impression upon many generally intelligent men even among our own mercantile community," while a gold standard Boston manufacturer observed that if Senate amended the Bland bill properly, "opposition in this region [to the Bland bill] will be confined to doctrinaires and experts."[53]

Monometallists were surprisingly strong, however, in some midwestern mercantile groups. At the 1877 National Board of Trade meeting, the Detroit delegation voted against remonetiza-

49. Unger, *Greenback Era,* pp. 333–34; Cincinnati *Commercial,* Nov. 20 and Nov. 21, 1877; Philadelphia *Inquirer,* Feb. 19, 1878; *Proceedings of the National Board of Trade for 1877,* p. 218.

50. Unger, *Greenback Era,* p. 333.

51. *Proceedings of the National Board of Trade for 1876* (Chicago, 1876), pp. 77–85.

52. *Proceedings . . . 1877,* p. 218; San Francisco *Chronicle,* Aug. 26, 1877; New York *Weekly Journal of Commerce,* July 26, 1877.

53. W. W. Warren to James A. Garfield, Feb. 4, 1878, Garfield MSS, LC; Henry C. Leach to Henry Teller, Jan. 5, 1878, Teller MSS, Denver Public Library.

tion while the Chicago and Milwaukee groups divided on the question. The pro-silver petition even came under attack by some members of the Cincinnati delegation that had sponsored it! The following year anti-greenback and anti-silver midwestern businessmen joined forces with the Honest Money League of the Northwest, a group that played an important role in electing sound money candidates during the 1878 campaign.[54]

Most western businessmen, whatever their personal views on the silver question, resented pressures applied by some eastern banking houses and mercantile groups to oppose the Bland bill or face economic reprisals. The New York *Journal of Commerce* had advised eastern merchants to insist on clauses in business contracts with western firms stipulating payment in gold and had urged bankers only to loan money on western or southern securities on the same basis, adding correctly that "the stronghold of this form of repudiation [pro-silver sentiment] is in the Western cities."[55] Many westerners deplored bitterly the charge that they hoped to damage the nation's finances by supporting remonetization.[56] "This arrogant and supercillious [sic] style . . . of argument which the advocates of an exclusive gold standard indulge in, is not calculated to impress Western people with the merits of their side of the question," one Nebraska businessman wrote *The Iron Age* in January 1878. Midwestern business interests favored restoration of legal tender silver, the writer noted, "because it is a product of our soil, will add to the

54. *Proceedings . . . 1877;* S. Lester Taylor to David A. Wells, July 5, 1877, Wells MSS, LC; Unger, *Greenback Era,* pp. 387–92; William Henry Smith to R. B. Hayes, Mar. 11, 1878, typescript, Hayes MSS, Fremont; Levi P. Morton to Whitelaw Reid, Dec. 27, 1877 and Jan. 14, 1878; H. C. Fahnestock to Reid, Dec. 7, 1877, Reid MSS, LC.

55. New York *Weekly Journal of Commerce,* Jan. 10, 1878.

56. Nichols, "John Sherman and the Silver Drive," p. 159. On western resentment towards eastern business firms, see William Henry Smith to Sherman, Mar. 4 and Mar. 15, 1878; Smith to R. B. Hayes, Mar. 9 and Mar. 31, 1878; Smith to Horatio Burchard, May 4, 1878; Smith Letterbooks, Hayes Library, Fremont.

currency of our country, is an important and valuable factor in commerce, and because resumption of specie payments is impossible without it!"[57]

Many western manufacturers also supported the Bland bill as "an important means toward the restablishment of industrial prosperity." A special Chicago meeting of the Textile Manufacturer's Association of the West and South in July 1877, attended by delegates from firms throughout the Midwest, unanimously adopted a resolution demanding restoration of the 412.5 grain silver dollar.[58] Leading business figures throughout the region urged the Hayes Administration not to veto the silver bill, and even in the East, a small minority braved prevailing local opinion to endorse remonetization.[59] In New York City alone, 193 "persons doing business" in lower Manhattan or three-quarters of the tradesmen and merchants in the area, petitioned Congress in favor of the measure.[60]

Few of the country's business and banking organizations, however, attempted to coordinate their members' opinions on the silver agitation, and since most merchants and manufacturers did not split on the issue along sectional lines, the available evidence of business response to the Bland bill often runs counter to the neo-Beardian view of a "traditional East-West rift" on the question.[61] American entrepreneurs, like the intellectual community, remained chaotically divided on remonetization during

57. William A. Gwyer (Omaha), Jan. 21, 1878, in *The Iron Age,* Jan. 31, 1878.

58. *Report of a Special Meeting of the Textile Manufacturers' Association of the West and South, Held July 19, 1877 at Chicago* (Chicago, 1877), copy in pamphlet collection, Hayes Library, Fremont.

59. John V. Farwell to William H. Smith, Jan. 23, 1878, Smith MSS, Ohio State Historical Society; C. W. Moulton to John Sherman, Aug. 14 1877; George B. Wright to Sherman, Feb. 14, 1878; Sherman MSS, LC; William Henry Smith to R. B. Hayes, Aug. 8, 1877, typescript, Hayes Library, Fremont.

60. Philadelphia, *Inquirer,* Feb. 12, 1878; Lewis H. Taylor to R. B. Hayes, Feb. 4, 1877, Hayes Library, Fremont.

61. The most sophisticated neo-Beardian analysis of this point is in Irwin Unger's excellent study, *Greenback Era,* pp. 333–34.

the 1870s, and no apparent single pattern of business reaction emerged. The occasional efforts by businessmen to publicize their opinions and influence government action were haphazard, hastily organized, and seldom of political consequence. Despite its economic importance, the struggle to restore legal bimetallism failed to stir a response from the business community even remotely comparable to its intense participation in the "battle of the standards" during the 1890s.

Congress' 1877 Christmas recess allowed legislators to return home for final political soundings on the silver question before voicing their opinions on both Stanley Matthews' bond payment resolution and on the Bland bill. By this time, debate raged furiously in most states over restoring the "dollar of the daddies," yet in some areas dominant opinion on the issue was not hard to determine. In the New England states, for example, vocal opponents of remonetization far outnumbered its supporters; "only in New England, New York [and] New Jersey . . . did a majority of the [local] press oppose silver."[62] The Massachusetts Conference of Unitarian Ministers petitioned Congress against passage of the Bland bill, and the religious press of the region, "although riddled with pro-silver heresy," generally brought God and the Gospels to the defense of the gold standard.[63] William Dean Howells, editor of the *Atlantic Monthly,* the economist Edward Atkinson, Boston aristocrats like Amos Lawrence, and other representatives of the region's self-conscious "respectable" element, peppered government officials with anti-silver pronouncements, while the Massachusetts legislature sent its predictable set of gold standard resolutions to Congress.[64]

62. Nichols, "John Sherman and the Silver Drive."

63. New York *Graphic,* Jan. 29, 1878. For a good summary of religious press opinion on the silver issue, see Unger, *Greenback Era,* p. 359.

64. Alexander H. Rice (Commonwealth of Massachusetts, Executive Department) to R. B. Hayes, Feb. 27, 1878, Hayes MSS, Fremont; W. D. Howells to James Garfield, Dec. 1, 1877, Garfield MSS, LC;

The two leading supporters of silver in the Bay State were actually greenbackers, the radical orator Wendell Phillips and Congressman Benjamin F. Butler, and Butler acknowledged often that a majority of his constituents differed with him on the question.[65] Opposition to silver in Massachusetts appeared to be concentrated in Boston and surrounding textile cities, articulated largely by businessmen and professionals. Elsewhere in New England, however, the small towns and agrarian areas showed marked hostility toward restoring the "dollar of the daddies." This was especially true among older Republicans, swayed less by economic arguments against restoration than by the stern pronouncements of bimetallism's "immorality" made by the region's leading legislators.

Senators Morrill and Edmunds of Vermont, along with Congressman Henry L. Dawes of Massachusetts, defended their support for the gold standard to local voters on the grounds that passage of the Bland bill would involve repudiation of the government's moral obligation to public creditors. Many of their constituents—"old soldiers," ex-Conscience Whigs or Free Soil Democrats long amalgamated into the Republican party—seemed to endorse this stand. To New Englanders of modest means, most of whom never owned a resumption bond, the silver movement appeared to be a continuation of earlier "repudiationist" campaigns to undermine the federal government. Southern secessionists and financial defaulters, alike, shared the common aim of destroying national stability, in this view, and differed only in their methods.

Edward Atkinson to David A. Wells, Nov. 20, 1877, Wells MSS, LC; Amos A. Lawrence to Justin S. Morrill, Feb. 4, 1878, Morrill MSS, LC. See also "No Repudiator" to James A. Garfield, Mar. 11, 1878, Garfield MSS; Reuben Brooks to Thomas F. Bayard, Feb. 6, 1878, and George Richard Minst to Bayard, Feb. 25, 1878, Bayard MSS, LC; N.S. Bartlett to David A. Wells, Mar. 8, 1878, Wells MSS, LC; E. H. Derby to John Sherman, May 12, 1877, Sherman MSS, LC.

65. New York *Graphic,* Jan. 29, 1878.

"I am very thankful that there is one man that dare lift his lance against such fraud and dishonesty," ran a typical letter from one Vermont farmer to Justin Morrill shortly after final approval of the silver bill. "I am shocked at the pasage [*sic*] of such a bill in what is suposed [*sic*] to be enlightened Congress and I fear lest such corruption shall prove our [undoing]."[66] Nowhere in the country was opposition to remonetization more intense than among the rank and file agrarian and rural New England voters of both major parties. Yet even here those hostile to silver did little to organize and spread their opinions through public meetings or other forms of political protest. Although New England cheered on its gold standard congressional delegation by offering editorials of praise and letters of encouragement, the region felt keenly its isolation from the mainstream of national sentiment, which favored remonetization. Instead of spearheading an aggressive attack on bimetallism, most New Englanders seemed content with their *moral* superiority on the issue. With significant exceptions like David A. Wells and Samuel Bowles of the Springfield *Republican,* they avoided noisy public protests against the silver drive. Only in New York City did the press, business, and banking communities campaign actively against the Bland bill.

The only notable anti-silver lobbying before the Senate Finance Committee, when it held open hearings on proposed amendments to the measure, came from the group organized by George S. Coe that represented the banking fraternity of New York City, Boston, Philadelphia, and Baltimore.[67] Most of its active members actually resided in or around Wall Street, and among all the Eastern cities, only in New York did most news-

66. J. B. Byck to Justin S. Morrill, Mar 1, 1878. See also J. R. Parrish to Morrill, Feb. 7, 1878; Justin K. Richardson to Morrill, Feb. 19, 1878; G. E. Fogg to Morrill, Feb. 19, 1878; M. M. Dikeman to Morrill, Feb. 22, 1878; Morrill MSS, LC.

67. Redlich, *The Molding of American Banking,* pp. 430–32; Unger, *Greenback Era,* p. 360.

papers vigorously oppose the silver drive. Journals such as the *Tribune,* the *Sun,* the *Times,* the *Herald,* and *Frank Leslie's Illustrated Newspaper* vied with one another in elaborate denunciations of remonetization.[68] At one point, the city's only silverite daily, the *Graphic,* presented a fanciful description of the appearance made by the gold standard New York editors and bankers to oppose the Bland bill before the Senate Finance Committee in November 1877:

> The Senate Committee on Finance had a wild meeting today . . . there were observed coming down the street, arm in arm, Messrs. Whitelaw Reid [of the *Tribune*], Dana [of the *Sun*], George Jones [of the *Times*], and the editor of the *Herald* . . . Behind them as a support were Messrs. Jay Gould, August Belmont, Story of the Chicago *Times,* and others not quite so well known. Following in the rear were 350 bankers, completely filling up the hall . . . .
>
> Dana (moving toward the door with George Jones, Jay Gould and others) (speaks)—You are all repudiationists! All the people of this country are repudiationists, except the bondholders![69]

Although the New York state legislature, like its Massachusetts counterpart, passed an anti-silver resolution, hostility toward the measure centered in New York City rather than elsewhere in the state.[70] Sizable pockets of silverite strength existed not

68. Thomson P. McElrath to David A. Wells, Jan. 23, 1878, Wells MSS, LC. See also Whitelaw Reid to Charles Storrs, Feb. 19, 1878, Reid MSS, LC.

69. In the *Graphic's* version of the encounter, a remarkable forerunner of the technique used skillfully by William H. Harvey in *Coin's Financial School* during the 1890s, John Percival Jones served as a self-appointed tutor to the assembled editors and bankers from New York, demolishing their arguments so easily that they fled in disarray. New York *Graphic,* Nov. 18, 1877.

70. New York *Tribune,* Jan. 28 and 29, 1878. For anti-silver sentiment in New York City, see the following: Theo. M. Lilienthal to Thomas F. Bayard, Bayard MSS, LC; Edmund Wright to Justin S.

only upstate but even in New York City, where several local congressmen voted for the Bland bill.[71]

If New York was a gold standard state with a prominent silverite minority, Pennsylvania, which boasted a predominantly bimetallist congressional delegation, possessed an active anti-silver contingent, especially in Philadelphia. There, as in other eastern cities, the banking community and "all proper thinking people" opposed remonetization.[72] Elsewhere in the state, although a few businessmen petitioned against restoration and some protectionist newspapers expressed skepticism over its "propriety," the silverites clearly held the field.[73] "Things such as the Bland or Silver bill iz [*sic*] getting up to blood heat hear [*sic*] in Chester County *Pa.,*" wrote one Keystone state goldbug. This local agitation changed no legislative votes, however, and the state's two Senators, Democrat William Wallace and Republican Don Cameron, joined in supporting remonetization.[74]

Delaware's congressional delegation, on the other hand, re-

Morrill, Dec. 10, 1877; L. E. Chittenden to Morrill, Feb. 7, 1878; August Belmont to Morrill, Feb. 18, 1878; Morrill MSS, LC; J. S. Moon to David A. Wells, July 22, 1877, Wells MSS, LC; Henry Kemp to R. B. Hayes, Feb. 13, 1878, Hayes Library, Fremont.

71. New York *Tribune,* Nov. 17, 1877. *Cong. Record,* 45th Cong., 1st sess., vol. 1, pp. 241–42; 2d sess., vol. 7, pt. 2, pp. 1419–20.

72. William Platt Pepper to Thomas F. Bayard, Feb. 27, 1878. See also George W. Biddle to Bayard, Dec. 18, 1877; Bayard MSS, LC; John W. Frazier to W. K. Rogers, Nov. 23, 1877, Hayes MSS, Fremont; A. Louden Snowden to James A. Garfield, Aug. 16, 1877, Garfield MSS, LC; Philadelphia *North American,* quoted in *The Bulletin of the American Iron and Steel Association,* August 1877.

73. Republican opponents of remonetization in Pennsylvania, finding few members of their own state party's congressional delegation sympathetic to their views, often wrote more congenial legislators to express hostility toward remonetization. See, for example, C. W. Shinn to James A. Garfield, Jan. 17, 1878; Evans Brothers to Garfield, Jan. 9, 1878; T. R. Kennedy to Garfield, April 6, 1878, Garfield MSS, LC. See also Silas Ward to Thomas Bayard, Feb. 6, 1878, Bayard MSS, LC.

74. Joseph Domdall to Thomas Bayard, Jan. 30, 1878, Bayard MSS, LC.

mained divided between backers of Senator Thomas F. Bayard, the leading monometallist on the mid-Atlantic seaboard, and silverite Senator Eli Saulsbury, both Democrats. Bayard's mail on the issue suggested that the state's voters also disagreed profoundly on silver legislation, although the gold monometallist Democrat received strong backing from the business and professional classes of Wilmington and other cities.[75] Bayard's anti-silver correspondents came largely from the state's urban communities and acknowledged that their view was "not the popular side" but went against "the current of public opinion" in Delaware.[76]

In the West and South, hostility toward remonetization outside the business community appeared even more scattered and disorganized than in the East. The brave, if outnumbered, band of newspapers in the Midwest that denounced the Bland bill isolated themselves from prevailing sentiment in their own towns and cities. Only in Ohio's Western Reserve did the area's press, public opinion, and congressional representative all remain hostile toward silver legislation. The Reserve's prominent congressman, James A. Garfield, alone among the state's House delegation in opposing silver, received substantial support from the Cleveland business community and from several important newspapers in the area, including the Cleveland *Herald* and Cleveland *Leader*.[77]

75. For a sampling of anti-silver Delaware and Mid-Atlantic state opinion, see the following letters to Thomas F. Bayard: Sidney Webster, Dec. 17, 1877; H. C. Snitcher, Jan. 28, 1878; "BLM" [?], Jan. 29, 1878; H. B. Tiddeman, Feb. 2, 1878; C. J. Hall, Feb. 5, 1878; S. J. Field (Justice, United States Supreme Court), Feb. 6, 1878; Henry Pepper, Feb. 8, 1878; John C. Gooden, Feb. 9, 1878; Joseph L. Carpenter, Feb. 23, 1878; L. G. Wales, Feb. 24, 1878; William T. Croasdale, Feb. 25, 1878; Bayard MSS, LC.

76. See especially C. J. Hall to Bayard, Feb. 5, 1878; Henry Pepper to Bayard, Feb. 8, 1878; and H. B. Tiddeman to Bayard, Feb. 2, 1878; ibid.

77. C. E. Henry to James A. Garfield, Feb. 4, 1878; W. S. Peterson to Garfield, July 4, 1877; Garfield MSS, LC.

Elsewhere in the Midwest, Cincinnati's influential German-language daily *Volksfreund* waged a lonely campaign for the gold standard against an impressive array of local public and business support for remonetization marshaled by Halstead's *Commercial.* The St. Paul (Minnesota) *Press* also struggled against its own silverite business community, and in Iowa, the Davenport *Gazette* kept a solitary beacon lit for any fearless monometallists bucking the blizzard of bimetallist opinion.[78]

Only in San Francisco, where the business community actively and almost unanimously supported the gold standard, did the major newspapers of any city west or south of New York remain hostile toward the silver drive.[79] Opponents of silver in the Midwest and on the Pacific Coast, like their eastern counterparts, were most numerous among bankers, businessmen, self-employed professionals, and government officials. Their inability or unwillingness to organize publicly prevents a more systematic occupational analysis. Apart from writing to sympathetic Washington officials, monometallists in the American heartland did little to challenge the intense widespread enthusiasm for the "dollar of the daddies."[80]

78. W. Jungst to David A. Wells, Apr. 2, 1878, Wells MSS, LC; Cincinnati *Commercial,* Dec. 19, 1876; H. R. Clausen to John Sherman, Nov. 26, 1877, Sherman MSS, LC; Leland L. Sage, *William Boyd Allison: A Study in Practical Politics* (Iowa City, Iowa, 1956), p. 154.

79. San Francisco *Chronicle,* Dec. 25, 1877, and passim.

80. For representative anti-silver opinion in Ohio, James A Garfield's papers are the most valuable source. The congressman received dozens of letters from monometallists in all section of his state, often writing as silent or embattled minority voices in their own communities. See, for example, the following 1878 letters to Garfield: John T. Strong, Jan. 31; H. Steele, Jan. 21; John Curtis, Jan. 28; J. C. Beatty, Feb. 7; W. Cannon, Feb. 10; William H. Libron, Mar. 4; Garfield MSS, LC. For Illinois opponents of the Bland bill, see C. E. Henry to Garfield, Dec. 6, 1877, Garfield MSS, LC; Elihu B. Washburne to Edward McPherson, Jan. 9, 1878, McPherson MSS, LC; Homer N. Hibbard to Justin S. Morrill, Feb. 11, 1878, Morrill MSS, LC; M. M. Kirkman to R. B. Hayes, Jan. 15, 1878, Hayes MSS, Fremont. On scattered anti-

Despite the southern business community's division over the silver question, there was little newspaper or public opposition to the Bland bill in the section. Southern voices raised against remonetization generally announced their own helplessness against the prevailing tide of silverite sentiment.[81] Only in the port cities of New Orleans, Savannah, and Mobile did monometallists display any strength, while in Congress, only the rare conservative like Senators Lamar of Mississippi and Hill of Georgia spoke against "silver inflation." Hill bowed to political necessity by voting for the silver bill, while Lamar violated the Mississippi legislature's explicit instructions and voted against the measure, a gesture that he claimed later had brought him "a great many complimentary letters from the North, very few from Mississippi."[82] So bitterly did many of Lamar's constituents view his defiance that the Mississippi legislature passed another resolution thanking its Negro senator, Blanche K. Bruce,

---

silver opinion elsewhere in the Middle West and Far West, see H. Walters to Thomas F. Bayard, Feb. 16, 1878, Bayard MSS, LC; James Harlan to W. B. Allison, Mar. 2, 1878, Allison MSS, Des Moines; Alex F. North to Garfield, Dec. 11, 1877; A. J. Loomis to Garfield, Jan. 28, 1878; and Wilbur F. Sanders to Garfield, Feb. 23, 1878; Garfield MSS, LC.

81. See, for example, L. A. Weaver to James A. Garfield, Feb. 21, 1878, Garfield MSS, LC; James N. Walker to Justin S. Morrill, Feb. 4, 1878, Morrill MSS, LC; William Frazier to T. F. Bayard, Feb. 11, 1878, Bayard MSS, LC. On southern support for remonetization, see Rev. D. Hillhouse Buel to Bayard, Feb. 9, 1878, and W. A. Montgomery to Bayard, Jan. 22, 1878, Bayard MSS, LC; also L. A. Sheldon to Garfield, Jan. 22, 1878, Garfield MSS, LC.

82. Woodward, *Reunion and Reaction,* p. 260. For the fullest account of Lamar's actions on the silver bill, see Edward Mayes, *Lucius Q. C. Lamar. His Life, Times and Speeches, 1825–1893* (Nashville, 1896), pp. 323–51. See also Wirt A. Cate, *Lucius Q. C. Lamar* (Chapel Hill, N.C., 1935); also W. A. Montgomery (Mississippi State Senate) to Thomas F. Bayard, Jan. 22, 1878, and William T. Croasdale to Bayard, Feb. 25, 1878, Bayard MSS, LC.

for voting in favor of remonetization.[83] Too much can be made of this unique action by a single southern state legislature, however, and apart from Lamar's dramatic stand against restoration, silver did not become a prominent local issue elsewhere in the region prior to passage of the Bland-Allison Act.

Despite scattered evidence of "the intensity of [Southern] regional sentiment on economic issues" at this time, political life still revolved largely around questions of home rule and the Negro. Therefore, remonetization never entered southern political debate to the degree it had elsewhere in the country by late 1877.[84] Although the South appeared to approve of bimetallism overwhelmingly, and although the section's congressional delegation solidly endorsed the Bland bill, leadership and public support for restoration of the 412.5 grain silver dollar came predominantly from politicians, publicists, businessmen, and voters in the urban Midwest.

The extent of agrarian involvement in the silver drive of the 1870s has also been exaggerated by historians, most of whom have simply projected the experiences of the nineties back into the earlier bimetallist campaign. By the time the country's major farm organization, the National Grange of the Patrons of Husbandry, belatedly endorsed legal bimetallism in November 1877 at its Cincinnati convention by a 34 to 9 vote, its action met with only cursory interest, even in the pro-silver press.[85] Far more

83. Woodward, *Reunion and Reaction.* The *Graphic* interviewed the Negro senator and discovered that "Bruce is very much flattered as he supposed it was impossible for him to do anything the Democrats of Mississippi would approve." New York *Graphic,* Feb. 7, 1878.

84. Occasionally Republicans repeated traditional appeals to their northern colleagues to use the financial question as a stalking horse with which to draw southern conservatives away from the race issue, an illusive hope that Mississippi's response to Bruce's vote on the silver bill must have encouraged momentarily. See, for example, James Atkins to James A. Garfield, Dec. 17, 1877, Garfield MSS, LC.

85. New York *Graphic,* Nov. 27, 1877; Philadelphia *Inquirer,* Nov. 28, 1877.

active and important than "the insistent voice of agrarian soft money" in campaigning for "free silver" during the agitation of the seventies were a large number of newspaper editors, bankers, merchants, lawyers, and politicians from the small towns and cities of the Midwest.[86] A half-dozen mass meetings were held in the Illinois cities of Springfield, Quincy, Bloomington, Peoria, and Princeton alone while the Senate debated the Bland bill, and most urban communities in the state sent delegations to an elaborate silver convention that met at Springfield in January 1878 to dispatch the customary petitions to Congress.[87] The State Grange, meeting at Peoria, telegraphed its support to the Springfield gathering, and silverites in the Illinois legislature sent their own memorial to the White House.[88] Joseph Medill of the Chicago *Tribune,* a major sponsor of the Illinois bimetallists, helped publicize a huge December 1877 rally in that city, attended reportedly by over five thousand people. Despite the opposition of some Chicago bankers, the silver drive in Illinois appeared to enjoy near-unanimous support.[89]

86. Unger, *Greenback Era,* p. 358. Unger offers the most sophisticated neo-agrarian analysis of the roots of silver agitation. The present writer disagrees with his contention, the basis for most previous discussions of the silver issue during the seventies, that agrarian soft-money forces organized, led, and provided most of the significant support for remonetization during the 1870s. The available evidence does not support this analysis.

87. Ibid.; Ernest Ludlow Bogart and Charles Manfred Thompson, *The Industrial State, 1870–1893,* vol. 9 of *The Centennial History of Illinois* (Springfield, 1920), pp. 126–27.

88. Ibid.; J. H. Kedzie to W. B. Allison on the following 1878 dates: Jan. 8, Jan. 10, and Jan. 23, Allison MSS, Des Moines.

89. Philadelphia *Inquirer,* Dec. 14, 1877; Philip Kinsley, *The Chicago Tribune, Its First Hundred Years, Vol. II, 1865–1880* (Chicago, 1945), pp. 261–66; Joseph Medill to R. B. Hayes, Jan. 15, 1878, Hayes MSS, Fremont; Bogart and Thompson, *The Industrial State,* pp. 126–27. On other Illinois silverites, see Samuel Hoard to Carl Schurz, May 18, 1877, Schurz MSS, LC; Samuel Hoard to John Sherman, April 26, 1877, and Crafts J. Wright to Sherman, Jan. 19, 1878, Sherman MSS, LC; J. H. Kedzie to R. B. Hayes, Dec. 17, 1877, Hayes MSS, Fremont.

Throughout the Midwest, both political parties endorsed remonetization during the fall campaign, and resolutions demanding Senate passage of the Bland bill came from several legislative bodies in the region, including the Ohio House of Representatives and the Minnesota State Senate. The Minnesota move was organized by the later Populist leader, Ignatius Donnelly.[90] Many Ohioans, responding to appeals by Halstead's *Commercial* and other silverite newspapers, wrote to the state's three leading opponents of remonetization—Hayes, Sherman, and Garfield—demanding immediate passage of the Bland bill. Dispirited administration supporters in Ohio acknowledged that "there is not one in ten who is not [for] Matthews' Silver Resolution, the Bland Bill, [and] Repeal of the Resumption [Act]."[91] Elsewhere in the region another mass meeting supporting passage of the silver bill was held in Indianapolis, jointly sponsored by Indiana Democrats and Independent-Greenbackers, while several similar gatherings took place in Dubuque and other Iowa cities.[92] The Iowa House of Representatives passed its expected pro-silver resolution, and the state's professionals—

90. Philadelphia *Inquirer,* Jan. 17, 1878; [?] Thorpe to James A. Garfield, Jan. 19, 1878, and J. S. Robinson to Garfield, Feb. 15, 1878, Garfield MSS, LC; Ridge, *Ignatius Donnelly,* p. 177; Unger, *Greenback Era.*

91. A. Denny to John Sherman, Jan. 30, 1878, Sherman MSS, LC. The files of Sherman and Garfield contain dozens of similar expressions of opinion from irate Ohio silverites, See, for example, James R. Challon to Sherman, Feb. 22, 1877; F. W. Powell to Sherman, Nov. 13, 1877; and John Welch to Sherman, Jan. 21, 1878, Sherman MSS, LC. See also E. R. Moore to Garfield, July 2, 1877; O. M. Woodward to Garfield, Dec. 29, 1877; L. Smith to Garfield, Dec. 25, 1877; Garfield MSS, LC. Friends of the Administration attempted to make Hayes, Sherman, and Garfield aware throughout the controversy of the depth of local feeling on the question. For example, L. C. Weir to R. B. Hayes, Jan. 9, 1878, Hayes MSS, Fremont; D. W. McClung to Garfield, Feb. 9, 1878, Garfield MSS, LC.

92. Unger, *Greenback Era;* Edward Guilberthy to W. B. Allison, Feb. 5, 1878, Allison MSS, Des Moines.

doctors, lawyers, and public officials—bombarded Allison with letters of support.[93]

In the Far West public enthusiasm for remonetization transformed the political life of Nevada by providing the state with an indigenous issue and a new popular hero, John Percival Jones, the "daddy of our dollars." In neighboring Colorado, Henry Moore Teller had just begun his long Senate career. Not yet identified with the silver movement, Teller supported Allison's amendments to the Bland bill and later acknowledged, in 1882, that he had "not heretofore been very radical on this question."[94] Reaction to the House measure by Teller's Colorado Senate colleague, Jerome B. Chaffee, and by California's Newton Booth illustrated the wide influence of greenback ideas on far western representatives. Although Teller, Chaffee, and Booth all supported remonetization, they also sponsored separate amendments to the Bland bill that provided for unlimited issues of paper currency backed either by silver bullion or by coin.[95] Even John Percival Jones himself became a "probationary convert" to greenbackism by mid-1877, although even then he expressed little enthusiasm for his western colleagues' various silver note schemes. Teller's Colorado mail ran almost entirely favorable to the silver bill, although local greenbacker correspondents considered it only a first step in their program of financial expansion.[96]

93. George A. Morse to Allison, Feb. 11, 1878. See also the following representative letters to Allison, primarily from Iowa professionals: R. W. Humphrey, Jan. 6, 1877; Charles Mason, Nov. 11, 1877; George C. Van Allen, Dec. 25, 1877; J. L. Husted, Dec. 29, 1877; S. D. Nichols, Jan. 7, 1878; D. N. Loose, Feb. 13, 1878; Robert Lowry, Feb. 17, 1878; John McKeon, Mar. 2, 1878; Allison MSS, Des Moines.

94. On Jones and silver politics in Nevada, see Chap. 3, passim. On Colorado silver politics during the 1870s see Elmer Ellis, *Henry Moore Teller* (Caldwell, Idaho, 1941), pp. 125–26.

95. Ibid. For debate over the Chafee and Booth amendments, see *Cong. Record,* 45th Cong., 2d sess., vol. 7, pt. 2, pp. 1102–05.

96. For representative Colorado silverite opinion, see the following letters to Teller: O. H. Harkett, Mar. 10, 1878; S. E. Browne, Feb. 2, 1878; Richard Irwin, Jan. 11, 1878; John Trask, Mar. 1, 1878; James

Mining state senators, on the whole, handled the silver issue gingerly in the seventies, despite recognition that support for restoration was "almost universal" in the Far West. Thus, after Newton Booth's amendment, which provided for an exchange of paper notes for deposits of silver coin, had been accepted by the Senate, both Teller and Booth took almost no further part in debate on the measure. William Sharon of Nevada, who opposed remonetization, remained in California and tended to his vast banking and brokerage interests until the silver issue had been disposed of, declining to risk his reelection chances by voting against the Bland-Allison Act. Chaffee's views on the monetary standard question confused even his own Colorado supporters, some of whom felt he was a secret greenbacker while others considered him a gold monometallist.[97] The Coloradan's Senate activities encouraged this confusion; although he voted for the silver bill's final amended version and for the Matthews Resolution, he also joined eastern conservatives in attempting unsuccessfully to subvert the bond-payment declaration with a preamble that endorsed the gold standard![98]

Only John Percival Jones, among far western congressmen in the late 1870s, supported remonetization consistently and vigorously. Republican Aaron Sargent of California reflected the opinions of his San Francisco business associates by opposing the Bland bill, and his Senate colleague Newton Booth was practically a greenbacker. Jones' Nevada Senate colleague, the absent William Sharon, also endorsed the gold standard, while Henry Teller "never spoke upon the question . . . possibly because he knew very little about it." Finally, although Jerome

---

B. Belford, Mar. 17, 1878; R. Weiser, Mar. 8, 1878. For Colorado Greenbackism, see the following letters to Teller: P. M. Housel, Feb. 14, 1878; William H. Davidson, Jan. 16 and Feb. 25, 1878; M. S. Taylor, Mar. 8, 1878; James Wolff (Chairman, Colorado Greenback Party), Nov. 12 and Nov. 24, 1877; Teller MSS, Denver Public Library.

97. P. P. Wilcox to Teller, Mar. 7, 1878; James Belford to Teller, Mar. 17, 1878; Richard Irwin to Teller, Jan. 11, 1878, ibid.

98. *Cong. Record.* 45th Cong., 2d sess., vol. 7, pt. 1, pp. 561–64.

Chaffee cast several ballots for silver, his "great wealth and growing eastern interests had given him much of the point of view of the gold standard advocates."[99] For all practical purposes, only Jones actively represented in Congress that majority of the electorate in the western mining states which strongly favored the return of legal bimetallism.

Although public opinion forced a number of reluctant western politicians to accept remonetization or risk political reprisal, the silver movement's strength in eastern states lay not in its numbers but in the relentless campaigning of a small group of publicists and politicians. In New York City, for example, only the *Graphic* among local dailies endorsed the Bland bill. Still, speeches by Congressman "Sunset" Cox of Brooklyn along with the writings of Thurlow Weed and other enthusiasts helped generate considerable popular support for silver. In February 1878, "a packed meeting [at Cooper Union] of businessmen, labor leaders, and soft money professionals" heard Weed, Henry D. Carey, and other venerable antebellum figures demand immediate passage of the congressional silver bill, and in the three months preceding Senate action on the measure, "Sunset" Cox and Roscoe Conkling introduced pro-silver petitions signed by over thirty thousand New Yorkers from all corners of the state.[100]

This effective petition campaign, organized by an Albany silverite, George Jones, may have influenced Conkling's decision to refrain from openly opposing the Bland bill until the last days of Senate debate, when pressures from influential gold-standard papers like the *Tribune* and the *Journal of Commerce* finally stirred him to denounce the legislation.[101] Despite their

99. Ellis, *Henry Moore Teller,* p. 125.

100. Unger, *Greenback Era,* pp. 336–37; New York *Graphic* on the following 1878 dates: Jan. 31, Feb. 2, and Feb. 5; David Lindsey, *"Sunset" Cox, Irrepressible Democrat* (Detroit, 1959), pp. 176–77.

101. New York *Graphic,* Feb. 2, 1878. For Conkling's silence on the silver question, see the *Graphic,* Feb. 5, 1878; New York *Journal of*

limited numbers, New York silverites like Thurlow Weed, *Graphic* editor D. G. Croly, J. Watson Webb, *Bankers' Magazine* editor I. S. Homan, bullion dealer J. B. Colgate, George Jones of Albany, and S. S. Cox of Brooklyn waged an extremely aggressive drive to solicit popular backing. They demonstrated that opinions in the state were more deeply divided on remonetization than the anti-silver stand taken by most Empire State congressmen would have indicated.[102]

Further down the eastern seaboard, silverites held a commanding majority of Pennsylvania's votes in Congress, and both state parties endorsed the Bland bill.[103] In Delaware, where Senator Thomas F. Bayard attempted to rally support for the gold standard, Wilmington's monometallist mayor confessed to Bayard in January 1878 that "outside of the [newspapers and] their dipendants [*sic*] we find nobody in favor of it." There was more interest aroused in Wilmington by a proposal to hold a pro-silver meeting, and one sad constituent complained to Bayard that "our people take sides with [silverite Senator] Saulsbury."[104] Even in New England, an unusual congressman like Ben Butler, an eccentric reformer like Wendell Phillips and a rare news-

---

Commerce, Feb. 5, 1878; Silas Ward to Thomas F. Bayard, Feb. 6, 1878, Bayard MSS, LC; and Thomas C. Platt to Whitelaw Reid, Feb. 20, 1878, Reid MSS, LC.

102. On the activities of New York silverites see the following: J. Watson Webb to Thurlow Weed, July 1, 1877, Weed MSS, New York Historical Society; M. C. Matteson to Cornelius Cole, Feb. 10, 1878, Cole MSS, UCLA Library; Horace Binney to James A. Garfield, Dec. 5, 1877, Garfield MSS, LC: Thurlow Weed to Whitelaw Reid, Nov. 2, 1877, and Weed to Reid, Feb. 4, 1878, Reid MSS, LC; D. G. Croly to John Sherman, Jan. 20, 1879 [*sic*], Sherman MSS, LC.

103. John Brooks (Pennsylvania House of Representatives) to John Sherman, Jan. 20, 1878, Sherman MSS, LC.

104. W. G. [?] to Thomas F. Bayard, Jan. 16, 1878; Abraham Payne to Bayard, Jan. 11, 1878; J. Turpin Wright to Bayard, Feb. 8, 1878; Delaware farmer [unsigned letter] to Bayard, Dec. 24, 1877; Bayard MSS, LC.

paper like the Nashua [New Hampshire] *Gazette* favored restoration of the double standard, although in splendid isolation.[105]

Elsewhere in the country, from New York City down the Atlantic coast to Georgia, throughout the Midwest and on the Pacific coast, "details of innumerable meetings and memorials filled the press and the congressmen's mail" while the Senate debated Allison's amendments, most of them favoring swift passage of a silver bill.[106] By the time Congress returned from its Christmas recess, these different barometers of public opinion suggested that a national mandate existed, except in New England, for the immediate restoration of legal bimetallism. A silver movement had been born.

105. Benjamin F. Butler to James M. Caller, Feb. 5, 1878, typescript, Butler MSS, LC; New York *Graphic,* Jan. 25, 1878, for the New Hampshire *Gazette's* opinions. On Phillips's support for silver, see Crafts J. Wright to John Sherman, Jan. 19, 1878, Sherman MSS, LC.

106. Nichols, "John Sherman and the Silver Drive," p. 158.

12

The Road to Bland-Allison: Climax and Compromise, 1878

The central figure in the silver drive's final phase was Iowa Republican William Boyd Allison, chairman of the Finance Committee and a man identified with the hard-money resumptionist bloc among midwestern Republicans. Although Allison came up for reelection in January 1878, his support for remonetization exceeded the political necessities imposed by a strongly pro-silver Iowa constituency.[1] Allison's role as Senate floor manager for the silver bill was only one factor in his near unanimous reelection by the Iowa legislature. Actually, as a leading congressional spokesman for western interests, he had been a highly popular figure in Iowa long before the silver agitation opened. Allison enjoyed substantial support from the state's Republican newspapers, especially James S. "Ret" Clarkson's widely circulated Des Moines *Register,* because of his outspoken opposition to Hayes' conciliatory southern policy.[2] The senator's biographer credits Clarkson's backing as the most important factor in Allison's hefty January 1878 majority in the state legislature, noting that because of the *Register's* obsessive hatred for the

1. For a contrasting opinion, see Nichols, "John Sherman and the Silver Drive," p. 158.

2. M. K. Jesup to Allison, Jan. 12, 1877; S. S. Farwell to Allison, Jan. 1, 1878; E. H. Nealley to Allison, Jan. 10, 1878; J. Fred Meyers to Allison, Jan. 28, 1878. For Iowa silverite endorsement of Allison's reelection bid, see E. W. Eastman to Allison, Jan. 1, 1878, Allison MSS, Des Moines; also Dan Elbert Clark, *History of Senatorial Elections in Iowa* (Iowa City, 1912), pp. 185–186.

President's efforts to placate the South, Clarkson's journal—the most influential in the state—"had little time and space for the silver fight then going on."[3]

Although smaller Iowa dailies devoted more attention to the Congressional struggle over the Bland bill, Allison's speeches and letters never betrayed particular concern for adjusting his personal views on remonetization to suit those of his constituents. The Iowa Republican had devoted as much time as had John Sherman or John Percival Jones to studying the monetary standard question. He believed that restoration of legal bimetallism followed by an international agreement would stabilize the world market ratio between gold and silver at a level that would insure their interchangeable use. Allison indicated the strength of this ideological commitment to silver during Senate debate in February 1878:

> Mr. President, this demand for remonetization [Allison observed] does not come from our country alone or any section of it. It receives the support of the best writers and thinkers in our own and in other countries. It does not have its origin in petty malice toward the public creditor, nor is it a dishonest demand made by debtors. It receives the sanction of the many men who have devoted their lives to the study of economic subjects, and if we follow such guidance we are not likely to be led astray. Those who favor this measure do not propose to violate any promise, and least of all to tarnish or impair the public credit, but rather to establish it upon more enduring foundations by increasing our ability to pay according to promise the heavy public burdens which now weight us down.[4]

The Iowa Republican knew at firsthand of international bimetallism's popularity among American economic analysts, hav-

3. Clark, History of Senatorial Elections, p. 150.

4. *Cong. Record,* 45th Cong. 2d sess., vol. 7, pt. 2, p. 1061, Feb. 15, 1878.

ing read their works and discussed the subject personally with many of the writers. While preparing his amendments, before Senate debate on the silver bill, he had studied carefully the writings of Ernest Seyd, Henri Cernuschi, and other European publicists while seeking advice at the same time from American agreement silverites like George Walker and S. Dana Horton.[5] More than most leading silverites, the Finance Committee chairman tried to maintain a dialogue on monetary standard policy with monometallists like Horace White, Edward Atkinson, and Samuel B. Ruggles.[6] The Iowan drew for his ideas on the writings of Dana Horton and George Walker, and the latter probably drafted the international conference provision that Allison included among his amendments to the Bland bill. The section eventually adopted by the Senate differed only in minor changes of wording from an earlier draft submitted by Walker to Allison.[7] Walker also continued to consult with the Iowa Republican during the final months of the silver drive, providing him with material for use during Senate debate.[8]

The international conference idea was one of three important

5. George Walker to Allison, Nov. 13, 1877, and Feb. 4, 1878; S. Dana Horton to Allison, Feb. 7, 1878, Allison MSS, Des Moines.

6. W. B. Allison to S. B. Ruggles, Nov. 23, 1877, Ruggles MSS, New York Public Library. See also S. B. Ruggles to Allison, Nov. 21, 1877; Horace White to Allison, Nov. 27, 1877; Thomas F. Bayard to Allison, Dec. 9, 1877; Allison MSS, Des Moines.

7. S. Dana Horton to Allison, Feb. 7, 1878; see also George Walker to Allison, Nov. 13, 1877; Allison MSS, Des Moines. Walker's draft amendment, included in his November 13 letter to Allison, differed only in minor changes of detail and wording from the amendment which eventually became part of the Bland-Allison Act. Allison's Finance Committee voted to reject the international conference amendment at its November 21 meeting but later reconsidered, and the provision was submitted to the Senate on behalf of the Committee by Allison on December 13. Allison to Samuel B. Ruggles, Nov. 23, 1877, Ruggles MSS, N.Y. Public Library; *Cong. Record* 45th Cong., 2d sess., vol. 7, pt. 1, pp. 177–78.

8. Walker to Allison, Feb. 5 and Mar. 2, 1878, Allison MSS, Des Moines.

changes made in the Bland bill by the Senate Finance Committee at a November 21 meeting. No official record survives of the group's deliberations, but "by common consent the committee turned to [Allison] for leadership."[9] He and Pennsylvania Democrat William A. Wallace, both moderate silverites, held the balance of power in the divided committee, since three eastern members of the group—Morrill, Dawes, and Bayard—firmly opposed any silver bill while three westerners—Jones, Howe, and Ferry—favored immediate passage of the House measure without revisions.[10] Allison and Wallace voted with their three fellow silverites to block a number of proposals by the committee's monometallists aimed at limiting silver's legal tender powers, but the pair aligned with the three eastern members to support several amendments that cut the inflationary heart out of the Bland bill.

Instead of *free* coinage, which would have awarded bullion sellers the difference between silver's market price and the currently higher mint purchase rate, the Finance Committee placed the metal's coinage on "government account," so that the Treasury now received all minting profits. The House measure had also provided for silver's *unlimited* coinage, but the committee limited the purchase of silver bullion to a modest two to four million dollars worth each month, an amendment that precluded serious currency inflation because of remonetization.[11]

Many silverites denounced the Finance Committee amendments immediately as unacceptable, because they deprived the House measure, in the New York *Graphic's* words, "of the greater part of its efficiency."[12] Bland himself warned that bi-

9. Sage, *William Boyd Allison,* p. 153.

10. Philadelphia *Inquirer,* Nov. 21, 1877; Unger, *Greenback Era,* pp. 361–62; Nichols, "John Sherman and the Silver Drive," p. 160.

11. Philadelphia *Inquirer,* Nov. 21, 1877; Chicago *Tribune,* Nov. 20 and Nov. 21, 1877; New York *Tribune,* Nov. 21 and Nov. 22, 1877; Cincinnati *Commercial,* Nov. 21 and Nov. 22, 1877.

12. New York *Graphic,* Nov. 21, 1877. See also Joseph Medill to W. B. Allison, Jan. 28, 1878, Allison MSS, Des Moines.

metallists in the lower chamber would bottle up all appropriation bills if the Senate did not pass his original silver bill intact, and the Missouri Democrat expressed confidence that all revisions would be voted down by Allison's colleagues.[13] Significantly, the Senate's leading silverite, John Percival Jones, found the amendments less troubling. Although Jones opposed them both in committee and in later Senate voting, he did so halfheartedly, as a political gesture on behalf of his Nevada constituents.

Allison had removed the Bland bill's "free and unlimited coinage" provisions partly in order to attract additional support from Senate moderates for the measure and thereby insure the two-thirds majority needed to override an expected presidential veto. The Iowa Republican recognized that Hayes would not approve the revised measure, since it failed to incorporate both the Chief Executive's recommendation for increasing the silver dollar's grain content and his demand that the public debt be exempted from payment in silver. Jones disagreed with Allison's strategy and contended that the Iowan's amendments "would not practically affect the operations of the bill in any way, or make it more acceptable to either of the two parties on the subject." The Nevadan agreed with Allison, however, that despite the limitations placed on complete remonetization, silver's market price would soon rise to a level substantially equal to gold once the double standard was restored, thereby providing the incentive for an international conference to stabilize a permanent mint ratio between the two metals.[14] Most historians have failed to credit the fact that Jones and Allison, the two Senate Republican leaders of the silver drive, along with most other bimetallists, supported remonetization not simply for political reasons but because they believed in its economic wisdom. Thus, Jones indicated in a letter to Murat Halstead that although he disap-

13. New York *Graphic,* Dec. 5, 1877, interview with Richard Bland.
14. Philadelphia *Inquirer,* Nov. 21, 1877.

proved of the Finance Committee's changes, he considered them negligible:

> If we have to accept a limitation of the coinage, I propose to have the Senate amendment amended so as to make three millions per month the minimum coinage and whenever the market price and mint price shall coincide, which they soon would do, the mint to be open to free coinage. This will satisfy those who clamor that the government shall receive the difference between the two and will be the best for us if the coinage is to be restricted.[15]

Jones' comments reflected the prevailing Senate desire for framing an acceptable compromise silver bill. Although few Senators believed that the House measure could be passed without amendments, almost none thought that it could be defeated. Debate centered around the precise nature of the revisions, and the upper chamber knocked down a number of attempts to alter the Bland bill more drastically than the Finance Committee had done. As early as December 6, at the very beginning of debate, Senator Ingalls of Kansas called for the bill's immediate passage and predicted that "no new arguments can be or will be adduced upon the subject; and, if the debate should continue in the Senate for months, I doubt very much whether a single vote would be changed or an opinion entertained that is not now held by the members of the Senate."[16]

The final February 1878 tally on the measure proved the Kansas Republican an accurate prophet. Along with his colleagues, however, Ingalls recognized that public attention had riveted upon the Senate. This allowed legislators to express their constituents' sentiments before a national audience. In the end, "thirty-two set speeches and ten 'respeeches' " droned on before an increasingly weary upper chamber from December 6, 1877,

15. John Percival Jones to Murat Halstead, Jan. 18, 1878, Halstead MSS, Cincinnati Historical Society; Washington *National Republican,* Jan. 10, 1878, interview with J. P. Jones.

16. *Cong. Record,* 45th Cong., 2d sess., vol. 7, pt. 1, p. 44.

when Allison brought up the revised Bland bill under a special order, to February 15, 1878, when it received final Senate approval.[17] Every Senator who had voted for the December 1877 special order ultimately voted for final passage and, similarly, opponents of the former ultimately rejected the bill itself. Only a few additional ballots changed a 41 to 18 December margin for remonetization to a 48 to 21 February tally.[18] (See Table 6.)

Before the Senate could begin debating the Bland bill, however, Republican Stanley Matthews of Ohio raised the related issue of the connection between silver policy and resumption. On December 6, immediately after Allison secured his special order, Matthews introduced a concurrent resolution which declared that payment of the federal debt, "principal and interest, at the option of the Government of the United States, in silver dollars . . . containing 412.5 grains each, of standard silver . . . is not in violation of the public faith, nor in derogation of the rights of the public creditor."[19] The Matthews Resolution seriously embarrassed those Republican moderates like Allison who had expected to secure floor action on the revised silver bill without rousing further the fears of government bondholders that they would be repaid in depreciated coinage.[20]

17. Ibid., pp. 43–47; Nichols, "John Sherman and the Silver Drive," p. 162.

18. *Cong. Record,* 45th Cong., 2d sess., vol. 7, pt. 1, p. 46; pt. 2 p. 1112.

19. Ibid., pt. 1, p. 47.

20. Before the Senate passed the Matthews Resolution, in fact, it may even have embarrassed its sponsor, a close friend of the President's. For when the declaration came up for debate on December 10, Hayes' principal Republican opponent in the battle for party leadership, Senator Roscoe Conkling of New York, tried unsuccessfully to change it from a concurrent to a joint resolution, the latter requiring the Chief Executive's signature. Hayes would undoubtedly have vetoed the Matthews Resolution, thereby further infuriating Republican silverites who represented a probable majority of the party in the Middle West and the South (Ibid., p. 92). For congressional debate on the Matthews Resolution, see ibid., pp. 87–94, 168–77, 549–64, 627–28.

Table 6

Vote on the Special Order Calling up the Bland Bill, Senate, December 6, 1877

	Ayes			Nays	
	Rep.	Dem.	Ind.	Rep.	Dem.
New England States					
Massachusetts				1	
Maine				2	
New Hampshire				2	
Vermont				1	
Connecticut					1
Rhode Island				2	
TOTALS				8	1
Middle Atlantic States					
New York					
Pennsylvania		1			
Maryland					1
Delaware					1
New Jersey					2
TOTALS		1			4
Midwestern States					
Ohio	1	1			
Illinois	1		1		
Indiana		2			
Wisconsin	2				
Minnesota	1				
Michigan	1			1	
Iowa	2				
Kansas	2				
Nebraska	2				
TOTALS	12	3	1	1	
Border States					
Kentucky		2			
Tennessee		2			
West Virginia		2			
Missouri					
TOTALS		6			

Table 6—Continued

	Ayes			Nays	
	Rep.	Dem.	Ind.	Rep.	Dem.
Southern States					
Virginia		2			
North Carolina		2			
South Carolina	1				
Georgia		1			1
Alabama		1			
Mississippi	1				1
Florida	1	1			
Louisiana					
Texas		2			
Arkansas	1	1			
TOTALS	4	10			2
Far Western States					
California			1	1	
Nevada	1				
Colorado	2				
Oregon				1	
TOTALS	3		1	2	
GRAND TOTALS	19	20	2	11	7

TOTAL AYES: 41

TOTAL NAYS: 18

Allison also sensed that the Matthews Resolution would distract public attention from the major question, "namely, what shall be done with silver; whether or not silver shall again take its place as a part of the money of the United States."[21] The Iowa Republican resented especially the implication in Matthews' declaration that silverites were "repudiators" who favored remonetization primarily as a device to scale down the public debt through its repayment in silver dollars worth less than their market weight in gold. Most monometallists saw the con-

21. For Allison's comments on the resolution, ibid., pp. 173–75.

current resolution in this light, as simply "a rascally scheme to dishonor the country."[22] Even staunch supporters of the original Bland bill like the New York *Graphic* considered the Ohio Republican's actions ill-advised and unnecessary, since "the law is clear and explicit [on repayment in either metal] as it stands."[23]

Matthews' reasons for having sponsored the resolution remain obscure. He claimed to have been inspired partly by a similar pro-silver declaration that passed the Ohio legislature several months earlier. More probably he reacted against Hayes' annual message, issued several days earlier, which had labeled any attempt to pay the public debt in silver as both illegal and immoral. Matthews had portrayed the President leaning toward support for remonetization in a number of newspaper interviews, and Hayes' message made him seem not only a poor prophet but a slightly ridiculous one. Shortly after introducing the resolution, one reporter found the Buckeye state's junior senator "somewhat reticent concerning the views of the President and his probable action on the bill, but . . . quite unreserved in reference to the position of Congress."[24]

The Senate resumed consideration of the Matthews Resolution following its Christmas recess on January 25 and rejected immediately, by a 23 to 29 vote, New York Republican Roscoe Conkling's attempt to embarass the President, his factional enemy in the party, by turning the declaration into a joint resolution that would require Hayes' signature. Almost all eastern gold standard Republicans, also stalwart opponents of the chief executive, voted with Conkling while Democrats split on the proposal. Following a lively debate between the Senate's leading

22. August Belmont to Thomas F. Bayard, Dec. 18, 1877, Bayard MSS, LC.

23. New York *Graphic,* Dec. 7, 1877.

24. *Cong. Record,* 45th Cong., 2d sess., vol. 7, pt. 1, p. 87; Nichols, "John Sherman and the Silver Drive", p. 158; New York *Graphic,* Dec. 20, 1877.

bimetallists—Matthews, Allison, and Jones—and the Vermont monometallist George F. Edmunds, the upper chamber defeated Edmund's attempt to proclaim government securities payable only in gold, 18 to 44. The upper chamber then passed the Matthews Resolution itself by a 43 to 22 vote. Several whimsical proposals by opponents to attach a gold standard preamble to the resolution were beaten down by similar margins before the Senate adopted Matthew's original declaration.[25]

The debate's high point came shortly before final voting, when John Gordon of Georgia warned fellow silverites against expecting passage of the Bland bill to provide immediate economic relief for the country. The causes of the prolonged depression, Gordon reminded his colleagues, were too complex to be resolved simply by expanding the currency. Demonetization, Gordon avowed, was primarily a wrong "to be righted," an "act of justice" owed to the people, that would assist in business recovery mainly by halting the "pernicious policy of [currency] contraction which . . . is the prime evil and agent in the destruction of our prosperity." The extended applause that followed Gordon's short address made the presiding officer, Vice-President Wheeler, threaten to clear the galleries, which remained packed with ardent silverites throughout the months of Senate debate.[26] (See Table 7.)

New England's senators, both Democratic and Republican, opposed the Matthews Resolution in the final tally while other northeastern legislators split on the question. Midwestern Republicans and southern Democrats accounted for almost half the declaration's votes, and support came also from a small band of southern Republicans and a larger contingent of border state Democrats. Both parties, on the whole, showed a more pronounced tendency toward sectional balloting than their House

25. *Cong. Record,* 45th Cong., 2d sess., vol 7, pt. 1, pp. 549–58, 561–64.

26. For this concluding Senate discussion of the Matthews Resolution, see ibid., pp. 549–64.

Table 7

Vote on the Matthews Resolution, Senate, January 25, 1878

	Ayes			Nays	
	Rep.	Dem.	Ind.	Rep.	Dem.
New England States					
Massachusetts				1	
Maine				2	
New Hampshire				2	
Vermont				2	
Connecticut					2
Rhode Island				2	
TOTALS				9	2
Middle Atlantic States					
New York				1	1
Pennsylvania	1	1			
Maryland		1			
Delaware		1			1
New Jersey					2
TOTALS	1	3		1	4
Midwestern States					
Ohio	1	1			
Illinois	1		1		
Indiana		2			
Wisconsin	2				
Minnesota	1			1	
Michigan	1			1	
Iowa	2				
Kansas	1				
Nebraska	1			1	
TOTALS	10	3	1	3	
Border States					
Kentucky		2			
Tennessee		1			
West Virginia		2			
Missouri		1			
TOTALS		6			

Table 7—Continued

	Ayes			Nays	
	Rep.	Dem.	Ind.	Rep.	Dem.
Southern States					
Virginia		2			
North Carolina		2			
South Carolina					
Georgia		1			
Alabama	1	1			
Mississippi	1				1
Florida	1	1			
Louisiana		1			
Texas		2			
Arkansas	1				
TOTALS	4	10			1
Far Western States					
California			1	1	
Nevada	1				
Colorado	2				
Oregon		1		1	
TOTALS	3	1	1	2	
GRAND TOTALS	18	23	2	15	7

TOTAL AYES: 43

TOTAL NAYS: 22

colleagues had done, although the direction of the Senate silver bill remained in Republican hands. (See Table 8.)

The House endorsed the Matthews Resolution swiftly, without debate, on January 28 by a lopsided 189 to 79 count that reflected accurately the strength of remonetization's supporters and opponents in the lower chamber.[27] The balloting was remarkably similar among midwestern, southern, and border state

27. For House action on the resolution, ibid., pp. 627–28. See also Philadelphia *Inquirer,* Jan. 26, and Feb. 1, 1878; and New York *Weekly Journal of Commerce,* Jan. 31, 1878.

Table 8

Vote on the Matthews Resolution, House of Representatives, January 28, 1878

	Ayes		Nays	
	Rep.	Dem.	Rep.	Dem.
New England States				
Massachusetts	1		9	1
Maine			5	
New Hampshire			2	1
Vermont			3	
Connecticut		1	1	2
Rhode Island			2	
TOTALS	1	1	22	4
Middle Atlantic States				
New York	1	2	13	12
Pennsylvania	7	8	8	1
Maryland		5		1
Delaware				1
New Jersey		1	3	2
TOTALS	8	16	24	17
Midwestern States				
Ohio	9	7	1	
Illinois	11	7		
Indiana	9	3		
Wisconsin	5	3		
Minnesota	2		1	
Michigan	5		1	1
Iowa	9			
Kansas	3			
Nebraska	1			
TOTALS	54	20	3	1
Border States				
Kentucky		9		
Tennessee	2	8		
West Virginia		3		
Missouri	3	8	1	
TOTALS	5	28	1	

Table 8—Continued

	Ayes		Nays	
	Rep.	Dem.	Rep.	Dem.
Southern States				
Virginia		5	1	
North Carolina	1	7		
South Carolina	2	2	1	
Georgia		8		
Alabama		8		
Mississippi		5		
Florida		1	1	
Louisiana		3	1	
Texas		5		1
Arkansas		4		
TOTALS	3	48	4	1
Far Western States				
California	2	1	1	
Nevada	1			
Colorado		1		
Oregon			1	
TOTALS	3	2	2	
GRAND TOTALS	74	115	56	23

TOTAL AYES: 189

TOTAL NAYS: 79

representatives to their earlier November 1877 division on the Bland bill, with only a handful of votes changing in each section. In the northeast, however, the tally indicated that public interest in the question had intensified, making it more difficult for legislators to abstain from voting as many had done the previous November. Party lines in the middle Atlantic states split badly; 65 congressmen balloted in January on the Matthews Resolution compared with 19 on the Bland bill. Republicans in the area voted 8 to 24 against the bond payment declaration, while Democrats divided more closely, 16 to 17, on the question. New

England House members, on the other hand, voted overwhelmingly, like their Senate counterparts, against the resolution, with a much larger number taking part in the balloting than had voted on the silver bill. Midwestern Republicans and southern Democrats registered more than half the House votes for the Matthews Resolution, although a higher proportion of overall support in the lower chamber came from Democrats.

For the next two weeks, from January 29 to February 15, several dozen senators introduced amendments to the House silver bill while presenting speeches on the question or inserting them into the *Record.* Final debate began at a marathon seventeen-hour session on February 15.[28] Justin Morrill opened the round of speechmaking with a long anti-silver polemic on January 29, sustained during the following days by similar orations from a small but able group of monometallists that included Thomas Bayard of Delaware, George Edmunds of Vermont, Henry L. Dawes of Massachusetts, William Eaton of Connecticut, Francis Kernan of New York, and Isaac Christiancy of Minnesota. William A. Wallace of Pennsylvania, speaking on behalf of the Finance Committee, served as keynoter for the silverite case on January 29. At subsequent meetings, Allen Thurman of Ohio, Eli Saulsbury of Delaware, John J. Ingalls of Kansas, John Percival Jones, and finally Allison himself all demanded remonetization.

From the opening moment of debate, silverite senators insisted that Allison's amendments had removed the inflationary threat posed by the House measure and that, therefore, the real issue was whether the country should continue under the gold standard or return to bimetallism. "This bill is not the Bland bill. The free-coinage feature is out of it," Wallace noted in his

28. For the speeches and Senate debate over the Bland bill, see *Cong. Record,* 45th Cong., 2d sess., vol. 7, pt. 1, pp. 607–18, 646–48, 666–71, 687–89, 726–35, 752–66, 786–96, 820–26, 842–54, 924–37, 957–59, 960–63, 976–95; pt. 2, pp. 1017–29, 1051–1112.

opening address. "The question before us is not, shall we make silver an unlimited legal tender, but shall we coin silver dollars?" All but the most intransigent Senate supporters of free and unlimited coinage disclaimed any inflationist sentiments and argued that "an additional amount of [silver] coin in the country [would produce] greater stability and regularity in financial affairs . . . aid in securing and maintaining resumption, encourage legitimate enterprise and industry, and assist in restoring a greater degree of prosperity . . ." Supporters of the Allison compromise repeatedly refuted "the principal point raised by the opponents of this bill . . . the assumption that its passage would tend to drive gold out of this country as a circulating medium." To counter this argument Senate silverites pointed out repeatedly that the Allison amendment which placed a monthly limit on silver coinage would allow for a transitional period, during which the metal's market price was expected to rise to that of gold. An international conference could then stabilize more permanently the legal relation between the two. As an added precaution Senator Beck and others even suggested that foreigners be barred from selling silver to the American mints until the metals were interchangeable in market price.[29]

A wide spectrum of opinions emerged in the Senate on remonetization during the last weeks of discussion. Rather than dividing into two monolithic silver and anti-silver blocs, legislators offered several distinct positions in their prepared speeches. Some defended the original House bill and denied the need for any amendments. Among these were John Percival Jones, Beck of Kentucky, Ferry of Michigan, and Coke of Texas, all of whom eventually voted for the revised measure.[30] A much larger bloc of senators followed moderates Allison and Wallace and endorsed remonetization but only with restrictions placed

29. Ibid., pt. 1, pp. 641, 726–27, 925.

30. Ibid., pp. 726–27, 758, 932–37; Philadelphia *Inquirer*, Feb. 14, 1878. See also *Cong. Record*, 45th Cong., 2d sess., vol. 7, pt. 2, pp. 1017–26.

on free and unlimited coinage. A third group led by William Windom of Minnesota, Angus Cameron of Wisconsin, and Augustus Merrimon of North Carolina were even more cautious than the Finance Committee and hoped for additional modifications in the Bland bill, usually by increasing the standard silver dollar to 420 or more grains, thus improving slightly its existing market relation to the gold dollar.[31] Despite their reservations this small group of "moderate moderates" also voted for the final bill.

Several senators claimed to favor bimetallism but, as Garfield had done in the House, ultimately voted against remonetizing the old dollar. Men such as L. Q. C. Lamar of Mississippi and James G. Blaine of Maine were caught between their gold standard economic beliefs and various political necessities. Coming from a solidly pro-silver state, Lamar's vote against the Bland-Allison Act represented a mark of high political courage. Blaine, on the other hand, while insisting that restoration of the double standard was both legally and morally justified, looked ahead primarily to his 1880 presidential bid and succeeded remarkably well in straddling the issue.[32] His general endorsement of remonetization pleased bimetallists, and a short February 8 speech on the question received applause from Senate galleries comparable to John Percival Jones' February 14 address. On the other hand, his final vote against the Bland-Allison compromise allowed Blaine to retain intact his New England hard money credentials. The New York *Journal of Commerce* referred admiringly to this political balancing feat as "Senator Blaine's Great Equestrian Act," and 'probationary converts' to bimetallism like Blaine and Garfield rarely convinced more knowledgeable

31. See, for example, 45th Cong., 2d sess., vol. 7, pt. 1, pp. 648, 758; pt. 2, pp. 1111–12.

32. The substitute bill that Blaine introduced, although retaining the unlimited coinage and full legal tender features of the House measure, raised the grain content of the standard silver dollar to 425 grains. Ibid., pp. 820–22. See also New York *Graphic,* Jan, 28, 1878; New York *Weekly Journal of Commerce,* Feb. 14, 1878.

silverites of their sincerity: "All men who want to add to the weight of the silver dollar," the New York *Graphic* stated flatly, "are enemies of that coin."[33] In the final Senate tally, while Blaine and Lamar opposed the modified Bland bill, Benjamin Hill of Georgia, also a monometallist but unwilling like Lamar to endanger his political career, merely paired against the measure without voting.[34]

Another small group of Senators also attempted to amend the House bill by raising the silver dollar's grain content, but unlike Blaine and Lamar, they proclaimed themselves monometallists and tried to obstruct restoration of the double standard. Eaton of Connecticut and Christiancy of Minnesota led an unsuccessful effort to substitute a 435 grain dollar or a coin of even greater weight for the 412.5 grain dollar. One moderate silverite noted caustically that "three-fourths of the Senators who have opposed this bill [are] in favor of remonetizing silver," and "only two or three Senators have taken a position . . . against . . . remonetization" in some form.[35] Actually, a half-dozen legislators including Morrill, Dawes, Bayard, and Eaton proposed retaining the gold standard, but Senate debate bypassed this demand and focused instead on amendments concerning the exact grain content, legal tender powers, and limitations to be placed on a remonetized silver dollar.[36]

Debate over the Allison amendments took place as public demands mounted for final action on the silver bill, and even the

33. New York *Weekly Journal of Commerce*, Feb. 14, 1878. *Cong. Record*, 45th Cong., 2d sess., vol. 7. See also Muzzey, *James G. Blaine*, p. 139.

34. *Cong. Record*, 45th Cong., 2d sess., vol 7, pt. 2, p. 1112. See also New York *Weekly Journal of Commerce*, February 14, 1878.

35. *Cong. Record*, 45th Cong., 2d sess., vol. 7, pt. 1, pp. 753, 796, 853–54.

36. For the opinions of bitter-end gold monometallists, see ibid., pp. 607–18 (Morrill), 644–46 (Dawes), 646–48 (Whyte), 728–35 (Bayard), and 753–61 (Eaton). See also Senator MacDonald's remarks, p. 957.

silverite majority began showing the strains that accompanied prolonged agitation of the issue. Senator Oglesby of Illinois probably spoke for many of his colleagues when he observed that "so deeply concerned are our constituents that from day to day they give us no rest, with their crying inquiries as to the time when this question shall be settled." Further discussion seemed increasingly useless, both to most supporters and opponents of the measure. "Public meetings are being held," observed Benjamin Hill of Georgia, "immense petitions are being sent in to this body, and perhaps a thousand newspapers are to-day engaged in the patriotic work of impressing the people of this country with the idea that one-half of the members of Congress have been bought up by the bullion-holders and the other half by the bondholders . . ."[37] More exhausted than exuberant, the Senate girded for a final test of strength in February 1878 between friends and enemies of remonetization.

The probable outcome seemed clear to many disconsolate goldbugs outside Congress. Secretary Sherman confided to his London bond sale agent late in January 1878 that "the Bland bill or some other bill very nearly as bad will pass both Houses by a two-thirds vote, and, although there may be some delay [i.e., a presidential veto], it is likely that silver will be remonetized."[38] Mint Director Linderman informed Sherman shortly afterwards that "speculative operation in silver" had already begun. He suggested that the government begin stockpiling bullion before congressional approval of the silver bill increased the metal's market price.[39] Republican monometallists lamented the loss of traditional hard-money allies like Allison to the bimetal-

37. Ibid., pp. 688, 765, 842, 957. On the bribery rumors, see New York *Graphic,* Jan. 14, 1878; Silas Ward to Thomas Bayard, Feb. 6, 1878, Bayard MSS, LC.

38. John Sherman to Charles Conant, Jan. 28, 1878, Sherman MSS, LC.

39. Henry Linderman to John Sherman, Feb. 5, 1878, Letterbooks, Director of the Mint, NA, RG 104.

list forces and, seeking a scapegoat, began blaming the party's division in Congress on Hayes' lack of executive leadership.

"The administration is utterly powerless to help preserve the national honor," William E. Chandler complained to Whitelaw Reid. "It hasn't 15 votes that it influences in both Houses! And Stanley Matthews leads the silver van!"[40] Even Republican friends and supporters of the President like Justin Morrill, James Garfield, and the former Iowa congressman John A. Kasson, then minister to Austria, decried the party's split on silver policy, although only Garfield blamed Hayes for the situation.[41] "The President was not only unable to influence a single vote but lost some in each House," the Ohio legislator wrote after congressional passage of the Bland bill. "He has pursued a suicidal policy toward Congress—and is almost without a friend."[42]

Whether Hayes could have influenced any votes is questionable, considering the predominantly pro-silver temper of Congress and of the country. In the weeks preceding passage of the Bland-Allison Act, the President was under increasing pressure, often surprisingly from gold-standard advocates, not to veto any compromise measure approved by Congress. Many opponents of remonetization shared the feeling expressed by the monometallist editor of the Cincinnati *Gazette* that "'anything would be better than the suspense that prevails." What troubled Republican politicians and newspapermen most was a fear that the fratricidal party battle over silver legislation would continue until the fall elections.[43] Hugh McCulloch confessed to Gar-

40. W. E. Chandler to Whitelaw Reid, Feb. 2, 1878. See also Chandler to Reid, Feb. 14, 1878, Reid MSS, LC.

41. Justin S. Morrill to Manton Marble, Jan. 5, 1878, Morrill MSS, LC; Silas Ward to Thomas F. Bayard, Feb. 6, 1878, Bayard MSS, LC; John A. Kasson to James A. Garfield, Jan. 27, 1878, Garfield MSS, LC.

42. Garfield Diary, Feb. 28, 1878, Garfield MSS, LC.

43. Richard Smith to James A. Garfield, Dec. 1, 1877, ibid. See also Henry Adams to Henry Cabot Lodge, Jan. 6, 1878, in Worthington Chauncey Ford, ed., *Letters of Henry Adams 1858–1891* (Boston, 1930), pp. 303–04; Whitelaw Reid to R. S. Brownson, Dec. 14, 1877, Reid MSS, LC.

field that he dreaded only two things more than passage of a silver bill:

> 1st. A continued and violent agitation of the currency question.
>
> 2nd. The submission of the question as a party and somewhat sectional question, to a popular vote [in the fall elections of 1878].

Should this happen, McCulloch felt, the result would be the election of an inflationist Congress, with both Houses controlled by the Democrats who would proceed to repeal the National Banking System, pass anti-resumption legislation, issue large amounts of additional greenbacks, and engage in other actions far "worse than silver." The Indiana banker considered most advocates of remonetization "honest" hard-money men, "not . . . repudiators," although they labored "under a delusion of which they can only be cured by a trial of their policy."[44]

Sentiment for compromise and for quieting the turmoil over remonetization even reached into the New York banking community, which had led business opposition to the Bland bill. H. C. Fahnestock of the First National Bank, a member of the Belmont Syndicate, wrote Hayes early in February 1878 urging that an agreement be reached between "the honest silver men and the anti-silver men who are open to conviction." Two Senate amendments to the House measure suggested by Fahnestock, a seigniorage on silver coinage and provision for an international conference, had already been included in the Finance Committee draft, and the New York banker indicated to the President the importance that he and fellow syndicate bankers attached to ending further agitation: "The greatest advantage of this compromise, in our opinion, is the avoidance of further discussion of the public credit question, which is left, as in the Bland bill, sub-

44. Hugh McCulloch to James A. Garfield, Jan. 30, 1878, Garfield MSS, LC. See also J. M. Forbes to Hugh McCulloch, Jan. 24, 1878, McCulloch MSS, LC.

ject to existing contracts."[45] Fahnestock, like McCulloch, Richard Smith of the Cincinnati *Gazette,* and other troubled opponents of bimetallism, viewed an unsettled silver issue as the opening wedge in a more sweeping challenge to the administration's resumption program. They urged compromise, therefore, for both political and economic reasons. As William Windom remarked before casting his Senate ballot for the Bland-Allison Act, "no evil, even in the House bill, [is] at all comparable to those which would follow from another year of agitation."[46] Most congressmen apparently agreed with Windom, for the amended silver bill passed the Senate early in the morning of February 16 after a marathon session.

Debate at the February 15–16 Senate meeting that approved the measure lasted seventeen hours, interspersed with roll call votes on several dozen amendments, most of which were rejected.[47] By the time the upper chamber had navigated this labyrinth of suggested changes to take a final vote at 4:40 A.M. on February 16, most senators were either dazed, drowsing, or drunk.[48] The discussion was conducted generally with much good humor and contained one moment of real drama when L. Q. C. Lamar explained his defiance of the Mississippi legislature's resolutions in a speech that began: "Mr. President, between these resolutions and my convictions there is a great gulf. I cannot pass it."[49] Most of the prolonged session was spent discussing and voting down an array of amendments introduced by opponents of remonetization in a fruitless effort to further emasculate the House measure.

Voting on these proposed additions to the Finance Committee amendments finally polarized Senators into two distinct blocs,

45. H. C. Fahnestock to R. B. Hayes, Feb. 1, 1878, Hayes MSS, Fremont.

46. *Cong. Record,* 45th Cong., 2d sess., vol. 7, pt. 2, p. 1112.

47. Ibid., pp. 1051–112.

48. Nichols, "John Sherman and the Silver Drive," p. 162.

49. *Cong. Record,* 45th Cong., 2d sess., vol. 7, pt. 2, p. 1061.

one willing to accept Allison's compromise measure and the other opposed to any version of the Bland bill. Monometallist James Blaine, for example, proposed at one point that the silver dollar be increased to 425 grains. Balloting for the Blaine Amendment showed the difficulty that waverers like Blaine, Lamar, and Windom faced in trying to hold aloof from one of the two major Senate groupings on remonetization. Moderate silverites like Cameron, Paddock, and Windom all voted against the amendment, while Lamar joined the Maine Republican in supporting the 425 grain coin. The basic Senate issue, however, involved response to the Allison amendments, and the 46 to 23 majority that defeated Blaine's proposal reflected accurately the division between those in the upper chamber who favored a compromise silver bill and those unalterably opposed to such a measure. Every effort by the outmanned group of single standard advocates to change the Finance Committee's draft went down to defeat by margins of more than two to one, and the only major addition to Allison's amendments accepted by the Senate was Newton Booth's silver certificate scheme.[50]

Booth had submitted an amendment late in January that allowed holders of silver coin to deposit and exchange amounts of more than ten dollars for legal tender paper notes. Coke of Texas and Chaffee of Colorado introduced substitutes for the Booth plan during the February 15 debate that authorized deposits of

50. Ibid., pp. 1099–100. Before silverites voted on the Finance Committee amendments, they turned down a variety of other revisions proposed by monometallists. Among those rejected were amendments limiting the yearly percentage of customs dues payable in silver (Morrill), prohibiting silver dollar coinage from interfering with the Mint's production of gold or subsidiary coins (Edmunds), raising the content of the standard silver dollar to 425 (Blaine) or to 440 grains (Eaton), restricting the legal tender of silver coins to twenty dollars (Whythe) or to five hundred dollars (Burnside), exempting the public debt and customs dues entirely from payment in silver (Sargent), and, finally, requiring withdrawal from circulation of an equal amount of greenbacks for all silver dollars issued (Morrill and Kernan). Ibid., pp. 1073, 1076–85, 1099–100, 1102, 1106, 1111.

bullion as well as *coin,* thereby making a blatantly inflationist device of Booth's simple plan to provide a convenient means for transporting silver coins. Allison denounced the Coke-Chaffee plan immediately as an attempt by bullion holders to retain the profits of coinage, thereby "in effect nullifying" the Finance Committee's seigniorage amendment. Booth's original proposal then passed by a lopsided 49 to 15 margin.[51]

The Finance Committee's major amendments, which altered the House bill's provisions for free and unlimited coinage, passed 49 to 22, supported by a Republican coalition of moderate bimetallists and gold standard advocates, with some Democratic silverites from the west and south joining John Percival Jones in opposing the change. Republicans approved the coinage limitations by an overwhelming 32 to 4 margin while Democrats divided, 16 to 17, on the proposal (see Table 9).

Republican party lines also held firm during balloting for the international conference amendment, which passed by a closer 40 to 30 margin (see Table 10). Again, Republican monometallists and silverites joined to modify the House bill, aided this time by an even smaller contingent of Democrats. Allison's insistence that an eventual worldwide monetary agreement was "of vast importance to the success of [American] silver coinage" provoked a round of nationalistic oratory, especially from southern Democrats who, like their House counterparts, denounced not only the proposed meeting but any other "foreign alliances, foreign entanglements, and foreign associations."[52] Southern balloting shifted from an 8 to 9 regional tally against the coinage restriction amendment to a more pronounced 4 to 13 vote against the international conference. Senate Republicans deliv-

51. Ibid., pt. 1, p. 687; pt. 2, pp. 1102–03. Even Blaine voted for the proposal, his only pro-silver ballot during the entire Senate debate (pp. 1102–05). Silverites voted down almost all amendments by the gold standard bloc (pp. 1074–76).

52. Ibid., pp. 1076, 1091. For debate on the international conference amendment, see pp. 1084–91.

Table 9

Vote on Allison Amendment Restricting Free and Unlimited Coinage, Senate, February 15, 1878

	Ayes			Nays		
	Rep.	Dem.	Ind.	Rep.	Dem.	Ind.
New England States						
Massachusetts	2					
Maine	2					
New Hampshire	2					
Vermont	2					
Connecticut		2				
Rhode Island	2					
TOTALS	10	2				
Middle Atlantic States						
New York	1	1				
Pennsylvania	1	1				
Maryland		1			1	
Delaware		2				
New Jersey		2				
TOTALS	2	7			1	
Midwestern States						
Ohio	1				1	
Illinois	1					1
Indiana		1			1	
Wisconsin	2					
Minnesota	2					
Michigan	2					
Iowa	2					
Kansas	2					
Nebraska	1			1		
TOTALS	13	1		1	2	1
Border States						
Kentucky					2	
Tennessee					1	
West Virginia		1			1	
Missouri					2	
TOTALS		1			6	

Table 9—Continued

	Ayes			Nays		
	Rep.	Dem.	Ind.	Rep.	Dem.	Ind.
Southern States						
Virginia		1			1	
North Carolina		2				
South Carolina		1				
Georgia						
Alabama				1	1	
Mississippi	1	1				
Florida				1	1	
Louisiana	1				1	
Texas					2	
Arkansas	1				1	
TOTALS	3	5		2	7	
Far Western States						
California	1		1			
Nevada				1		
Colorado	2					
Oregon	1				1	
TOTALS	4		1	1	1	
GRAND TOTALS	32	16	1	4	17	1

TOTAL AYES: 49

TOTAL NAYS: 22

ered a 29 to 5 majority in favor of the meeting while Democrats divided 10 to 24 against it. Senate Democrats felt less disturbed apparently by the crippling of free and unlimited coinage than by the possibility of a world monetary treaty!

Despite some minor disagreements among senators favorable to remonetization, Allison held the bimetallist ranks together firmly as floor leader, displaying remarkable stamina and equanimity during the exhaustive seventeen-hour debate on February 15 while nudging the weary lawmakers toward a final vote. By midnight strained nerves and a free bar in the Democratic

Table 10

Vote on the International Monetary Conference Amendment, Senate, February 15, 1878

	Ayes			Nays	
	Rep.	Dem.	Ind.	Rep.	Dem.
New England States					
Massachusetts	2				
Maine	2				
New Hampshire	2				
Vermont	1			1	
Connecticut		2			
Rhode Island	2				
TOTALS	9	2		1	
Middle Atlantic States					
New York	1	1			
Pennsylvania	1	1			
Maryland		1			1
Delaware		1			1
New Jersey		2			
TOTALS	2	6			2
Midwestern States					
Ohio	1				1
Illinois	1		1		
Indiana					2
Wisconsin	2				
Minnesota	2				
Michigan	2				
Iowa	2				
Kansas				1	
Nebraska	2				
TOTALS	12		1	1	3
Border States					
Kentucky					2
Tennessee					1
West Virginia					2
Missouri					2
TOTALS					7

Table 10—Continued

	Ayes			Nays		
	Rep.	Dem.	Ind.	Rep.	Dem.	Ind.
Southern States						
Virginia					2	
North Carolina					2	
South Carolina		1				
Georgia					1	
Alabama				1	1	
Mississippi		1				
Florida				1	1	
Louisiana	1				1	
Texas					2	
Arkansas	1				1	
TOTALS	2	2		2	11	
Far Western States						
California	1					1
Nevada				1		
Colorado	2					
Oregon	1				1	
TOTALS	4			1	1	1
GRAND TOTALS	29	10	1	5	24	1

TOTAL AYES: 40

TOTAL NAYS: 30

cloakroom had left many senators in high if not good spirits, and one monometallist, George Edmunds, resisted Allison's attempt to restrict debate on the remaining amendments by invoking with effective irony the spectre of a "Crime of 1878."[53] "To

53. The senators considered the tipsiest among a boozy assemblage of legislators during the all-night meeting were Eaton, Thurman and Booth. Thomas C. Platt to Whitelaw Reid, Feb. 20, 1878, Reid MSS, LC. For lively discussions of the "bibulous session," see Philadelphia *Inquirer*, Feb. 16, 1878; New York *Graphic*, Feb. 16, 1878; and Nichols, "John Sherman and the Silver Drive," p. 162.

that I object," Edmunds protested, when Allison suggested limiting further discussion:

> I do not intend to have somebody when this operation turns out to be disastrous to every honest man in the country, tell us hereafter as we are told now about the action of 1873, that it was hustled through and people did not have an opportunity to understand it . . . I have no doubt that in three or four years we should hear the Senator from Iowa saying that the thing was not perfectly understood, that debate was choked off. (Laughter) Mr. ALLISON. I will say that now to the Senator from Vermont. Mr. EDMUNDS. I think the Senator is quite right. I doubt if it is understood. (Laughter) I judge by the votes.[54]

Five more hours of debate and voting on amendments followed before the entire bill came to a final ballot at 4:40 A.M. on February 16. The Senate then passed the revised measure by a 48 to 21 majority and, as Ingalls had predicted, not a single vote had been changed during three months of debate[55] (see Table 11).

Northeastern gold monometallists from both parties who supported Allison's amendments voted against the finished product, while southern and border-state Democrats, who fought the Finance Committee changes, returned to the silverite fold and endorsed the final bill. Allison's most consistent backers, senators who voted for his amendments and for the final bill, consisted only of eighteen fellow Republicans, mainly from the Midwest. The Iowa Republican, starting from this small core of moderate bimetallists, had added votes either from more radical silverites or from monometallists, depending on the circumstances, and steered the silver bill deftly through a divided Senate.

When the amended measure returned to the House on February 21, the importance of partisan rather than sectional politics in the first silver drive became even more apparent. The original

54. *Cong. Record,* 45th Cong., 2d sess., vol. 7, pt. 2, p. 1091.
55. Ibid., p. 1112.

House measure had been a Democratic bill passed with some Republican support. The Bland-Allison Act represented a Republican-sponsored Senate revision that secured reluctant approval from the upper chamber's Democratic bimetallists, and at no point was there "the slightest contact or collaboration between Bland and Allison on the act that bears their name."[56]

The only attempt made to construct a bipartisan sectional coalition during the struggle for remonetization, composed almost entirely of western and southern silverites in the House, collapsed abruptly following Senate passage of the silver bill. During the months that the upper chamber debated the Bland Act, several dozen House Democratic and Republican supporters of the measure had caucused privately to discuss ways of rousing public support for bimetallism, especially through distributing appropriate pamphlet literature "in the eastern states to counteract the prevailing . . . sentiment." The group defined its long-range purposes in the vaguest terms, since it numbered among its members congressmen who differed fundamentally on most other financial questions; these included hard-money Republican resumptionists like Jacob Cox of Ohio and Joseph Cannon of Illinois, Republican inflationists such as Benjamin F. Butler and "Pig-Iron" Kelley as well as Democratic soft-money enthusiasts like Richard Bland and Thomas Ewing of Ohio.[57]

A good deal of inconclusive discussion among caucus members occurred at several January 1878 meetings, at which various participants proposed the repeal of the Resumption Act, expansion of the greenback supply, and abolition of the national banking system. However, as one of those attending the caucus confided to a questioner, "so far its primary object is to remonetize silver."[58] In order to underscore the priority that it gave to

56. Sage, *William Boyd Allison*, p. 156.

57. Unger, *Greenback Era*, pp. 358–59.

58. Benjamin F. Butler to B. S. Heath, Jan. 29, 1878, typescript, Butler MSS, LC. See also New York *Weekly Journal of Commerce*, Jan. 17, 1878.

Table 11

Vote on Final Passage of the Bland-Allison Act, Senate February 15, 1878

	Ayes			Nays	
	Rep.	Dem.	Ind.	Rep.	Dem.
New England States					
Massachusetts				2	
Maine				2	
New Hampshire				2	
Vermont				2	
Connecticut					1
Rhode Island				2	
TOTALS				10	1
Middle Atlantic States					
New York				1	1
Pennsylvania	1	1			
Maryland		1			1
Delaware		1			1
New Jersey					2
TOTALS	1	3		1	5
Midwestern States					
Ohio	1	1			
Illinois	1		1		
Indiana		2			
Wisconsin	2				
Minnesota	2				
Michigan	1			1	
Iowa	2				
Kansas	2				
Nebraska	2				
TOTALS	13	3	1	1	
Border States					
Kentucky		2			
Tennessee		1			
West Virginia		2			
Missouri		2			
TOTALS		7			

Table 11—Continued

	Ayes			Nays	
	Rep.	Dem.	Ind.	Rep.	Dem.
Southern States					
Virginia		2			
North Carolina		1			
South Carolina					
Georgia		1			
Alabama	1	1			
Mississippi	1				1
Florida	1	1			
Louisiana	1	1			
Texas		2			
Arkansas	1	1			
TOTALS	5	10			1
Far Western States					
California			1	1	
Nevada	1				
Colorado	2				
Oregon		1		1	
TOTALS	3	1	1	2	
GRAND TOTALS	22	24	2	14	7

TOTAL AYES: 48

TOTAL NAYS: 21

passage of the Bland bill, the bipartisan caucus adopted the name "Silver Union," and its executive committee began collecting funds to finance an educational campaign in eastern gold standard strongholds.[59] This was the first of several efforts in the late nineteenth century to organize congressional bimetallists into an ideological coalition that cut across sectional lines. It disintegrated quickly once the Senate had approved the Bland-Allison Act, when the caucus found it impossible to agree upon

59. Philadelphia *Inquirer,* Jan. 29 and Feb. 19, 1878; Unger, *Greenback Era.*

a response toward the revised measure that all bimetallists in the House could accept.

At a February 18 meeting attended by sixty members of the "Silver Union," a large minority favored "concurrence" with the Allison bill as a first step toward eventual free and unlimited coinage, while two-thirds of those present supported "committal" of the measure to inflationist Democrat Buckner's Banking and Currency Committee, which would then report the original Bland bill for House approval. Although a few Democrats like Eden of Illinois recommended accepting the Senate compromise, most Democrats at the meeting followed Thomas Ewing and Buckner, the caucus chairman, in demanding its rejection.[60]

Republican participants in the "Silver Union," however, almost unanimously favored immediate passage of the revised bill, having joined the alliance with Democratic anti-resumptionists only to help secure remonetization. "Instead of being dismayed at finding Butler, Bland, Ewing, and Vorhees, with me," Jacob Cox wrote his friend David A. Wells, "I felt that their being so, and the getting them to accept this measure first, was the only way to prevent their accomplishing *really* dangerous things . . . *We* [Republican bimetallists] have been simply using them . . ."[61]

The "Silver Union's" February 18 meeting proved to be its last, indeed the last held by any bipartisan group of congressional silverites for over a decade. Before disbanding, however, the caucus' Democratic majority voted overwhelmingly—roughly along partisan lines—to support committal of the Senate bill. A lone pair of Republicans, Butler and Joseph Cannon, supported this caucus decision, Butler being a professed Greenbacker while Cannon was hardpressed in his rabidly inflationist Illinois district.[62] In the voting that followed, these two were alone among Republican silverites in voting against passage of the amended

60. Philadelphia *Inquirer,* Feb. 19, 1878; New York *Weekly Journal of Commerce,* Feb. 21, 1878.

61. Jacob D. Cox to David A. Wells, Feb. 28, 1878, Wells MSS, LC.

62. Philadelphia *Inquirer,* Feb. 19, 1878.

Bland bill.[63] Most Republican bimetallists in the House found the Allison amendments both politically acceptable and economically sound, which ended the need for further cooperation with anti-resumption Democrats. As a result, party lines hardened still further during February 21 House debate on the Senate measure.

Gold standard opponents of remonetization scarcely entered the hour-long discussion, as practically all Republican silverites (joined by a sizeable Democratic minority) urged concurrence, while a procession of Democrats—and Ben Butler—supported the "Silver Union's" committal strategy. Even the more ardent Republican bimetallists like Phillips of Kansas, who privately opposed the Allison amendments, now recommended their acceptance on the grounds that the silver movement had achieved its prime object in returning the 412.5 grain dollar as a full legal tender. More moderate Republicans like James Monroe of Ohio took pains to distinguish their party's view of the silver drive from that of the Democrats'. "I am not in favor of a poor or a cheap silver dollar," Monroe insisted, "[and] in supporting this bill I would not retard the resumption of specie payments. I am opposed to paper inflation as well as to silver inflation." Richard Bland appeared to accept this argument—that Republican silverites believed silver would aid in resumption while House Democrats viewed remonetization primarily as an inflationary tactic—when he rose to defend his surprising endorsement of the Senate bill. If the expansion of silver coinage did not prove sufficient for inflationists, Bland told a crowded House gallery, there would be time enough for soft money enthusiasts to pass additional legislation "issuing paper money enough to stuff down the bondholders until they are sick."[64]

Opposition to the amended bill came both from gold mono-

63. *Cong. Record,* 45th Cong., 2d sess., vol. 7, pt. 2, p. 1285.

64. Speaking in favor of the Senate compromise were Republican congressmen Phillips, Monroe, Shallenberger, Hanna, Henderson, Kiefer, Bundy, Ellsworth, Bacon, Evans of Pennsylvania, Thompson and White

metallists and from greenback inflationists like Ewing and Butler, who refused to join Bland in accepting the Allison compromise. William Frye of Maine stated the gold standard position crisply in a one sentence speech: "I am for the amendments and against the bill." Ewing, on the other hand, denounced the Finance Committee amendments as a "delusive compromise" that perverted the intentions of the original House measure, and he urged silverites to vote against the revised statute. In the end even many gold monometallists voted for the Senate bill "for fear of something worse," and Abram Hewitt's motion to defer final approval failed by a three to one margin of 71 to 205. The Senate amendment limiting free and unlimited coinage of silver then passed by a 203 to 72 vote and the international conference provision by a 196 to 71 tally.[65] (See Tables 12 and 13.)

All factions in the House Republican party—monometallists, moderate bimetallists, and inflationists—joined to endorse these Senate amendments, along with most Democratic goldbugs and some silverites who followed Bland's lead. Ewing and a majority of the Democratic party's inflationist wing voted against the revised measure. Republicans supported the coinage limitation amendment by a 128 to 4 margin and the conference provision by an equally striking 118 to 11 vote. Democrats, on the other hand, divided 75 to 68 on the former and 78 to 60 on the international meeting. With this extraordinary display of House Republican unity in supporting their Senate colleagues' compromise measure, the Bland-Allison Act went to the White House.

Hayes had expressed privately, as early as February 3, his be-

---

of Pennsylvania, along with Democrats Stephens, Bland, Sayler, Southard, Finley, Cox of New York, Sampson, Harrison, Wilson, Townshend and Wright. Republican Ben Butler along with Democrats Buckner, Whitthorne, Atkins, Ewing, Bright, Springer, Sparks, Robbin, Turner, Steele, and Bragg all opposed the compromise and supported "committal." For the entire House debate, see ibid., pp. 1243–85.

65. Ibid., pp. 1257, 1263–64, 1273, 1279, 1284–85. For voting on the Hewitt motion, p. 1283.

lief that the measure would pass "in such shape that I must withhold my signature," largely on the grounds that holders of resumption bonds and other government securities would be threatened with repayment in depreciated silver dollars, thereby undermining American public credit.[66] Considering his remarks on remonetization in the December 1877 annual message, the President would probably have vetoed any bill which did not provide for payment of government securities in gold. Having elevated his concern for protecting investors to the status of an inviolable moral principle, Hayes cared little whether or not others shared his concern. His February 1878 correspondence and diary entries indicate that he "luxuriated in the thought of a veto and could afford it politically."[67] Other Republicans were far more troubled than Hayes over the political implications of a veto.

"Pardon me if I say to you that the Silver Bill amended is verry [sic] popular," the party's Ohio state chairman, J. P. Robinson, informed James Garfield. The Ohio congressman had stood practically alone among western House Republicans in opposing remonetization, and Robinson warned: "You will need to thicken your skin, or moral courage, [for] . . . the storm is raging."[68] The congressman's closest Ohio political associate, Harmon Austin, also assured Garfield "that the majority of the republican voters are opposed to the demonetization of silver as it now stands."[69] Garfield agreed reluctantly with these estimates and complained that he had "never seen a craze equal to that which now possesses the public mind in regard to silver."[70] For this reason, the two leading editorial advocates of remone-

66. Charles Williams, ed., *Diary and Letters of R. B. Hayes,* vol. 3, p. 459, Feb. 3, 1878. See also the diary entries for Feb. 6, Feb. 17 and Feb. 23. Ibid., pp. 459–61.

67. Nichols, "John Sherman and the Silver Drive," p. 163.

68. J. P. Robinson to James A. Garfield, Feb. 21, 1878, Garfield MSS, LC.

69. Harmon Austin to James A. Garfield, Feb. 12, 1878, ibid.

70. Garfield to Austin, Feb. 20, 1878, ibid. See also Garfield to Austin, Mar. 3, 1878.

Table 12

Vote on Allison Amendment Restricting Free and Unlimited Coinage, House of Representatives, February 21, 1878

	Ayes		Nays	
	Rep.	Dem.	Rep.	Dem.
New England States				
Massachusetts	8		1	2
Maine	5			
New Hampshire	2	1		
Vermont	3			
Connecticut	1	3		
Rhode Island	2			
TOTALS	21	4	1	2
Middle Atlantic States				
New York	16	8	1	5
Pennsylvania	16	8		
Maryland		3		2
Delaware		1		
New Jersey	3	4		
TOTALS	35	24	1	7
Midwestern States				
Ohio	11	6		1
Illinois	9	3	1	4
Indiana	9	2		2
Wisconsin	5	1		2
Minnesota	3			
Michigan	7	1		
Iowa	8			
Kansas	3			
Nebraska	1			
TOTALS	56	13	1	9
Border States				
Kentucky				9
Tennessee	2	1		5
West Virginia		3		
Missouri	4	5		4
TOTALS	6	9		18

Table 12—Continued

	Ayes		Nays	
	Rep.	Dem.	Rep.	Dem.
Southern States				
Virginia	1	6		2
North Carolina		3	1	4
South Carolina	3	1		1
Georgia		4		3
Alabama		5		3
Mississippi		2		4
Florida	1	1		
Louisiana	1	1		4
Texas		1		5
Arkansas		1		3
TOTALS	6	25	1	29
Far Western States				
California	2			2
Nevada	1			
Colorado				1
Oregon	1			
TOTALS	4			3
GRAND TOTALS	128	75	4	68

TOTAL AYES: 203

TOTAL NAYS: 72

tization, midwestern Republicans Halstead and Medill, both warned Hayes and Sherman that his vetoing the silver bill would result in the election of a far more radical Congress in the fall. Both editors insisted that if Democratic inflationists like Ewing, aided by a presidential veto, managed to keep the issue alive by preventing repassage of the Bland-Allison Act, "they will carry both branches of the next congress, and . . . raise hell—the largest crop ever seen."[71] Sherman tried to calm the fears of Republi-

71. Joseph Medill to R. B. Hayes, Feb. 25, 1878; Murat Halstead to Hayes, Feb. 20, 1878, Hayes MSS, Fremont. See also Halstead to John Sherman, Feb. 20 and Feb. 26, 1878, Sherman MSS, LC; Halstead to Carl Schurz, Feb. 24, 1878, Schurz MSS, LC.

Table 13

Vote on the International Monetary Conference Amendment, House of Representatives, February 21, 1878

	Ayes		Nays	
	Rep.	Dem.	Rep.	Dem.
New England States				
Massachusetts	9	1	1	
Maine	5			
New Hampshire	2	1		
Vermont	3			
Connecticut	3	2		1
Rhode Island				
TOTALS	22	4	1	1
Middle Atlantic States				
New York	12	11	3	2
Pennsylvania	14	7	2	
Maryland		3		2
Delaware		1		
New Jersey	3	4		
TOTALS	29	26	5	4
Midwestern States				
Ohio	11	6		1
Illinois	9	4	1	3
Indiana	7	1	2	3
Wisconsin	5	1		2
Minnesota	3			
Michigan	6	1		
Iowa	9			
Kansas	3			
Nebraska				
TOTALS	53	13	3	9
Border States				
Kentucky		3		6
Tennessee	1	1	1	5
West Virginia		3		
Missouri	4	4		5
TOTALS	5	11	1	16

Table 13—Continued

	Ayes		Nays	
	Rep.	Dem.	Rep.	Dem.
Southern States				
Virginia	1	6		2
North Carolina		3	1	4
South Carolina	3			2
Georgia		4		3
Alabama		5		3
Mississippi		3		2
Florida	1			1
Louisiana		1		2
Texas		1		5
Arkansas		1		3
TOTALS	5	24	1	27
Far Western States				
California	2			2
Nevada	1			
Colorado				1
Oregon	1			
TOTALS	4			3
GRAND TOTALS	118	78	11	60

TOTAL AYES: 196

TOTAL NAYS: 71

cans such as Robinson and Halstead by assuring them privately that the silver bill would be repassed despite a veto, after which he "would execute the law according to the spirit and intent of those who pass it."[72]

Even many opponents of the legislation preferred accepting the Senate compromise measure to continued agitation. White-

72. Sherman to Halstead, Feb. 25, 1878, Halstead MSS, Cincinnati Historical Society; Sherman to J. S. Robinson, Feb. 25, 1878; Sherman to C. W. Moulton, Feb. 15, 1878; both in Sherman MSS, LC. See also New York *Graphic,* Feb. 27, 1878, and Sherman to Wilson J. Vance, Mar. 7, 1878, Sherman MSS, LC.

law Reid, whose New York *Tribune* led the nation's gold standard press in denouncing restoration, now agreed with Republican bimetallists that it was "for the best to let the silver lunatics take the bill they have carried—with the hope that this would remove a most dangerous question from the fall elections."[73] More surprisingly, August Belmont, leader of the resumption syndicate, informed Sherman that, like Fahnestock of the First National Bank, he feared "the effects of a veto [and] prefers the bill should be approved, *bad* as he thinks it is."[74] Belmont and other eastern bankers may have been impressed by the reception given by New York and London bond markets to news that Congress had passed the Bland-Allison Act. The price of gold did not fluctuate greatly as many had previously feared, and government securities actually increased in value![75] Other business interests reacted similarly to passage of the measure. One large delegation of Cincinnati bankers wired Hayes asking him not to extend business uncertainty through a veto, and "a surprisingly large part of the President's mail from both eastern and western businessmen also urged him to sign to avoid prolonging the silver agitation."[76]

73. Whitelaw Reid to George Walker, Feb. 27, 1878; William M. Grosvenor to Whitelaw Reid, Feb. 26, 1878, Reid MSS, LC.

74. Charles Williams, ed., *Diary and Letters of R. B. Hayes,* vol. 3, diary entry for Feb. 26, 1878, pp. 461–62.

75. Philadelphia *Inquirer,* Feb. 25, 1878; London *Times,* Feb. 19, 1878, quoted in New York *Weekly Journal of Commerce,* Feb. 21, 1878; New York *Graphic,* Feb. 19, 1878; New York *Tribune,* Feb. 19, 1878. Even George S. Coe expressed his confidence to one silverite newspaper reporter that bond prices would continue to remain stable and would not decline, *Graphic,* Feb. 18, 1878.

76. D. J. Fullis, President, Merchants National Bank, et al. (nine other Cincinnati bankers) to R. B. Hayes, Feb. 25, 1878, typescript, Stanley Matthews MSS, Hayes Library, Fremont; Unger, *Greenback Era,* p. 363. In Philadelphia, Lorin Blodgett, Secretary of the Associated Industries of the United States, an organization of manufacturers concerned with encouraging export trade, declared his pleasure and relief that financial uncertainty had ended with passage of the Bland-Allison

Hayes was bewildered but unmoved by the depth of goldbug willingness to accept the Senate compromise. "You have no idea how our friends were stampeded at the critical moment," he later wrote William Henry Smith. "Sixteen anti-silver Republicans from New York preferred to have the bill signed, or allowed to become a law by lapse of time . . . The [Cincinnati] *Gazette* [Richard Smith's monometallist daily] . . . advised me to sign; also the Indianapolis *Journal,* and eastern men in considerable number."[77]

Some gold standard advocates did favor a veto. A few influential Republicans urged such a course, including Justin Morrill and Benjamin H. Bristow, the latter still a political favorite of the party's reformers.[78] A number of eastern bankers, including syndicate member Levi P. Morton, disagreed with Belmont and Fahnestock that a modified silver bill was preferable to continued agitation and demanded instead that the bill be returned with a strong veto message.[79] Clergymen, small businessmen, and ordinary citizens from all sections of the country who considered the legislation "dishonest" and "unjust" supported Hayes' decision to reject it, although the chief executive does not appear to

---

Act which, Blodgett insisted, did not worry him in the least. Other Philadelphia merchants and businessmen were equally grateful that the period of agitation had ended with a compromise measure, New York *Graphic,* Feb. 18, 1878.

77. R. B. Hayes to William Henry Smith, Mar. 6, 1878, in Williams, *Diary and Letters of R. B. Hayes,* vol. 3, pp. 465–66.

78. Justin S. Morrill to John Sherman, Feb. 17, 1878, Sherman MSS, LC; Benjamin H. Bristow to Carl Schurz, Feb. 27, 1878, Schurz MSS, LC.

79. For Eastern banking opposition to Hayes' signing the silver bill, see the following: Levi P. Morton to John Sherman, Feb. 28, 1878, Sherman MSS, LC; Elbert P. Cook (Havana, New York) to Hayes, Feb. 23, 1878; C. P. Williams (Albany, N.Y.) to Hayes, Feb. 23, 1878; S. H. Tingley (Providence, R.I.) to Hayes, Feb. 15, 1878; Hayes MSS, Fremont. See also Unger, *Greenback Era.*

have been swayed in either direction by his correspondence on the subject.[80]

At a February 26 cabinet meeting, Hayes read his veto message, which denounced the Bland-Allison Act for committing "a grave breach of the public faith" in making the remonetized 412.5 grain dollar a full legal tender, thus raising the possibility that both customs dues and the public debt might be paid in "a silver dollar of less commercial value than any dollar, whether of gold or paper, which is now lawful money in this country." The President called the measure "an act of bad faith [which] . . . will in the end defraud not only creditors, but all who are engaged in legitimate business."[81] Hayes apparently wrote the veto message himself, although Sherman may have suggested certain changes before its submission to Congress.[82]

Navy Secretary Richard Thompson of Indiana, who supported the silver bill, spoke against the veto as did Sherman and Secretary of War George McCrary of Iowa. The latter two both opposed remonetization but preferred to see the measure pass, thereby ending further discussion of the issue. Except for Thompson, however, the entire Cabinet voted to endorse Hayes' actions, although Sherman and McCrary acted "with some doubts."[83] The chief executive sent his letter rejecting the Bland-Allison Act to Congress on February 28. The following day, after the bill's hasty repassage, Hayes lamented in his diary: "I am not liked as President by the politicians in office, in the

80. W. S. Grosvener to Carl Schurz, Feb. 23, 1878, Schurz MSS, LC; Henry G. Seaver (New York City) to Hayes, Jan. 26, 1878; J. Benton Farley (Atlanta) to Hayes, Feb. 22, 1878; A. W. Sepis (New York City) to Hayes, Feb. 22, 1878; H. A. Gray to Hayes, Feb. 23, 1878; Hayes MSS, Fremont; Unger, *Greenback Era.*

81. For Hayes' veto message, see *Cong. Record,* 45th Cong., 2d sess., vol. 7, pt. 2, pp. 1418–19.

82. Hayes to Sherman, Dec. 19, 1885, and Sherman to Hayes, Dec. 24, 1885, Hayes MSS, Fremont; Nichols, "John Sherman and the Silver Drive."

83. Williams, ed., *Diary and Letters of R. B. Hayes,* vol. 3, diary entry for Feb. 26, 1878, pp. 461–62.

press, or in Congress. But I am content to abide the judgment—the *sober second thought*—of the people."[84] (See Tables 14 and 15.)

Congressional treatment of the veto message confirmed the President's estimate of his political standing, even among members of his own party.[85] After a reading of the veto message, which Democrat S. S. Cox of New York called "a charge of fraud by a fraud," referring to the disputed 1876 election, the House approved the Bland-Allison Act once again without debate by a 196 to 73 margin. Ewing's intransigents now joined moderate silverites who had previously supported the Allison amendments in voting for repassage, while northeastern monometallists and a handful of other representatives, mainly Republicans, sustained the President.[86] Among the chief executive's midwestern friends and associates, silverite ranks held firm, and 56 of the 79 Republican votes to override the veto came from that section. The Democrats added a solid 117 to 22 majority for the revised silver bill. Even in the northeast, Republicans divided by a close 15 to 19 tally on the measure. Repassage of the Bland-Allison Act came almost on the anniversary of Hayes' inauguration after the electoral crisis, and House Democrats must have savored watching the President's own closest political allies in the lower chamber repudiate his leadership on the silver question.

Republican silverites also stood together in the Senate, which disposed of the veto message that same day, February 28, by a 46 to 19 vote.[87] Eleven midwestern Republicans voted to override the veto, and only Cameron of Wisconsin and Oglesby of Illinois withdrew their earlier support for the measure. Silverite

84. Ibid., entry for Mar. 1, 1878, p. 463.

85. James A. Garfield to Harmon Austin, Mar. 3, 1878, Garfield MSS, LC; William E. Chandler to Whitelaw Reid, Feb. 27, 1878; Reid to Chandler, Feb. 28, 1878; and Garfield to Reid, Mar. 19, 1878, Reid MSS, LC.

86. *Cong. Record,* 45th Cong., 2d sess., vol. 7, pt. 2, pp. 1419–20.

87. Ibid., pp. 1409–11.

Table 14

Vote to Override Hayes' Veto and Repass the Bland-Allison Act, House of Representatives, February 28, 1878

	Ayes		Nays	
	Rep.	Dem.	Rep.	Dem.
New England States				
Massachusetts	1		9	1
Maine			5	
New Hampshire			2	1
Vermont			3	
Connecticut		2		1
Rhode Island			2	
TOTALS	1	2	21	3
Middle Atlantic States				
New York	3	3	14	12
Pennsylvania	7	6	8	1
Maryland		3		
Delaware				1
New Jersey		1	2	2
TOTALS	10	13	24	16
Midwestern States				
Ohio	9	7	1	
Illinois	11	6		
Indiana	9	4		
Wisconsin	5	3		
Minnesota	2		1	
Michigan	7		1	1
Iowa	9			
Kansas	3			
Nebraska	1			
TOTALS	56	20	3	1
Border States				
Kentucky		10		
Tennessee	2	8		
West Virginia		2		
Missouri	4	9		
TOTALS	6	29		

Table 14—Continued

	Ayes		Nays	
	Rep.	Dem.	Rep.	Dem.
Southern States				
Virginia		6		
North Carolina	1	7		
South Carolina	2	2	1	
Georgia		9		
Alabama		8		
Mississippi		6		
Florida		1	1	
Louisiana		3		1
Texas		5		1
Arkansas		3		
TOTALS	3	50	2	2
Far Western States				
California	1	2	1	
Nevada	1			
Colorado		1		
Oregon	1			
TOTALS	3	3	1	
GRAND TOTALS	79	117	51	22

TOTAL AYES: 196

TOTAL NAYS: 73

Don Cameron of Pennsylvania also absented himself during the balloting, along with several other eastern Republicans—George Edmunds, Henry Anthony, and Ambrose Burnside—who disliked Hayes even more than silver. On the whole, however, the balloting for repassage followed closely the earlier Senate vote on the Bland-Allison Act. A Republican majority again approved the measure, this time by a 20 to 10 count, while Democrats divided 25 to 9 for the legislation.

Rarely had a presidential veto been overridden so quickly and so casually. Not one opponent of silver even bothered to praise

Table 15

Vote to Override Hayes' Veto and Repass the Bland-Allison Act, Senate, February 28, 1878

	Ayes			Nays	
	Rep.	Dem.	Ind.	Rep.	Dem.
New England States					
Massachusetts				2	
Maine				2	
New Hampshire				2	
Vermont				1	
Connecticut					2
Rhode Island					
TOTALS				7	2
Middle Atlantic States					
New York				1	1
Pennsylvania		1			
Maryland		1			1
Delaware		1			1
New Jersey					2
TOTALS		3		1	5
Midwestern States					
Ohio	1	1			
Illinois			1		
Indiana		2			
Wisconsin	1				
Minnesota	2				
Michigan	1				
Iowa	2				
Kansas	2				
Nebraska	2				
TOTALS	11	3	1		
Border States					
Kentucky		2			
Tennessee		2			
West Virginia		2			
Missouri		1			
TOTALS		7			

Table 15—Continued

	Ayes			Nays	
	Rep.	Dem.	Ind.	Rep.	Dem.
Southern States					
Virginia		2			
North Carolina		1			
South Carolina	1				1
Georgia		2			
Alabama	1	1			
Mississippi	1				1
Florida	1	1			
Louisiana	1	1			
Texas		2			
Arkansas	1	1			
TOTALS	6	11			2
Far Western States					
California				1	
Nevada	1				
Colorado	2				
Oregon		1		1	
TOTALS	3	1		2	
GRAND TOTALS	20	25	1	10	9

TOTAL AYES: 46

TOTAL NAYS: 19

Hayes' action, and Congress even denied him the customary courtesy of delaying legislative response for at least a day. "He [was] absolutely treated with contempt," observed one silverite daily, "and no one resents it." With Hayes' leadership repudiated even by Republicans who agreed with his views on the bill, the Bland-Allison Act entered the statute books, restoring as full legal tender the 412.5 grain "dollar of the daddies."[88]

88. Philadelphia *Inquirer,* Mar. 1, 1878. See also New York *Tribune,* Mar. 1, 1878; Chicago *Tribune,* Mar. 1, 1878; Cincinnati *Commercial,* Mar. 1, 1878; New York *Graphic,* Mar. 1, 1878. Roscoe

Despite widespread popular support for the measure, Congress' graceless handling of the veto message offended many private citizens, and the President received a small flood of congratulatory letters and telegrams, mainly from gold standard advocates but also from some bimetallists. "My own views on the silver question do not coincide with yours," a typical letter of condolence began, "but I cannot avoid a feeling of contempt for a public body that will so treat a public officer when he has discharged an unpleasant duty evidently according to his conscience and sense of duty."[89] Once the President's anger at Congress had cooled, he felt relieved that the silver question had been disposed of, expecting that Republicans would now unite to defend his resumption policies. Within a few weeks, the chief executive even managed to convince himself that only the threat of his veto had enabled "Republicans in the Senate to improve the Bland bill" through the Allison amendments![90]

The President assessed his party's mood on the currency issue accurately, however, since Republican monometallists and sil-

---

Conkling later claimed to have appealed privately for a twenty-four-hour postponement "more from a desire to maintain the dignity of the Senate than to show respect to the President, but he was hooted by every Senator he approached." Thomas C. Platt to Whitelaw Reid, May 6, 1878, Reid MSS, LC. Other observers, however, witnessed Conkling placing the bill at the head of the Senate calendar because "he thought it ought to be disposed of." Philadelphia *Inquirer,* Mar. 1, 1878.

89. William Cam to R. B. Hayes, Mar. 11, 1878, Hayes MSS, Fremont. Also complaining of the President's unfair treatment were the following correspondents: R. Moffett to James A. Garfield, May 26, 1878, Garfield MSS, LC, and Horace White to Whitelaw Reid, Mar. 12, 1878, Reid MSS, LC. Dozens of 1878 letters endorsing Hayes' stand can be found in his papers at Fremont, Ohio. See also Levi P. Morton to Whitelaw Reid, Mar. 19, 1878, Reid MSS, LC; also W. H. Mason to John Sherman, Mar. 5, 1878, Sherman MSS, LC.

90. Williams, ed., *Diary and Letters of R. B. Hayes,* vol. 3, diary entry for April 14, 1878, p. 479. See also R. B. Hayes to William Henry Smith, Mar. 6, 1878, pp. 465–66.

verites alike now rallied behind the Treasury Department's efforts to secure resumption—to redeem paper currency at face value in gold—on schedule by January 1879.[91] Republicans defeated an attempt by Democratic inflationists later in the year to gain Senate approval of Thomas Ewing's House measure that repealed the crucial resumption-day section of the 1875 act.[92] Republican silverites in the House had opposed this Democratic bill in November 1877 before its passage, and now Senate Republican bimetallists rallied against it successfully in April 1878.[93] The party's solidarity on the resumption question remained strong, in the end, despite two bruising years of controversy over remonetization.

The economic effect of the Bland-Allison Act went almost unnoticed after the measure's passage. Remonetization did not depress the price of American securities in world bond markets, as Hayes and other opponents had expected, but neither did it fulfill silverite expectations by turning "the wheels of trade, to the manifest benefit of the whole people" or by helping "to start up not a few of our dropping industries."[94] American recovery from the prolonged business depression began in 1878 and owed more to the depleted granaries of Europe than to the minor addition of 24 to 48 million dollars worth of standard silver dollars to the nation's circulating currency.[95] Economic analysts soon concluded, even in 1878, that as an instrument of

91. Murat Halstead to R. B. Hayes, Mar. 6, 1878, Hayes MSS, Fremont; Carl Schurz to Benjamin Bristow, Mar. 16, 1878, Bristow MSS, LC.

92. Nichols, "John Sherman and the Silver Drive," pp. 164–65; Unger, *Greenback Era,* pp. 364–73.

93. For a skillful description of these maneuvers, see Unger, *Greenback Era,* pp. 353–55, 371–73.

94. Philadelphia *Inquirer,* Mar. 1, 1878; *Rocky Mountain Daily News* (Denver), Mar. 2, 1878.

95. James Kindahl, "Economic Factors in Specie Resumption: The United States, 1865–1879," *The Journal of Political Economy,* 69 (1961), 47–48; Friedman and Schwartz, *Monetary History,* pp. 79–88.

monetary policy, "both the friends and opponents of the [silver bill] will be greatly disappointed."[96]

More significant was the Bland-Allison Act's political impact. Agitation for free and unlimited coinage subsided quickly after passage of the amended silver bill, and most bimetallists appeared to agree with John Sherman that their most important immediate task was to insure the law's "fair and just enforcement."[97] "The silver question has passed out of the range of discussion," publicist George Walker informed Whitelaw Reid. Walker vowed to withhold further newspaper articles on the subject in order not "to weary a tired audience with any more talk about it." Instead, Walker announced, he would devote himself to preparing for the forthcoming international monetary conference authorized by the silver bill.[98]

Even in the President's home state, where the controversy had raged only weeks earlier, passage of the Bland-Allison Act satisfied all but a few bimetallists. One Ohio legislator informed James Garfield in late March that "all the excitement about silver is dying out, nearly gone in fact."[99] Throughout the country, politicians, businessmen, and other participants in the debate over remonetization expressed satisfaction that the issue had been successfully compromised and agitation stilled so quickly.[100] Hayes weathered almost without political loss, therefore,

96. Roscoe Conkling, quoted in Philadelphia *Inquirer,* Mar. 2, 1878. See also James A. Garfield to Harmon Austin, Mar. 3, 1878, Garfield MSS, LC; Albany *Evening Journal,* Feb. 28, 1878; Edward Atkinson to W. B. Allison, Mar. 3, 1878, Allison MSS, Des Moines.

97. John Sherman to Thomas L. Young, Feb. 28, 1878, Sherman MSS, LC.

98. George Walker to Whitelaw Reid, Feb. 28, 1878, Reid MSS, LC.

99. J. M. Thorp to James A. Garfield, Mar. 26, 1878, Garfield MSS, LC.

100. See, for example, the following: William M. Grosvenor to Whitelaw Reid, Apr. 20, 1878, Reid MSS, LC; William Henry Smith to William T. Baker, May 25, 1878, Smith Letterbooks, Ohio Historical Society (Columbus); George Harrington to Justin S. Morrill, Mar. 10,

the storm created by his veto. With the silver dollar partly restored to its former place in the coinage system, most Americans appeared to believe, at least for the moment, that "the Crime of 1873" had been avenged.

1878, Morrill MSS, LC; J. B. Harrison (First National Bank of Cincinnati) to Murat Halstead, Oct. 22, 1878, Halstead MSS, Cincinnati Historical Society; William Henry Smith to R. B. Hayes, Nov. 12, 1878, typescript, Hayes MSS, Fremont.

Epilogue: The Significance of Silver

Since I have been in Congress I have seen nearly all of the predictions of financial men come to grief. I was here through the refunding process, and every attempt to reduce the rate of interest was declared to be dangerous; bonds would not be floated at par at such low rates, etc., etc.; and yet we succeeded every time in establishing a lower rate. When the Bland Bill was passed everybody seemed to think the price of silver would increase but it decreased. . . . Now where is wisdom to be found in these financial questions?

Senator William P. Frye to Wharton Barker,
Dec. 4, 1894, Barker MSS, LC

Silver is a forgotten issue in American life, dead and buried, but it manages an occasional ghostly murmur. On the ninetieth anniversary of the Bland-Allison Act in 1968, for example, the government's silver market finally reached the sixteen to one market ratio with gold hoped for by Gilded Age bimetallists. The same year, a few companies announced the reopening of certain previously-abandoned Comstock Lode mines. Both actions were grandly irrelevant, of course, to the shape of American monetary problems in the mid-twentieth century, and the public ignored these curious events just as it had ignored silver's original demonetization in 1873. The monetary standard question lost its importance as a serious political issue following McKinley's 1896 victory.

When the silver question first arose during the 1870s, however, it did not have the clear sectional and class support that it enjoyed among American agrarians by 1896. Instead, it hung uncomfortably between past and future crises in nineteenth-century American life. On the one hand, it served as an aborted prelude to Populism by offering a brief foretaste of the class conflicts over tariff and currency questions that would divide both major parties during the 1890s. At the same time, the issue arose during a severe business depression in the context of a political debate that concerned the unsettled problem of resuming specie payments. In this connection the silver drive of the seventies was a postscript to earlier disputes over government financial policy making which had their roots during the Civil War. The contradictions and sometimes confusing nature of early silver politics can be understood best through its ambiguous genesis, as both an issue of the past and a problem for the future. Demands for a bimetallic currency came first from urban hard money forces but had penetrated deeply into the folklore of agrarian inflationists by the nineties. Similarly, silver coinage itself was scorned contemptuously by the great mineowners of the seventies but became the subject of reverent idolatry by their counterparts two decades later. Finally, an issue that divided Democrats, Republicans, and Greenbackers along party lines during the late Reconstruction era became, by 1896, a sectional-class conflict bitter enough to provoke schisms in both major parties. These are a few of the residual paradoxes of the silver question.

When congressional debate over remonetization began in 1876, the issue lacked definition: few legislators understood it and almost none cared. But by the time Congress agreed to an inconclusive compromise settlement in February 1878, the terms under which Americans would debate monetary policy for the next two decades had been established. Programs and ideologies that characterized silver politics during the nineties developed during the eighteen months of legislative and public discussion that preceded passage of the Bland-Allison Act; hence, the significance of the first silver drive. Most historians of the silver question, however, have projected upon the issue during the 1870s an analysis derived from studying the "battle of the standards" during the 1890s.[1] Groups that responded to silver in a certain way by 1896, they have assumed, reacted similarly at the movement's outset. Such arguments have little basis in fact.

The campaign to remonetize silver during the seventies, for one thing, did not originate primarily among agrarians and mineowners. Nor did it find its earliest and most important roots of support among monetary inflationists. Most important western holders of silver bullion during this decade, including the dominant Bonanza Kings, remained indifferent toward remonetization or actively opposed it. This aloofness also characterized almost all western legislators during the 1870s except for Nevada's John Percival Jones who, although a mineowner, endorsed the silver drive largely for political reasons. Silver began as an urban movement, furthermore, not an agrarian crusade. Its original strongholds were the large towns and cities of the Midwest and middle Atlantic states, not the country's farming communities. The first batch of bimetallist leaders were a loosely knit collection of hard money newspaper editors, businessmen, academic reformers, bankers, and commercial groups. Only a few agrarian inflationist leaders participated meaningfully in the silver drive, and most greenbackers provided only tepid support for remonetization.

Nor was silver agitation limited exclusively to southern and western power bases. The early bimetallist movement enjoyed broad popular approval in every section but New England. Silver was a nationally based movement during the seventies and

1. See, for example, the following: Richard B. Morris, ed., *Encyclopedia of American History,* rev. ed. (New York, 1961), p. 254; Hicks, Mowry, and Burke, *The American Nation 2,* 58–59; Garraty, *The American Nation,* pp. 613–14; Current, Williams, and Freidel, *American History,* p. 559.

gold a sectional one. There existed, moreover, neither the concern nor the machinery for a bipartisan silverite coalition of southern and western congressmen similar to that of the nineties. The politics of silver during its formative period remained bitterly partisan. Democratic inflationists in the House tried to use remonetization as a convenient stalking-horse to ride down Republican chances for successful resumption of specie payments. Republican Senate leaders, for their part, endorsed restoration of the double monetary standard mainly to provide a larger specie basis with which to sustain resumption. Conflict over silver legislation concerned this underlying partisan dispute over resumption policy, and bipartisan cooperation among congressional bimetallists proved brief and unsuccessful. Viewed as an episode in the evolution of American political parties, therefore, the silver issue enhanced party cohesion during the 1870s and strengthened the influence of legislative caucuses. This role, which emerges when examining congressional voting behavior, contrasts starkly with the issue's divisive political impact during the nineties.

The timing of the early silver question confronts historians with a difficult problem of periodization, one that resembles somewhat the dilemma of that medieval knight in the cartoon who explained while stripping from his armor into an elegant cloth garment: "The Middle Ages are over. We're in the Renaissance now." Does Reconstruction end in a similarly abrupt fashion for the historian of national politics with the Compromise of 1877? Even if this were the case, the fact remains that the Gilded Age silver issue arose and was first debated in a Reconstruction setting. A Republican senate caucus such as the one that developed the 1875 Resumption Act performed a similar compromise role in shaping the Bland-Allison Act. Although specie resumption in 1879 rendered academic any further political controversy over the gold convertibility of greenbacks, it left unresolved the monetary standard question. Silver emerged as a distinct issue only when it lost its original identification with the resumption question. Although monetary standard myths and policies evolved during the brief silver drive of the seventies, the absence of sustained interest by politicians and public alike explains the swift demise of further controversy on the issue for almost a decade following passage of the Bland-Allison Act.

Historians of early silver politics squat awkwardly, therefore, upon a fencepost dividing two periods in American history. The struggle over silver during the seventies was fought along familiar partisan lines and disposed of temporarily in 1878 without arousing strong class or sectional divisions. Within a decade, the monetary standard question, however, had shed its early association with resumption and had assumed its own distinctive character. In similar manner, the slavery problem had proven a manageable partisan issue during the 1830s when raised in context of the nullification struggle over tariff policy. Slavery, like the silver question, ended by disrupting the political system two decades later once it lost its partisan moorings and became grounded in apparently irreconcilable differences of principle. The history of the money question after Bland-Allison concerns the process by which this transformation occurred on the silver issue. By the 1890s, supporters of both bimetallism and the gold standard had become clearly identified with different class and sectional interest groups, and they defended their respective claims with far greater passion than displayed during the seventies.

Any complete account of the silver issue would also have to recognize that, although it spanned the formative decades of American industrial growth, the question marked another chapter in the continuing struggle to shape government financial policy that reached back into the Jeffersonian and Jacksonian eras. There exist discernible resemblances between the coalition that opposed rechartering the Second Bank of the United States during the 1830s and the bimetallist forces of the 1870s. Both movements contained incongruous lineups of hard money "bullionists" and paper note inflationists. Any comparison of the two movements, however, must recognize the half-century that separated them and avoid overdrawing the similarities. Elements of Jacksonian rhetoric characterized both silverites and goldbugs in the earliest battle over remonetization. In some cases direct links existed, as in the activities of aging Jacksonian political figures during the silver drive. But even here the evidence for direct links is hardly clear. Thomas Olcott, a longtime Albany Jacksonian Democrat and banker, became a prominent silverite but so did Thurlow Weed, the old New York Whig strategist. The leading gold standard advocate in New York City throughout the 1870s, on the other hand, was another old Jacksonian, industrialist Abram S. Hewitt, whose famous father-in-law, Peter Cooper, was the Greenback party's vice-presidential choice. Throughout the South, former pre-War Whig and Democratic politicians joined in endorsing bimetallism, although notable gold standard holdouts among these antebellum survivors included John Gordon of Georgia, L. Q. C. Lamar of Mississippi, and John Tyler, Jr., of Virginia. There existed no obvious pattern of partisan or sectional continuity among politicians from the Bank War to Bland-Allison.

Gold standard advocates and bimetallists alike, furthermore, employed Jacksonian terminology in denouncing the "money power," although each group located the enemy in the other's tents. Abram S. Hewitt, E. L. Godkin, and other gold monometallists believed that millionaire silver mineowners had sponsored and paid for the political agitation over remonetization. John Percival Jones, Richard Bland, and their fellow silverites, on the other hand, were equally convinced that international bankers and bondholders had not only financed silver's demonetization but that they continued to underwrite congressional opposition to remonetization. Both sides in the monetary standard question during the 1870s claimed to speak on behalf of the country's small-holding entrepreneurs, not as avowed representatives of class or sectional interests.

Although some scholars have described the first struggle over silver policy as an early confrontation between America's assertive business community and its divided farmer-labor *jacquerie,* such a rigorously Beardian analysis bears small relation to the realities of the conflict.[2] To begin with, differences in rhetoric between gold standard advocates and bimetallists were not absolute but involved shadings and stresses. Goldbugs presented themselves as representatives of the country's "producing classes," defending an "honest" currency system threatened by the special-interest schemes of mineowners and silver speculators. Silverites claimed to represent these same "producers" against the encroachments of millionaire bondholders interested in overvaluing gold to increase the value of their securities. In short, "producerism" was the dominant ideology during the 1870s of most politicians and of substantial numbers of businessmen, many of whom joined the campaign to remonetize silver. There existed no special economic class positions on the battle over silver policy during the seventies, any more than such self-conscious class or sectional identification could be found at this time on most major economic policy questions in American life.

The depression of the 1870s left in its wake, in Robert Wiebe's words, a society marked strongly by "dislocation and bewilderment" rather than by the class or interest-group "polarization" detected by neo-Beardian historians. "America in the late nineteenth century was a society without a core . . . [lacking] those national centers of authority and information which might have given order to such swift changes." The basic unit of both class and political identification still remained the local community, and most groups—whether farmers, laborers, professionals, or businessmen—had yet to create appropriate national organizations for influencing or directing the process of government economic policy making. "American institutions were still

2. N. 1, passim. See especially Nugent, *Money and American Society,* pp. 267–69. See also pp. 205–18.

oriented toward a community life where family and church, education and press, professions and government, all largely found their meaning by the way they fit one with another inside a town or a detached portion of a city." In such a "distended society," to use Wiebe's phrase, "a great many looked upon economic downturns as a moral judgment, precise punishment for the country's sins."[3]

It is at the level of political symbolism and not through an unwarranted division of the country into warring classes during the seventies that we can find continuity between the Jacksonian anti-Bank coalition and the early silver movement. Their affinity lay in their analogous moral claims rather than in similar class composition. Uniting the disparate elements that opposed Biddle's "Monster Bank," as Marvin Meyers has shown, had less to do with economic class interests or specific "material injuries" than with the cultural fears, anxieties, and ambitions felt by Jacksonian contemporaries in an era of rapid economic growth and accompanying social dislocation. "Many found in the anti-Bank crusade, and in the Jacksonian appeal generally," Meyers pointed out, "a way to damn the unfamiliar, threatening, sometimes punishing agents in the changing order by fixing guilt upon some single protean agent."[4] In comparable fashion both bimetallists and gold standard advocates expressed their differences more often in terms of contrasting *moral* judgments on one another rather than in judgments on their respective *economic* policies.

The Coinage Act of 1873 represented for the ordinary silverite a secret betrayal of America's constitutional monetary standard, gold *and* silver, and restoration of the old silver dollar appeared for many of them a simple "act of justice." Even John Sherman recognized this obsession with ethical rather than eco-

3. Robert H. Wiebe, *The Search for Order, 1877–1920* (New York, 1967), pp. 2, 12.

4. Marvin Meyers, *The Jacksonian Persuasion, Politics and Belief* (Stanford, Calif., 1957), p. 8.

nomic principles as the essential root of silver agitation when he acknowledged that "right or wrong, its demonetization is regarded as a grand error if not a crime."[5] The impulse to "restore" the traditional coinage system remained as deep among bimetallists of the seventies as the desire for restoration of earlier banking patterns had been for many Jacksonians. Gold monometallists felt equally indignant at what they believed was the bimetallists' desire to "repudiate" legitimate government financial obligations through repaying the public debt in depreciated silver coinage. Goldbugs dwelt in their speeches and writings on those widows, orphans, and war veterans who, along with wealthier bondholders, had accepted greenbacks and federal bonds during the Civil War, expecting their eventual "redemption" in gold. Both sides on the monetary standard question agreed, in fact, on the essentially moral meaning of money, arguing primarily over whether financial virtue was to be found by "restoring" silver or by "redeeming" gold.

The intense preoccupation of nineteenth-century Americans with the ethics of financial policy, beginning with the Bank War and ending with the "free silver" campaign of 1896, may appear to some in retrospect as shallow and irrational. So a few recent historians, armed with modern investment theory, have argued.[6] One scholar has even termed "the whole enrapturement of Americans with the money question a blunder," one that he holds largely responsible for the failure of Gilded Age Americans "to come to terms rationally with the international trends of urbanization and industrialization."[7] Goldbugs, silverites, and

5. John Sherman to J. H. Tuleston, Mar. 1, 1878. See also H. S. Bundy to John Sherman, Dec. 23, 1876, Sherman MSS, LC.

6. See, for example, Richard Hofstadter. "Free Silver and the Mind of 'Coin' Harvey," in *The Paranoid Style in American Politics and Other Essays* (New York, 1965), pp. 238–315, passim; Nugent, *Money and American Society,* pp. 3–5, 33–55, 199–202, 263–75.

7. Nugent, *Money and American Society,* p. 5, 264. Some of Nugent's other remarks are also relevant in this connection (see pp. 3–5, 199–202, 263–75).

greenbackers, in this view, all lost the opportunity "to create for themselves, by rational choice, individual and collective self-images adequate to their changing environment."[8] Whether groups such as the Populists, Knights of Labor, or Bellamy Nationalists actually lacked such adequate "self images" might be questioned. A more persuasive charge leveled by modern economic historians, however, concerns the ignorance displayed by all groups during the late nineteenth century of the manner in which government monetary policy conditioned and influenced private investment behavior.[9] The evidence suggests that no economic analyst in the silver drive of the seventies, whether bimetallist or gold advocate, understood except in overly simplified fashion precisely how the adoption of different monetary standards would affect the interest rates of national or private banks. Furthermore, these same ideologists also betrayed no clear sense of the role which changes in the interest rates for borrowing money played in altering the propensity of businessmen to shift available funds into investment channels.

That such confusion existed among the semiprofessional economic publicists of the Gilded Age should come as little surprise, especially when economists continue even today to dispute the precise relationship between monetary policy, investment behavior, and economic recovery in America during the depressions of the 1870s and 1890s. Milton Friedman and Anna Jacobson Schwartz concluded, for example, after assessing the alternatives available to government policy makers during these decades, that adoption of a silver rather than a gold standard

8. Ibid., p. 264.

9. See, for example, the following: Friedman and Schwartz, *Monetary History,* esp. pp. 3–134; Richard H. Timberlake, Jr., "Ideological Factors in Specie Resumption and Treasury Policy," *Journal of Economic History,* 24 (March 1964), 29–52; James K. Kindahl, "Economic Factors in Specie Resumption: The United States, 1865–1879"; Rendig Fels, *American Business Cycles, 1865–1879* (Chapel Hill, N.C., 1959), especially pp. 62–112.

would have contributed best to rapid economic recovery and subsequent growth.[10] Rendig Fels, on the other hand, blamed the prolonged decline in the business cycle during the seventies on the absence of a functioning gold standard prior to resumption. Had the gold standard existed when the Panic of 1873 occurred, he argued, "the recovery of physical output [by 1877] would have been vigorous: the date of the cyclical upturn . . . would have come two years earlier; and the depression of the seventies would never have come to be regarded as outstanding in the history of cycles."[11]

Still a third economic historian, Richard Timberlake, drew attention to the critical role of strategic decisions made by different secretaries of the Treasury in securing specie resumption and thereby assisting economic recovery. Silver policy played a negative but determining role in this process, according to Timberlake, for "even though little silver currency actually came into circulation before 1879 [it] exerted phantom leverage on the course that resumption policy actually took." The major reason for this, in his view, was the importance of a falling price level as "both a necessary and sufficient condition for resumption." To help secure a falling price level the money stock would have to decline or to increase less rapidly than the output of goods and services. Yet the American public demanded additional currency issues throughout the mid-seventies to provide relief from the depression. John Sherman's policy as Treasury Secretary of retiring high-interest government notes while accumulating a gold reserve to sustain resumption—thereby encouraging a declining price level—was possible, Timberlake believes, partly because "the cheap money movement presumed that silver was 'in.' "[12] The author credits Sherman with too much foresight,

10. Friedman and Schwartz, *Monetary History,* esp. p. 134.

11. Fels, *American Business Cycles,* p. 73.

12. Timberlake, "Ideological Factors in Specie Resumption," pp. 30, 51–2.

however, since he believes that the Ohioan used bimetallism as a deliberate stalking-horse to "delude the public" and divert it from more extreme inflationist demands. Still, Timberlake suggests an even more ironic possibility, that the Senate's compromise silver bill—by defusing inflationist demands—rescued Sherman's resumption program despite the secretary's personal disapproval. In such ironies and in the persistent disputes of professional analysts lurk the hidden economic meanings of the silver issue.

Life remained simpler for most contemporary economic ideologists. Greenbackers, bimetallists, and gold standard advocates shared the basic assumption that once their particular monetary scheme had been enacted into law, business confidence would be restored, private investment returned to high levels, and prosperity assured. This easy confidence underscored the rudimentary state of economic knowledge among all Americans, whatever their class, when confronting the problems of an industrializing society. In the sense that they claimed no special understanding of economic processes beyond the conceptual grasp of ordinary Americans, bimetallists and gold standard advocates both resembled earlier Jacksonian political economists rather than modern analysts: "the broad vision clearly dominated their thought. Means mattered very little . . . Basically all of these theorists offered a feeling, an ethic, and a hope."[13]

As for the politics of silver during the seventies, a Beardian or sectional-class analysis does not explain adequately the development of the early silver movement. For one thing, the business community divided in disorderly fashion on the issue, as did most other economic classes in American life. During the seventies, neither in Congress nor elsewhere, did significant sectional-class alliances exist on the silver question. Instead, the battle over coinage policy began as a partisan issue and remained so for

13. Wiebe, *The Search for Order,* p. 140.

the eighteen months preceding passage of the Bland-Allison Act. This interpretation of the monetary standard issue relates closely to previous studies of Reconstruction finance by Robert Sharkey, Stanley Coben, and Irwin F. Unger.[14] As Sharkey concluded, "if the material interests of capitalists and other groups were so divergent and conflicting, it becomes obviously impossible to see economic forces as constituting a decisive factor in the determination of Reconstruction policy. One of the effects therefore of the work of Coben, Unger, and myself has been to help to restore primacy to the political interpretation of Reconstruction."[15] The present analysis of silver substantiates and reinforces Sharkey's assessment.

What remains to be said, then, concerning the direction taken by silver politics following passage of Bland-Allison? If historians have argued correctly that sectional and class factors outweighed partisan loyalties in the struggle over silver during the 1890s, they have neglected to account for an important transitional stage. Recent studies of Gilded Age politics have stressed the growth of party cohesion during the nineties, especially in Congress, which raises the question of why politicians failed to keep silver within the bounds of partisan dispute as successfully as other issues.[16] A poet once lamented the passing of a time "when . . . historians left blanks in their writings . . . for things they didn't know."[17] In the past, the silver question has been studied through the prism of the 1896 campaign, when both

14. Unger, *Greenback Era,* passim; Robert P. Sharky, *Money, Class and Party;* Stanley Coben, "Northeastern Business and Radical Reconstruction: A Re-examination," *Mississippi Valley Historical Review,* 46 (1959), 67–90.

15. Sharkey, *Money, Class and Party,* p. 12.

16. See, for example, Wiebe, *The Search for Order,* pp. 188–89, and David J. Rothman, *Politics and Power: The United States Senate, 1869–1901* (Cambridge, Mass., 1966), esp. pp. 73–108.

17. Ezra Pound, *The Cantos of Ezra Pound* (New York, 1948), p. 60.

parties split into opposing camps. Scholars have assumed from this that bipartisan and sectional-class alignments characterized the coinage question from the beginning. The assumption is erroneous, but only a fresh look at the issue from Bland-Allison to Bryan can describe more faithfully the subsequent course of silver politics and fill in the appropriate blanks.

Appendix: Government Transactions with the Bonanza Kings

1. *Government Silver Purchases from Bonanza Firm Companies, January 1875–April 1876*

Place and date of sale (selling company)	Weight of silver (ounces)	Rate per ounce (cents)	Purchase price in gold coin
San Francisco Mint			
Jan. 13, 1876 (Nevada Bank)	250,785.39	120.5	$ 302,196.39
Feb. 27, 1876 (Nevada Bank)	200,147.57	116	232,171.20
Feb. 1876 (Nevada Bank)*			302,291.52
Mar. 23, 1876 (Nevada Bank)	101,651.13	114	115,882.29
Mar. 1876 (Nevada Bank)*			303,712.48
Carson City Mint			
July 16, 1875 (Con. Va. Mining Co.)	248,039.28	119	295,166.69
Sept. 3, 1875 (Con. Va. Mining Co.)	138,749.81	121	167,887.26
Feb. 18, 1876 (Con. Va. Mining Co.)	108,099.93	118.5	128,098.44
Mar. 15, 1876 (Con. Va. Mining Co.)	96,835.05	116	112,328.62

Appendix Table 1—Continued

Philadelphia Mint			
Feb. 3, 1876			
(Nevada Bank)	500,677.82	119.25	597,058.29
Mar. 26, 1876			
(Nevada Bank)	300,376.00	117	351,439.92
New York Assay Office			
June 1, 1875			
(Con. Va. Mining Co.)	750,237.61	121.5	820,384.83
TOTAL SILVER PURCHASED (EQUIVALENT IN GOLD COIN)			$3,728,617.93

*Local purchases in addition to those transcribed in the records of the Bureau of the Mint (monthly totals in San Francisco Mint records).
Sources: Recordbook, Silver Purchases, Bureau of the Mint, NA, RG104; Silver Purchases, San Francisco Mint, NA, RG217, Records of the First Auditor, Treasury Department.

2. *Government Silver Purchases from Bonanza Firm Companies, April 1876–August 1876*

Place and date of sale (selling company)	Weight of silver (ounces)	Rate per ounce (cents)	Purchase price in gold coin†
San Francisco Mint			
April 1, 1876			
(Nevada Bank)	299.918.23	114.5	$ 343,406.37
April 19, 1876			
(Nevada Bank)	300,750.36	117	351,877.91
April 1876			
(Pacific Refining and Bullion Company)*			214,262.91
July 8, 1876			
(Nevada Bank)	548,077.63	104.5	572,741.12
May 1876			
(Nevada Bank)*			650,354.50
May 1876			
(Pacific R. & B. Co.)*			294,074.22
June 1876			
(Pacific R. & B. Co.)*			432,944.11
August 1876			
(Pacific R. & B. Co.)*			107,743.85
August 1876			
(Nevada Bank)*			680,953.54
Carson City Mint			
April 20			
(Con. Va.)	199,262.00	114.5	228,154.99
May 11			
(Nevada Bank)	199,674.08	117.2	233,618.67
June 14			
(Nevada Bank)	303,477.39	114.5	347,481.61
July 8			
(Nevada Bank)	298,356.92	104.5	311,782.98
July 8			
(Nevada Bank)	198,315.56	104.5	207,239.76

Philadelphia Mint			
April 19			
(Nevada Bank)	1,500,022.38	118	1,770,026.41
May 24			
(Nevada Bank)	200,375.31	114.25	228,928.79
July 8			
(Nevada Bank)	749,649.30	103.84	778,435.84
New York Assay Office			
June 1876			
(Nevada Bank)	331,398.59	114.25	340,760.59
TOTAL SILVER PURCHASED (EQUIVALENT IN GOLD COIN)			$8,094,788.17

*Local purchases in addition to those transcribed in the records of the Bureau of the Mint (monthly totals in San Francisco Mint records).

Sources: Recordbook, Silver Purchases, Bureau of the Mint, NA, RG104; Silver Purchases, San Francisco Mint, NA, RG217, Records of the First Auditor, Treasury Department.

3. Government Bonds Acquired by the Bonanza Kings in 1876: 5 Percent

Agent of Bonanza firm listed on bond and date purchased	Number of bonds	Denomination	Total amount
John W. Mackay			
May 26	13	$50,000	$ 650,000
	1		5,000
	1		1,000
June 13	19	50,000	950,000
	3	1,000	3,000
Aug. 13	1	(assorted)	35,000
	7	50,000	350,000
	1	(assorted)	6,000
Oct 5	5	1,000	5,000
	3	5,000	15,000
	1		10,000
	1		20,000
	39	50,000	1,950,000
Louis McLane, President, Nevada Bank			
Aug. 16	1	(assorted)	650
	3	1,000	3,000
	1		5,000
	1		20,000
	5	50,000	250,000
Oct. 5	40	50,000	2,000,000
TOTAL AMOUNT IN 5 PER CENT BONDS ACQUIRED IN 1876			$6,278,650

Source: Ledgerbooks, Bonds purchased, United States 5 per cent funded loan of 1881 (vols. 3–4), Records of the Bureau of the Public Debt, NA, RG53.

4. *Government Bonds Acquired by the Bonanza Kings through February 1878*

Agent of Bonanza firm listed on bond and date purchased	Number of bonds	Denomination	Total amount
Total through Dec. 1876 (See Appendix 3)			$ 6,278,650
James C. Flood (5 percent bond purchases)			
April 6, 1877	4	$50,000	$ 200,000
April 7, 1877	4	50,000	200,000
April 11, 1877	4	50,000	200,000
	4	50,000	200,000
April 13	4	50,000	200,000
Aug. 29	10	50,000	500,000
Dec. 20	10	50,000	500,000
Dec. 21	10	50,000	500,000
Dec. 28, 1877	25	50,000	1,250,000
Louis McLane, President, Nevada Bank			
Jan. 9, 1877	4	50,000	200,000
Jan. 11	4	50,000	200,000
	4	50,000	200,000
	5	50,000	250,000
	1		10,000
Jan. 13	8	50,000	400,000
	1		20,000
Jan. 15	4	50,000	200,000
Feb. 1	1		20,000
Feb. 2	6	50,000	300,000
Feb. 13	4	50,000	200,000
Feb. 15	6	50,000	300,000
Mar. 14	5	50,000	250,000
May 1	5	50,000	250,000
May 2	5	50,000	250,000
May 19	5	50,000	250,000

May 28	4	50,000	200,000
June 9	6	50,000	300,000
June 25	5	50,000	250,000
June 26	5	50,000	250,000
Aug. 29	10	50,000	500,000
Dec. 20	10	50,000	500,000
Dec. 21	10	50,000	500,000
Dec. 28	25	50,000	1,250,000
TOTAL 5 PERCENT BONDS PURCHASED IN 1877			10,800,000
James C. Flood—TOTAL PURCHASES OF 4.5 PERCENT BONDS IN 1877			5,000,000
TOTAL BOND-HOLDINGS OF THE BONANZA KINGS THROUGH FEB. 1878:			$22,078,000

Sources: Ledgerbooks, 5% and 4.5% funded loans, Records of the Bureau of the Public Debt, NA, RG53. (4.5% 15-year funded loan of 1891; 5% funded loan of 1881.)

5. *Government Silver Purchases from Bonanza Firm Companies, January 1875–March 1, 1878*

Place and date of sale (selling company)	Weight of silver (ounces)	Rate per ounce (cents)	Purchase price in gold coin
TOTAL SILVER PURCHASED, JAN. 1875–APRIL 1876:			$ 3,728,617.93
TOTAL SILVER PURCHASED, APRIL 1876–AUG. 1876:			8,094,788.17
San Francisco Mint			
Sept. 1876 (Nevada Bank)*			302,181.57
Sept. 1876 (Pacific Refining & Bullion Co.)*			201,839.92
Oct. 1876 (Nevada Bank)*			80,450.54
Nov. 21, 1876 (Nevada Bank)	1,000,958.50	118.5	1,186,135.82
Dec. 1876 (Nevada Bank)*			274,707.81
Jan. 1877 (Nevada Bank)*			271,691.65
Mar. 8, 1877 (Nevada Bank)	300,613.83	122.75	369,003.40
Apr. 6, 1877 (Nevada Bank)	500,200.25	116.75	583,983.79
Sept. 10, 1877 (Nevada Bank)	150,017.27	118	177,020.38
Sept. 14, 1877 (Nevada Bank)	249,716.48	118.2	295,164.88
Carson City Mint			
Nov. 25, 1876 (Nevada Bank)	299,644.37	118.5	355,078.58
Jan. 12, 1877 (Nevada Bank)	249,941.69	125	312,427.11

Jan. 29			
(Nevada Bank)	500,761.39	126	630,959.35
Mar. 12			
(Nevada Bank)	201,063.56	123	247,308.16
Sept. 17			
(Nevada Bank)	82,773.40	118.2	97,838.15
Sept. 21			
(Nevada Bank)	130,159.38	118.2	153,848.36
Sept. 27			
(Nevada Bank)	36,070.76	118.2	42,635.66
Dec. 11, 1877			
(Nevada Bank)	150,193.05	119	178,729.73
Mar. 1, 1878			
(Nevada Bank)	500,075.58	120.5	602,591.08
Philadelphia Mint			
Oct. 27, 1876			
(Nevada Bank)	500,239.89	118.75	594,034.85
Mar. 9, 1877			
(Nevada Bank)	509,649.91	124.25	633,240.02
Mar. 23, 1877			
(Nevada Bank)	228,153.05	117.5	338,579.83
Sept. 9, 1877			
(Nevada Bank)	1,000,826.89	118.2	1,182,977.38
Feb. 27, 1878			
(Nevada Bank)	499,934.60	120.5	602,421.20
			$21,538,255.32

TOTAL SILVER PURCHASED (EQUIVALENT IN GOLD COIN), JAN. 1875–MAR. 1, 1878 $21,538,255.32

*Local purchases in addition to those transcribed in the records of the Bureau of the Mint (monthly totals in San Francisco Mint records). *Sources: Recordbook,* Silver Purchases, Bureau of the Mint, NA, RG104; Silver Purchases, San Francisco Mint, NA, RG217, Records of the First Auditor, Treasury Department.

Critical Bibliography and Listing of Major Sources

Any brief evaluation of the materials important to this study would have to omit a number of primary and secondary sources that aided analysis at vital stages. Those that contributed most meaningfully to the book's development will be discussed in the following pages, reserving the appended listing for a fuller catalog of major sources consulted.

Several works served as points of departure for the entire project. Anyone who hopes to explore currency politics in the immediate post-Civil War period must begin by examining carefully two invaluable works on the subject. Both Robert Sharkey's *Money, Class and Party: An Economic Study of Civil War and Reconstruction* (Baltimore, Johns Hopkins Press, 1959) and Irwin Unger's *The Greenback Era: A Social and Political History of American Finance, 1865–1879* (Princeton, Princeton University Press, 1964) survey skillfully the dimensions of monetary politics during the Reconstruction era, and I am deeply indebted to both men for their insights and superb scholarship. Although the present work questions a number of conclusions reached by Unger on the silver issue, it builds appreciatively upon his findings. Unger and Sharkey disagree on the basic motives underlying public and political response to Reconstruction's financial issues. Sharkey argues that economic interests generally governed reaction to currency questions while Unger stresses relevant moral and cultural determinants of political behavior along with economic factors. Their dispute has helped to clarify my own ideas on the question. Joseph Dorfman's *The Economic Mind in American Civilization* (New York, The Viking Press, 1946–59) and Milton Friedman and

Anna Jacobson Schwartz' *A Monetary History of the United States* (Princeton, Princeton University Press, 1963) have also been extremely useful guides from the beginning of my research.

The only previous modern article on the silver question during this period, Jeannette P. Nichols' "John Sherman and the Silver Drive of 1877–1878: The Origins of the Gigantic Subsidy," *Ohio State Archeological and Historical Quarterly*, 46 (1937), also provided useful introductory material. Walter T. K. Nugent's *Money and American Society, 1865–1880* (New York, The Free Press, 1968) and the same author's *The Money Question during Reconstruction* (New York, W. W. Norton and Co., 1967), both published after completion of the dissertation on which this book was based, verify my own analysis of silver's demonetization. Nugent's books do not otherwise modify greatly earlier interpretations of silver politics during the 1870s. They add significantly, however, to our understanding of international monetary trends during this period.

To understand the background of silver's demonetization in 1873 required familiarity with the records of both the Treasury Department and the Philadelphia Mint, which contain many useful letters exchanged among mint officials involved in the episode as well as important correspondence with chairmen of the various congressional committees concerned with coinage policy. Treasury and mint records throughout the post-Civil War period proved a vital untapped source of information on the process through which government monetary policy took shape during the years covered by this book. The published *Annual Reports of the Secretary of the Treasury* and the *Annual Reports of the Director of the Philadelphia Mint* for the years 1867–73 also contained a surprising amount of helpful material on the motives behind demonetization, especially the 1872 Treasury report which distilled the findings of an earlier special report to Secretary Boutwell from Henry Richard Linderman.

Although congressional committee records, also found in the National Archives, contained few items of interest for this period, the Congressional correspondence of the Treasury Secretary and of leading mint officials unearthed many significant indications of House and Senate opinion on the resumption and silver questions.

Despite a thorough examination of Treasury and mint records, however, no reassessment of the traditional story of demonetization would have been possible without first consulting Paul M. O'Leary's pioneering article, "The Scene of the Crime of 1873 Revisited: A Note," *Journal of Political Economy, 68* (August 1960), on which my own analysis of the episode is based.

Several manuscript collections at the Library of Congress proved to be indispensable in studying the emergence of silver as a political issue in the mid-1870s. The papers of Benjamin H. Bristow, James A. Garfield, Justin S. Morrill, and Whitelaw Reid, all at the Library of Congress, were particularly rich in items concerning currency politics. But I began my research with and returned constantly to the incoming mail and letterbooks of John Sherman, a central figure in the politics of finance during Reconstruction.

The papers of John Percival Jones were divided after his death between the Huntington Library and U.C.L.A. Library. Of the two collections, the Huntington owns a far richer mass of manuscript material, including Jones's valuable letters to his wife, which often discuss Washington political affairs. U.C.L.A. has a number of Jones's scrapbooks with important clippings on financial matters. The present analysis of Jones's political motives for opening the congressional silver drive relied heavily on his personal papers. They afforded unique clues to the character and ambitions of this enthusiastic Nevada politician and entrepreneur. Other materials in western archives, including miscellaneous collections at the Huntington Library, the Bancroft Library, and the Nevada Historical Society, also helped to clarify the nature and extent of mining state response to the silver drive. This response turned out upon examination to have been considerably less during the seventies than generally assumed by historians.

The belief that major silver mineowners had sponsored the political agitation for remonetization during this period, for example, proved to be false, a fact revealed through careful study of the Bonanza firm, the country's leading producers of silver bullion. Most important Nevada mineowners, who also operated large banks in San Francisco, opposed restoration of the double standard, both publicly in the San Francisco press and privately in letters to mint officials. The richest source for study of the Bonanza firm proved to be Mint Bureau records. They showed the extent of government cooperation with the mineowners prior to passage of the Bland-Allison Act. The chapter on mining king involvement relied heavily on correspondence contained in Mint Bureau files, supplemented by government silver purchase and resumption bond purchase records.

The degree to which silver emerged first as an important question in 1876 among business groups, academics, and reformers rather than as an agrarian demand became evident only after extensive research in the entire range of sources. Certain manuscript collections revealed the genesis and development of business and reform response to the monetary standard issue, especially the John Sherman, Carl Schurz, and David A. Wells papers at the Library of Congress and the Samuel Ruggles papers at the New York Public Library. Periodicals like the *Bankers' Magazine, Commercial and Financial Chronicle,* and *The Nation* were filled with articles by economic analysts on the silver issue, and newspapers such as the New York *Tribune,* Chicago *Tribune,* Cincinnati *Commercial,* and New York *Journal of Commerce* also followed the emergence of business and academic opinion on remonetization from the moment silver became a political question. Furthermore, Treasury and mint records often contained correspondence from bankers, merchants, and reformers which shed light upon class and group response to the silver issue.

At all stages of research the examination of legislative action on monetary policy questions involved careful study of the debates published in the Congressional *Globe* and its successor, the *Record.* Furthermore, no attempt to understand the politics of the Hayes administration could proceed very far without consulting the President's own papers at the Hayes Memorial Library in Fremont, Ohio. This well-administered library contains not only Hayes' personal papers, which are more important for the chief executive's incoming political correspondence than for his own cautious replies, but also the papers of politicians and friends of the President like Stanley Matthews and William Henry Smith. John Sherman's papers at the Library of Congress are even more valuable than the Hayes collection in understanding the monetary politics and policy making of the late 1870s. When supplemented by Sherman's official Treasury Department correspondence in the National Archives, a full picture could be constructed of the economic and political difficulties faced by the Hayes administration in grappling with the silver issue.

The sections on business reaction to remonetization used material collected from various manuscript collections, business publications, Treasury records, periodicals, and newspapers. The tentativeness and uncertainty of much business response to the Bland bill can be seen in the scarcity of organized efforts either on behalf of the measure or against it. The one exception remained George S. Coe's work in organizing eastern banking opposition to restoration of the double standard, and Fritz Redlich's discussion of Coe's work in *The Molding of American Banking: Men and Ideas,* vol. 2, pt. II (New York, Hafner Publishing Company, 1951) provided a useful and informative introduction to the political activities of national bankers during the 1870s.

The book's final two chapters maintain two basic assumptions: that partisan rather than sectional considerations dominated congressional voting behavior during the closing months of the first silver drive and that widespread popular support for some form of remonetization did not come primarily from the West and South alone but emerged in all but the New England states. Newspaper discussions of the issue, the incoming mail of public officials and other evidence indicated that moral repugnance at the so-called "Crime of 1873" accounted for this high degree of public enthusiasm for silver even more than any widespread belief in the economic benefits that would flow from returning to a dual monetary standard.

Party influence on congressional voting patterns on the silver issue became more observable after analyzing more than a dozen crucial legislative votes. Newspaper and manuscript sources also helped to document the swift abandonment by House Republicans of the bipartisan coalition known as the "Silver Union" once William Boyd Allison's amended silver bill had passed the Senate. Allison's own papers in the Iowa State Department of History and Archives at Des Moines were particularly important in understanding Republican congressional handling of the remonetization issue during the Hayes administration. Allison's close relationships with leading international bimetallists and his concern for preserving party unity by rallying congressional Republicans around a compromise silver bill were two of the points that emerged from examining this rich but poorly maintained collection. Only the Sherman and Garfield papers at the Library of Congress were as important in understanding financial politics during the late 1870s.

Certain additional materials used in my research deserve mention, although they did not influence particular chapters of the book as keenly as previously discussed sources. Several manuscript collections, especially their incoming mail, indicated reaction to remonetization by different economic classes and political groups. Thomas F. Bayard's papers at the Library of Congress, for example, contained numerous letters from eastern and southern businessmen opposed to the Bland bill, while the Benjamin F. Butler collection in the same repository helped to document the reluctant and ambiguous quality of Greenback involvement in the silver drive. Henry Teller's Colorado constituents expressed their enthusiasm for silver in correspondence housed at the Denver Public Library, while Democratic politicians bombarded House Speaker Samuel J. Randall, whose papers are found at the University of Pennsylvania, with suggestions concerning party strategy on the issue. The small Murat Halstead collection at the Cincinnati Historical Society contained some important letters from leading silverite politicians and newspapermen. Correspondence among intransigent Democratic silverites opposed to the Senate compromise measure were found in the Thomas Ewing papers at the Library of Congress and in some fascinating letters to Ewing from midwestern agrarian inflationists in the Salmon P. Chase collection at the Pennsylvania Historical Society.

Several published congressional reports supplemented material taken from the *Globe,* the *Record* and committee papers. Two publications were particularly useful. The 1868 Finance Committee report on Samuel Ruggles' proposal that the United States adopt his scheme for an international gold standard, reprinted as *International Coinage* (Washington, D.C., 1868), focused congressional attention on the monetary standard question for the first time during the Reconstruction period. The Monetary Commission's two-volume 1877 *Report (Senate Report No. 703,* 44th Congress, 2d Session) contained the various majority and minority recommendations as well as an extremely informative volume of testimony by business, banking, and academic witnesses.

Newspapers and periodicals not previously mentioned that

proved helpful in tracing public response to remonetization included the Chicago *Inter-Ocean;* the Cincinnati *Enquirer,* a leading midwestern Democratic journal; Richard Smith's Cincinnati *Gazette;* James S. Clarkson's Des Moines *Iowa State Register;* the *Economist* of London, especially for trends in the international bullion markets; the Indianapolis *Sun* and Philadelphia *Inquirer,* both important Greenback dailies; Henry Watterson's Louisville *Courier-Journal,* which kept a shrewd eye on political developments and opinion throughout the South; the Boston *Journal of Commerce* and Boston *Globe,* which chronicled the eastern business community's political activities and reactions; the *North American Review,* which published a number of articles dealing with government monetary policy; the Washington *National Republican's* daily, thorough accounts of the city's political life; and finally the San Francisco *Chronicle,* Nevada's Virginia City *Territorial Enterprise,* and Denver's *Rocky Mountain Daily News,* all superb sources for western mining state response to the silver drive.

The pamphlet literature on the silver question had become voluminous within a year or two after the issue arose, and only a small fraction of contemporary tracts on the subject have been mentioned in the appended listing. Excellent collections of pamphlets on remonetization can be found at the Hayes Memorial Library, the Library of Congress, and the New York Public Library. Rarely did these tracts add to the arguments developed on all sides of the silver question in the 1877 congressional *Report of the Monetary Commission,* and most of the pamphlet writers borrowed heavily, usually without acknowledgment, from this report. Among contemporaries whose writings on silver assumed special significance because of their involvement in congressional action on the monetary standard question were Samuel F. Cary, Thomas Ewing Jr., Murat Halstead, S. Dana Horton, John Percival Jones, Henry Richard Linderman, Henry Varnum Poor, Samuel B. Ruggles, Carl Schurz, Ernest Seyd, John Sherman, Francis Amasa Walker, and David A. Wells. Their publications are described both in the book and in the listing of major sources consulted.

A number of contemporary memoirs also provided important material for this study, including the reminiscences of Carl Schurz, William Morris Stewart, Wells Drury, Harry Gorham, Mary

Logan, and George Lyttleton Upshur. Two memoirs were especially useful. George S. Boutwell's *Reminiscences of Sixty Years in Public Affairs* (New York, McClure, Phillips and Company, 1902) offered evidence concerning Boutwell's motives for wishing silver demonetized quickly in 1872. John Sherman's *Recollections of Forty Years in the House, Senate and Cabinet* (Chicago, The Werner Company, 1896) contained the *apologia* of a major architect of government silver policy during the post-Civil War period. The *Garfield-Hinsdale Letters, Correspondence Between James Abram Garfield and Burke Aaron Hinsdale* (Ann Arbor, University of Michigan Press, 1949), edited by Mary L. Hinsdale, reprinted some valuable letters by the Ohio Republican on his difficulties with the remonetization issue.

The annual reports of commercial and banking organizations provided a major source of insight into business response to the monetary standard question. The reports of the American Bankers' Association, Boston Board of Trade, Cincinnati Chamber of Commerce, National Board of Trade, and New York State Chamber of Commerce were extremely helpful in this regard. The academic-reform community debated the silver issue at the 1876 and 1877 annual meetings of the American Social Science Association, and the division of opinion among American economic experts on silver policy can be followed in the *Transactions of the . . . Association for the Years 1875–1879*. State and national party platforms were compiled in *Appleton's Annual Cyclopedia* and in Edward McPherson's yearly *Handbook of Politics,* and both publications included much useful information on local political response to silver.

Almost every page of the book builds on the work of previous historians, but special mention might be given to a few particularly helpful works. Neil Carothers' *Fractional Money* (New York, 1930), for example, initiated the author into some of the mysteries of American coinage policy and remains the best available study of the subject. Richard Hofstadter has woven a remarkably challenging analysis of the entire silver movement into his introduction to William H. Harvey's *Coin's Financial School* (Cambridge, Harvard University Press, 1963). No recent historian has explored as perceptively the economic and cultural dimensions of the silver question in post-Civil War America.

Rodman Paul's *Mining Frontiers of the Far West, 1848–1880* (New York, Holt, Rinehart and Winston, 1963) provides the best introduction to American silver mining during the 1870s. For a fuller understanding of Nevada mining and politics in this decade, Paul's study should be supplemented by Grant H. Smith's helpful volume, *A History of the Comstock Lode, 1850–1920* (Reno, University of Nevada Bulletin, 37, no. 3, 1943). Robert Wiebe's *The Search for Order, 1877–1920* (New York, Hill and Wang, 1967) scrutinizes with fresh insight the sources of American political and cultural change during the Gilded Age and Progressive periods.

Four biographies proved particularly helpful in the course of research. Harry Barnard's *Rutherford B. Hayes and His America* (Indianapolis, The Bobbs-Merrill Company, 1954) summarized the President's response to the silver issue, while Leland L. Sage assessed Senate handling of the Bland bill in *William Boyd Allison, A Study in Practical Politics* (Iowa City, State Historical Society of Iowa, 1956). Martin Ridge's *Ignatius Donnelly, The Portrait of a Politician* (Chicago, University of Chicago Press, 1962) shed light on Greenback reaction to the silver drive, while Daniel G. B. Thompson traced the career of an important but little-known monetary reformer in *Ruggles of New York: A Life of Samuel B. Ruggles* (New York, Columbia University Press, 1946). Modern biographies are sorely needed of several major post-Civil War political figures important in silver politics during the 1870s, especially James A. Garfield, James G. Blaine, Richard Parks Bland, John Percival Jones, Roscoe Conkling, and Justin S. Morrill. There is also no modern biography of John Sherman, an important gap in American political historiography.

A number of articles influenced the present analysis of silver politics, including Stanley Coben's "Northeastern Business and Radical Reconstruction: A Re-examination," *Mississippi Valley Historical Review*, 46 (June 1959), which, along with the Sharkey and Unger studies, revised previous historical opinion concerning the relationship between northern business interests and Radical policies toward the South during the Reconstruction period. Richard A. Timberlake, Jr., developed a set of categories for dealing with ideological response to the resumption question in his article "Ideological Factors in Specie Resumption and Treasury

Policy," *Journal of Economic History, 24* (March 1964) that suggested some of my own interpretations in this book. James K. Kindahl's "Economic Factors in Specie Resumption: The United States, 1865–1879," *Journal of Political Economy, 69* (February 1961) summarized the findings of Kindahl's dissertation on the question. Three articles by Jeannette Paddock Nichols, other than her previously mentioned article on the silver drive itself, contributed to my understanding of monetary politics and policy making in the 1870s: "John Sherman: A Study in Inflation," *Mississippi Valley Historical Review, 21* (September 1934), "The Monetary Problems of William McKinley," *Ohio History, 72* (October 1963), and "Silver Diplomacy," *Political Science Quarterly, 48,* no. 4 (1933). Several major articles by Irwin Unger on business response to resumption politics were included later in *The Greenback Era.*

The most insightful discussion of silver politics in all the unpublished dissertations consulted came from Irwin Unger's "Men, Money and Politics: The Specie Resumption Issue, 1865–1879" (Columbia University, 1958).

Source Materials

Manuscripts

Allen, William. Papers. Library of Congress.

Allison, William Boyd. Papers. Iowa State Department of History and Archives, Des Moines.

Bancroft, Hubert Howe. Papers and Collections. Bancroft Library, Berkeley, California.

Barker, Wharton. Papers. Library of Congress.

Bateman, Warner. Papers. Western Reserve Historical Society, Cleveland.

Bayard, Thomas F. Papers. Library of Congress.

Blaine, James G. Papers. Library of Congress.

Blair Family Papers. Library of Congress.

Bristow, Benjamin. Papers. Library of Congress.

Butler, Benjamin F. Papers. Library of Congress.

Cameron, Simon. Papers. Library of Congress.

Carey, Henry C. Papers. Historical Society of Pennsylvania.

Chandler, John Winthrop. Papers. New York Historical Society.
Chandler, William E. Papers. Library of Congress.
Chandler, Zachariah. Papers. Library of Congress.
Chase, Salmon P. Papers. Historical Society of Pennsylvania.
Colfax, Schuyler. Papers. Library of Congress.
Clarkson, James S. Papers. Library of Congress.
———. Papers. Iowa State Department of History and Archives, Des Moines.
Cole, Cornelius. Papers. U.C.L.A. Library, Los Angeles.
Comly, James M. Papers. Ohio State Historical Society, Columbus.
Conger, A. L. Papers. Hayes Memorial Library, Fremont, Ohio.
Cooke, Jay. Papers. Historical Society of Pennsylvania.
Cooper, Peter. Papers. The Cooper Union, New York City.
Cox, Jacob D. Papers. Oberlin College Library, Oberlin, Ohio.
Daggett, Rollin Mallory. Papers. Bancroft Library, Berkeley, California.
Dawes, Henry L. Papers. Library of Congress.
Dick, Charles. Papers. Ohio State Historical Society, Columbus.
Dodge, Grenville M. Papers. Iowa State Department of History and Archives, Des Moines.
Ewing Family Papers. Library of Congress.
Fish, Hamilton. Papers. Library of Congress.
Foraker, Joseph B. Papers. Historical and Philosophical Society of Ohio, Cincinnati.
Garfield Family Papers. Library of Congress.
Garfield, James A. Papers. Library of Congress.
Godkin, Edwin L. Papers. Harvard University.
Grant, Ulysses S. Papers. Library of Congress.
Halstead, Murat. Papers. Historical and Philosophical Society of Ohio, Cincinnati.
Harrison, Benjamin. Papers. Library of Congress.
Hayes, Rutherford B. Papers. Hayes Memorial Library, Fremont, Ohio.
———. Papers. Library of Congress.
Jones, John Percival. Papers. Huntington Library, San Marino, California.
———. Papers. U.C.L.A. Library, Los Angeles.
Knox Family Papers. New York Historical Society.
Laughlin, J. Lawrence. Papers. Library of Congress.

Logan, John A. Papers. Library of Congress.
Marble, Manton. Papers. Library of Congress.
Matthews, Stanley. Papers. Hayes Memorial Library, Fremont, Ohio.
———. Papers. Historical and Philosophical Society of Ohio, Cincinnati.
McCulloch, Hugh. Papers. Library of Congress.
McKinley, William A. Papers. Library of Congress.
McPherson, Edward. Papers. Library of Congress.
Morrill, Justin. Papers. Library of Congress.
Morton, Levi P. Papers. New York Public Library.
Olcott, Thomas. Papers. Columbia University.
Randall, Samuel J. Papers. University of Pennsylvania Library.
Reid, Whitelaw. Papers. Library of Congress.
Robertson J. Barr. Papers. Bancroft Library, Berkeley, California.
Ruggles, Samuel. Papers. New York Public Library.
Schuckers, Jacob W. Papers. Library of Congress.
Schurz, Carl. Papers. Library of Congress.
Sherman, John. Papers. Library of Congress.
———. Papers. Ohio State Historical Society, Columbus.
Sherman, W. T. Papers. Library of Congress.
Smith, William Henry. Papers. Hayes Memorial Library, Fremont, Ohio.
———. Papers. Ohio State Historical Society, Columbus.
Stewart, William M. Papers. Nevada Historical Society, Reno.
Teller, Henry. Papers. Denver (Colorado) Public Library.
Walker, Francis Amasa. Papers. Library of Congress.
Watterson, Henry. Papers. Library of Congress.
Weed, Thurlow. Papers. New York Historical Society.
Wells, David A. Papers. Library of Congress.
———. Papers. New York Public Library.

Government Documents and Publications

Bureau of the Mint. *Annual Reports of the Director of the Mint for the Years 1873–1878.*
———. Records, 1873–78. National Archives, Record Group no. 104.
Congressional *Globe,* 1867–73.
Congressional *Record,* 1874–79.

International Coinage. Washington, Government Printing Office, 1868.

Philadelphia Mint. *Annual Reports of the Director of the Philadelphia Mint for the Years 1867–1873.*

———. Records, 1867–78. National Archives, Record Group no. 104.

United States Comptroller of the Currency. *Annual Reports for the Years 1867–1878.*

United States House of Representatives. *Executive Document No. 9 (Specie Resumption and Refunding of National Debt).* 46th Congress, 2d Session.

———. *Executive Document No. 307 (Report on the Proposed Mint Bill, 1870).* 41st Congress, 2d Session.

———. *Miscellaneous Document No. 62. (Resumption of Specie Payments).* 45th Congress, 2d Session.

———. Records of the Committee on Banking and Currency, 1867–78. National Archives.

———. Records of the Committee on Coinage, Weights and Measures, 1867–78. National Archives.

———. Records of the Committee on Mines and Mining, 1867–78. National Archives.

———. Records, Miscellaneous Petitions, 1873–78. National Archives.

United States Senate. *Executive Document No. 51 (Report on Examination of the San Francisco Mint).* 41st Congress, 2d Session.

———. *Executive Document No. 58 (Report and Proceedings of the International Monetary Conference, 1878).* 45th Congress, 3d Session.

———. *Finance Committee (Interview of the Committee on Finance . . . with the Hon. John Sherman . . . in Regard to the Repeal of the Resumption Act).* Washington, Government Printing Office, 1878.

———. *Miscellaneous Document No. 132 (Documentary History of the Coinage Act of February 12, 1873).* 53rd Congress, 2d Session.

———. Records of the Committee on Finance, 1867–78. National Archives.

———. Records, Miscellaneous Petitions, 1873–78. National Archives.

———. *Report No. 235 (Coinage Laws of the United States, 1792 to 1894).* 53rd Congress, 2d Session.

———. *Report No. 703 (Report of the Monetary Commission, 2 vols.).* 44th Congress, 2d Session.

United States Treasury Department. *Annual Reports of the Secretary of the Treasury on the State of the Finances for the Years 1866–1879.*

———. Records, Bureau of the Public Debt. National Archives, Record Group no. 53

———. Records, Mint Correspondence of the Secretary of the Treasury, 1866–78. National Archives, Record Group no. 56.

Newspapers and Periodicals

Atlantic Monthly
Baltimore *Sun*
Bankers' Magazine
Boston *Evening Transcript*
Boston *Globe*
Boston *Herald*
Boston *Journal of Commerce*
Boston *Transcript*
Bulletin of the American Iron and Steel Institute
Bulletin of the National Association of Wool Manufacturers
Chicago *Daily Tribune*
Chicago *Inter-Ocean*
Chicago *Times*
Cincinnati *Commercial*
Cincinnati *Inquirer*
Cincinnati *Gazette*
The Commercial and Financial Chronicle (New York City)
Cleveland *Leader*
Des Moines *Iowa State Register*
Detroit *Evening News*
The Economist (London)
The Financier (The Public)
Gold Hill *News* (Nevada)

Harper's Weekly
Indianapolis *Sun*
International Review
Iron Age
Journal of Social Science
Louisville *Courier-Journal*
Merchant's Magazine and Commercial Review (Hunt's)
Mining Journal and American Railroad Gazette
The Nation
Nevada State Journal (Reno)
New York *Daily Tribune*
New York *Evening Post*
New York *Graphic*
New York *Herald*
New York *Journal of Commerce*
New York *Times*
The North American Review
Ohio State Journal (Columbus)
Philadelphia *Inquirer*
Rocky Mountain *Daily News* (Denver)
San Francisco *Alta*
San Francisco *Bulletin*
San Francisco *Commercial Herald*
San Francisco *Chronicle*
Virginia City *Chronicle*
Virginia City *Territorial Enterprise*
Washington *National Republican*

Contemporary Writings, Memoirs, and Collections of Printed Letters

Bancroft, Frederic, and Dunning, William A., eds. *The Reminiscences of Carl Schurz.* 3 vols. New York, The McClure Co., 1907.

Blaine, James G. *Twenty Years of Congress: From Lincoln to Garfield.* 2 vols. Norwich, Conn., The Henry Bill Co., 1886.

Brown, George Rothwell, ed. *Reminiscences of Senator William M. Stewart.* New York, Neale Publishing Co., 1908.

Boutwell, George Sewall. *Reminiscences of Sixty Years in Public Affairs.* New York, McClure, Phillips and Co., 1902

Butler, Benjamin F. *Autobiography and Personal Reminiscences of Major-General Benjamin F. Butler: Butler's Book.* Boston, A. M. Thayer and Co., 1892.

Carpenter, Frances, ed. *Carp's Washington.* New York, McGraw-Hill, 1960.

Cater, Harold Dean, ed. *Henry Adams and His Friends: A Collection of His Unpublished Letters.* Boston, Houghton Mifflin Company, 1947.

Cole, Cyrenus. *I Remember, I Remember: A Book of Recollections.* Iowa City, The State Historical Society of Iowa, 1936.

Cullom, Shelby M. *Fifty Years of Public Service.* Chicago, A. C. McClurg and Co., 1911.

Drury, Wells. *An Editor on the Comstock Lode.* New York, Farrar and Rinehart, 1936.

Ford, Worthington Chauncey, ed. *Letters of Henry Adams, 1858–1891.* Boston, Houghton Mifflin Company, 1930.

Goodwin, Charles Carroll. *As I Remember Them.* Salt Lake City, 1913.

Gorham, Harry M. *My Memories of the Comstock.* Los Angeles, 1939.

Hinsdale, Burke A. ed. *The Works of James Abram Garfield.* 1882.

Hinsdale, Mary L., ed. *Garfield-Hinsdale Letters, Correspondence Between James Abram Garfield and Burke Aaron Hinsdale.* Ann Arbor, University of Michigan Press, 1949.

Logan, Mary. *Reminiscences of a Soldier's Wife, An Autobiography.* New York, Charles Scribner's Sons, 1913.

Mayre, George Thomas, Jr. *From '49 to '83 in California and Nevada.* San Francisco, A. M. Robertson, 1923.

McCulloch, Hugh. *Men and Measures of Half a Century* New York, Charles Scribner's Sons, 1906.

Sherman, John. *Recollections of Forty Years in the House, Senate and Cabinet.* Chicago, The Werner Co., 1896.

Thorndike, Rachel Sherman, ed. *The Sherman Letters: Correspondence Between General and Senator Sherman from 1837 to 1891.* New York, Charles Scribner's Sons, 1894.

Upshur, George Lyttleton. *As I Recall Them, Memories of Crowded Years.* New York, Wilson-Erickson, 1936.

Williams, Charles Richard, ed. *Diary and Letters of Rutherford Birchard Hayes, Nineteenth President of the United States.* 5

vols. Columbus, The Ohio State Archeological and Historical Society, 1924.

Contemporary Pamphlets, Books, and Printed Speeches

Baird, Henry Carey. *Remonetization of Silver, Testimony of Henry Carey Baird before the United States Monetary Commission . . . October 31, 1876.* Philadelphia, 1878.

Beecher, Henry Ward. *Past Perils and the Peril of Today.* New York, 1877.

Boutwell, George S. *Mr. Boutwell's Speech on the Mint Bill of 1873.* Boston, 1896.

Brindle, William. *Catechism on the Money Question.* Philadelphia, 1877.

Brown, J. Ross, and Taylor, James W. *Report upon the Mineral Resources of the United States.* Washington, 1867.

Brown, William. *The Money Question in the United States.* Montreal, 1878.

Cary, Samuel F. *On the Aims of the Greenback Party: The Issues of the Campaign.* New York, 1876.

Cernuschi, Henri. *The Bland Bill: Its Grounds, Its Alleged Dishonesty, Its Imperfections, Its Future. Paris, 1878.*

———. *Nomisma or Legal Tender.* New York, 1877.

Ensley, Enoch. *The Philosophy of Money.* Memphis, 1877.

Ewing, Thomas, Jr. *Speech of General Thomas Ewing at the Democratic Ratification Meeting at Lancaster, Ohio, July 15, 1876.* n.p., n.d.

Frothingham, Frederick. *The Bland Silver Bill: A Sermon Preached in the First Unitarian Church of Buffalo, N.Y.* December 16, 1877. Buffalo, 1877.

Grubb, Joseph C. *Remarks before the Convention of the American Bankers' Association . . . By a "Merchant of Philadelphia."* Wilmington, 1877.

Halstead, Murat. *The Silver Question: Remonetization before Resumption. . . .* New York, 1877.

Harston, Edward F. B. *The Silver Coinage: Why Has It Depreciated?* San Francisco, 1876.

Harvey, William H. *Coin's Financial School.* Edited by Richard Hofstadter. Cambridge, Harvard University Press, 1963.

———. *A Tale of Two Nations.* Chicago, 1894.

Honest Money League of the Northwest. *Extracts from Some of the Communistic, Inflationary and Treasonable Documents Circulated by the National Greenback Party.* Chicago, 1878.

Horton, S. Dana. *Silver and Gold and Their Relation to the Problem of Resumption.* Cincinnati, Robert Clarke and Co., 1876.

———. *The Silver Bill in Congress.* New York, 1876.

———. *The Monetary Situation: An Address Delivered by Request of the American Social Science Association in Cincinnati, May 21, 1878.* Cincinnati, 1878.

Hughes, Robert William. *A Popular Treatise on the Currency Question Written from a Southern Point of View.* New York, 1879.

Jackson, George N. *The Present and Future of Silver: Bi-Metallism or Inconvertible Paper Money the World's Alternative.* Chicago, 1879.

Jones, John Percival, *Banking and Currency.* Washington, Government Printing Office, 1874.

———, *Resumption and the Double Standard, or The Impossibility of Resuming Specie Payments in the United States Without Restoring the Double Standard of Gold and Silver.* Washington, 1876.

Keeler, Bronson. *History of Demonetization.* n.p., 1896.

Keith, E. Charles. *Silver in the American Finances, Reprinted from The New Century* (vol. 1, 1877). n.p., 1877.

Linderman, Henry Richard. *The Free Coinage of Gold. . . .* Philadelphia, 1872.

———. *Money and Legal Tender in the United States.* New York, 1877.

Marie, Peter. *Ought We to Remonetize Silver?* New York, 1878.

"A Merchant of Philadelphia." *"The Financial Situation" Considered . . .* Washington, 1877.

Moore, Joseph Solomon. *Letters on the Silver Question.* New York, 1877.

Nichol, Thomas. *Honest Money: An Argument in Favor of a Redeemable Currency.* Chicago, 1878.

Parsons, George M. *The Silver Question.* Columbus, 1877.

Perry, Arthur Latham. *An Introduction to Political Economy.* New York, Charles Scribner's Sons, 1877.

Poor, Henry Varnum. *Money and Its Laws.* New York, 1877.
———. *Resumption and the Silver Question....* New York, 1878.
Ruggles, Samuel Buckley. *International Coinage: Supplemental Report to the Department of State.* New York, 1870.
———. *Vital Necessity of Preliminary International Monetary Conference for Establishing the Relative Legal Values of Gold and Silver Coin....* New York, 1877.
Schurz, Carl. *The Currency Question.* Washington, 1878.
Seyd, Ernest. *Bullion and Foreign Exchanges Theoretically and Practically Considered.* London, 1868.
———. *Suggestions in Reference to the Metallic Currency of the United States of America.* London, 1871.
Sherman, John. *The Coinage Act of 1873.* Washington, 1888.
———. *Speech Delivered by Hon. John Sherman, Secretary of the Treasury at Mansfield, Ohio . . . August 17, 1877.* Washington, 1877.
———. *Speeches and Reports on Finance and Taxation.* Washington, 1879.
Shinn, Charles Howard. *The Story of the Mine.* New York, D. Appleton and Company, 1896.
The Silver Dollar of the United States. New York, Clark and Zugalla, 1889.
Stewart, William Morris. *Bondholders' Conspiracy to Demonetize Silver . . .* San Francisco, 1885.
———. *Speech of Hon. William M. Stewart of Nevada.* Washington, 1893.
Sumner, William Graham. *A History of American Currency,* New York, Henry Holt and Company, 1874.
Taft, Alphonso. *Speech on Remonetization of Silver, Delivered at Sandusky, Ohio, September 13, 1877.* Cincinnati, 1877.
Walker, Francis Amasa. *Money.* New York, Henry Holt and Company, 1877.
Wells, David A. *Robinson Crusoe's Money.* New York, 1876.
———. *The Silver Question: The Dollar of the Fathers Versus the Dollar of the Sons.* New York, 1877.
Weston, George. *The Silver Question.* New York, 1878.
———. *Money.* New York, 1880.
Wright, William (Dan DeQuille, pseud.). *The Big Bonanza.* Reprint. New York, Knopf, 1947.

Proceedings, Reports, and Memorials

American Bankers' Association. *Reports of Proceedings at Conventions, 1875–1878.*

American Iron and Steel Association. *Annual Reports for 1873–1878.*

Baltimore Board of Trade. *Annual Reports for 1876–1878.*

Boston Board of Trade. *Annual Reports for 1873–1878.*

Chicago Board of Trade. *Annual Reports for 1876–1878.*

Cincinnati Chamber of Commerce. *Annual Reports for 1875–1878.*

Committee of the Banks of . . . New York, Boston, Philadelphia, and Baltimore. *The Silver Question: Memorial to Congress, January 1878.* New York, 1878.

National Board of Trade. *Proceedings of Annual Meetings for 1867–1878.*

New York Board of Trade. *Memorial to Congress on the Currency of the United States (1876).*

New York State Chamber of Commerce. *Annual Reports for 1866–1878.*

Philadelphia Board of Trade. *Proceedings and Annual Reports for 1875–1878.*

Report of a Special Meeting of the Textile Manufacturer's Association of the West and South, Held July 19, 1877 at Chicago. Chicago, 1877.

Transactions of the American Social Science Association for the Years 1875–1879.

Miscellaneous Source Materials

Appleton's Annual Cyclopedia. New York, D. Appleton and Company, 1875–79.

Huntington, A. T., and McWhinney, Robert J., eds. *Laws of the United States Concerning Money, Banking and Loans, 1778–1909.* Washington, Government Printing Office, 1910.

McPherson, Edward. *Handbook of Politics.* Philadelphia and New York, 1873–78.

———, ed. *New York Daily Tribune Almanac for 1876–1878.*

Richardson, James D., ed. *A Compilation of the Messages and Papers of the Presidents.* n.p., Bureau of National Literature, 1897.

U.S. Bureau of the Census. *Historical Statistics of the United States, 1789–1945.* Washington, Government Printing Office, 1952.

Wilson, James G., and Fiske, John, eds. *Appleton's Cyclopedia of American Biography.* 6 vols. New York, D. Appleton and Company, 1888–89.

Secondary Materials

General Histories, Monographs, and Special Studies

Abell, Aaron Ignatius. *The Urban Impact on American Protestantism, 1865–1900.* Cambridge, Harvard University Press, 1943.

Alexander, DeAlva S. *A Political History of the State of New York,* vol. 3, 1861–82. New York, Henry Holt and Company, 1909.

Andreano, Ralph, ed. *The Economic Impact of the American Civil War.* Cambridge, Schenkman Publishing Company, 1962.

Angel, Myron, ed. *History of Nevada.* Oakland, Calif., Thompson and West, 1881.

Bancroft, Hubert Howe. *History of Nevada, Colorado and Wyoming.* San Francisco, The History Company, 1890.

Barrett, Don Carlos. *The Greenbacks and Resumption of Specie Payments, 1862–1879.* Cambridge, Harvard University Press, 1931.

Beale, Howard K. *The Critical Year: A Study of Andrew Johnson and Reconstruction.* New York, Harcourt, Brace and Company, 1930.

Beard, Charles A., and Mary R. *The Rise of American Civilization.* 2 vols. New York, The MacMillan Company, 1927.

Benson, Lee. *Merchants, Farmers and Railroads: Railroad Regulation and New York Politics, 1850–1887.* Cambridge, Harvard University Press, 1955.

Binkley, Wilfred E. *American Political Parties: Their Natural History.* 4th ed. New York, Alfred Knopf, 1965.

Bogart, Ernest Ludlow, and Thompson, Charles Manfred. *The Industrial State, 1870–1893.* Vol. 4 of *The Centennial History of Illinois.* Springfield, Ill., Illinois Centennial Commission, 1920.

Bogue, Allan G. *Money at Interest: The Farm Mortgage on the Middle Border.* Ithaca, Cornell University Press, 1955.

Bolles, Albert Sidney. *The Financial History of the United States from 1861 to 1885.* New York, D. Appleton and Co., 1886.

Bruce, Robert V. *1877: Year of Violence.* Indianapolis, The Bobbs-Merrill Company, 1959.

Buck, Paul, A. *The Road to Reunion, 1865–1900.* Boston, Little, Brown and Company, 1937.

Buck, Solon Justus. *The Agrarian Crusade: A Chronicle of the Farmer in Politics.* New Haven, Yale University Press, 1920.

———. *The Granger Movement: A Study of Agricultural Organization and Its Political, Economic and Social Manifestations, 1870–1880.* Cambridge, Harvard University Press, 1913.

Bullock, Charles J. *Essays on the Monetary History of the United States.* New York, The Macmillan Company, 1900.

Cagan, Phillip. *Determinants and Effects of Changes in the Stock of Money, 1875–1960.* New York, Columbia University Press, 1965.

Carothers, Neil. *Fractional Money.* New York, J. Wiley and Sons, 1930.

Clancy, Herbert J. *The Presidential Election of 1880.* Chicago, Loyola University Press, 1958.

Clapham, J. H. *The Economic Development of France and Germany, 1815–1914.* Cambridge, Cambridge University Press, 1951.

Clark, Dan Elbert. *History of Senatorial Elections in Iowa.* Iowa City, State Historical Society of Iowa, 1912.

Clark, Victor S. *History of Manufactures in the United States.* Vol. 2, 1860–93. New York, Peter Smith, 1949.

Cochran, Thomas. *Railroad Leaders, 1845–1890: The Business Mind in Action.* Cambridge, Harvard University Press, 1953.

———, and Miller, William. *The Age of Enterprise: A Social History of Industrial America.* New York, The Macmillan Company, 1942.

Cole, Arthur Harrison. *The American Wool Manufacture.* Cambridge, Harvard University Press, 1926.

Coletta, Paolo E. *William Jennings Bryan, I. Political Evangelist, 1860–1908.* Lincoln, University of Nebraska Press, 1964.

Commons, John R., and associates. *History of Labor in the United States.* New York, The Macmillan Company, 1918–35.

Copeland, Melvin Thomas. *The Cotton Manufacturing Industry of the United States.* Cambridge, Harvard University Press, 1912.

Coulborn, W. A. L. *A Discussion of Money.* London, Longmans, Green and Company, 1950.

Cross, Ira B. *Financing an Empire: A History of Banking in California.* 4 vols. San Francisco, 1927.

Curti, Merle. *The Growth of American Thought.* 3d ed. New York, Harper and Row, 1964.

Davis, Sam P. *The History of Nevada.* Los Angeles, The Elm Publishing Company, 1913.

De Santis, Vincent P. *Republicans Face the Southern Question: The New Departure Years, 1877–1897.* Baltimore, Johns Hopkins Press, 1959.

Destler, Chester McArthur. *American Radicalism, 1865–1901: Essays and Documents.* New London, Connecticut College, 1946.

Dewey, Davis Rich. *Financial History of the United States.* 7th ed. New York, Longmans, Green and Company, 1934.

Diamond, Sigmund. *The Reputation of the American Businessman.* Cambridge, Harvard University Press, 1955.

Dilla, Harriet M. *Politics of Michigan, 1865–1878.* New York, Columbia University Studies in History, Economics and Public Law, no. 118, 1912.

Dorfman, Joseph. *The Economic Mind in American Civilization.* New York, The Viking Press, 1946–59.

Dunne, Gerald T. *Monetary Decisions of the Supreme Court.* New Brunswick, Rutgers University Press, 1960.

Durden, Robert F. *James Shepherd Pike, Republicanism and the American Negro, 1850–1880.* Durham, N.C., Duke University Press, 1957.

Eiselen, Malcolm Rogers. *The Rise of Pennsylvania Protectionism.* Philadelphia, the author, 1932.

Eliot, Clara. *The Farmer's Campaign for Credit.* New York, D. Appleton and Company, 1927.

Esary, Logan. *History of Indiana from Its Exploration to 1922.* Dayton, Ohio, Historical Publishing Company, 1924.

Fels, Rendig. *American Business Cycles, 1865–1897.* Chapel Hill, University of North Carolina Press, 1959.

Ferguson, E. James. *The Power of the Purse: A History of American Public Finance, 1776–1790.* Chapel Hill, University of North Carolina Press, 1961.

Ferleger, Herbert Ronald. *David A. Wells and the American Revenue System, 1865–1870.* New York, 1942.

Fine, Nathan. *Labor and Farmer Parties in the United States, 1828–1928.* New York, Rand School of Social Science, 1928.

Fine, Sidney. *Laissez Faire and the General-Welfare State: A Study of Conflict in American Thought, 1865–1901.* Ann Arbor, The University of Michigan Press, 1956.

Foner, Philip. *History of the Labor Movement in the United States.* New York, International Publishers, 1947.

Franklin, John Hope. *Reconstruction after the Civil War.* Chicago, University of Chicago Press, 1961.

Friedman, Milton, and Schwartz, Anna Jacobson. *A Monetary History of the United States, 1867–1960.* Princeton, Princeton University Press, 1963.

Gardner, Charles M. *The Grange: Friend of the Farmer.* Washington, The National Grange, 1949.

Gibson, Florence E. *The Attitudes of the New York Irish toward State and National Affairs, 1848–1892.* New York, 1951.

Gilchrist, David T., and Lewis, W. David, eds. *Economic Change in the Civil War Era.* Greenville, Delaware, Eleutherian Mills-Hagley Foundation, 1965.

Ginger, Ray. *Age of Excess: The United States from 1877 to 1914.* New York, The Macmillan Company, 1965.

Glad, Paul W. *McKinley, Bryan and the People.* Philadelphia and New York, J. B. Lippincott, 1954.

Glasscock, C. B. *The Big Bonanza.* New York, Grosset and Dunlap, 1934.

Gras, N. S. B., and Larson, Henrietta M. *Casebook in American Business History.* New York, Appleton-Century-Crofts, Inc., 1939.

Greer, Thomas H. *American Social Reform Movements. Their Pattern since 1865.* New York, Prentice-Hall, Inc., 1949.

Greever, William S. *The Bonanza West, the Story of the Western Mining Rushes, 1848–1900.* Norman, University of Oklahoma Press, 1963.

Grimes, Alan Pendleton. *The Political Liberalism of the New*

York Nation, 1865–1932. Chapel Hill, University of North Carolina Press, 1953.

Grob, Gerald. *Workers and Utopia: A Study of Ideological Conflict in the American Labor Movement, 1865–1900.* Evanston, Ill., Northwestern University Press, 1961.

Hacker, Louis M. *The Triumph of American Capitalism.* New York, Columbia University Press, 1947.

Hammond, Bray. *Banks and Politics in America, from the Revolution to the Civil War.* Princeton, Princeton University Press, 1957.

Harris, Seymour E., ed. *American Economic History.* New York, McGraw-Hill Book Company, 1960.

Harrod, Roy. *The Dollar.* London, Macmillan and Company, 1953.

Hartz, Louis. *The Liberal Tradition in America.* New York, Harcourt, Brace and World, Inc., 1955.

Hays, Samuel P. *The Response to Industrialism, 1885–1914.* Chicago, The University of Chicago Press, 1957.

Haynes, Fred E. *Third Party Movements since the Civil War, with Special Reference to Iowa: A Study in Social Politics.* Iowa City, The State Historical Society of Iowa, 1916.

Hepburn, A. Barton. *A History of Currency in the United States.* New York, The Macmillan Co., 1924.

Hicks, John D. *The Populist Revolt: A History of the Farmer's Alliance and the People's Party.* Minneapolis, The University of Minnesota Press, 1931.

Higham, John, et al. *History.* Englewood Cliffs, New Jersey, Prentice-Hall, 1965.

Hirshon, Stanley P. *Farewell to the Bloody Shirt: Northern Republicans and the Southern Negro, 1877–1893.* Bloomington, Indiana University Press, 1962.

Hofstadter, Richard. *The Age of Reform, from Bryan to F.D.R* New York, Alfred Knopf, 1956.

———. *The American Political Tradition and the Men Who Made It.* New York, Alfred Knopf, 1949.

———, ed. *Coin's Financial School,* by William H. Harvey. Cambridge, Harvard University Press, 1963.

———. *The Paranoid Style in American Politics and Other Essays.* New York, Alfred Knopf, 1965.

Hoogenboom, Ari. *Outlawing the Spoils: A History of the Civil*

Service Reform Movement, 1865–1883. Urbana, University of Illinois Press, 1961.

Hubbard, Henry Clyde. *The Older Middle West, 1840–1880.* New York, D. Appleton-Century, 1936.

Hulse, James W. *The Nevada Adventure: A History.* Reno, University of Nevada Press, 1963.

Hunt, R. L. *A History of Farmer Movements in the Southwest, 1873–1925.* n.p., n.d.

James, Frank C. *The Growth of Chicago Banks.* New York, Harper, 1938.

Johnson, Emory R., et al. *History of Domestic and Foreign Commerce of the United States.* Washington, Carnegie Institution of Washington, 1915.

Jordan, Phillip D. *Ohio Comes of Age, 1873–1900.* Vol. 5 of *The History of the State of Ohio.* Columbus, Ohio State Archeological and Historical Society, 1943.

Josephson, Matthew. *The Politicos, 1865–1896.* New York, Harcourt, Brace and Co., 1938.

———. *The Robber Barons: The Great American Capitalists, 1861–1901.* New York, Harcourt, Brace and Company, 1934.

Kemmerer, Edwin W. *Gold and the Gold Standard.* New York, McGraw-Hill Book Company, 1944.

King, Joseph L. *History of the San Francisco Stock and Exchange Board by the Chairman.* San Francisco, privately printed, 1910.

Kinsley, Philip. *The Chicago Tribune: Its First Hundred Years, Vol. II, 1865–1880.* Chicago, Chicago Tribune, 1945.

Kirkland, Edward Chase. *Business in the Gilded Age.* Madison, University of Wisconsin Press, 1952.

———. *Dream and Thought in the Business Community, 1860–1900.* Ithaca, Cornell University Press, 1956.

———. *Industry Comes of Age: Business, Labor, and Public Policy, 1860–1897.* New York: Holt, Rinehart, and Winston, 1961.

Knox, John Jay. *A History of Banking in the United States.* New York, Bradford Rhodes and Company, 1900.

———. *United States Notes: A History of the Various Issues of Paper Money by the Government of the United States.* New York, Charles Scribner's Sons, 1884.

Lamar, Howard R. *Dakota Territory, 1861–1889: A Study of Frontier Politics.* New Haven, Yale University Press, 1956.

Larson, Henrietta M. *The Wheat Market and the Farmer in Minnesota, 1858–1900.* New York, Columbia University Press, 1926.

Laughlin, J. Laurence. *The History of Bimetallism in the United States.* New York, D. Appleton and Company, 1893.

Lewis, Oscar. *Silver Kings: The Lives and Times of Mackay, Fair, Flood and O'Brien, Lords of the Nevada Comstock Lode.* New York, Knopf, 1947.

Lord, Eliot. *Comstock Mining and Miners.* Washington, Government Printing Office, 1883.

Madeleine, Sister M. Grace. *Monetary and Banking Theories of Jacksonian Democracy.* Philadelphia, 1943.

Mayer, George H. *The Republican Party, 1854–1964.* New York, Oxford University Press, 1964.

McCloskey, Robert G. *American Conservatism in the Age of Enterprise.* Cambridge, Harvard University Press, 1951.

Merrill, Horace Samuel. *Bourbon Democracy of the Middle West 1865–1896.* Baton Rouge, Louisiana State University Press, 1953.

Michelson, Miriam. *The Wonderlode of Silver and Gold.* Boston, The Stratford Company, 1934.

Miller, William, ed. *Men in Business: Essays on the Historical Role of the Entrepreneur.* New York, Harper and Row, 1962.

Mints, Lloyd W. *A History of Banking Theory in Great Britain and the United States.* Chicago, The University of Chicago Press, 1945.

Mitchell, Wesley Clair. *Gold, Prices and Wages under the Greenback Standard.* Berkeley, The University [of California] Press, 1908.

———. *A History of the Greenbacks, with Special Reference to the Economic Consequences of Their Issue, 1862–1865.* Chicago, The University of Chicago Press, 1903.

Morgan, H. Wayne, ed. *The Gilded Age: A Reappraisal.* Syracuse, Syracuse University Press, 1963.

Murad, Anatol. *The Paradox of a Metal Standard: A Case History of Silver.* Washington, 1939.

Myers, Margaret G. *The New York Money Market.* New York, Columbia University Press, 1931.

Nash, Howard P. *Third Parties in American Politics.* Washington, Public Affairs Press, 1959.

Nichols, Jeannette P., and Randall, J. G., eds. *Democracy in the Middle West, 1840–1940.* New York, D. Appleton-Century Co., 1941.

Noyes, Alexander Dana. *Thirty Years of American Finance: A Short Financial History of the Government and People of the United States since the Civil War, 1865–1896.* New York, G. P. Putnam's Sons, 1898.

Nugent, Walter T. K., *Money and American Society, 1865–1880.* New York, The Free Press, 1968.

———. *The Money Question during Reconstruction.* New York, W. W. Norton and Co., 1967.

Nussbaum, Arthur. *A History of the Dollar.* New York, Columbia University Press, 1957.

Nye, Russell Blaine. *Midwestern Progressive Politics, 1870–1950.* East Lansing, Michigan State College Press, 1951.

O'Conner, Michael J. L. *Origins of Academic Economics in the United States.* New York, Columbia University Press, 1944.

Ostrander, Gilman M. *Nevada, The Great Rotten Borough, 1859–1964.* New York, Knopf, 1966.

Paine, A. E. *The Granger Movement in Illinois.* Urbana, The University [of Illinois], 1904.

Patterson, Robert T. *Federal Debt-Management Policies, 1865–1879.* Durham, Duke University Press, 1954.

Paul, Rodman W. *Mining Frontiers of the Far West, 1848–1880.* New York, Holt, Rinehart and Winston, 1963.

Plumb, Ralph Gordon. *Badger Politics, 1836–1930.* Manitowoc, Wis., Brandt Printing and Binding Co., 1930.

Pollack, Norman. *The Populist Response to Industrial America.* Cambridge, Harvard University Press, 1962.

Porter, George H. *Ohio Politics during the Civil War Period.* New York, 1911.

Randall, J. G., and Donald, David. *The Civil War and Reconstruction.* 2d edition. Boston, D. C. Heath and Company, 1961.

Ratner, Sidney. *American Taxation: Its History as a Social Force in Democracy.* New York, W. W. Norton and Co., 1942.

Redlich, Fritz. *Essays in American Economic History.* n.p., 1944.

———. *The Molding of American Banking: Men and Ideas.* vol. 2, pt. II. New York, Hafner Publishing Company, 1951.

Rhodes, James Ford. *History of the United States from the Compromise of 1850 to the Final Restoration of Home Rule at the South in 1877.* New York, The Macmillan Company, 1893–1927.

Robertson, Ross. *History of the American Economy.* 2d. ed. New York, Harcourt, Brace and World, 1964.

Roll, Eric. *A History of Economic Thought.* New York, Prentice-Hall, Inc., 1942.

Roseboom, Eugene. *A History of Presidential Elections.* New York, The Macmillan Company, 1958.

———. *The Civil War Era, 1850–1873.* vol. 4 of *The History of the State of Ohio.* Columbus, Ohio State Archeological and Historical Society, 1944.

Ross, Earle Dudley. *The Liberal Republican Movement.* New York, Henry Holt and Company, 1919.

Rothman, David J. *Politics and Power: The United States Senate, 1869–1901.* Cambridge, Harvard University Press, 1966.

Russell, Henry B. *International Monetary Conferences, Their Purposes, Character, and Results. . . .* New York and London, Harper and Brothers, 1898.

Saloutos, Theodore. *Farmer Movements in the South, 1865–1933.* Berkeley, University of California Press, 1960.

Schultz, William J., and Caine, M. R. *Financial Development of the United States.* New York, Prentice-Hall, 1937.

Shannon, Fred A. *The Farmer's Last Frontier: Agriculture, 1860–1897.* New York, Rinehart and Co., Inc., 1945.

Sharkey, Robert P. *Money, Class and Party: An Economic Study of Civil War and Reconstruction.* Baltimore, Johns Hopkins Press, 1959.

Silbey, Joel. *The Shrine of Party: Congressional Voting Behavior, 1841–1852.* Pittsburgh, University of Pittsburgh Press, 1967.

Smith, Grant H. *History of the Comstock Lode, 1850–1920.* Reno, University of Nevada Bulletin, *37,* no. 3 (Geology and Mining Series no. 37), 1943.

Smith, Timothy L. *Revivalism and Social Reform in Mid-Nineteenth Century America.* New York, Abingdon Press, 1962.

Sparks, Earl Sylvester. *History and Theory of Agricultural Credit in the United States.* New York, Thomas Y. Crowell Company, 1932.

Spence, Clark C. *British Investments and the American Mining Frontier, 1860–1901.* Ithaca, Cornell University Press, 1958.

Sproat, John C. *"The Best Men": Liberal Reformers in the Gilded Age.* New York, Oxford University Press, 1968.

Stampp, Kenneth M. *The Era of Reconstruction, 1865–1877.* New York, Knopf, 1966.

Stedman, Murray S., Jr., and Stedman, Susan W. *Discontent at the Polls: A Study of Farmer and Labor Parties, 1827–1948.* New York, Columbia University Press, 1950.

Stewart, Robert E., and Stewart, Mary F. *Adolph Sutro.* Berkeley, University of California Press, 1962.

Stover, John F. *The Railroads of the South, 1865–1900. A Study in Finance and Control.* Chapel Hill, University of North Carolina Press, 1955.

Studenski, Paul, and Krooss, Herman E. *Financial History of the United States.* 2d ed. New York, McCraw-Hill Book Company, Inc., 1963.

Swank, James M. *History of the Manufacture of Iron in All Ages. . . .* Philadelphia, American Iron and Steel Association, 1892.

Taussig, Frank W. *The Tariff History of the United States.* New York, G. P. Putnam's Sons, 1931.

Taxay, Don. *The U.S. Mint and Coinage.* New York, Arco Publishing Company, 1966.

Taylor, Charles H., ed. *History of the Board of Trade of the City of Chicago.* Chicago, Robert O. Law Co., 1917.

Thomson, Alexander M. *A Political History of Wisconsin.* Milwaukee, 1902.

Unger, Irwin. *The Greenback Era: A Social and Political History of American Finance, 1865–1879.* Princeton, Princeton University Press, 1964.

Upton, Jacob K. *Money in Politics.* Boston, D. Lothrop and Co., 1884.

Usher, Ellis B. *The Greenback Movement of 1875–1884 and Wisconsin's Part in It.* Milwaukee, 1911.

Ware, Norman J. *The Labor Movement in the United States, 1860–1895: A Study in Democracy.* New York, D. Appleton and Company, 1929.

Watson, D. K. *A History of American Coinage.* New York, G. P. Putnam's Sons, 1899.

Weisenburger, Francis Phelps. *Idol of the West, The Fabulous Career of Rollin Mallory Daggett.* Syracuse, Syracuse University Press, 1965.

White, Horace. *Money and Banking.* Boston, Ginn and Co., 1895.

White, Leonard D. *The Republican Era: A Study in Administrative History, 1869–1901.* New York, The Macmillan Company, 1958.

Wiebe, Robert H. *The Search for Order, 1877–1920.* New York, Hill and Wang, 1967.

Wildman, Murray S. *Money Inflation in the United States: A Study in Social Pathology.* New York, 1905.

Willem, John M., Jr. *The United States Trade Dollar.* New York, privately printed, 1959.

Williamson, Harold Francis, ed. *The Growth of the American Economy.* New York, Prentice-Hall, 1951.

Wish, Harvey. *The American Historian: A Social-Intellectual History of the Writing of the American Past.* New York, Oxford University Press, 1960.

Woodward, C. Vann. *Origins of the New South, 1877–1913.* Baton Rouge, Louisiana State University Press, 1951.

———. *Reunion and Reaction: The Compromise of 1877 and the End of Reconstruction.* Boston, Little, Brown and Company, 1951.

Woolfolk, George R. *The Cotton Regency: The Northern Merchants and Reconstruction, 1865–1880.* New York, Bookman Associates, 1958.

Wright, Benjamin C. *Banking in California, 1849–1910.* San Francisco, 1910.

Wright, Ivan. *Bank Credit and Agriculture under the National and Federal Reserve Banking Systems.* New York, McGraw-Hill Book Company, 1922.

Biographies

Barnard, Harry. *Rutherford B. Hayes and His America.* Indianapolis, The Bobbs-Merrill Company, Inc., 1954.

Barnes, James A. *John C. Carlisle.* New York, Dodd, Mead and Company, 1931.

Barrows, Chester L. *William M. Evarts: Lawyer, Diplomat, Statesman.* Chapel Hill, University of North Carolina Press, 1941.

Bronson, S. A. *Life and Public Services of the Hon. John Sherman.* Columbus, Ohio, H. W. Derby and Company, 1880.

Burton, Theodore E. *John Sherman.* Boston, Houghton Mifflin and Company, 1906.

Byars, William Vincent. *An American Commoner: The Life and Times of Richard Parks Bland.* Columbia, Mo., E. W. Stephens, 1900.

Caldwell, Robert Granville. *James A. Garfield: Party Chieftain.* New York, Dodd, Mead and Company, 1931.

Cary, Edward. *George William Curtis.* Boston, Houghton Mifflin and Co., 1894.

Cate, Wirt A. *Lucius Q. C. Lamar.* Chapel Hill, University of North Carolina Press, 1935.

Chandler, Alfred D. *Henry Varnum Poor: Business Editor, Analyst and Reformer.* Cambridge, Harvard University Press, 1956.

Chidsey, Donald Barr. *The Gentleman from New York: A Life of Roscoe Conkling.* New Haven, Yale University Press, 1935.

Conkling, Alfred R. *The Life and Letters of Roscoe Conkling, Orator, Statesman, Advocate.* New York, Charles L. Webster and Company, 1899.

Cortissez, Royal. *The Life of Whitelaw Reid.* 2 vols. New York, Charles Scribner's Sons, 1921.

Dawson, Charles Francis. *Life and Services of Gen. John A. Logan.* Chicago and New York, Belford, Clarke and Company, 1887.

Eckenrode, Hamilton James. *Rutherford B. Hayes, Statesman of Reunion.* New York, Dodd, Mead and Company, 1930.

Ellis, Elmer. *Henry Moore Teller, Defender of the West.* Caldwell, Idaho, Caxton Printers Ltd., 1941.

Flick, Alexander C. *Samuel Jones Tilden: A Study in Political Sagacity.* New York, Dodd, Mead and Company, 1939.

Foulke, William Dudley. *Life of Oliver P. Morton.* Indianapolis, The Bowen-Merrill Company, 1899.

Fuess, Claude Moore. *Carl Schurz, Reformer.* New York, Dodd, Mead and Company, 1932.

Green, Arnold W. *Henry Charles Carey, Nineteenth Century Sociologist.* Philadelphia, University of Pennsylvania Press, 1951.

Grodinsky, Julius. *Jay Gould: His Business Career, 1867–1892.* Philadelphia, University of Pennsylvania Press, 1957.

Hesseltine, William B. *Ulysses S. Grant, Politician.* New York, Dodd, Mead and Company, 1935.

Hollister, Ovanda James. *Life of Schuyler Colfax.* New York, Funk and Wagnalls, 1886.

Holzman, Robert S. *Stormy Ben Butler.* New York, The Macmillan Company, 1954.

Howe, George Frederick. *Chester A. Arthur: A Quarter-Century of Machine Politics.* New York, Dodd, Mead and Company, 1934.

Joyner, Fred Bunyan. *David Ames Wells, Champion of Free Trade.* Cedar Rapids, Iowa, The Torch Press, 1939.

Kaplan, Abraham D. H. *Henry Charles Carey, A Study in American Economic Thought.* Baltimore, The Johns Hopkins Press, 1931.

Kerr, W. S. *John Sherman.* 2 vols. Boston, Sherman, French and Co., 1908.

King, Willard L. *Lincoln's Manager,* David Davis. Cambridge, Harvard University Press, 1960.

Larson, Henrietta. *Jay Cooke, Private Banker.* Cambridge, Harvard University Press, 1936.

Leonard, Lewis Alexander. *Life of Alphonso Taft.* New York, Hawke Publishing Company, 1920.

Lindsey, David. *"Sunset" Cox, Irrepressible Democrat.* Detroit, Wayne State University Press, 1959.

Lowitt, Richard. *A Merchant Prince of the Nineteenth Century, William E. Dodge.* New York, Columbia University Press, 1954.

Mack, Edward C. *Peter Cooper, Citizen of New York.* New York, Duell, Sloan and Pearce, 1949.

Manter, Ethel. *Rocket of the Comstock, The Story of John William Mackay.* Caldwell, Idaho, Caxton Printers, 1950.

Mayes, Edward. *Lucius Q. C. Lamar, His Life, Times and Speeches, 1825–1893.* Nashville, Barbee and Smith, 1896.

McElroy, Robert. *Levi Parsons Morton, Banker, Diplomat, and Statesman.* New York, G. P. Putnam's Sons, 1930.

McGrane, Reginald Charles. *William Allen, A Study in Western Democracy.* Columbus, The Ohio State Archeological and Historical Society, 1925.

Merriam, George S. *The Life and Times of Samuel Bowles*. New York, The Century Company, 1885.

Milne, Gordon. *George William Curtis and the Genteel Tradition*. Bloomington, Indiana University Press, 1956.

Morgan, H. Wayne. *William McKinley and His America*. Syracuse, Syracuse University Press, 1963.

Munroe, James Phinney. *Francis Amasa Walker*. New York, H. Holt and Company, 1923.

Muzzey, David Saville. *James G. Blaine: A Political Idol of Other Days*. New York, Dodd, Mead and Company, 1934.

Neilson, James W. *Shelby M. Cullom, Prairie State Republican*. Urbana, University of Illinois Press, 1962.

Nevins, Allan. *Abram S. Hewitt, With Some Account of Peter Cooper*. New York, Harper and Brothers, 1935.

———. *Hamilton Fish: The Inner History of the Grant Administration*. 2 vols. New York, Dodd, Mead and Company, 1936.

Oberholtzer, Ellis Paxson. *Jay Cooke, Financier of the Civil War*. Philadelphia, George W. Jacob and Co., 1907.

Ogden, Rollo ed. *Life and Letters of Edwin Lawrence Godkin*. 2 vols. New York, 1907.

Parker, William Belmont. *The Life and Public Services of Justin Smith Morrill*. Boston and New York, Houghton Mifflin Company, 1924.

Richardson, Leon Burr. *William E. Chandler, Republican*. New York, Dodd, Mead and Company, 1940.

Ridge, Martin. *Ignatius Donnelly, The Portrait of a Politician*. Chicago, The University of Chicago Press, 1962.

Sage, Leland L. *William Boyd Allison, A Study in Practical Politics*. Iowa City, State Historical Society of Iowa, 1956.

Samuels, Ernest. *The Young Henry Adams*. Cambridge, Harvard University Press, 1948.

Sherman, Ellen Ewing. *Memorial of Thomas Ewing of Ohio*. New York, The Catholic Publication Society, 1948.

Sherwin, Oscar. *Prophet of Liberty: The Life and Times of Wendell Phillips*. New York, Bookman Associates, 1958.

Smith, Theodore Clarke. *The Life and Letters of James Abram Garfield*. 2 vols. New Haven, Yale University Press, 1925.

Stanwood, Edward. *James Gillespie Blaine*. Boston, Houghton Mifflin Company, 1905.

Starr, Harris E. *William Graham Sumner.* New York, Henry Holt and Company, 1925.

Tansill, Charles C. *The Congressional Career of Thomas Francis Bayard, 1868–1885.* Washington, Georgetown University Press, 1946.

Thompson, E. Bruce. *Matthew Hale Carpenter, Webster of the West.* Madison, State Historical Society of Wisconsin, 1954.

Thompson, Daniel G. B. *Ruggles of New York: A Life of Samuel B. Ruggles.* New York, Columbia University Press, 1946.

Vanderbilt, Kermit. *Charles Eliot Norton, Apostle of Culture in a Democracy.* Cambridge, The Belknap Press, 1959.

Williams, Charles R. *The Life of Rutherford Birchard Hayes, Nineteenth President of the United States.* Columbus, The Ohio State Archeological and Historical Society, 1918.

Williamson, Harold Francis. *Edward Atkinson, The Biography of an American Liberal, 1827–1905.* Boston, Old Corner Book Store, 1934.

Younger, Edward. *John A. Kasson, Politics and Diplomacy from Lincoln to McKinley.* Iowa City, State Historical Society of Iowa, 1955.

Articles

Anderson, George L. "The Proposed Resumption of Silver Payments in 1873," *Pacific Historical Review, 8* (September 1939).

———. "The South and Post Civil War Finance," *Journal of Southern History, 9* (May 1943).

Barnett, Paul. "The Crime of 1873 Re-examined," *Agricultural History, 37* (July 1964).

Barsalou, F. W. "The Concentration of Banking Power in Nevada: An Historical Analysis," *Business History Review, 29* (December 1955).

Burr, Susan S. "Money Grows Up in American History," Service Center for Teachers of History, *Publication Number 43.*

Carleton, William G. "The Money Question in Indiana Politics, 1865–1890," *Indiana Magazine of History, 42* (June 1946).

———. "Why Was the Democratic Party in Indiana a Radical Party, 1865–1890?," *Indiana Magazine of History, 42* (September 1946).

Coben, Stanley. "Northeastern Business and Radical Reconstruction: A Re-examination," *Mississippi Valley Historical Review* (June 1959).

Cooper, Vernon. "William Boyd Allison," *University of Iowa Studies,* n. s. *10* (1932).

Eckler, A. R. "A Measure of the Severity of Depressions, 1873–1932," *Review of Economic Statistics, 15* (May 15, 1933).

Ellis, Lewis Ethan. "A History of the Chicago Delegation in Congress, 1843–1925," *Transactions of the Illinois Historical Society* (1930).

Farmer, Hallie. "The Economic Background of Frontier Populism," *Mississippi Valley Historical Review, 10* (March 1924).

Garnett, Porter. "History of the Trade Dollar," *American Economic Review, 1* (March 1917).

Graham, Frank D. "International Trade Under Depreciated Paper: The United States, 1862–1879," *Quarterly Journal of Economics, 36* (February 1922).

Hafen, LeRoy. "Currency, Coinage and Banking in Pioneer Colorado," *The Colorado Magazine, 10* (1933).

Hesseltine, William B. "Economic Factors in the Abandonment of Reconstruction," *Mississippi Valley Historical Review, 22* (September 1935).

———. "Regions, Classes, and Sections in American History," *Journal of Land and Public Utility Economics,* 20 (February 1944).

Hicks, John D. "The Political Career of Ignatius Donnelly," *Mississippi Valley Historical Review,* 7 (June–September 1921).

Hoogenboom, Ari A. "An Analysis of Civil Service Reformers," *The Historian, 23* (November 1960).

House, Albert V. "Men, Morals and Manipulation in the Pennsylvania Democracy of 1875," *Pennsylvania History, 23* (April 1956).

Jordan, Henry D. "Daniel Wolsey Voorhees," *Mississippi Valley Historical Review,* 6 (March 1920).

Kindahl, James K. "Economic Factors in Specie Resumption: The United States, 1865–1879," *The Journal of Political Economy,* 69 (February 1961).

Klement, Frank. "Middle Western Copperheadism and the Genesis of the Granger Movement," *Mississippi Valley Historical Review, 38* (March 1952).

Leach, J. A. "Public Opinion and the Inflation Movement in Missouri, 1875–1879," *Missouri Historical Review, 24* (1930–31).

Lester, Richard A. "Inflation and the Farmer," *Journal of Farm Economics, 16* (April 1924).

Libby, Orin G. "A Study of the Greenback Movement, 1876–1884," *Transactions of the Wisconsin Academy of Sciences, Arts and Letters,* vol. 12 p. II (1900).

McGrane, Reginald C. "Ohio and the Greenback Movement," *Mississippi Valley Historical Review, 11* (March 1925).

Martin, Roscoe C. "The Greenback Party in Texas," *The Southwest Historical Quarterly, 30* (January 1927).

Miller, Raymond C. "The Background of Populism in Kansas," *Mississippi Valley Historical Review, 11* (March 1925).

Mittleman, Edward B. "Chicago Labor in Politics, 1877–1896," *The Journal of Political Economy, 28* (May 1920).

Moore, Clifford H. "Ohio in National Politics, 1865–1896," *Ohio Archeological and Historical Publications, 37* (1928).

Musson, A. E. "The Great Depression in Britain, 1873–1896: A Reappraisal," *The Journal of Economic History, 19* (June 1959).

"New Luster for the White Metal, I. Crime of '73: Case Closed," Federal Reserve Bank of San Francisco, *Monthly Review, 50* (June 1964).

Nichols, Jeannette Paddock. "Bryan's Benefactor: Coin Harvey and His World," *Ohio Historical Quarterly, 67* (October 1958).

———. "John Sherman and the Silver Drive of 1877–1878: The Origins of the Gigantic Subsidy," *Ohio State Archeological and Historical Quarterly, 46* (1937).

———. "John Sherman: A Study in Inflation," *Mississippi Valley Historical Review, 21* (September 1934).

———. "The Monetary Problems of William McKinley," *Ohio History, 72* (October 1963).

———. "Silver Diplomacy," *Political Science Quarterly, 48,* no. 4 (1933).

O'Leary, Paul M. "The Scene of the Crime of 1873 Revisited: A Note," *Journal of Political Economy, 68* (August 1960).

Redlich, Fritz. " 'Translating' Economic Policy into Business Policy:

An Illustration from the Resumption of Specie Payments in 1879," *Bulletin of the Business Historical Society,* 20 (December 1950).

Rezneck, Samuel. "Distress, Relief, and Discontent in the United States During the Depression of 1873–1878," *The Journal of Political Economy,* 58 (December 1950).

Ridge, Martin. "Ignatius Donnelly and the Greenback Movement," *Mid-America, An Historical Review,* 39 (July 1957).

Roach, Hannah Grace. "Sectionalism in Congress (1870–1890)," *American Political Science Review,* 19 (August 1925).

Ruggles, Clyde O. "The Economic Basis of the Greenback Movement in Iowa and Wisconsin," *Proceedings of the Mississippi Valley Historical Association for the Year 1912–1913,* vol. 6.

Saloutos, Theodore. "The Spring-Wheat Farmer in a Maturing Economy, 1870–1920," *Journal of Economic History,* 6 (November 1946).

Schell, Herbert S. "The Grange and the Credit Problem in Dakota Territory," *Agriculture History,* 10 (April 1935).

Thompson, Thomas Gray. "The Far Western Mining Frontier: Trends and Unsolved Problems," *The Colorado Magazine,* 41 (Spring 1964).

Timberlake, Richard A., Jr. "Ideological Factors in Specie Resumption and Treasury Policy," *Journal of Economic History,* 24 (March 1964).

Unger, Irwin. "The Business Community and the Origins of the 1875 Resumption Act," *The Business History Review,* 35 (Summer 1961).

———. "Business and Currency in the Ohio Gubernatorial Campaign of 1875," *Mid-America, An Historical Review,* 41 (January 1959).

———. "Business Men and Specie Resumption," *Political Science Quarterly,* 74 (March 1959).

Wall, C. James. "Gold Dust and Greenbacks," *Montana: The Magazine of Western History,* 7 (Spring 1957).

Wells, O. V. "Depression of 1873–1879," *Agricultural History,* 11 (July 1937).

Wilcox, Benton H. "An Historical Definition of Northwestern

Radicalism," *Mississippi Valley Historical Review, 26* (December 1939).

Woodward, C. Vann. "The Populist Heritage and the Intellectual," in Woodward, *The Burden of Southern History*. New York, Vintage, 1961.

Unpublished Doctoral Dissertations

Gutman, Herbert G. "Social and Economic Structure and Depression: American Labor in 1873 and 1874." University of Wisconsin, 1959.

Haswell, Harold Alanson. "The Public Life of Congressman Richard Parks Bland." University of Missouri, 1951.

James, Edward T. "American Labor and Political Action, 1865–1896: The Knights of Labor and Its Predecessors." Harvard University, 1954.

Lewis, E. Gilmore. "Some Contributions of John Sherman to Public and Private Finance, 1855–1881." University of Illinois, 1932.

Kindahl, James K. "The Economics of Resumption: The United States, 1865–1879." University of Chicago, 1958.

Mack, Effie M. "Life and Letters of William Morris Stewart, 1827–1909." University of California, 1930.

Merrifield, Robert B. "Nevada, 1859–1881: The Impact of an Advanced Society upon a Frontier Area." University of Chicago, 1957.

Ricker, Ralph R. "The Greenback-Labor Movement in Pennsylvania." Pennsylvania State University, 1955.

Scheidler, Lawrence J. "Silver and Politics, 1803–1896." Indiana University, 1936.

Shipley, Max L. "The Greenback Issue in the Old Northwest, 1865–1880." University of Illinois, 1929.

Silbey, Joel. "The Shrine of Party: Congressional Voting Behavior, 1841–1852." University of Iowa, 1963.

Tucker, David Milton. "The Mugwumps and the Money Question, 1865–1900." University of Iowa, 1965.

Unger, Irwin. "Men, Money and Politics: The Specie Resumption Issue, 1865–1879." Columbia University, 1958.

Unpublished Master's Thesis

Buckner, Philip E. "Silver Mining Interests in Silver Politics . . ." Columbia University, 1954.

Miscellaneous Secondary Materials

Biographical Dictionary of the American Congress, 1774–1949. 81st Congress, 2d Session. *House Document no. 607.*

Burnham, W. Dean. *Presidential Ballots, 1836–1892.* Baltimore, The Johns Hopkins Press, 1955.

Johnson, Allen, and Malone, Dumas, eds. *Dictionary of American Biography.* New York, Charles Scribner's Sons, 1932.

Larson, Henrietta M. *Guide to Business History. Materials for the Study of American Business History and Suggestions for Their Use.* Cambridge, Harvard University Press, 1948.

Morris, Richard B., ed. *Encyclopedia of American History.* New York, Harper and Brothers, 1961.

National Cyclopedia of American Biography. New York, James T. White and Company, 1928–.

Porter, Kirk H., and Johnson, Donald Bruce. *National Party Platforms, 1840–1964.* Urbana, University of Illinois Press, 1966.

Index